MAJOR EUROPEAN AUTHORS

MOLIÈRE

BOOKS IN THIS SERIES

BY THE SAME AUTHOR

Life and Letters in France: the Seventeenth Century, London, 1965.
(With C. L. Walton) *Explications: the Technique of French Literary
Appreciation*, Oxford, 1971.
(Ed. with Merlin Thomas) *Molière: Stage and Study: Essays in honour of
W. G. Moore*, Oxford, 1973.
Sublime and Grotesque: a Study of French Romantic Drama, London, 1975.
(Ed.) *Comic Drama: the European Heritage*, London, 1978.

Editions of French texts:

Anouilh, *Pauvre Bitos,* London, 1958.
Le Bal des voleurs, London, 1960.
Becket, London, 1962.
Molière, *Dom Juan*, Oxford, 1958.
L'École des femmes and La Critique de l'École des femmes, Oxford, 1963.

MOLIÈRE
A PLAYWRIGHT
AND HIS AUDIENCE

W. D. Howarth
Professor of Classical French Literature
University of Bristol

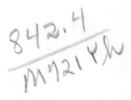
CAMBRIDGE UNIVERSITY PRESS
Cambridge
London   New York   New Rochelle
Melbourne   Sydney

Published by the Press Syndicate of the University of Cambridge
The Pitt Building, Trumpington Street, Cambridge CB2 1RP
32East 57th Street, New York, NY 10022, USA
296 Beaconsfield Parade, Middle Park, Melbourne 3206, Australia

First published 1982

Printed in Great Britain at the University Press, Cambridge

Library of Congress catalogue card number: 81–18173

British Library Cataloguing in Publication Data
Howarth, W. D.
Molière: a playwright and his audience.
– (Major European authors)
1. Molière
I. Title   II. Series
842'.4   PQ 1860

ISBN 0 521 24425 0 hard covers
ISBN 0 521 28679 4 paperback

Dans les pièces sérieuses, il suffit, pour n'être point blâmé, de dire des choses qui soient de bon sens et bien écrites; mais ce n'est pas assez dans les autres, il y faut plaisanter; et c'est une étrange entreprise que celle de faire rire les honnêtes gens.

(*La Critique de l'École des femmes*, scene vi)

Contents

Illustrations

Plates

Between pp. 50 and 51

Figure

General Preface to the Series

This series was initiated within the Cambridge University Press as an at first untitled collection of general studies. For convenience it was referred to inside the Press as 'the Major European Authors Series'; and once the initial prejudice against the useful word 'major' was overcome, the phrase became the official title.

The series was always meant to be informal and flexible, and no very strict guidelines are imposed on the authors. The aim is to provide books which can justifiably be given a title which starts simply with the name of the author studied; therefore to be general, introductory and accessible. When the series started, in the 1960s, there was an assumption that a biographical approach or an approach via historical background was old-fashioned, and in practice the student or general reader can usually find adequate biographies or literary histories. Yet it is still relatively hard to find books which address themselves directly to the works as literature or as drama, and try to give a direct sense of the general intention, the structure and effect of poetry, or the way drama works with an audience. So the aim has consistently been to give a critical introduction to the whole *oeuvre* or the most important works; to help the reader form or order his own impressions by giving liberal quotation and judicious analysis; to assume little prior knowledge, and in most cases to quote in English or to add a translation to quotations in the original.

It is hoped that the series will help to keep some classics of European literature alive and active in the minds of present-day readers; both those working for a formal examination in literature and the educated general reader – a class which exists, though it may be small.

Professor Howarth's study is conceived within the general framework of the series; but to do justice to his author he has necessarily to take some account of the history of the stage in Molière's time, and of Molière's activity as leader of a troupe of players. The essentially social nature of comedy also entails more than a glance at the nature and preoccupations of the French society which gave him his original audience.

Acknowledgements

Thanks are due to Gordon Kelsey of the Arts Faculty Photographic Unit, University of Bristol, for help with the preparation of illustrations.

To Sylvie Chevalley for her kind help over matters concerning Molière at the Comédie-Française.

To generations of students, at Oxford and at Bristol, with whom I have so much enjoyed studying Molière, and to whom this book owes a great deal.

And to my wife, for her invaluable help with the proofs and indexing.

Introduction

Chaque génération, depuis trois siècles, [a] déformé ou transformé à sa
guise un texte dont la vertu essentielle est d'être indéfiniment adaptable
à toutes les tendances et à toutes les turpitudes.   (Louis Jouvet)[1]

To justify the writing of yet another book about a playwright on
whom so much has been published is not easy. However, every
scholar who undertakes such a task is presumably motivated by the
belief that there is something new to be said, and that even if he
cannot lay claim to complete originality either of subject-matter or of
method, he nevertheless has a worthwhile contribution to make in
terms of interpretation and emphasis. In the present case, to try to
define that contribution at the outset was an essential preliminary to
the planning of a new study of Molière, and I hope it may also help to
justify to the reader the adding of yet another title to the copious
critical bibliography that already exists.

Any moliériste surveying the critical literature of the post-war decades must acknowledge the pioneer work of the late W. G. Moore.
His Molière: A New Criticism (1949) has rightly been seen as a landmark, which more than any other single work helped to turn the
academic interpretation of Molière's comedy away from a twin preoccupation, with autobiographical sources and with moral 'message',
towards a more detached, objective examination of the plays as plays.
The substitution of the aesthetic for the moral approach is the most
important development in Molière criticism – French, British and
American – during the last thirty years; and this period has seen a
number of valuable studies inspired by the Anglo-American New
Criticism, as well as others, of more limited value, inspired by the
structuralist disciplines of 'la nouvelle critique'. But running through
much of this post-war reinterpretation, however valuable, has been
an unfortunate polarisation between the 'form' and the 'content' of
the plays, based on the assumption – perhaps implicit in Moore,

---

[1] Témoignages sur le théâtre (Paris, 1952), p. 22. For translation of French quotations, see
section at end of book.

certainly explicit in Bray's *Molière, homme de théâtre* (1954) – that the aesthetic approach excludes the moral. The obsession of earlier generations with the 'message' of the plays has too often given way to a refusal to look for, even to recognise, a positive point of view on moral and social matters. 'Molière pense-t-il?' asks a chapter-heading in Bray's book, and the reader is invited to answer in the negative.

Such a restrictive approach is an undue limitation of what Molière's comedy has to offer; moreover, it hardly corresponds with what most spectators experience when they see Molière performed in the theatre. There have, it is true, been recent attempts to reconcile form and content in this context, one of the most interesting being Robert McBride's *The Sceptical Vision of Molière* (1977), which appeared while the present book was being written. However, whereas Dr McBride sets out to relate Molière – via the opinions expressed by his characters – to contemporary *moraliste* writers, and to line him up with the sceptical tradition represented by Montaigne and his seventeenth-century followers, my own starting-point is nearer to that of René Bray. I have tried to situate Molière as accurately as possible in the professional milieu in which he worked, on the one hand by studying his particular gifts as an actor, the resources of his company, and his commitment as *chef de troupe,* and on the other hand by characterising the tastes, the prejudices and the preoccupations of the audiences. It was from the interplay of these factors – Molière the actor–manager, catering for audiences first in the provinces, then in Paris and at Court – that Molière the playwright was born. But whereas Bray's 'homme de théâtre' appeared to be defined in terms of exclusively material and technical considerations: 'Pour comprendre comment le *Misanthrope* a été composé, il importe moins de savoir si son auteur était taciturne ou atrabilaire que de connaître le nombre et la qualité des actrices dont il disposait'[2] – I hope that by attempting to relate the plays to the intellectual and moral climate of the age in which Molière lived, I may have succeeded in preserving an essential component in the make-up of Molière the playwright that Bray's 'technicien' seemed to have lost.[3]

As with any figure of the past who left no diaries, memoirs or letters, it is a good deal easier to piece together the external details of Molière's existence as a professional man of the theatre than to know

[2] *Molière, homme de théâtre* (Paris, 1954), p. 19.
[3] 'Son dessein est celui d'un technicien, nullement d'un psychologue ou d'un moraliste', *ibid.,* p. 340.

what went on in his mind. As far as the story of his private and domestic life is concerned, Molière's early biographers, from Grimarest onwards, no doubt unconsciously so combined fact and fiction as to produce a legendary Life in which the true and the apocryphal are inextricably mixed. Evoking a litany of anecdotal clichés about the playwright's family background and schooling, his provincial travels and his relationships with his friends and his servants, Robert Jouanny comments with good-humoured scepticism: 'Voici quelques beaux contes entrelacés de suggestifs détails dont l'imagination de l'homme a besoin pour illustrer à toute force dans la grisaille quotidienne notre cohabitation avec le génie.'[4]

But if we turn to Molière's public life, the picture is more reliable. From the factual record left by La Grange of the day-to-day activities of Molière and his troupe,[5] and accounts such as Chappuzeau's of the seventeenth-century theatre in general,[6] as well as from the patient researches of historians of our own day,[7] we can obtain enough evidence of the material conditions in which Molière worked for our knowledge of his professional life to be based on reasonably firm foundations, and for the way in which the demands of his professional life influenced his evolution as a creative writer to be quite accurately assessed.

However, Molière the actor–manager is only a starting-point; and although I think a knowledge of his professional career is an essential point of departure, it cannot explain the whole Molière. As Ramon Fernandez wrote: 'L'interprétation comique du monde implique une vision, qui implique à son tour une philosophie.'[8] To limit Molière's 'comic vision' to matters of theatrical – or even theatrical and literary – technique would be to be content with externals: it is the unique combination of craftsmanship and 'philosophy' that defines his genius. And when we come to consider his moral ideas and his

[4] Molière, *Oeuvres complètes*, ed. R. Jouanny (Paris, 1962), I, p. viii.
[5] *Le Registre de La Grange, 1659–1685*, ed. B. E. and G. P. Young (2 vols., Paris, 1947).
[6] *Le Théâtre français* (1674), ed. G. Monval (Paris, 1875).
[7] See e.g. P. Mélèse, *Le Théâtre et le public à Paris sous Louis XIV, 1659–1715* (Paris, 1934); P. Mélèse, *Répertoire analytique des documents contemporains d'information et de critique concernant le théâtre à Paris sous Louis XIV* (Paris, 1934); M. Jurgens and E. Maxfield-Miller, *Cent ans de recherches sur Molière, sur sa famille et sur les comédiens de sa troupe* (Paris, 1963); G. Mongrédien, *La Vie quotidienne des comédiens au temps de Molière* (Paris, 1966); G. Mongrédien (ed.), *Recueil des textes et des documents du xviie siècle relatifs à Molière* (2 vols., Paris, 1966).
[8] 'Molière', in *Tableau de la littérature française de Corneille à Chénier*, ed. Alain *et al.* (Paris, 1939), p. 86.

outlook on life, we need to look at the audiences for whom he wrote, and to try to define their attitudes as well.

Molière has suffered less than, for instance, Racine from the attentions of those *nouveaux critiques* who approach a text with a resolutely anti-historical bias, whose object is to reinterpret a seventeenth-century author in twentieth-century terms, or in other words to impose on his writings a 'structure' valid for our own day (derived from Marx, Freud or Jung as the case may be), however much this may do violence to the 'univers imaginaire' of the author concerned. Fortunately, it is less easy in Molière's case to ignore the specific fact that Molière was a seventeenth-century playwright writing for a seventeenth-century audience; for whereas Racine chose as settings for his tragedies periods and places that were almost as remote from the *siècle de Louis XIV* as they are from us today, the text of nearly all of Molière's plays is rich with allusions to a precise temporal and social context, that of the contemporary spectators for whom he wrote. All these allusions they, no doubt, took for granted; for the twentieth-century reader or spectator, such references serve to give the plays a coherent historical setting, even if a certain amount of elucidation may sometimes be necessary.

That is not to say that Molière is ever difficult of access. Compared not only with writers of comedy from the ancient world like Aristophanes or Plautus, but also with a near-contemporary such as Ben Jonson, Molière is much more readily accessible, and he has seldom chosen to portray the sort of details of seventeenth-century life that keep the uninitiated reader or spectator at arm's length. When we read Plautus, the French Renaissance dramatists, or Jonson, their society of courtesans, pimps and parasites requires a good deal more deliberate acclimatisation on our part, a good deal more 'suspension of disbelief', than does the bourgeois household of *Tartuffe* or Célimène's *salon* in *Le Misanthrope*.

Nor am I advocating the pedantic reconstruction of the historical setting of Molière's plays for its own sake. Molière has been pretty well worked over by the *sourciers*, and only in a few cases can a knowledge of the out-of-the-way sources they have brought to light be said to be essential to the appreciation of the play concerned. On the other hand, I do consider it vital to build up as full a background as possible in a more general sense, to establish a parallel between Molière's 'univers imaginaire' and the world in which he himself lived and moved, in an attempt to define the moral outlook, the taste,

4

and the habits of thought of the spectators for whom he wrote. We need a well-documented, reliable account of the relationship between the playwright and his audience, so that we can judge how far this relationship is still valid for us today. Once we have the feel of such a relationship, we can better understand certain ways in which it may not fully work for us because we no longer have the same habits of thought, or the same moral outlook, as the audiences for whom he wrote; and we can give ourselves the best possible chance of re-establishing a valid rapport, so as to appreciate the comic vision, and the underlying philosophy, that the playwright was seeking to communicate to his original audiences.[9]

[9] May I refer the reader to my *Life and Letters in France: The Seventeenth Century* (London, 1965), which attempts, in a rather more general way, to define the habits of thought of the seventeenth-century reading public, and the moral climate in which a number of the outstanding works of the period were written.

PART I

The background

I

The formation of an actor

Son jeu . . . a plu à assez de gens pour lui donner la vanité d'être le premier farceur de France. (A. B. de Somaize, April, 1660)[1]

(i) 'Le premier farceur de France'

At about the time of Molière's return to Paris in 1658 from his thirteen years of provincial wanderings, Tallemant des Réaux, the writer of gossipy memoirs, who had already written a paragraph in his *Historiettes* about Madeleine Béjart ('Je ne l'ai jamais vue jouer; mais on dit que c'est la meilleure actrice de toutes. Elle est dans une troupe de campagne'), made this interesting marginal addition to his manuscript:

> Un garçon, nommé Molière, quitta les bancs de Sorbonne pour la suivre; il en fut longtemps amoureux, donnait des avis à la troupe, et enfin s'en mit et l'épousa. Il a fait des pièces où il y a de l'esprit. Ce n'est pas un merveilleux acteur, si ce n'est pour le ridicule. Il n'y a que sa troupe qui joue ses pièces; elles sont comiques.[2]

In spite of its inaccuracy in certain particulars – Madeleine Béjart was Molière's mistress, but never his wife – this laconic paragraph is a most valuable text. It contains the earliest known assessment of Molière's qualities as an actor; and the difference in the wording of the two references could well be taken as an indication that in the later addition Tallemant is speaking at first hand, having seen the new troupe perform since their arrival in Paris.[3] In its form – the backhanded compliment to Molière as a comic actor only partly offsets a distinctly unfavourable judgement of his aptitude for tragedy – Tallemant's comment observes the priority universally accorded to the latter genre, by the acting profession as well as by their public. There is no doubt that Molière aspired to recognition as a tragic actor – one of the best-known portraits depicts him in the role of

---

[1] Quoted Mongrédien (ed.), *Recueil*, p. 123.
[2] *Historiettes*, ed. A. Adam (2 vols., Paris, 1960–1), II, p. 778.
[3] Adam is positive that this is so: *ibid.*, p. 1525.

César in Corneille's *Pompée*[4] – and little doubt, either, that he must have been mortified by the public's refusal to take him seriously in tragic roles. Tallemant's contrast between mediocrity in tragedy and implied excellence in comedy is echoed by a number of contemporaries, from the hostile comments emanating from the rival Hôtel de Bourgogne troupe at the time of the 'Guerre comique':

> Il faut que tout cède au bouffon d'aujourd'hui;
> Sur mon âme, à présent on ne rit que chez lui,
> Car pour le sérieux à quoi l'Hôtel s'applique,
> Il fait, quand on y va, qu'on ne rit qu'au comique;
> Mais au Palais-Royal quand Molière est des deux,
> On rit dans le comique et dans le sérieux[5]

to Charles Perrault, eulogising Molière at the end of the century as one of the great men of his age:

> Il a été si excellent acteur pour le comique, quoique très médiocre pour le sérieux, qu'il n'a pu être imité que très imparfaitement par ceux qui ont joué son rôle après sa mort.[6]

His first biographer, Grimarest, writing in 1705, summed up contemporary opinion on this score:

> Il est vrai que Molière n'était bon que pour représenter le comique; il ne pouvait entrer dans le sérieux, et plusieurs personnes assurent qu'ayant voulu le tenter, il réussit si mal la première fois qu'il parut sur le théâtre, qu'on ne le laissa pas achever. Depuis ce temps-là, dit-on, il ne s'attacha qu'au comique, où il avait toujours du succès, quoique les gens délicats l'accusassent d'être un peu grimacier.[7]

It seems likely that Molière lacked the necessary presence and carriage to impose himself in tragic roles; and although Montfleury's portrait is obviously a satirical caricature:

> Il vient le nez au vent,
> Les pieds en parenthèse, et l'épaule en avant,
> Sa perruque qui suit le côté qu'il avance,
> Plus pleine de lauriers qu'un jambon de Mayence,
> Les mains sur les côtés d'un air peu négligé,
> La tête sur le dos comme un mulet chargé,

---

[4] This portrait, by Nicolas Mignard (painted 1657–8) is in the Comédie-Française. See Plate I.
[5] Montfleury, *L'Impromptu de l'Hôtel de Condé* (1664), lines 103–8. See *La Querelle de l'École des femmes*, ed. G. Mongrédien (2 vols., Paris, 1971), p. 226; and cf. similar references in other texts, *ibid.*, pp. 98–9, 133–6.
[6] *Les Hommes illustres* (1696), in Mongrédien (ed.), *Recueil*, p. 702.
[7] *La Vie de M. de Molière*, ed. G. Mongrédien (Paris, 1955), pp. 99–100.

Les yeux fort égarés, puis débitant ses rôles,
D'un hoquet éternel sépare ses paroles[8]

the impediment of speech here mentioned is also acknowledged by
Grimarest. He, however, suggests how this disadvantage was mini-
mised in comic roles:

> Dans les commencements qu'il monta sur le théâtre, il reconnut qu'il
> avait une volubilité de langue, dont il n'était pas le maître et qui rendait
> son jeu désagréable. Et des efforts qu'il se faisait pour se retenir dans la
> prononciation, il s'en forma un hoquet, qui lui demeura jusques à la fin.
> Mais il sauvait ce desagrément par toute la finesse avec laquelle on peut
> représenter. Il ne manquait aucun des accents et des gestes nécessaires
> pour toucher le spectateur. Il ne déclamait point au hasard, comme ceux
> qui, destitués des principes de la déclamation, ne sont point assurés dans
> leur jeu: il entrait dans tous les détails de l'action.[9]

What is quite certain is that Molière's manner as a tragic actor was
very much at variance with the current fashion: that is, the pompous,
declamatory style in favour at the Hôtel de Bourgogne, which
Molière himself sarcastically recommends to his colleagues in the
Impromptu de Versailles (1663):

> Comment? vous appelez cela réciter? C'est se railler: il faut dire les
> choses avec emphase. Écoutez-moi . . . Voyez-vous cette posture? Re-
> marquez bien cela. Là, appuyer comme il faut le dernier vers. Voilà ce
> qui attire l'approbation et fait faire le brouhaha. (scene i)

In contrast, this same passage from the *Impromptu* repeatedly advo-
cates a delivery which should aim at being 'as natural as possible';
and it is clear that whatever Molière's shortcomings as a heroic actor
may have been, he deliberately rejected the notion of a tragic performance as a mere exercise in rhetoric, offering scope for stylised
virtuoso playing, in favour of a more lifelike interpretation of consistent, coherent characters. Already in *Les Précieuses ridicules* (1659) he
had satirised the emphatic manner in vogue at the Hôtel de Bourgogne, in a passage which indicates clearly enough, by means of
antiphrasis, his own positive ideal as an actor and director of tragic
drama; Mascarille, the bogus *marquis*, boasts of having written a play:

> — A quels comédiens la donnerez-vous?
> — Belle demande! Aux Grands Comédiens! Il n'y a qu'eux qui soient
> capables de faire valoir les choses. Les autres sont des ignorants qui
> récitent comme l'on parle: ils ne savent pas faire ronfler les vers, et
> s'arrêter au bel endroit; et le moyen de connaître où est le beau vers si le

---

[8] *L'Impromptu*, lines 131–8.   [9] *La Vie de M. de Molière*, p. 99.

comédien ne s'y arrête, et ne vous avertit par là qu'il faut faire le brouhaha? (scene ix)

Throughout the years in the provinces the tragedies of Corneille, Rotrou, Tristan and Du Ryer had formed the staple repertory of Molière and his company, as they pursued their itinerary via Lyon, Avignon, Toulouse, Bordeaux, Nantes, Rouen and who knows where besides. And when finally the 36-year-old actor-manager decided once more to try his fortune in the capital, it was still on Corneille's heroic tragedy that their repertory was based. *Nicomède* was their choice, on 24 October 1658; and to quote Grimarest's account:

> Leur début fut heureux; et les actrices surtout furent trouvées bonnes. Mais comme Molière sentait bien que sa troupe ne l'emporterait pas pour le sérieux sur celle de l'Hôtel de Bourgogne, après la pièce il s'avança sur le théâtre, et fit un remerciement à Sa Majesté, et la supplia d'agréer qu'il lui donnât un des petits divertissements, qui lui avaient acquis un peu de réputation dans les provinces. En quoi il comptait bien de réussir, parce qu'il avait accoutumé sa troupe à jouer sur-le-champ de petites comédies, à la manière des Italiens.[10]

Le Docteur amoureux (the text is lost)[11] succeeded, and it was with 'divertissements' – probably of his own composition, certainly tried and tested in the provinces as a vehicle for his own acting talents – that Molière began to impose himself on the Parisian public, as well as on the Court. Tragedies were still played, but the growing reputation of the Troupe de Monsieur was due to their creation of *L'Étourdi* and *Dépit amoureux* (1658 – though both had been played before in the provinces); while after the production of *Les Précieuses ridicules*, performed with Corneille's *Cinna* in November 1659, they never looked back. As Molière's self-confidence grew, with each new play in his own characteristic manner that made its mark – *Sganarelle ou le Cocu imaginaire* (May 1660), *L'École des maris* (June 1661), *L'École des femmes* (December 1662) – the place of tragedy in his repertory gradually grew less important;[12] and it is perhaps significant that the

[10] *Ibid.*, pp. 45–6.
[11] The undated play with this title discovered and published by A. J. Guibert (Geneva–Paris, 1960) may possibly be the *Docteur amoureux* of 1658. As A. Gill has shown, in his review of the above (*French Studies*, xv (1961), 54–7), this text is largely made up of scenes from *Le Déniaisé* by Gillet de la Tessonnerie, which feature Jodelet as valet and Pancrace as pedant doctor.
[12] See R. Bray, 'Le Répertoire de la troupe de Molière', *Mélanges . . . offerts à Daniel Mornet* (Paris, 1951), pp. 91–8. Bray's analysis underlines the fact that in the last six years of Molière's life only two new tragedies were created (one being the 'tragédie-ballet' *Psyché* in which he had himself collaborated). See Appendix iii below.

only real failure among his own early plays was his single attempt at a more elevated comedy in the heroic style, *Dom Garcie de Navarre* (February 1661).[13]

What was there so remarkable in the eyes of his contemporaries about the kind of comedy Molière offered them, and why were they so impressed with his originality? In the short space of time remaining before his early death, certain discerning judges were already hailing him as the greatest comic dramatist of all time – witness the tributes paid to him on his death in 1673[14] – yet for his contemporaries at large he remained primarily a performer, an entertainer. Confirmation of this can be seen in the painting, now in the possession of the Comédie-Française, of the 'Farceurs français et italiens depuis soixante ans et plus', a painting which was executed in 1670, and in which Molière appears alongside such figures as Turlupin, Jodelet. and Scaramouche.[15] The following anecdote related by Louis Racine may well be apocryphal:

> Le Roi demandant un jour (à Boileau) quel était le plus rare des grands écrivains qui avaient honoré la France pendant son règne, il lui nomma Molière: 'Je ne le croyais pas', répondit le Roi, 'mais vous vous y connaissez mieux que moi.'[16]

At any rate the King's reported surprise strikes an authentic note: the royal patronage extended to Molière, however valuable, was really no more than condescension towards a talented actor who had the knack of amusing His Majesty. And Boileau's own assessment is more fully represented in the well-known lines from his *Art poétique*. Molière, says Boileau, would perhaps have been without equal as a writer of comedy,

> Si, moins ami du peuple, en ses doctes peintures,
> Il n'eût point fait souvent grimacer ses figures,
> Quitté, pour le bouffon, l'agréable et le fin,
> Et sans honte à Térence allié Tabarin.
> Dans ce sac ridicule où Scapin s'enveloppe,
> Je ne reconnais plus l'auteur du *Misanthrope*.[17]

[13] I have argued elsewhere ('*Dom Garcie de Navarre* or *Le Prince Jaloux?*', *French Studies*, v (1951), 140–8) that the affinities of this play with later comedies are more important than the untypical elevation of style. Molière was not attempting to create a hybrid genre, still less to write a tragedy (cf. 'Molière's one attempt at a tragedy . . .', R. J. Nelson, 'Molière: the Metaphysic of Comedy', *Esprit Créateur*, xv, 1–2 (1975), 129). See pp. 134ff. below.

[14] See Mongrédien (ed.), *Recueil*, pp. 437–77.   [15] See Plate III.

[16] *Mémoires* (1747) (Paris, 1885), pp. 270–1; quoted Mongrédien (ed.), *Recueil*, p. 434.

[17] *Art poétique* (1674), III, lines 395–400.

The qualification is all-important: for Boileau, Molière's claim to supremacy as a comic dramatist was compromised by the survival, through to some of his later works, of those features of popular farce that he had depended on when playing before provincial audiences, and which had characterised his early Parisian 'divertissements'.

Long before Molière's return to Paris in 1658, traditional farce had virtually disappeared from the Parisian stage. This genre, as it had developed in the mediaeval theatre, had taken the form of brief sketches with the simplest of plots, often of the 'biter bit' variety. They offered satirical portraits of social types such as the monk, the scholar, or the lawyer, or else presented a caricatural view of the conjugal relationship, with henpecked husband and domineering wife; but satire and caricature were by no means incompatible with homely domestic realism. The popularity of this indigenous kind of farce had declined steadily from the early years of the seventeenth century; it proved unable to stand up to competition with a more literary form of comedy on the one hand, and with *commedia dell'arte* farce on the other. In the 1620s, however, it was still being successfully maintained at the Hôtel de Bourgogne by a famous trio of *farceurs*: Turlupin, Gros-Guillaume and Gaultier-Garguille.[18] On the latter's death in 1633 he was replaced by an equally talented successor in Guillot-Gorju,[19] but Gros-Guillaume too died in 1634, and Turlupin in 1637, and with their departure the days of French farce were over. Actors like these also played serious roles, of course, but they made their reputation as *farceurs*; and when the young Molière was taken to the Hôtel de Bourgogne at the age of ten or so by a grandfather who was devoted to the theatre, it was their farcical sketches that he saw and remembered. By this time, the native French style had been much influenced by the livelier and more inventive manner of the *commedia dell'arte*. Turlupin, for instance, wore a costume modelled on that of the Italian valet, Brighella, and an Italian-style mask (though Gros-Guillaume preserved the French practice of covering his face with flour instead of wearing a mask), and the farces offered by the Hôtel de Bourgogne appear to have been based on an amalgam of the two styles; as with the Italian *commedia*, much was left to last-minute improvisation, and that is no doubt why virtually no texts have survived.

[18] These were the professional names respectively of Henri Legrand, Robert Guérin and Hugues Guéru. See G. Mongrédien, *Les Grands Comédiens du xviie siècle* (Paris, 1927), pp. 1–9.　　[19] *Ibid.*

This was the tradition perpetuated by Molière during his provincial wanderings; to quote Grimarest:

> Il avait accoutumé sa troupe à jouer sur-le-champ de petites comédies, à la manière des Italiens. Il en avait deux entre autres, que tout le monde en Languedoc, jusqu'aux personnes les plus sérieuses, ne se lassaient [*sic*] point de voir représenter. C'étaient les *Trois Docteurs rivaux* et le *Maître d'école*, qui étaient entièrement dans le goût italien.[20]

Half a dozen titles of these early sketches, or *canevas* in the Italian manner, presumably composed by Molière, have come down to us, listed by La Grange in his *Registre*: in addition to those already mentioned (here called *Le Docteur amoureux, Les Trois Docteurs* and *Gros-René écolier*), there are *Le Docteur pédant, La Casaque, Gorgibus dans le sac* and *Le Fagotier*. The two latter were most likely primitive versions respectively of *Les Fourberies de Scapin* and *Le Médecin malgré lui*; and the whole group of titles suggests *commedia*-type intrigue, slapstick, and fixed, stereotyped characters. Besides these bare titles, two plays from that period have survived, which can with some confidence be attributed to Molière. In *La Jalousie du Barbouillé* the central character is the traditional *mal-marié* of the farces, deceived and outwitted by his wife: his name indicates the actor's floured face, intended, like the Italian mask, to denote a fixed stereotype. This sketch provides the first draft of the last act of *George Dandin* (1668), in which the jealous husband is fooled by his flighty wife; it also contains scenes of absurd verbal comedy featuring the traditional pedant. Even if Molière was not the author, and even if it is most likely that Du Parc (and not Molière himself) played Le Barbouillé,[21] it would be difficult to overestimate the importance of this character in the development of his own theatre, for here is to be seen the ancestor of many of his characteristic comic dupes. *Le Médecin volant* is recognisably Italian in its inspiration: more visual in its appeal to the spectator, it calls for great suppleness and agility in the principal role of the resourceful valet. Its plot is more complicated, and is based on lovers' intrigue, not on the conjugal relationship: it depends on disguise and mistaken identity, with the valet as *meneur du jeu*.

In April 1659, Molière recruited for his company the most celebrated comic actor of his generation, Jodelet 'le Fariné', who alone

[20] *La Vie de M. de Molière*, pp. 45–6.
[21] This is pure conjecture as regards the first performances in the provinces; but if the play recorded by La Grange as *La Jalousie de Gros-René* is the same as *La Jalousie du Barbouillé*, the part must have been taken in Paris by Du Parc.

had preserved, at the Théâtre du Marais, something of the manner of the earlier *farceurs*, with whom he provides the most tangible link. Jodelet played a thoroughly conventional valet's role under his own name in burlesque comedies, or plot-comedies in the Spanish manner, written by Scarron and others in the middle years of the century. Molière was to revive some of these plays as a vehicle for his new colleague,[22] and in *Les Précieuses ridicules* wrote a part for him, still with his flour-daubed face and under his own name (as 'le Vicomte de Jodelet') alongside his own Mascarille.

According to contemporary commentators, Molière's own acting style owed much to the Italians with whom he shared the Petit-Bourbon theatre on first returning to Paris;[23] and here again, valuable testimony is provided by his jealous detractors. Somaize, for instance, wrote at the time of the controversy over *Les Précieuses ridicules*:

> Il a imité par une singerie dont il est seul capable le *Médecin volant* et plusieurs autres pièces des . . . Italiens, qu'il n'imite pas seulement en ce qu'ils ont joué sur leur théâtre, mais encore en leurs postures, contre-faisant sans cesse sur le sien et Trivelin et Scaramouche; mais qu'attendre d'un homme qui tire toute sa gloire des *Mémoires* de Guillot-Gorju qu'il a achetés de sa veuve et dont il s'adopte tous les ouvrages?[24]

There is abundant evidence of the esteem in which Molière held his colleague Tiberio Fiorelli, famous on stage as Scaramouche:

> Molière aimait fort Scaramouche pour ses manières naturelles; il le voyait jouer fort souvent, et il lui a servi à former les meilleurs acteurs de sa troupe.[25]

The following epigram from a biography of the Italian pays a handsome compliment to the talents of both actors:

> Cet illustre comédien
> Atteignit de son art l'agréable manière.
> Il fut le maître de Molière,
> Et la nature fut le sien[26]

while even the following hostile comment pays unwitting tribute to

[22] For instance, Scarron's *Jodelet ou le Maître-valet* and *Don Japhet d'Arménie*, and Thomas Corneille's *Jodelet prince*. These plays all remained in the company's repertoire after Jodelet's death at Easter 1660.

[23] Until July 1659.   [24] Mongrédien (ed.), *Recueil*, p. 117.

[25] From the *Recueil de Tralage* (1966), quoted *ibid.*, p. 262. And cf. *Ménagiana* (1693): 'Molière, original français, n'a jamais voulu perdre une représentation de cet original italien' (*ibid.*, p. 665).

[26] A. Constantini, *Vie de Scaramouche* (1695), quoted *ibid.*, p. 691.

the thoroughness of Molière's technical preparations for each part he played:

> Chez le grand Scaramouche il va soir et matin.
> Là, le miroir en main et ce grand homme en face,
> Il n'est contorsion, posture ni grimace
> Que ce grand écolier du plus grand des bouffons
> Ne fasse et ne refasse en cent et cent façons.[27]

As has been seen, a major reason for Molière's lack of success in serious roles was that he was too 'natural': he refused to adopt the stylised, emphatic declamation of his rivals at the Hôtel de Bourgogne, and was therefore judged to lack dignity and presence. But in comedy, things were different: here, we may suppose that the substitution of a less emphatic acting style was in keeping with the taste of at least the more refined element among the spectators; and it seems that Molière (with or without the aid of Scaramouche) did effect a significant revolution in the comic actor's technique. His attention to detail, both in his own acting and as manager of his company, training his colleagues in the technical minutiae of their craft, is well documented. Donneau de Visé may be indulging in picturesque exaggeration when he writes of *L'École des femmes*:

> Jamais comédie ne fut si bien représentée ni avec tant d'art; chaque acteur sait combien il doit faire de pas et toutes ses oeillades sont comptées.[28]

There is, however, ample corroboration of the spirit of his remark in the following analysis of Molière's performance as Sganarelle in the play of that name:

> Il ne s'est jamais rien vu de si agréable que les postures de Sganarelle, quand il est derrière sa femme: son visage et ses gestes expriment si bien la jalousie, qu'il ne serait pas nécessaire qu'il parlât pour paraître le plus jaloux des hommes . . .[29]

L'Impromptu de Versailles, that invaluable portrait of Molière the actor–manager, makes it clear that all these efforts tended in the direction of a convincingly natural acting style, and away from the rigid stereotypes of mid-century burlesque. As La Fontaine was later to write:

---

[27] Le Boulanger de Chalussay, *Élomire hypocondre* (1670), in *Molière Mocked: Three Contemporary Hostile Comedies*, ed. F. W. Vogler (Chapel Hill, N.C., 1973), p. 127.

[28] *Nouvelles nouvelles* (1663), quoted Mongrédien (ed.), *Recueil*, p. 177.

[29] La Neufvillenaine, *Arguments du Cocu imaginaire* (1660), quoted in Molière, *Oeuvres*, ed. E. Despois and P. Mesnard (Paris, 1873–1900), II, p. 174.

Nous avons changé de méthode;
Jodelet n'est plus à la mode,
Et maintenant il ne faut pas
Quitter la nature d'un pas.[30]

What Molière learned from his frequenting of Scaramouche was almost certainly physical flexibility and mobility of features. For whereas previous Scaramouches had been masked, Fiorelli, the most famous of them all, being the 'prince des grimaciers', merely powdered his face; and his influence must have been of paramount importance in the evolution from the stylised techniques associated with farce, towards the more naturalistic manner of Molière's maturity.

(ii) The actor–manager

The opening page of La Grange's *Registre*, recording the company's Paris debut, reads as follows:

> Le Sr de Molière et sa troupe arrivèrent à Paris au mois d'octobre 1658 et se donnèrent à Monsieur, frère unique du Roi, qui leur accorda l'honneur de sa protection et le titre de ses Comédiens avec 300*l*. de pension pour chaque comédien.[31]

Even though a marginal addition indicates that 'les 300 *l*. n'ont point été payées', we may assume that Monsieur's protection did fulfil the really vital function of providing Molière and his colleagues with a chance to perform in public at the Louvre. In recognition of their success on this occasion, and as a token of the King's favour, the newly-arrived company were allowed to share the Salle du Petit-Bourbon, alongside the Louvre, with the resident Italian troupe, the Italians retaining the fashionable days of the week – Sundays, Tuesdays and Fridays – while Molière was given the 'jours extraordinaires'.[32] This was a slim enough base from which to challenge the theatrical establishment of Paris, and no doubt the confidence to make such a challenge came only gradually. For the distance separating the new arrivals, with their precarious toe-hold in the Petit-Bourbon, from the 'Grands Comédiens' at the Hôtel de Bourgogne with half a century of tradition behind them, was immense. The prestige of the Hôtel de Bourgogne had been shared for a

---

[30] *Lettre à Maucroix* (1661), quoted *ibid.*, p. 101.   [31] *Registre*, II, p. 1.
[32] This arrangement remained in force until July 1659, when the Italian troupe was disbanded.

while in the 1630s and 1640s by Mondory's company at the Théâtre du Marais, where all of Corneille's early successes were staged; but more recently the Hôtel had achieved a virtual monopoly of the best serious theatre,[33] while the Marais – too remote in any case to compete on equal terms – had begun to specialise in machine-plays.

Molière's achievement in imposing his unknown troupe on this theatrical scene, against all odds, is quite remarkable. No doubt his success depended to some extent, from the beginning, on royal favour; but the Troupe de Monsieur was by no means cushioned from adversity, and survival more than once depended on Molière's ability to defend his interests and those of his colleagues. At Easter 1659, at the end of the theatrical season, Du Parc and his wife, who had been with Molière in the provinces, left to join the Marais, while Dufresne, whose troupe had amalgamated with that of Molière and the Béjarts at an early point in their provincial journeyings, chose that moment to go into retirement. This loss of three experienced actors from a company of ten[34] might have been a bad omen; not only, however, did Molière fill the gaps more than satisfactorily by taking in the experienced Jodelet and his brother, but he built better than he knew in recruiting three 'acteurs nouveaux à Paris', Du Croisy and his wife and above all La Grange, whose services to the company must in any reckoning come second only to those of Molière himself.[35] A more serious crisis faced the troupe in October 1660, when extensions to the Louvre caused the Salle du Petit-Bourbon to be demolished; and so precarious was their tenure that this could take place without prior notice.[36] On that occasion Monsieur's protection, and the King's favour, were all that stood between the company and complete disaster: the King granted Molière the use of the Palais-Royal theatre,[37]

---

[33] According to Tallemant, writing in 1657–8, 'le théâtre du Marais n'a pas un seul bon acteur, ni une seule bonne actrice' (*Historiettes*, II, p. 778). In a letter of May 1658 (Mongrédien (ed.), *Recueil*, p. 100), Thomas Corneille suggests that if Molière's troupe (then still in the provinces) could amalgamate with the Marais company, that might change the latter's fortunes, though it would need a 'miracle'.

[34] Six men, four women.

[35] La Grange succeeded Molière as *orateur de la troupe* in 1664, and gradually replaced Madeleine Béjart as business manager. His *Registre*, and his Preface to the 1682 edition of the dramatist's works, provide the most valuable first-hand account of Molière's career in Paris; and after Molière's death it was La Grange's administrative ability that held the company together.

[36] La Grange reports that Ratabon, Surintendant des Bâtiments du Roi, 'n'avait pas cru qu'il fallait entrer en considération de la comédie pour avancer le dessein du Louvre' (*Registre*, II, p. 26).

[37] Built for Richelieu in the 1630s in what was then called the Palais-Cardinal.

and ordered that renovations should be paid for out of the public purse. In the three months during which they were without a theatre, the company faced a further threat: attempts by both the other Paris theatres to entice Molière's colleagues away from him:

> Mais toute la troupe de Monsieur demeura stable; tous les acteurs aimaient le sieur de Molière, leur chef, qui joignait à un mérite et une capacité extraordinaire une honnêteté et une manière engageante qui les obligea tous à lui promettre qu'ils voulaient courre sa fortune et qu'ils ne le quitteraient jamais, quelque proposition qu'on leur fît et quelque avantage qu'ils pussent trouver ailleurs.[38]

However, once installed at the Palais-Royal, Molière was well housed, in a central position; and it was there that all the master-pieces of his mature creative period were presented to the public. If the one-act *Sganarelle* of May 1660 can be regarded as the last product of Molière's long apprenticeship, then the move into the Palais-Royal, in addition to its critical importance for the fortunes of the troupe, acquires a symbolic value in the evolution of Molière the playwright. From now onwards the Troupe de Monsieur was a permanent, and an increasingly popular, feature of the Paris theatrical scene.

Further tangible marks of the King's favour came when they were most needed. First, during the controversy following the success of *L'École des femmes*, when a cabal of jealous actors, rival playwrights and their noble patrons produced a spate of pamphlets and plays attacking Molière not only in his professional activities but also in his private life – the episode that is often called 'la Guerre comique'[39] – the King granted Molière a pension of 1000 *l.*, lent his authority to *L'Impromptu de Versailles*, Molière's riposte to the Hôtel de Bourgogne, and scotched the scurrilous rumours about Molière's marriage by standing as godfather to the playwright's first child in February 1664.[40] The following year, 1665, brought Molière's first serious

---

[38] La Grange, *Registre*, I, pp. 25–8.
[39] For a collection of all the relevant texts, see *La Querelle de l'École des femmes*, ed. Mongrédien.
[40] In February 1662 Molière had married Armande Béjart, the young sister of his former mistress, Madeleine; however, in view of the difference between the ages of the two Béjarts (forty-four and twenty), there was some speculation that they were not sisters, but mother and daughter. According to a letter written by Racine (November 1663), Montfleury, the actor of the Hôtel de Bourgogne, had addressed a 'requête contre Molière' to the King: 'Il l'accuse d'avoir épousé la fille, et d'avoir autrefois couché avec la mère. Mais Montfleury n'est point écouté à la Cour' (Mongrédien (ed.), *Recueil*, p. 195).

brush with the ecclesiastical authorities. It is not known how far the suppression of *Dom Juan*, by far the most successful of Molière's plays judged by box-office receipts, after fifteen performances[41] was due to the direct intervention of the censor; what is certain is that the play was attacked by the *dévots*, and that far from heeding their appeal,[42] Louis chose this moment to put his patronage on a more permanent footing: Molière's company now became 'la troupe du Roi au Palais-Royal', with an increased pension of 6000 *l*.

Finally, in his protracted attempt to secure the unimpeded performance of *Tartuffe*, Molière had an ally in the King. For their own reasons, Louis XIV and Colbert were seeking to destroy the influence of the 'cabale des dévots', and though the King's hands were tied by the powerful opposition of the Queen Mother, the Archbishop of Paris and the President of the Parlement de Paris, the hope that he could ultimately count on the royal support that he did receive openly in 1669 must have been an important factor in persuading Molière not to abandon the struggle.

But these marks of royal favour towards one who, for a period of a dozen years or so, was evidently the King's favourite entertainer, were not purchased without cost. Most obviously, recipients of royal pensions were expected to earn their keep; Chapelain, submitting his list of recommended names to Colbert in 1663, wrote:

> Je ne fais, Monsieur, que vous indiquer ceux que je crois dignes de ces faveurs, suivant l'ordre que vous m'avez donné, afin d'avoir plusieurs trompettes des vertus du Roi.[43]

While it would be a gross exaggeration to see Molière as a servile or sycophantic writer, nevertheless the 'Remercîment au Roi' of 1663, and the eulogy of the 'prince ennemi de la fraude' that appears in *Tartuffe* (lines 1906–44) are both in their own way acknowledgements of favours received. A more equivocal case is that of *Amphitryon*, which has frequently been seen – and I think with some justice – as an indulgent commentary on the King's adulterous relationship with Madame de Montespan. There is no means of judging how far this sort of homage to the Sun King may have conflicted with Molière's

---

[41] For details, see my edition of the play (Oxford, 1958), pp. xxxii–xxxiii.

[42] Rochemont's *Observations sur une comédie de Molière intitulée le Festin de pierre* (1665) concluded with an appeal to the King: 'Nous avons tous sujet d'espérer que ce même bras qui est l'appui de la religion abattra tout à fait ce monstre et confondra à jamais son insolence.'

[43] Quoted by G. Mongrédien, *La Vie littéraire au xviie siècle* (Paris, 1947), p. 264.

private opinions: in any case, such compromises were an essential corollary of any system of royal patronage.

As officially pensioned entertainers, Molière and his troupe were expected to be at the call of the King and his Court; and not the least important information provided by the *Registre* as a log-book of the company's activities is the record of the *visites*, the performances which took place by royal command at Court, or by invitation in various princely or noble houses. René Bray has shown, in a most interesting analysis of this information, that the latter – nearly a hundred performances away from the Petit-Bourbon or the Palais-Royal, excluding those given at Court – took place predominantly during the early years, and indeed that during the second half of Molière's Paris career there were virtually no *visites* outside the restricted circle of 'la très haute aristocratie' (Monsieur at the Luxembourg, Condé at Chantilly):

> A partir du moment où la réputation de la compagnie fut établie les visites furent moins recherchées et peut-être évitées: Molière et ses camarades se consacrèrent au service quasi exclusif du public et du Roi.[44]

As for the royal command performances, during the latter period visits to one or other of the royal Courts – Versailles, Saint-Germain, Chambord – became an increasingly important part of the company's routine, and Bray has estimated that if one added together the periods spent in the King's service in this way, it would produce the remarkable total of a whole year's activity.[45]

Not only, as this indicates, was a significant proportion of Molière's time and energy devoted to the business of entertaining the King; but the majority of the new plays he wrote during the second half of his Paris career, from 1666 onwards, were first performed at Court. The constraints imposed by Molière's position as Court entertainer on his development as a writer have often been the subject of critical comment, many writers deploring the extent of his involvement in such undertakings as the 'Plaisirs de l'Ile enchantée' of 1664, the 'Ballet des Muses' of 1666, or the 1671 entertainments at the Tuileries.[46] However, to assume that without such constraints there would have been a greater flow of plays more in keeping with the taste of modern

---

[44] *Molière, homme de théâtre*, p. 165.   [45] *Ibid.*, p. 171.

[46] *La Princesse d'Élide* (together with the three-act version of *Tartuffe*) was created for the festivities at Versailles in 1664; *Mélicerte, La Pastorale comique* and *Le Sicilien* for the 'Ballet des Muses' (Saint-Germain, 1666); and *Psyché* (in collaboration with Corneille and Quinault) at the Tuileries for the Carnival season in 1671.

spectators or readers would be quite unjustified; and Bray is surely right when he remarks, 'Ceux qui regrettent qu'il ne nous ait pas donné davantage de *Misanthropes* se méprennent singulièrement sur son génie comique.'[47] The complete Molière is the Molière of Versailles, Chambord and Saint-Germain as well as the Molière of the Palais-Royal.

The organisation of Molière's company was similar to that of other seventeenth-century troupes – and indeed, not unlike that of the Comédie-Française today. The actors formed an association, each having the right to a share (in the case of new or inexperienced members, sometimes a half- or quarter-share) of the profits after expenses had been met; and La Grange's *Registre* gives for each day's performance the name of the play, the total takings, and the amount of an individual share. To begin with, as we have seen, the Troupe de Monsieur comprised ten *parts*: six men, four women, all of whom had acted together for five years in the provinces. The complement increased to twelve at Easter 1659, and that number was maintained in the following season, despite the deaths of Joseph Béjart and Jodelet, by the return of Du Parc (Gros-René) and his wife from the Marais – in itself surely a tribute to the successful start made by Molière and his colleagues. In 1662 the actors numbered fifteen, and in 1663 fourteen, each with a full *part*; but because of deaths and retirements – Gros-René, for instance, died in 1664 and his widow, the celebrated Marquise du Parc, now Racine's mistress, left to play Andromaque at the Hôtel de Bourgogne in 1667 – Molière allowed numbers to fall to eleven by 1668 or so. Possibly, as Bray suggests,[48] this was a precautionary measure, taken because of an appreciable loss of income between 1666 and 1668, and a consequent uncertainty as to future prospects. At all events, when the success of *Tartuffe* in 1669 brought renewed prosperity, more engagements were made, such as those of the young Baron and the Beauval couple from a provincial company, to enable the complement to be maintained at thirteen. For special purposes – for example, when the performance at the Palais-Royal of one of the *comédies-ballets* that had been premièred at Court called for musicians and dancers[49] – extras would be hired; but essentially,

---

[47] *Molière, homme de théâtre*, p. 171.   [48] *Ibid.*, p. 74.
[49] Cf. La Grange, *Registre*, pp. 125–6 (La Grange's note on exceptional expenses for musicians and dancers required for *Psyché*); p. 144 (similar note concerning *Le Malade imaginaire*).

Molière's resources were those of a company seldom exceeding about a dozen in number. While one or two members of the company were entitled, because of their physical appearance, professional expertise or reputation, to specialise in a narrow range of roles (Jodelet and Gros-René are examples), it goes without saying that for the most part the members of a small troupe, playing both comedy and tragedy, had to be fairly adaptable. There was no room for the hierarchical attitudes on the part of established members of a company, jealously defending the roles to which their seniority entitled them, such as marked the Comédie-Française for much of the eighteenth and nineteenth centuries; on the contrary, one has the impression of a genuine atmosphere of loyalty and solidarity in this company, which succeeded remarkably well in preserving the family spirit that had sustained it during its years in the provinces.[50] Of the twenty-two actors besides Molière himself who were members of the company during the fourteen-year period in Paris up to the latter's death, there was a permanent nucleus formed by the Béjart family: Madeleine and Geneviève, Joseph (who died in 1659), Louis (who retired in 1670) and Armande (who made her debut in 1662); by de Brie and his wife, who had been with them in the provinces; and by La Grange and Du Croisy, who joined after the first months at the Petit-Bourbon.[51]

As a portrait of Molière and his troupe in action, *L'Impromptu de Versailles* carries complete conviction. It suggests something, at least, of the particular attributes of each actor and actress; it gives an excellent indication of Molière's professional relationship with his colleagues; and although it stands in a class by itself as an example of the means by which Molière the dramatic author catered for the needs of his company, it illustrates remarkably well in a more general sense, too, the way in which the activities of the actor–manager and the playwright complemented each other.

Other actors among Molière's contemporaries turned their hands to writing plays: Dorimon and Villiers, authors of the two Don Juan plays in French which preceded Molière's; Brécourt, who was for a time a member of Molière's troupe; Poisson and Hauteroche of the

[50] The only evidence of jealousy concerns the women members of the troupe, during the first Paris season; this was no doubt the reason for the departure of Mlle du Parc. See Bray, *Molière, homme de théâtre*, pp. 70–1.
[51] See Appendix II; and for further details, see A. Copin, *Histoire des comédiens de la troupe de Molière* (Paris, 1886).

Hôtel de Bourgogne, among others. But none of these was a *chef de troupe*; none wrote more than a handful of plays; and virtually none of the plays concerned has retained more than a minor historical significance. Molière, on the contrary, wrote over thirty plays: that is to say, a good third of his company's repertory during their fifteen Paris seasons if one counts the titles of works performed, and well over two-thirds if one counts the number of performances. Moreover, his own plays were consistently the most successful, in box-office terms as well as in their impact on the public; and from the earliest successes, *Les Précieuses ridicules* and *Sganarelle, ou le Cocu imaginaire* onwards, there were few new plays by other authors that could compete with those Molière himself wrote for his troupe.[52] From this point of view it is obviously correct to say, as Mongrédien does: 'C'est donc bien Molière, auteur, qui soutint et fit vivre la troupe de Molière, acteur':[53] the benefits conferred on the company by their leader's activities as a playwright hardly need spelling out. Our concern is in any case with the reverse effect of the relationship between the playwright and the actor–manager: the influence of Molière's theatrical career, the need to provide a constant supply of new plays, on his evolution as a dramatist. Bray's provocative remark, that in studying the genesis of a play like *Le Misanthrope* we should look first of all at 'le nombre et la qualité des actrices dont [Molière] disposait',[54] was perhaps not meant to be taken literally. Insofar as such considerations are valid, they will at best affect details of the structure of a play, not its central comic principle; and while there may be a limited number of cases in which Molière does seem to have had the specific talents of one of his colleagues in mind in writing a part for him (the Vicomte de Jodelet in the *Précieuses ridicules* is a case in point), it would be wrong to attach too much importance to factors of this sort.[55] There is one technical consideration, however, the importance of which it would be difficult to overestimate: the nature of Molière's own gifts as a comic actor. Even if he began to write for the theatre in response to the needs of his company as a whole, the development from the provincial farces to the mature comedies of the last ten years of his life reflects the evolution of his own acting skills. Other, less tangible, factors no doubt played an important part in this development: the playwright's reaction to the critical reception of his early plays, his response to the

---

[52] See Appendix III.   [53] *Vie quotidienne*, p. 195.   [54] See above, p. 2.
[55] Bray's deductions from a comparison of the roles played by each of Molière's colleagues (*Molière, homme de théâtre*, pp. 284ff.) are ingenious rather than convincing.

views of those spectators whose judgement he valued. But whatever the influence of these external factors, it seems certain that a compelling personal motive was the consciousness of his own particular theatrical talent, and it is here that we must seek, in the first place, the key to Molière the comic dramatist.

(iii) Mascarille into Sganarelle

From the two provincial farces, *La Jalousie du Barbouillé* and *Le Médecin volant*, which stand at the threshold of Molière's career and most probably represent his own earliest compositions, it does not require too much imagination to see developing two distinct types of comic role which between them embrace nearly the whole of Molière's later work, and which can be identified with the names of two of the earliest parts he created for himself as an actor. One of these, which we may call the Mascarille type, has a brief but brilliant career, and is thereafter only very occasionally seen again, notably in the Scapin of *Les Fourberies*; the other, however, the Sganarelle type, develops from Le Barbouillé through the half-dozen early Sganarelles into a whole series of major comic roles which dominate Molière's mature comedy. The most important development of Molière's early years in Paris, from the point of view of his subsequent career both as actor and as playwright, was without a doubt the abandonment of Mascarille for Sganarelle. We do not know why, some eighteen months after the return to Paris – between the *Précieuses ridicules* of November 1659 and *Sganarelle, ou le Cocu imaginaire* of May 1660 – Molière should have decided not to exploit the success he had achieved as the Mascarille of *L'Étourdi* (created at Lyon, probably in 1655) and of the *Précieuses*, and to develop instead a very different role for himself. Where Mascarille had been Italian in inspiration, Sganarelle was French; where Mascarille was probably masked,[56] and certainly belonged to a masked tradition, Sganarelle was played without a mask. Mascarille was a mercurial, resourceful, extrovert role; Sganarelle was introspective and self-absorbed, and at first sight offered less scope for theatrical effect. But experience was to show that the Mascarille type had a

---

[56] This was for a long time disputed, though it is now generally accepted. Important in this connection is a mention by Christian Huyghens of a performance in January 1661: 'A la comédie au Palais-Royal, vu jouer ... les Précieuses ridicules de Molière. Mascarille masqué, le [vi]comte enfariné' (Mongrédien (ed.), *Recueil*, p. 141). See also L. Lacour, *Molière acteur* (Paris, 1928), p. 49.

much more restricted range, while the simple Sganarelle contained unlimited potential for development: whereas Mascarille was wholly a product of the theatre, Sganarelle had his roots in the observation of ordinary life.

It has been said that the essence of Molière's characteristic comedy resides in the confrontation between the *fourbe* and his dupe; between naïvety and cunning. Already, in the *Précieuses*, the dramatic interest had been shared between the rogues and their victims; Molière was shortly to discover that his own potential as an actor lay rather in the portrayal of the gullible dupe than in further exploitation of the traditional valet's cunning; and with the creation of the Sganarelle type in 1660, the foundations of his mature comedy were laid.

Sganarelle's theatrical antecedents are not to be found in the scheming valets of the *commedia dell' arte* (though one or two of the characters bearing this name have a certain affinity with the cowardly Arlecchino), but in the henpecked husbands of the mediaeval French farces. In spite of the Italian source of the name (it derives almost certainly from *sgannare*, 'to disabuse', the opposite of *ingannare*, 'to dupe'),[57] the role has no counterpart in Italian comedy. On the other hand, the first Sganarelle had appeared in the provinces in *Le Médecin volant* where, as we have seen, certain features of the plot were strongly reminiscent of the Italian tradition, and where Sganarelle's role had been that of the active valet, pressed into service to help his master's amorous designs. The theatricality of this early play is well characterised by Jouanny:

> Cette farce est un curieux exercice de voltige par quoi un acteur peut apprendre à connaître les dimensions d'un plateau de théâtre, les entrées et les sorties rapides, les déguisements multiples et presque simultanés, les jeux de scène les plus extravagants. La pièce est entraînée à une cadence qui va s'accélérant et s'écarte de plus en plus du vrai, pour nous arrêter devant cette maison dont les fenêtres laissent jaillir de drôles de corps. Le placide Gros-René en est éberlué; mais nous, nous sommes dans le secret; nous savons qu'il s'agit d'un monde burlesque et unique comme seul le théâtre peut en créer.[58]

It would no doubt have been a good deal neater for the purposes of our argument if this early Sganarelle had been called Mascarille. Indeed, the author of a recent article, 'Les Métamorphoses de Sganarelle', faced with the same dilemma, argues ingeniously that

[57] See H. Fritsche, 'Réponse à M. Baluffe', *Le Moliériste*, VI (1884), 82–4.
[58] Molière, *Oeuvres complètes*, ed. Jouanny, I, p. 4.

Sganarelle may not have been his original name: since we do not know the date of the manuscript in which the text of *Le Médecin volant* survived (it was not brought to light until the eighteenth century, and was published for the first time in the nineteenth), the name may have been changed long after the character was first created for that of a character Molière had subsequently created and made famous.[59]

But this is pure speculation, and perhaps not very plausible; what one can say with some certainty is that *Le Médecin volant* was an early farce, written at an unknown date during the years in the provinces, and before Molière had yet fixed the traits of the role which was later to be labelled Sganarelle; and moreover, that even the early Sganarelle of *Le Médecin volant* offers more hints of potential in terms of real character-development than the Arlecchino, Trivelino or Scappino of the *commedia*. Even in this early sketch he seems to be something of an amateur at the job he is reluctantly called on to do – certainly if we compare him with the confident, expert Mascarille of other early plays. 'C'est un lourdaud qui gâtera tout', says his master, 'mais il faut s'en servir faute d'autre' (scene i); and he already prefigures what one might call the 'anti-hero' characteristics of the Sganarelles of *Le Cocu imaginaire*, *Dom Juan* or *Le Médecin malgré lui*.

We do not know what costume Molière may have worn when playing this first Sganarelle. With the Sganarelle type as created in the early 1660s, however, we are on surer ground. A well-known portrait of Molière shows him in the traditional posture of the *orateur de la troupe*; it is undated, but the contemporary engraver bestowed on it the caption: 'Le vrai portrait de M. de Molière en habit de Sganarelle'.[60] The simple, plain costume with skull-cap, ruff and short cloak, seems to be modelled on that of Scaramouche in similar posture;[61] nevertheless, there should be little difficulty in accepting the caption as accurate, since corroboration is not lacking. First of all, there seems to be a marked resemblance between the costume of 'Molière en orateur de la troupe' and the indications given in the inventory of Molière's wardrobe made after his death, with regard to the costumes of the next two Sganarelles, the central figures of *Sganarelle ou le Cocu imaginaire* (1660): 'haut-de-chausses, pourpoint et manteau, col et souliers, le tout de satin rouge cramoisi', and of *L'École des maris* (1661): 'haut-de-chausses, pourpoint, manteau, col,

---

[59] J.-M. Pelous, 'Les Métamorphoses de Sganarelle: la permanence d'un type comique', *Revue d'Histoire Littéraire de la France*, LXXII (1972), 821–49.
[60] See Plate IIb.   [61] See Plate IIa.

escarcelle et ceinture, le tout de satin couleur de musc'.[62] And the resemblance is underlined by the engraver of the earliest frontispieces of these two plays, which show Sganarelle in a recognisably similar costume, and one which in both cases contrasts sharply with the fashionable lace and frills of the gallant lover whom the engraver has chosen also to portray.[63] In other words, when Sganarelle is transposed into a comfortable bourgeois milieu, his plain, unadorned costume is at once a reminder of his origins in the valet of the farce tradition, and a distinguishing feature of a certain kind of bourgeois. The more realistic the setting of the plays in which he appears, the more his dress gives visual emphasis to his naïvety, his gullibility, his alienation from the world surrounding him.

Whatever the reason which determined Molière to turn away from the Mascarille roles that he had previously created, it was not lack of success. Even Le Boulanger de Chalussay, author of the hostile *Élomire hypocondre* (1670), is forced to recognise that *L'Étourdi* had been an unqualified success for both author and actor. It may well be that Molière's accomplishments as a comic actor are deliberately introduced as a contrast, to point up his lack of success in tragedy[64] – but even so, the evidence is valuable:

> . . . Au lieu des pièces de Corneille,
> Je jouai l'*Étourdi*, qui fut une merveille;
> Car à peine on m'eut vu la hallebarde au poing,
> A peine on eut ouï mon plaisant baragouin,
> Vu mon habit, ma toque, et ma barbe et ma fraise,
> Que tous les spectateurs furent transportés d'aise,
> Et qu'on vit sur leurs fronts s'effacer ces froideurs
> Qui nous avaient causé tant et tant de malheurs.
> Du parterre au théâtre, et du théâtre aux loges,[65]
> La voix de cent échos fait cent fois mes éloges;
> Et cette même voix demande incessamment
> Pendant trois mois entiers ce divertissement.[66]

Both Mascarilles are extrovert, exhibitionist roles, displays of

---

[62] Jurgens and Maxfield-Miller, *Cent ans*, pp. 569–70.

[63] These engravings have often been reproduced: see for instance the Pléiade *Album Théâtre classique*, ed. Sylvie Chevalley (Paris, 1970), pp. 87, 92.

[64] Cf. Thomas Corneille's remark: 'le grand monde qu'ils ont eu à leur farce des *Précieuses* . . . fait bien connaître qu'ils ne sont propres qu'à soutenir de semblables bagatelles, et que la plus forte pièce tomberait entre leurs mains' (letter to Abbé de Pure, 1 December 1659, quoted Mongrédien (ed.), *Recueil*, p. 114).

[65] 'Le théâtre': i.e. the seats on the stage.

[66] Quoted Mongrédien (ed.), *Recueil*, p. 105.

theatrical virtuosity.[67] In the first case, Molière's costume appears to have been a functional one: 'un autre habit pour l' *Étourdi*, consistant en pourpoint, haut-de-chausse, manteau de satin';[68] but in the second, the extravagant costume was an essential part of the role. The Mascarille of the *Précieuses* has always been an illustrator's delight, and the following account is proof that the early engravers were not letting their imagination run away with them:

> Imaginez-vous, Madame, que sa perruque était si grande qu'elle balayait la place à chaque fois qu'il faisait la révérence, et son chapeau si petit qu'il était aisé de juger que le marquis le portait bien plus souvent dans la main que sur la tête; son rabat se pouvait appeler un honnête peignoir, et ses canons semblaient n'être faits que pour servir de cache aux enfants qui jouent à la cligne-musette. . . . Un brandon de glands lui sortait de la poche comme d'une corne d'abondance, et ses souliers étaient si couverts de rubans qu'il ne m'est pas possible de vous dire s'ils étaient de roussi, de vache d'Angleterre ou de maroquin; du moins sais-je bien qu'ils avaient un demi-pied de haut, et que j'étais bien en peine de savoir comment des talons si hauts et si délicats pouvaient porter le poids du marquis, ses rubans, ses canons et sa poudre.[69]

In his extravagances of dress, speech and behaviour, the 'Marquis de Mascarille' combines the fantasy of comic invention with a portrayal of observed reality. He is at once a variation on a fixed role – that of a valet adept at assuming disguises – and (something new in Molière) a satirical portrait of a social type. Though as a vehicle for social satire, the valet or servant disguised offered only limited possibilities: one has only to look at early eighteenth-century comedy to see how repetitive the device can become.

Compared with the brilliance of the Mascarille roles, the Sganarelle of 1660 may seem disappointingly sober. It has, indeed, been suggested that now he was nearing the age of forty, Molière may have felt the need to settle down to a style of acting more suited to his years:

> Mascarille avait fait son temps: valet de l'Étourdi et mystificateur hardi des Précieuses, Mascarille nous représente la jeunesse de Molière, qui

---

[67] There is yet another Mascarille, that of *Dépit amoureux* (created at Béziers in 1656), but that part was not taken by Molière, who played Albert. It has often been remarked that this Mascarille is a much less brilliant creation: indeed, like the Sganarelle of *Le Médecin volant*, Mascarille in *Dépit amoureux* represents something of a hybrid of the two types of role.

[68] Jurgens and Maxfield-Miller, *Cent ans*, p. 570.

[69] Mlle Desjardins, *Récit de la farce des Précieuses* (1660), quoted by Lacour, *Molière acteur*, p. 63.

s'en allait tantôt passée. A l'âge de trente-huit ans et plus, il lui fallait un caractère plus mûr, moins pétulant, moins moqueur. Sganarelle est dans ces conditions.[70]

But this explanation, with its suggestion of a *pis aller*, is not wholly convincing; nor is the interesting suggestion, made by Lancaster, that the Sganarelle of 1660 was originally conceived for Jodelet as a natural sequel to the role he had played under his own name in the *Précieuses*. Arguing from plot-resemblances between *Sganarelle* and the Jodelet plays of Scarron, as well as from similarities between the two characters, Lancaster writes: 'These resemblances suggest that Molière, who must have begun the play before Easter, 1660, intended the role of Sganarelle for Jodelet himself, but, as the latter died before it was performed, the author replaced him.'[71]

What is certain is that the Sganarelle roles, if they called for different talents, were no less demanding than Mascarille had been. Perhaps the most important difference between the two, from the actor's point of view, is that Mascarille's was a masked role, whereas Sganarelle was from the beginning played without a mask, allowing full scope for facial grimace as well as bodily gesture. And it is the range of facial expressions, and of gestures, that Molière brought to the latter that is particularly noted in La Neufvillenaine's commentary on the play.

All that is known of this personage is what he tells us himself. Having seen *Sganarelle* so often that he had learned the text by heart, and having written the text out together with a commentary for the benefit of a friend in the provinces, he then found, he says, that other parties were planning to bring out a pirated edition, and therefore arranged with the publisher Ribou to get in first with his own edition. Molière naturally took legal action (he had already had a brush with Ribou over the *Précieuses*), but the matter was settled fairly amicably. To this curious episode we owe a commentary on the play which puts *Sganarelle* in a decidedly privileged position. We are able to follow, scene by scene, and build up a convincing mental picture of Molière the actor at work, as seen by a contemporary spectator:

> Il faudrait avoir le pinceau de Poussin, le Brun et Mignard pour vous représenter avec quelle posture Sganarelle se fait admirer dans cette

[70] A. Bazin, *Notes historiques sur la vie de Molière* (1851), quoted in Molière, *Oeuvres*, ed. Despois and Mesnard, II, p. 160.
[71] *A History of French Dramatic Literature in the Seventeenth Century* (9 vols., Baltimore, 1929–42), III, i, p. 230.

scène, où il paraît avec un parent de sa femme (scene xii). L'on n'a jamais vu tenir de discours si naïfs, ni paraître avec un visage si niais, et l'on ne doit pas moins admirer l'auteur pour avoir fait cette pièce, que pour la manière dont il la représente. Jamais personne ne sut si bien démonter son visage, et l'on peut dire que dedans cette pièce il en change plus de vingt fois . . .[72]

La Neufvillenaine's *Arguments* would have been a precious adjunct to any of Molière's plays; they are doubly so, as a commentary on the creation of the new role of Sganarelle the *imaginaire*. They help us to visualise with remarkable clarity the actor's new-found style: no longer a virtuoso demonstration of theatricality, but a synthesis of lifelike gestures and expressions, just sufficiently stylised to suggest the dominance of an *idée fixe*; and already in this early play of 1660 we can discern the happy marriage of the performer's techniques and the writer's talents on which Molière's mature comedy was so largely to depend.

[72] La Neufvillenaine, *Arguments*, quoted in Molière, *Oeuvres*, ed. Despois and Mesnard, II, p. 189. Cf. also the passage quoted above, p. 17.

2

' A playwright and his audience

Le moins qu'un honnête homme puisse avoir affaire à ces animaux qu'on nomme comédiens, le mieux cela vaut pour lui.

(A court official (eighteenth-century))[1]

(i) Seventeenth-century audiences

Anyone writing about the social background to seventeenth-century literature should guard against the danger of circular argument: authors of a given period wrote as they did because they were catering for the tastes of their readers; and what better evidence have we of the tastes of those for whom they were writing, than the imaginative literature of the period? It is an insidious danger, because the evidence provided by the novels and plays of the past is more familiar to most of us than the documentary evidence furnished by letters, diaries and memoirs. To take a case in point: in *La Critique de l'École des femmes* Molière purports to present a cross-section of the audiences who had seen *L'École des femmes* itself, and to show the different reactions of a *précieuse*, a *marquis*, a man of letters, an *honnête homme* and their hostesses, two *salon* ladies of good taste. Of all his plays, the *Critique*, together with *L'Impromptu de Versailles*, seems to be the least marked by the caricatural exaggeration that is part and parcel of the creative process of any comic dramatist: it is a lifelike little conversation-piece, with characters whom we have no difficulty in accepting as representative. But do Climène, the Marquis and Lysidas represent observed reality? Are the ideas and opinions they express those of their counterparts in real life, or are they the prejudices Molière chose to attribute to certain groups of people with whom he had clashed since his return to Paris? Any evidence from Molière's own pen – or from that of any imaginative writer – must be used with caution; and where (as is sometimes the case) this is the only sort of evidence available, we must always be on the look-out for, and be ready to

[1] Quoted by J. Charon, *Moi, un comédien* (Paris, 1975), p. 193.

discount, any element of exaggeration for polemical purposes or for comic effect.

As it happens, we are reasonably well informed about the material conditions in which Molière and his troupe played at the Palais-Royal, and there is a fair amount of information about the composition of the theatre audiences of the period. A good deal of miscellaneous contemporary documentation exists, and modern historians, especially Lancaster, Mélèse, Mongrédien and Lough,[2] have performed an invaluable service in bringing together and interpreting this seventeenth-century material.

However, where much material does exist, it is tantalising that we lack the information that would complete the picture. For instance, while La Grange gives full particulars of the relative success, in terms of frequency of performance and of box-office takings, of all the plays put on by Molière's company, he does not provide details of the size of the audiences, or of the distribution of spectators between the various parts of the theatre: essential information if one is to attempt to assess the social composition of the audience with any accuracy. On the other hand, the *Registre* which his colleague Hubert kept, and which has been preserved for the 1672–3 season, does give these necessary statistics. We do not know the capacity of the Palais-Royal theatre with any certainty, but the largest number of paying spectators during the season in question was 925, with an average, over the 131 performances throughout the year, of approximately 400. Spectators were divided between the following locations, in descending order of cost:

	maximum number recorded
théâtre (seats on stage)	36
loges (front row of boxes)	99
amphithéâtre	124
loges hautes (second row of boxes)	206
loges du troisième rang	69
parterre	514
hypothetical total capacity	1048

With the reservation that Hubert's figures, strictly speaking, relate to a single season only, we may nevertheless take them as a rough guide

[2] Lancaster, *History*; Mélèse, *Théâtre*; Mélèse, *Répertoire*; Mongrédien, especially *Recueil*; J. Lough, *Paris Theatre Audiences in the Seventeenth and Eighteenth Centuries* (London, 1957).

to conditions obtaining throughout Molière's tenure of the Palais-Royal theatre.[3]

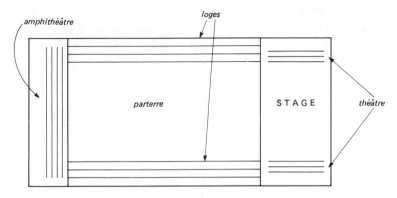

Fig. 1 Seating-plan of Molière's theatre at the Palais-Royal

Two of the locations in figure 1 call for particular comment:[4] the *théâtre* and the *parterre*, since each is identified with a specific class of spectator. The presence of spectators on stage – two or three rows of 'chaises de paille' on each side, and possibly also, if we are to believe the evidence of a contemporary engraving,[5] a number standing – was an abuse tolerated by the actors because these were the best-paying places.[6] The *théâtre* was an exclusively male preserve – as was the *parterre*, for different reasons. There is evidence that Molière himself

[3] See W. L. Schwarz, 'Molière's Theater in 1672 3: Light from *Le Registre d'Hubert*', *PMLA*, LVI (1941), 395–427. Schwarz's total of 1048 is reached by adding together the largest number of spectators recorded during the year in each part of the house. See also Schwarz's article analysing an earlier *Registre*: 'Light on Molière in 1664 from *Le Second Registre de la Thorillière*', *PMLA*, LIII (1938), 1054–75.

[4] The rectangular form derives from the *jeux de paume* (tennis-courts) used as theatres during the first half of the seventeenth century; this traditional shape was to influence French theatre design up to the Revolution, and can be seen in modified form in the present-day Comédie-Française (built in 1790).   [5] See Plate v.

[6] Introduced as a temporary measure, we are told, at the Marais during the successful run of *Le Cid*, the practice of seating fashionable spectators on stage soon became standard in Paris theatres (it seems that as early as the 1620s the 'recoins de théâtre' had been used by pages and lackeys); see S. W. Deierkauf-Holsboer, *L'Histoire de la mise en scène dans le théâtre français à Paris de 1600 à 1673* (Paris, 1960), p. 143. The practice was to last at the Comédie-Française until 1759. A. Adam, in his edition of Tallemant's *Historiettes* (II, p. 1526), states, though without indicating his source, that 'vers l'époque de Tallemant, on vit jusqu'à deux cents personnes sur la scène'. Schwarz's evidence would seem to be more reliable as regards the probable numbers on stage at the Palais-Royal.

35

took a seat on stage at the Hôtel de Bourgogne to observe the 'Grands Comédiens',[7] but generally speaking, these seats were occupied exclusively by young noblemen – moreover, fashionable, exhibitionist noblemen who went to the play to be seen, and who would not for the world mix with the common run of spectators in the *parterre*. François Doneau, whose admiration for Molière's *Sganarelle* took the form of plagiarism, writes in the Preface to his own *Cocue imaginaire*:

> Quoique Paris fût, ce semble, désert, il s'y est néanmoins encore assez trouvé de personnes de condition pour remplir plus de quarante fois les loges et le théâtre du Petit-Bourbon et assez de bourgeois pour remplir autant de fois le parterre.[8]

Other contemporary texts suggest that social divisions were not quite as rigid as Doneau implies. Wealthy bourgeois with their wives and families would occupy *loges* or the *amphithéâtre* – though the 'premières loges' are normally associated with ladies of quality – and there is plenty of evidence of members of the aristocracy, especially officers and pages, going into the *parterre*.

While the *loges* represented that informed, influential opinion to which playwrights found it expedient to defer, the *théâtre* and the *parterre* both contained sections of the audience to whose presence the actors were particularly sensitive. Both were restless and volatile; and both were potential sources of the kind of disturbance that could easily ruin the success of a performance.

It is for their nuisance value that the spectators on stage seem to have been particularly commented on. We must discount the exaggeration, for satirical purposes, of Molière's most celebrated portrait of such a spectator, one of the *fâcheux* in the play of that name:

> J'étais sur le théâtre, en humeur d'écouter
> La pièce, qu'à plusieurs j'avais ouï vanter;
> Les acteurs commençaient, chacun prêtait silence,
> Lorsque d'un air bruyant et plein d'extravagance,
> Un homme à grands canons est entré brusquement,
> En criant: 'Holà-ho! un siège promptement!'
> Et de son grand fracas surprenant l'assemblée,
> Dans le plus bel endroit a la pièce troublée. (lines 13–20)

It seems more than likely that this character's most outrageous behaviour belongs to the realm of fantasy:

---

[7] See Donneau de Visé, *Réponse à l'Impromptu de Versailles, ou la Vengeance des marquis* (1664), I, iii.   [8] Quoted Mongrédien (ed.), *Recueil*, p. 132.

> Les acteurs ont voulu continuer leurs rôles;
> Mais l'homme pour s'asseoir a fait nouveau fracas,
> Et traversant encor le théâtre à grands pas,
> Bien que dans les côtés il pût être à son aise,
> Au milieu du devant il a planté sa chaise,
> Et de son large dos morguant les spectateurs,
> Aux trois quarts du parterre a caché les acteurs. (lines 28–34)

But other details are less extravagant. The *fâcheux* arrives late, effusively greets an acquaintance, changes his place in order to sit beside him, keeps up a running commentary on the play:

> Et jusques à des vers qu'il en savait par coeur,
> Il me les récitait tout haut avant l'acteur (lines 57–8)

– and finally leaves, like all *gens du bel air*, before the end. Molière's satirical portrait is matched by similar vignettes from other dramatists – Regnard, for instance – and if their evidence, as that of interested parties, is felt to be suspect, it is worth noting that Tallemant, in his *Historiettes*, denounces the presence of spectators on stage as 'une incommodité épouvantable . . . cela gâte tout, et il ne faut quelquefois qu'un insolent pour tout troubler'.[9] Similarly, the Abbé de Pure, writing in 1668, gives a wholly convincing description of the effect of these spectators on theatrical illusion:

> Combien de fois, sur ces morceaux de vers: 'Mais le voici . . . mais je le vois', a-t-on pris pour un comédien et pour le personnage qu'on attendait, des hommes bien faits et bien mis qui entraient alors sur le théâtre, et qui cherchaient des places après même plusieurs scènes déjà exécutées?[10]

If the *théâtre* constituted a constant irritant, the *parterre*, or pit, represented, at any rate potentially, a much more disturbing influence. The *parterre* was not seated,[11] and its body of spectators, by that very fact, possessed some of the same characteristics as today's promenaders at the Albert Hall; even, at times, those we associate with football supporters on the terraces. The social composition of the *parterre* in Molière's time was mixed; though there is little evidence of a genuinely popular (in the sense of plebeian) element in the theatre audiences of the 1660s. Even Boileau's disparaging reference to that aspect of the comedy of Molière 'ami du peuple', which 'De mots sales

---

[9] II, p. 778.
[10] *Idée des spectacles anciens et nouveaux*, quoted by Mélèse, *Théâtre*, p. 211.
[11] The first Paris theatre to provide seats for the *parterre* was the one into which the Comédie-Française moved in 1784.

et bas [charme] la populace', although it is quoted by Lough in this context,[12] should probably be seen as expressing a dismissive attitude towards spectators of whose taste he disapproves, rather than as a precise indication of their class. Otherwise, evidence is fragmentary and somewhat contradictory, but it can be said with confidence that artisans and 'rude mechanicals' formed at most a negligible proportion of the *parterre*, and that this body of spectators was composed for the most part of 'solid bourgeois':[13] members of the professions, lawyers' clerks, shop assistants, with a leavening of men of letters and members of the nobility on the one hand,[14] and on the other of lackeys (their presence is well attested: they were presumably in attendance on the *gens de qualité* in the *loges*) and the military. Apart from the incidence of pickpockets, and minor quarrels of a personal nature, serious disturbances in the *parterre* seem to have been largely due to the last element, especially the *mousquetaires* and other troops of the royal household. Brawls, often involving the military, were a common feature of the *parterre* throughout the period, and the unruly behaviour of soldiers and pages was the subject of numerous edicts and decrees. Many of the incidents arose from attempts to enter without paying; Grimarest has an account of a fracas in which members of the King's household killed the porter of Molière's theatre,[15] but this ought perhaps to be treated with caution since it finds no echo in La Grange.

However undependable, the *parterre* was, as Hubert's figures show, by far the most numerous part of the audience; and the bourgeois in the *parterre* was to that extent a more representative spectator than the *marquis* on stage or the *grande dame* in her *loge*. In the first half of the century it had been normal for playwrights, as well as scholarly theorists of the drama, to express scorn for the taste of this section of the audience, as a collection of the most ignorant and uncultivated spectators; but by the end of the century dramatists were tending to show a much greater respect for their opinions, even if the academic writers still affected to look down on the judgement of the ordinary playgoer: Père Bouhours, for instance, writing in 1687, contrasts the taste of the *parterre* with that of 'personnes raisonnables'.[16] It seems clear that insofar as there was a change in the attitude of those writing

[12] *Paris Theatre Audiences*, p. 67.   [13] *Ibid.*, p. 81.
[14] Not, of course, the *grands seigneurs*. The playwright Boyer, writing of the exceptional success of his *Agamemnon* in 1680, claims that 'le théâtre [fut] si rempli, qu'on vit beaucoup de personnes de la première qualité prendre des places dans le parterre' (quoted by Lough, *ibid.*, p. 94).   [15] *La Vie de M. de Molière*, pp. 77–8.
[16] Quoted by Lough, *Paris Theatre Audiences*, p. 103.

for the theatre, it was Molière who led the way. To return to the *Critique de l'École des femmes*: on the one hand we have the satirical portrait of the affected Marquis and his kind, the spectators on stage:

> Tu es donc, Marquis, de ces Messieurs du bel air, qui ne veulent pas que le parterre ait du sens commun, et qui seraient fâchés d'avoir ri avec lui, fût-ce de la meilleure chose du monde? Je vis l'autre jour sur le théâtre un de nos amis, qui se rendit ridicule par là. Il écouta toute la pièce avec un sérieux le plus sombre du monde; et tout ce qui égayait les autres ridait son front. A tous les éclats de rire, il haussait les épaules, et regardait le parterre en pitié; et quelquefois aussi le regardant avec dépit, il lui disait tout haut: 'Ris donc, parterre, ris donc'. Ce fut une seconde comédie, que le chagrin de notre ami. (scene v)

On the other, we have the views of the enlightened Dorante, who diplomatically (but not necessarily insincerely) expresses Molière's respect both for the taste of the Court (excluding the self-opinionated *marquis*):

> Sachez, s'il vous plaît, Monsieur Lysidas, que les courtisans ont d'aussi bons yeux que d'autres; qu'on peut être habile avec un point de Venise et des plumes, aussi bien qu'avec une perruque courte et un petit rabat uni; que la grande épreuve de toutes vos comédies, c'est le jugement de la Cour; que c'est son goût qu'il faut étudier pour trouver l'art de réussir; qu'il n'y a point de lieu où les décisions soient si justes; et sans mettre en ligne de compte tous les gens savants qui y sont, que, du simple bon sens naturel et du commerce de tout le beau monde, on s'y fait une manière d'esprit, qui sans comparaison juge plus finement des choses que tout le savoir enrouillé des pédants (scene vi)

and for the judgement of the *parterre*:

> Apprends, Marquis . . . que le bon sens n'a point de place déterminée à la comédie; que la différence du demi-louis d'or et de la pièce de quinze sous[17] ne fait rien du tout au bon goût; que debout et assis, on peut donner un mauvais jugement; et qu'enfin, à le prendre en général, je me fierais assez à l'approbation du parterre, par la raison qu'entre ceux qui le composent, il y en a plusieurs qui sont capables de juger d'une bonne pièce selon les règles, et que les autres en jugent par la bonne façon d'en juger, qui est de se laisser prendre aux choses, et de n'avoir ni prévention aveugle, ni complaisance affectée, ni délicatesse ridicule. (scene v)

The similarity between the last two passages is quite striking. Sound judgement, says Dorante, depends neither on social nor on intellectual eminence, but on common sense; and that is a commodity

---

[17] The prices, respectively, of seats on stage or in the 'premières loges', and entry to the *parterre*.

more likely to be found among ordinary playgoers than among opinionated pedants or self-conscious men of fashion. Through his
spokesman Dorante, Molière here clearly and unequivocally declares
his faith in the judgement of 'la Cour et la Ville'.[18]

(ii) King and Court

'La Cour et la Ville': this phrase resounds through the literature of
the second half of the century, expressing in a singularly evocative
formula the attraction of the twin magnets of the capital and the
Court (the Louvre at the beginning of Louis XIV's personal reign,
Versailles increasingly from then onwards) for Molière's wealthy and
educated contemporaries. Rarely can there have been a civilisation so
metropolitan, so insular and so self-sufficient. Largely ignorant of
anything that was taking place outside France, disdainful of the
provinces,[19] the courtiers of the Roi-Soleil benefited, for the short
period of that civilisation's most splendid achievements, from these
very factors, which helped to create a homogeneity of taste and values
favourable to the forced growth of a hothouse culture; though from
the 1680s onwards, when the splendour of Versailles began to be
dimmed in all sorts of ways, two of the factors which contributed to
the decline in the arts were no doubt a complacent self-esteem, and a
lack of sufficient stimulus from outside.

There was of course a certain overlap between the ideas represented by the two concepts 'Cour' and 'Ville'; and in practice, the
identity of those composing the two communities overlapped considerably, even if the predominant connotations are respectively

[18] See E. Auerbach's excellent article 'La Cour et la ville' in *Vier Untersuchungen zur
Geschichte der französischen Bildung* (Berne, 1951), pp. 12–50. The formula adopted by
Vaugelas in the matter of linguistic usage provides a useful gloss on the phrase: when
he writes of 'la façon de parler de la plus saine partie de la Cour, conformément à la
façon d'écrire de la plus saine partie des auteurs du temps', he goes on to specify:
'Quand je dis la Cour, j'y comprends les femmes et les hommes, et plusieurs
personnes de la ville où le prince réside, qui, par la communication qu'elles ont avec
les gens de la Cour, participent à sa politesse' (Preface to *Remarques sur la langue
française*, 1647).

[19] Mascarille's '. . . hors de Paris il n'y a pas de salut pour les honnêtes gens' (*Pr. rid.*,
scene ix) is matched in real life by a phrase from one of Balzac's letters: 'hors Paris, il
n'y a point de salut pour les belles, ni pour les honnêtes gens' (quoted by
R. Lathuillière, *La Préciosité*, I (Paris, 1966), p. 537). Voiture, on a visit to Lorraine,
writes to Mme de Rambouillet: 'Quelque galante que soit la Cour de Lorraine . . . je
me souviens d'avoir vu quelquefois meilleure compagnie dans les ruisseaux de Paris
que je n'en ai encore rencontré dans la chambre de la duchesse' (*ibid.*, p. 536); and a
similar prejudice is to be found throughout Scarron's *Roman comique* (the author was
a Parisian, exiled at Le Mans).

aristocratic and bourgeois. This is especially the case when we are dealing with the early years, when the Court was still centred on the Louvre; it is said that one of the motives behind the building of Versailles was a political one: the young King's determination to have his Court outside Paris, so that in times of unrest he should never risk the indignities that the royal family had been subjected to during the Frondes. But the real detachment of Versailles from Paris did not come about until much later, and was due to the ascendancy of Mme de Maintenon and the climate of austerity that came to prevail at Court, as well as to Louis's willing connivance in the idolatrous pomp and ceremony which isolated him increasingly from the rest of his subjects in the outside world.

It was Molière's good fortune to be the entertainer of a young king who was still interested in the world outside his Court, who had a passion for the arts, especially the theatre, and whose relations with those of his subjects he favoured were remarkably informal compared with the stiff, hierarchical protocol of the later years. From the very beginning, Molière and his troupe were frequently summoned to Court to perform, and performances were also often arranged by noblemen at private houses at which the King was a guest. The information given by La Grange concerning the plays presented at Court during such visits is not complete; nor do we know whose responsibility it was to decide what play should be performed. Nevertheless, it is a reasonable assumption that the information we have is representative, and that whoever chose the plays did so with the King's preferences in mind. If we may make such an assumption, the statistics tell us a number of interesting things about the taste of King and Court.[20] Among the plays most often performed were *Les Fâcheux*, Molière's first *comédie-ballet*, and *La Princesse d'Élide*, a 'comédie galante mêlée de musique et d'entrées de ballet'. Others performed frequently *en visite* include the early successes: *L'Étourdi*, *Dépit amoureux*, *Sganarelle* and the two *Écoles* (at least partly for the reason that, being produced earlier in Molière's career, they had more chance to be performed), as well as farces like *Le Mariage forcé* and *Les Précieuses ridicules*. Insofar as generalisation from these figures is legitimate, they confirm what is suggested by other evidence: that the King and his Court favoured *comédie-ballet* and other forms of composite entertainment, and that among straight plays, the more light-hearted

[20] See Appendix III.

41

and farcical comedies were much more popular than 'la haute comédie'. Of plays by authors other than Molière, only one tragedy appears; Molière's own 'serious' comedy *Dom Garcie de Navarre* appears low down on the list, and *L'Avare* and *Les Femmes savantes* were performed respectively twice and once only. The only five-act verse comedies to appear in a high position are *L'École des femmes* and *Tartuffe* – the latter surely because of its notoriety – and *Le Misanthrope* was not performed at Court at all. It would be wrong to give the last fact too much importance on its own; however, taken together with the other evidence, the absence of *Le Misanthrope* is perhaps significant. Even as regards its appeal to audiences at the Palais-Royal, this play is often said to have been too much of a connoisseur's piece, 'caviar to the general'; Grimarest goes so far as to allege that *Le Misanthrope* was a failure with Paris audiences until Molière paired it in a double bill with the popular *Médecin malgré lui*:

> A la quatrième représentation du *Misanthrope* il donne son Fagotier, qui fit bien rire le bourgeois de la rue Saint-Denis. On en trouva le *Misanthrope* bien meilleur, et insensiblement on le prit pour une des meilleures pièces qui ait jamais paru.[21]

This is not borne out by the information given in the *Registre*, however; and in the six seasons remaining before Molière's death, *Le Misanthrope* had no fewer than fifty-nine performances: a very respectable total indeed. It could be purely accidental that such a play was never performed at Court; but one suspects that this may well be valid evidence of the difference between the taste of the Court and that of the capital.

There is no doubt at all of the King's own liking for spectacle, for musical entertainment, and for the kind of performance in which he and his courtiers could participate. Louis was himself a proficient dancer, and the early years of his reign gave a great impetus to the vogue for the *ballet de cour*, a spectacular entertainment drawing on the resources of poet, musician, choreographer and *machiniste*, in which the courtiers, and often the King himself, indulged their talents as actors and dancers under a skilful producer.[22] Molière was himself no stranger to this art form: in the *Ballet des Incompatibles, dansé à Montpellier*

[21] *La Vie de M. de Molière*, p. 93. Grimarest is wrong in saying that *Le Misanthrope* was paired with *Le Médecin* after only three performances: that did not happen until the twenty-second performance of *Le Misanthrope*.

[22] See M. McGowan, *L'Art du ballet de cour en France* (Paris, 1963); M.-F. Christout, *Le Ballet de cour de Louis XIV: 1643–1672* (Paris, 1967); and Chapter 8 below.

devant le Prince et la Princesse de Conti in 1655, he had appeared in two *entrées*, as a Poet and a Fishwife; though it is doubtful whether he wrote more than a fraction of the text.[23] But the magnificent entertainment staged at Vaux-le-Vicomte for the King and Court by Nicolas Fouquet, Louis's finance minister, in August 1661, was quite another matter; for it included as one of its principal items *Les Fâcheux*. The ostentation and extravagance of the spectacle were to be one of the factors that led to Fouquet's downfall, trial for appropriation of public money, and imprisonment for life; but the immediate impression, as recorded in the *Gazette*, was one of harmony and splendour:

> Cette auguste compagnie . . . fut traitée par le surintendant des finances avec toute la magnificence imaginable, la bonne chère ayant été accompagnée du divertissement d'un fort agréable ballet, de la comédie, et d'une infinité de feux d'artifice . . . de manière que ce superbe régal se trouva assorti de tout ce qui se peut souhaiter dans les plus délicieux, et que Leurs Majestés . . . témoignèrent en être merveilleusement satisfaites.[24]

By a cruel irony the Italian Torelli, the genius who had masterminded Fouquet's superb entertainment, also suffered the King's displeasure at his subject's ostentation: he was exiled from France, the victim of an entertainment that was to serve as a model for those at Versailles.[25] Fortunately the King bore no grudge against the members of the Troupe de Monsieur for their association with the disgraced minister, and within a week of the creation of *Les Fâcheux* at Vaux-le-Vicomte they were summoned to present the play at Fontainebleau: an auspicious visit, for *Les Fâcheux* was the first of Molière's *comédies-ballets*, and therefore the precursor of such masterpieces in the genre as *Le Bourgeois gentilhomme* (created at Chambord in 1670) and *Le Malade imaginaire* (although presented at the Palais-Royal, originally intended for performance at Court).

Given the pre-eminence of ballet among the young King's artistic interests, and the competition Molière faced from established composers and choreographers, the playwright might well have been content merely to ensure the continuance of the royal favour by producing elegant trifles which made the minimum demands on his time and his talent. On the contrary, he constantly rose to the challenge of working to order at short notice (he informs us that *Les*

[23] See Molière, *Oeuvres*, ed. Despois and Mesnard, Appendix to Volume i.
[24] Quoted *ibid.*, iii, p. 4.   [25] See Christout, *Le Ballet de cour*, p. 106.

43

Fâcheux was conceived, written, learned and performed all in a fort-
night), and achieved the *tour de force* of integrating genuine literary
comedy into these composite entertainments without either sacrificing his own distinctive manner or yet producing a completely incongruous whole. In the Preface to *Les Fâcheux* Molière tells us that the
association between comedy and the arts of music and dance ('un
mélange qui est nouveau pour nos théâtres') was a fortunate one born
of expediency:

> Le dessein était de donner un ballet aussi; et, comme il n'y avait qu'un
> petit nombre choisi de danseurs excellents, on fut contraint de séparer les
> entrées de ce ballet, et l'avis fut de les jeter dans les entr'actes de la
> comédie, afin que ces intervalles donnassent temps aux mêmes baladins
> de revenir sous d'autres habits. De sorte que, pour ne point rompre aussi
> le fil de la pièce par ces manières d'intermèdes, on s'avisa de les coudre
> au sujet du mieux que l'on put, et ne faire qu'une seule chose du ballet et
> de la comédie.

The play makes brilliant use of this formula. Its plot is of the slightest:
a lover is confronted by a series of society bores, who prevent him
from keeping a rendezvous with the woman he loves. This episodic
structure, adaptable to any number of *fâcheux* – the mute dancers of
the interludes as well as the voluble bores of the comedy itself –
provides both the playwright and the actor in Molière (who played a
number of the bores himself) with the opportunity for a series of
thumbnail sketches of social types based on observed reality but with
just enough caricatural exaggeration to sharpen the satirical impact.
We have already noted the portrait of the *fâcheux* displaying himself
on stage: other sketches include those of the *amateur de ballet*, the
gambler, the fanatical huntsman – and one thing all the bores have in
common is that they are courtiers. Not only at Vaux-le-Vicomte and
later at Court, but also at the Palais-Royal, *Les Fâcheux* was played
before the same young fashionables as are portrayed in the play.

However, it would be wrong to think of Molière as a licensed jester
whom the King's favour allowed to get away with anything he
wanted. The subtitle of Donneau de Visé's play, *La Réponse à l'Impromptu de Versailles, ou la Vengeance des marquis* (1663), suggests that
there was a body of courtiers who felt they had a score to settle with a
playwright who had taken too many liberties; and such courtiers were
not always content to avenge themselves by means of the pen. The
following anecdote also relates to the time of the 'Querelle de l'École
des femmes':

Le duc de la Feuillade . . . s'avisa d'une vengeance aussi indigne d'un homme de sa qualité qu'elle était imprudente. Un jour qu'il vit passer Molière par un appartement où il était, il l'aborda avec des démonstrations d'un homme qui voulait lui faire caresse. Molière s'étant incliné, il lui prit la tête, et en lui disant: 'Tarte à la crême, Molière, tarte à la crême', il lui frotta le visage contre ses boutons qui, étant fort durs et fort tranchants, lui mirent le visage en sang. Le Roi, qui vit Molière le même jour, apprit la chose avec indignation, et le marqua au Duc, qui apprit à ses dépens combien Molière était dans les bonnes grâces de Sa Majesté.[26]

And there is another from the time of *Le Misanthrope*:

Cette pièce fit grand bruit, et eut grand succès à Paris avant que d'être jouée à la Cour. Chacun y reconnut M. de Montausier, et prétendit que c'était lui qui Molière avait en vue. M. de Montausier le sut, et s'emporta jusqu'à faire menacer Molière de le faire mourir sous le bâton.[27]

The fact that the boorish behaviour of the first courtier was reproved by the King, and that in the second case the *coups de bâton* did not materialise, does not affect the point that summary vengeance of this nature was one of the risks that had to be accepted when one was dealing with courtiers who were touchy about their rank. There could be no more telling indication of the gulf that separated the *gens de qualité* from one who, even though he had his entrées at Court, was in their eyes a common entertainer. There is a revealing anecdote about a certain courtier, who was, like Molière, a Valet de Chambre du Roi, and who apparently did not find it all beneath his dignity to make the royal bed; but when it was his turn to share this duty with Molière, '[il] se retira brusquement en disant qu'il ne le ferait point avec un comédien'.[28] Grimarest's account of Molière's advice to the young man of good family who wanted to go on the stage is no doubt apocryphal, but there is a ring of truth about the playwright's supposed reflections on the facts of life:

Il est vrai que nous sommes en apparence recherchés des grands seigneurs, mais ils nous assujettissent à leurs plaisirs; et c'est la plus triste de toutes les situations, que d'être l'esclave de leur fantaisie.[29]

If Molière had reason to be grateful for the enlightened taste, and the generous patronage, of certain *grands seigneurs* like the Prince de

[26] La Martinière, *Vie de Molière* (1725), quoted Mongrédien (ed.), *Recueil*, p. 167.
[27] Dangeau, *Journal* (1690), quoted Mongrédien (ed.), *Recueil*, p. 260. As we have seen, there is no truth in the assertion that *Le Misanthrope* was played at Court.
[28] Titon du Tillet, *Le Parnasse français* (1732), quoted Mongrédien (ed.), *Recueil*, p. 795.
[29] *La Vie de M. de Molière*, p. 106.

Condé,[30] we may be sure that his dealings with the Court also brought him into contact with others whose attitude to the arts was capricious and unreliable, indeed whose first requirement of any work of art was that it should flatter their vanity and obsession with rank.[31] 'La qualité', 'les gens de qualité', 'un homme de ma qualité' are phrases with a thoroughly seventeenth-century ring; as La Bruyère writes of his Périandre:

> Il a commencé par dire de soi-même: 'un homme de ma sorte'; il passe à dire: 'un homme de ma qualité'. Il se donne pour tel; et il n'y a personne de ceux à qui il prête de l'argent, ou qu'il reçoit à sa table, qui est délicate, qui veuille s'y opposer.[32]

Contemporary memoirs, from Tallemant's malicious gossip in the 1650s to Saint-Simon's authoritative portrait of his age at the end of the century, give abundant anecdotal evidence of the vanity and ambition of seventeenth-century courtiers; but it is La Bruyère who generalises from the individual instances, and produces the most telling critique of this aspect of the civilisation of Versailles:

> Il y a un pays où les joies sont visibles, mais fausses, et les chagrins cachés, mais réels. Qui croirait que l'empressement pour les spectacles, que les éclats et les applaudissements aux théâtres de Molière et d'Arlequin, les repas, la chasse, les ballets, les carrousels, couvrissent tant d'inquiétudes, de soins et de divers intérêts, tant de craintes et d'espérances, des passions si vives et des affaires si sérieuses?[33]

From the opening paragraph of the chapter 'De la Cour':

> Le reproche, en un sens, le plus honorable que l'on puisse faire à un homme, c'est de lui dire qu'il ne sait pas la Cour: il n'y a sorte de vertus qu'on ne rassemble en lui par ce seul mot . . .

to the closing one:

> La ville dégoûte de la province; la Cour détrompe de la ville, et guérit de la Cour. Un esprit sain puise à la Cour le goût de la solitude et de la retraite,

the picture La Bruyère gives is of a society of false appearances and artificial values, a highly competitive society of show and ostentation.

---

[30] Condé's esteem for Molière is pithily illustrated in this anecdote from the period following the playwright's death: 'Un poète présentant à M. le Prince l'épitaphe de Molière, M. le Prince lui dit: "J'aimerais bien mieux que ce fût lui qui m'apportât la vôtre"' (*Ménagiana* (1694), quoted Mongrédien (ed.), *Recueil*, p. 446).

[31] Cf. J. Lough, *Writer and Public in France* (Oxford, 1978), pp. 127-8.

[32] *Caractères*, 'Des Biens de fortune', para. 21.　　[33] *Ibid.*, 'De la Cour', para. 63.

The Court audience for whom Molière produced such a large number of his plays was an audience which looked first and foremost to be entertained – even if, as Pascal, La Bruyère and Bossuet all tell us, the search for *divertissement* was a cover for varying degrees of chagrin, disillusionment and *angoisse*. In the case of the King himself, as we have seen, the favourite entertainments were of the spectacular kind, embracing music and ballet; but the taste of many of his courtiers favoured light-hearted, farcical comedy: the sort of entertainment we should no doubt be inclined to label 'popular' if we did not have this evidence about the taste of the Court. By contrast, there was in Molière's town theatre an important and influential element among the spectators who looked down on such simple and unsophisticated forms of drama, and who expected even comedy to provide them with intellectual stimulus; and we must now attempt to characterise the taste of 'la Ville'.

(iii) Education and the professions

We may suppose the cultural taste of those who were most influential among Molière's contemporaries, the leaders of opinion among his audiences, to have been formed in the first place by the education they received, though this factor was modified in important ways by other considerations: attitudes which may have been associated with the profession to which an individual belonged; the extent to which he came into contact with the Court; and perhaps above all, whether or not he moved in *salon* circles.

Formal education in the seventeenth century remained very largely in the hands of the Church, and was almost entirely concerned with the upbringing of boys: when the author of a recent article on women's education in the period writes that the only progress one can discern in that field is 'a very slow decline in illiteracy among women',[34] the observation should by no means be taken as referring only to women of the lower classes. Although the Oratorians and the *solitaires* of Port-Royal introduced curricular reforms and modernised their educational systems, French education in general was still very backward-looking, based firmly on the use of Latin – not only as a medium for the study of classical authors, but also as the language in

[34] E. T. Dubois, 'The Education of Women in Seventeenth-Century France', *French Studies,* xxxII (1978), 1.

which other academic disciplines were taught.[35] Together with this went an uncritical veneration of authority in the universities and the colleges, especially the authority of Aristotle. In 1625 the Parlement de Paris had forbidden the publication of anti-Aristotelian theses on pain of death; and the attitude of the official educational establishments remained resolutely hostile to 'la nouvelle philosophie' (that is, the ideas of Descartes in particular, but also, a phrase from Boileau's *Arrêt burlesque* of 1671 suggests, those of Gassendi and Harvey).[36] In the same year the University of Paris had tried to get the Parlement to prohibit the teaching of any other philosophy than that of Aristotle; the success of Boileau's satire was one of the reasons why the Parlement refused, but the University achieved the same result by means of an order from the King.[37]

This was an educational system, then, which still retained many of those legacies of the Middle Ages that Montaigne had criticised in the previous century,[38] it was reactionary as regards its curriculum, and its teaching methods were those of mediaeval scholasticism: 'Chez les Jésuites, l'exercice essentiel est constitué par la *prelectio*: le maître lit un passage, l'explique, le commente, le paraphrase; l'élève le recopie, l'apprend par coeur, et aussi le prend comme base d'imitation, de narration, de discours en latin.'[39]

It was designed to encourage in the pupil the ability to reason, but only so long as this activity was conducted according to a formal pattern of argument prescribed by Aristotelian logic; and the caricatural portraits of pedants we find in Molière's plays can be compared with Pascal's treatment of the Jesuit spokesmen in his *Lettres provinciales* (1656–7), as well as with Boileau's satire in his *Arrêt burlesque*.

As for women's education, girls were taught at home, or else in convents whose academic standards were acknowledged to be mediocre. The genuinely educated ladies of the period acquired their intellectual formation through a combination of their own determin-

---

[35] The Jesuit *Ratio Studiorum* proclaimed that 'the master shall constantly speak in Latin', and M. de Jouvency, writing at the end of the seventeenth century, confirms what Sorel's *Francion* had indicated in 1622, that pupils were expected to converse among themselves in Latin (quoted by G. Snyders, *La Pédagogie en France aux xviie et xviiie siècles* (Paris, 1965), pp. 60–1).

[36] 'Cartésiens, nouveaux philosophes, circulateurs et Gassendistes'. Harvey's discovery of the circulation of the blood had been published in 1628, but was still outlawed in the medical faculties of French universities at the time when Molière was writing.

[37] See J. S. Spink, *French Free-Thought from Gassendi to Voltaire* (London, 1960), p. 190.

[38] *Essais,* Book 1 (1580), chs. xxv, xxvi. [39] Snyders, *La Pédagogie,* pp. 60–1.

ation: 'Alors que les garçons ferment leurs livres en quittant le collège, nombre de filles les ouvrent en sortant du couvent',[40] and the help of an enlightened *abbé* or man of letters employed in the family as secretary or tutor: an *ad hoc* form of adult education which in many cases worked wonders. And if these women lacked the structured mental training based on the traditional exercises of formal rhetoric, that was more than compensated for by liberal educational methods which developed their sensibility.[41]

The reactionary nature of most formal education in the seventeenth-century colleges was matched, in the case of those going into the professions – the Church, law and medicine – by the training they went on to receive in the universities. The scientific and intellectual advances of the century took place outside the seats of learning; they were due either to thinkers working, and experimenting, on their own, like Descartes and Pascal, or else to groups of seekers after truth such as formed round Gassendi[42] or, later in the century, created the Académie des Sciences. The Académie Française had of course been founded in 1635; but during the first half-century of its existence neither its intellectual standing nor its achievements would justify its being considered as a major seat of independent, liberal thought. The professional man of letters was in any case at this period a pretty lowly individual. Few authors were able to live by the products of their pen, and those who can be regarded as full-time writers – journalists, translators, reviewers – were far from being the most illustrious. For the rest, royal or princely patronage was thought to be much less demeaning than professional status as a writer: when Boileau, nominated with Racine to the office of historiographer royal in 1677, writes of 'ce glorieux emploi qui m'a tiré du métier de la poésie',[43] I do not think this should be interpreted wholly ironically. Moreover, the noteworthy literary works of the age were for the most part written by gentlemen of independent means, or by members of the *noblesse de robe* whose administrative offices provided them with an income – and

[40] R. Duchêne, 'L'École des femmes au xviie siècle' in *Mélanges historiques et littéraires sur le xviie siècle offerts à G. Mongrédien* (n.p., 1974), p. 148.   [41] *Ibid.*, pp. 149ff.
[42] Gassendi taught at the Collège de France, an institution which even in the seventeenth century was more independent, and intellectually more distinguished, than the universities of France. According to Grimarest (*La Vie de M. de Molière*, p. 39), Gassendi 'ayant remarqué dans Molière toute la docilité et toute la pénétration nécessaires pour prendre les connaissances de la philosophie, se fit un plaisir de la lui enseigner . . .'. This is not now generally accepted, though Molière certainly had close ties with Chapelle and Bernier, who were taught by Gassendi.
[43] Preface to the 1683 edition of his works.

with the leisure – which enabled them to pursue a career in *belles-lettres*. When Molière's Alceste tells the Court poet Oronte:

> . . . n'allez point quitter, de quoi que l'on vous somme,
> Le nom que dans la Cour vous avez d'honnête homme,
> Pour prendre, de la main d'un avide imprimeur,
> Celui de ridicule et misérable auteur (*Mis.*, lines 369–72)

he is expressing the same aristocratic disdain for the professional writer that Guez de Balzac had expressed in a letter of 1637:

> Est-il possible qu'un homme . . . à qui il n'a point été fait de commandement de par le Roi, et sur peine de la vie, de faire des livres, veuille quitter son rang d'honnête homme qu'il tient dans le monde, pour aller prendre celui d'impertinent et de ridicule parmi les docteurs et les écoliers?[44]

This is an attitude that is summed up in Saint-Simon's laconic praise of Racine: 'Rien du poète, tout de l'honnête homme'.[45]

On the part of courtiers and men of fashion who themselves had literary ambitions, such an attitude may strike us as pure affectation; but among the members of polite society as a whole, there is no doubt of the strength of this prejudice. The professional writer, like the professional scholars to whom Balzac refers, was outside the pale; and what is said of the merchant in the following passage: 'Il suffit d'être négociant pour être regardé avec mépris . . . Alors le négociant quitte son commerce pour se retirer à la campagne ou achète une charge pour lui-même pour sortir de cet esclavage',[46] could just as easily be said of the liberal professions.[47]

In fact, there was only one profession compatible with the bearing of an aristocratic name: that of soldier; and the ethos of Court and high society had remained to a very large extent that of a military caste. To those of the old school, earlier in the century, the military virtues had sufficed, and there was little room for social graces or for intellectual accomplishments; as late as 1679–80 the Italian diplomat Primi Visconti could write:

> En France, en effet, on n'estime que les titres de guerre; ceux des lettres et de toute autre profession sont méprisés et l'on considère comme vil l'homme de qualité qui sait écrire; je sais que les seigneurs d'Urfé ont honte que leur aïeul Honoré d'Urfé ait écrit le poème de l'*Astrée*.[48]

[44] Quoted in Molière, *Oeuvres*, ed. Despois and Mesnard, v, pp. 466–7.
[45] Quoted by Auerbach, 'La Cour et la ville', p. 45.
[46] Quoted by P. Sagnac, *La Formation de la société française moderne:* 1 (*1661–1715*) (Paris, 1945), p. 162.
[47] Cf. Lough, *Writer and Public,* ch. iii, 'The Seventeenth Century'.
[48] *Mémoires sur la cour de Louis XIV,* trans. J. Lemoine (Paris, 1908), pp. 225–6.

Plate 1 Molière the tragic actor: as César in Corneille's *Pompée* (attributed to
Nicolas Mignard)
Collections de la Comédie-Française

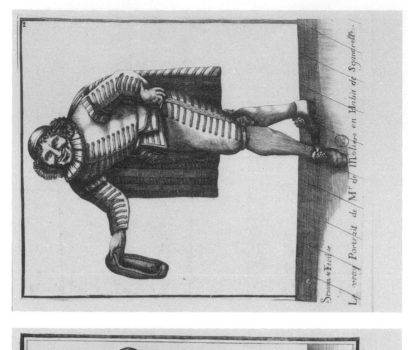

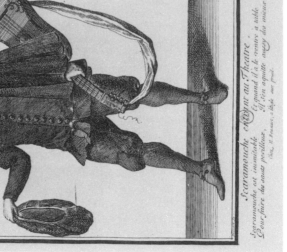

Plate IIa Scaramouche
Phot. Bibl. Nat. Paris

Plate IIb Molière as Sganarelle (attributed to Simonin)
Phot. Bibl. Nat. Paris

Plate III Farceurs français et italiens, 1670 (Collections de la Comédie-Française)

Plate IV Frontispiece to *Oeuvres* (1666), Vol. I: Molière as Mascarille and as
Sganarelle (Chauveau)
Phot. Bibl. Nat. Paris

ô bien don Ie fuis ton feruiteur.

Plate v Spectators on stage (Le Pautre)
Phot. Bibl. Nat. Paris

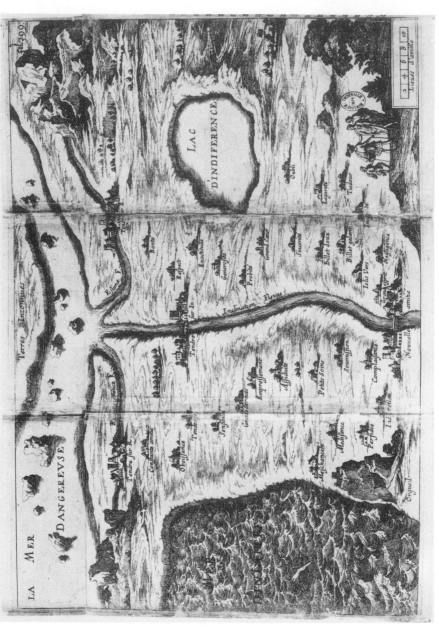

Plate vi La Carte de Tendre (from Mlle de Scudéry, *Clélie*, Vol. i (1654))
Phot. Bibl. Nat. Paris

Plate VII Les Vierges sages (detail) (Abraham Bosse)
Phot. Bibl. Nat. Paris

Plate VIII Alizon: a male actor in an elderly woman's role
Phot. Bibl. Nat. Paris

Such extreme forms of aristocratic prejudice had no doubt largely disappeared long before then – though they presumably survived longer in the provinces, and away from Court. In Paris, the civilising process had been more rapid and more thorough; and by the middle of the century, as a result of the *salon* movement, society in the capital had acquired that refinement and cultural discernment that we associate with the spectators and the reading public of the Grand Siècle. It is a most paradoxical development that in a century when, as we have seen, women's education remained in such a rudimentary state, a relatively small number of women, largely self-educated, should have been able to wield a wholly disproportionate influence.

(iv) The 'salons'

The history of the *salon* movement has often been written.[49] The beginnings are particularly well known: the installation of the young Marquise de Rambouillet in her town house near the Louvre, which she had redesigned to accommodate social gatherings in the civilised Italian manner as an alternative to the uncouth, uncomfortable military atmosphere of the Court, and her success in attracting almost all the literary and intellectual figures of the capital, as well as the flower of the nation's aristocracy. From the 1620s to the time of the Frondes and beyond, 'la divine Arthénice', from her 'chambre bleue', set the tone of polite French society: a tone that was cultured without being bookish, and marked by intellectual curiosity rather than by pedantry: 'Chapelain, Conrart et Balzac, derrière eux toute l'Académie, n'ont pu agir si puissamment sur le goût que grâce à l'Hôtel et parce que l'Hôtel leur assurait l'audience de la bonne société.'[50] This refining influence complemented others, more specifically literary: in particular, that of the pastoral literature on which a whole generation of readers was brought up. Like Honoré d'Urfé in *L'Astrée*, the Marquise de Rambouillet in her *salon* was responsible for introducing refinement of thought, delicacy of feeling, and a care for purity of expression to the men and women who were to form Molière's audiences.

---

[49] See for instance R. Picard, *Les Salons littéraires et la société française, 1610–1789* (New York, 1943); Mongrédien, *Vie littéraire*; D. A. L. Backer, *Precious Women* (New York, 1974); C. C. Lougee, *Le Paradis des femmes: Women, Salons, and Social Stratification in Seventeenth-Century France* (Princeton, 1976).
[50] A. Adam, *Histoire de la littérature française au xviie siècle*, I (Paris, 1956), p. 268.

However, in the years following the Frondes, the most influential *salon* was no longer that of the Marquise. Among the hostesses of other *salons* that had started up in imitation of the Hôtel de Rambouillet – including ladies of the highest quality – several had inclined to more serious intellectual pursuits, some could perhaps even be called bluestockings. It is in these *salons*, not in the 'chambre bleue', that the origins of preciosity are to be sought; and when we come to the *salon* of Mlle de Scudéry, the high-priestess of the cult, the emphasis is very different from that of the Hôtel de Rambouillet. Her two novels, *Le Grand Cyrus* (1649–53) and *Clélie* (1654–60) were the favourite reading of Molière's spectators (at any rate, the women among them): they were long, episodic romances which portrayed, under transparent historical disguises (Condé as Cyrus, Mme de Longueville as Mandane) persons well known at the Hôtel de Rambouillet and at Mlle de Scudéry's own *samedis*, and elaborated, even more fully than *L'Astrée* had done, courtship rituals interrupted by estrangements, misunderstandings, kidnappings and every kind of romanesque obstacle.[51] The first volume of *Clélie* contains the celebrated 'Carte de Tendre', an allegorical map charting the way from Nouvelle Amitié to the cities of Tendre sur Estime, Tendre sur Reconnaissance and Tendre sur Inclination.[52] This ingenious invention is a perfect illustration of the intellectual and moral character of mid-century preciosity: it shows a real interest in the detailed psychology of relations between the sexes – but an interest that remained very largely cerebral (for even when the lover arrived at Tendre, he stayed safely on the terra firma of a platonic relationship, without venturing across the Mer Dangereuse to the Terres Inconnues of physical passion); and together with this, a somewhat pedantic tendency to push an amusing conceit too far. If the literary productions of the *salons* – the novels, the *portraits*, and the *poésie galante* – expressed their members' absorbing interest in the affairs of the heart, it also seems certain that the literature in its turn influenced the behaviour of its devotees, and in the well-publicised platonic courtships of the time, such as that of Pellisson and Mlle de Scudéry herself, we can see a clear case of life imitating art.

The relationship between life and art is central to the debate about 'true' and 'false' preciosity, about 'préciosité' and 'préciosité ridicule', with which is linked the question whom Molière was satirising

[51] Cf. *Pr. rid.*, scene iv.
[52] See Plate VI; and cf. the helpful commentary on the 'Carte de Tendre' in Backer, *Precious Women*, pp. 194ff.

in his play of November 1659.[53] We shall return to this question in a later chapter; here, suffice it to say that the distinction between 'true' and 'false' that Molière draws in his Preface seems to have been well established by other writers in the years preceding the performance of *Les Précieuses ridicules*. The Abbé de Pure, writing in 1658, uses terms very like Molière's own:

> Je connais trop le peu de rapport qu'il y a entre des fausses précieuses et un véritable précieux, entre de défectueuses copies et un parfait original.[54]

Saint-Évremond writes, in a note attached to his satirical poem 'Le Cercle' (1656), that:

> le corps des précieuses n'est autre chose que l'union d'un petit nombre de personnes, où quelques-unes véritablement délicates ont jeté les autres dans une affectation de délicatesse ridicule.[55]

And Scarron, in a poem published in 1659, writes:

> Mais revenons aux fâcheux, aux fâcheuses,
> Au rang de qui je mets les précieuses,
> Fausses, s'entend, et de qui tout le bon
> Est seulement un langage ou jargon,
> Un parler gras, plusieurs sottes manières,
> Et qui ne sont enfin que façonnières,
> Et ne sont pas précieuses de prix
> Comme il en est deux ou trois dans Paris,
> Que l'on respecte autant que des princesses.[56]

If the 'précieuses de prix' were those who, like the Marquise de Rambouillet, played a large part in forming the taste of the cultivated readers and spectators of the 1660s, they had numerous imitators who lacked the vital qualities of tact and discernment:

> Si l'on y réfléchit bien, le phénomène précieux porte en lui-même un germe de corruption et engendre spontanément sa propre caricature. Non seulement le sublime est voisin du ridicule, mais il est et doit être rare par essence: s'il fait l'objet d'une mode, il est aussitôt absorbé par ce qu'il prétendait fuir. D'autre part, l'art exquis d'enchanter la vie quotidienne ne peut être l'effet de la seule intention: il y faut du tact, du goût, une imagination délicate, une aristocratie d'esprit et de manières.[57]

[53] See Lathuillière, *La Préciosité*, pp. 201–18: 'Un faux problème: les vraies et les fausses précieuses'; and Introduction to *Les Précieuses ridicules*, ed. M. Cuénin (Paris, 1973).
[54] *Le Roman de la Précieuse*, ed. E. Magne (Paris, 1939), II, p. 187 (dedicatory letter to Book IV, addressed to the Abbé de Tonnerre).
[55] *Oeuvres choisies*, ed. M. Hippeau (Paris, 1866), p. 362.
[56] Quoted in Lathuillière, *La Préciosité*, I, p. 201.
[57] Cuénin, Introduction to *Les Précieuses ridicules*, p. lxviii.

It was these imitators who sought to impose fashions of speech and behaviour which were ridiculous because of their extravagance, and standards of critical taste whose exclusiveness made them harmful.

If we leave on one side the question of 'préciosité ridicule' – indeed, it may be better to avoid the term *préciosité* altogether, because of its ambiguity – we can readily appreciate the positive achievements of seventeenth-century *salon* culture. The *salons* created an intelligent lay-public passionately interested in the things of the mind, and especially in the critical discussion of literature; and although that sometimes took a trivial form, as in the controversy over the respective merits of Voiture's 'Sonnet d'Uranie' and Benserade's 'Sonnet de Job' which divided the polite world in 1648, nevertheless a considerable number of major works were read by their authors to *salon* audiences – from *Polyeucte* onwards, including the *Tartuffe* of 1664–5,[58] not counting works like La Rochefoucauld's *Maximes* or *La Princesse de Clèves*, conceived and created within a *salon* environment. By their intelligent criticism, and through intellectual pursuits such as the 'questions d'amour' – the debating of problems relating to the psychology of the passions – the *habitués* of the *salons* helped to shape an analytical vocabulary capable of dealing with the finer nuances of the emotions, and at the same time influenced the content of the works which were written for them. We take it for granted in the case of *La Princesse de Clèves*, of the *Maximes*, or of *Phèdre*, that such works were written to cater for a public who appreciated psychological finesse; but a similar influence is also to be seen in the case of *Le Misanthrope* or *Les Femmes savantes*, for these were the discerning spectators whom Molière too sought to please.

'The *salon* hid origins well, for . . . its most famous personages often came from the most obscure backgrounds':[59] rather than constituting a threat to the social structure, as some seventeenth-century writers evidently thought, *salons* helped to counter such a threat by assimilating talented persons of non-noble birth into a culture which, in spite of its egalitarian appearances, retained much of its aristocratic character.[60] However, the *salons* and the *précieux* movement were subversive in another sense, in the challenge they posed to traditional male supremacy. Seventeenth-century feminism is a complex phenomenon, and certain aspects of it are certainly bound up with the question of 'préciosité ridicule'. However emancipated, a woman had

[58] Molière, *Oeuvres complètes*, ed. Jouanny, I, pp. 623–4.
[59] Lougee, *Le Paradis des femmes*, p. 226.   [60] *Ibid.*, pp. 212–13.

to be careful not to make a parade of her learning if she was not to fall foul of the gossips and the satirists; Balzac had told Mme des Loges in 1628 that he could 'no more approve a learned female than a woman on a horse',[61] and Mlle de Scudéry herself makes it clear in this passage from *Le Grand Cyrus* that the bluestocking was as unwelcome as the male pedant:

> Encore que je voulusse que les femmes sussent plus de choses qu'elles n'en savent pour l'ordinaire, je ne veux pourtant jamais qu'elles agissent ni qu'elles parlent en savantes. Je veux donc bien qu'on puisse dire d'une personne de mon sexe qu'elle sait cent choses dont elle ne se vante pas, qu'elle a l'esprit fort éclairé, qu'elle connaît finement les beaux ouvrages, qu'elle parle bien, qu'elle écrit juste et qu'elle sait le monde; mais je ne veux pas qu'on puisse dire d'elle: c'est une femme savante. Ce n'est pas que celle qu'on n'appellera point savante ne puisse savoir autant et plus de choses que celles à qui on donnera ce terrible nom; mais c'est qu'elle se sait mieux servir de son esprit, et qu'elle sait cacher adroitement ce que l'autre montre mal à propos.[62]

But alongside the sometimes aggressive determination to prove that women were the intellectual equals of men, was a more widespread reaction against the very real social, legal and economic disadvantages from which they suffered. The feminist aspirations of the *précieuses* originated above all in their revulsion from the *mariage de convenance* with its inequality and injustice. Their attitude is well expressed by a character in the Abbé de Pure's novel *La Précieuse* (1656–8), who asks 'quelle règle on pourrait apporter au désordre du mariage pour en adoucir la rigueur de l'esclavage, la dureté des fers; et ce qui peut-être est encore plus fâcheux que tous les deux ensemble, la durée de l'un et de l'autre'; and the same character is led to wonder 's'il fallait dire se marier *contre* quelqu'on ou à quelqu'un'.[63] Incompatibility between the two partners in what was primarily a business deal arranged for family or dynastic interests; excessively frequent pregnancies; a double standard of morality; the impossibility of a divorce: the realities of marriage were the complete antithesis of the ideal union imagined by the *précieuses* and their allies, brought up on the enlightened treatises of polite manners and the romanesque novels of their day, as a free and unconstrained exchange between equal partners. No wonder that some advanced *précieux* circles looked with favour on theoretical projects with a thoroughly twentieth-

[61] Quoted by Backer, *Precious Women*, p. 112.
[62] Quoted by C. Livet in his edition of Somaize, *Le Grand Dictionnaire des précieuses* (Paris, 1856), II, p. 373.   [63] *Le Roman de la Précieuse*, ed. Magne, pp. 15, 17.

century flavour such as trial marriages or the communal upbringing of children. And in practice, while many women no doubt merely sought, as their husbands did, to realise their ideal in an extra-marital relationship, there were also many who, with a greater respect for the marriage-tie, or because they were disillusioned with adultery as well as with marriage, preferred to take refuge in the platonic concept of 'honnête amitié'.

The theorists of the Women's Liberation movement of the 1960s and 1970s rightly claimed the *précieuses* of three hundred years ago as their precursors, seeing them as part of 'une première *intelligentsia* féminine qui forgera les premières revendications (droit au divorce, à la jouissance sexuelle, à la culture, à l'instruction, aux emplois, à la vie politique)'.[64] But this is only part of the picture; and to claim that 'le qualificatif de "ridicules" ressort d'une vision antiféminine'[65] is a serious over-simplification. And nowhere is this more so than in the case of Molière himself, whose attitudes towards preciosity are complex, and certainly cannot be dismissed in such a summary way. If Boileau (who certainly was anti-feminist, and even a misogynist) could hail Molière as the scourge of the *précieuses*:

> une précieuse,
> Reste de ces esprits jadis si renommés
> Que d'un coup de son art Molière a diffamés,[66]

on the other hand a modern writer was able to entitle a study of the playwright *Molière auteur précieux*.[67] And as with Molière himself, so no doubt with his audiences. The 'woman question', which had been kept alive during the late Middle Ages and the Renaissance as a theme for literary debate, had suddenly acquired a new topicality. The *salons* had given it a new social dimension, and the *précieuses* of the 1650s were trying to turn the feminist cause from a subject for academic debate into a militant campaign. As a cross-section of literate society, Molière's audiences no doubt represented all shades of opinion, from passionate support, through well-disposed, or mocking, amusement, to uncomprehending hostility. From *Les Précieuses ridicules* onwards, Molière was to return time and again to the 'woman question'; and as the *Critique de l'École des femmes* suggests, his standpoint was not always understood, even by those for whom he tried to show sympathy.

[64] N. Benoît *et al.*, *La Femme majeure: nouvelle féminité, nouveau féminisme* (Paris, 1973), p. 14. [65] *Ibid.* [66] *Satire* x, lines 438–40. [67] F. Baumal (Paris, 1923).

(v) The 'honnêtes gens'

Like the *précieuse*, the *honnête homme* was essentially a product of polite
society outside the Court; but whereas preciosity was characterised
by ostentation and the desire to stand out from one's fellows, *honnêteté*
on the contrary implied modesty, discretion and the refusal to assert
oneself. In social intercourse, the *honnête homme* was a good listener,
who did not monopolise the conversation; as a critic, he was the
cultured amateur, never the professional. Indeed, it is significantly
easier to define the *honnête homme* by negatives: he is the antithesis of
the specialist, as of the pedant; according to La Rochefoucauld's
lapidary definition, 'Le vrai honnête homme est celui qui ne se pique
de rien.'[68] Saint-Évremond, who was universally acclaimed by contemporaries as the perfect type of the *honnête homme*, wrote an essay
'Sur les sciences où peut s'appliquer un honnête homme' in which,
after considering (and rejecting) theology and philosophy, he has this
to say about mathematics:

> Quand je songe aux profondes méditations qu'elles exigent, comme elles
> vous tirent de l'action et des plaisirs pour vous occuper tout entier, ses
> démonstrations me semblent bien chères, et il faut être fort amoureux
> d'une vérité pour la chercher à ce prix-là . . . Je vous l'avouerai ingénu-
> ment: il n'y a point de louanges que je ne donne aux grands mathémati-
> ciens, pourvu que je ne le sois pas. J'admire leurs inventions, et les
> ouvrages qu'ils produisent; mais je pense que c'est assez aux personnes
> de bon sens de les savoir bien employer, car, à parler sagement, nous
> avons plus d'intérêt à jouir du monde qu'à le connaître.[69]

All professional specialisation is repugnant; to quote the Chevalier de
Méré, whose writings crystallise the doctrine of *honnêteté*:

> C'est un malheur aux honnêtes gens d'être pris à leur mine pour des gens
> de métier,[70] et quand on a cette disgrâce, il s'en faut défaire à quelque
> prix que ce soit.[71]

---

[68] *Maximes* (1665), no. 203. An alternative interpretation takes 'se piquer' here in the
sense of 'se fâcher'; though the rendering 'se vanter' is supported by the editor of the
'Grands Écrivains' edition (*Oeuvres*, ed. D. L. Gilbert, I (Paris, 1868), p. 111) among
other commentators.   [69] *Oeuvres choisies*, ed. Hippeau, p. 231.

[70] Like, for instance, La Bruyère's specialist 'qui, borné et renfermé dans quelque
art . . . , ne montre hors de là ni jugement, ni mémoire, ni vivacité, ni moeurs, ni
conduite . . . un musicien, par exemple, qui après m'avoir comme enchanté par ses
accords, semble s'être remis avec son luth dans un même étui', *Caractères*, XII,
para. 56. When Molière makes Adraste in *Le Sicilien* say: 'Tu sais que . . . parfois je
manie le pinceau, contre la coutume de France, qui ne veut pas qu'un gentilhomme
sache rien faire' (scene ix), he is surely indulging in a satirical comment on the
extremes to which this attitude could be taken.

[71] 'Le Commerce du monde', *Oeuvres* (3 vols., Paris, 1930), III, p. 142.

The man of culture and breeding must have an unobtrusive all-round competence without affecting any single expertise in particular: even the military profession, by general consent the most fitting for a gentleman, is subject to the same reservation:

> La guerre est le plus beau métier du monde, il en faut demeurer d'accord; mais, à le bien prendre, un honnête homme n'a point de métier. Quoiqu'il sache parfaitement une chose, et que même il soit obligé d'y passer sa vie, il me semble que sa manière d'agir ni son entretien ne le font point remarquer.[72]

Defined in this light, the calling of *honnête homme* was the most arduous, and the most difficult to live up to. Its appeal was to the aesthetic rather than to the ethical sense, as Méré suggests:

> C'est la quintessence de toutes les vertus; et ceux qui ne l'ont point, sont mal reçus parmi les personnes de bon goût, et même quand ils parlent des choses du monde, c'est pour l'ordinaire de si mauvaise grâce, qu'on ne les peut souffrir. Cette science est proprement celle de l'homme, parce qu'elle consiste à vivre et à se communiquer d'une manière humaine et raisonnable.[73]

It is true that certain problems of terminology do exist, and that not all references to *honnêteté* in the seventeenth century relate to the exclusive aristocratic ideal, as defined in the *Dictionnaire de l'Académie* of 1694:

> On appelle aussi *honnête homme* un homme en qui on ne considère alors que les qualités agréables et les manières du monde. Et en ce sens, *honnête homme* ne veut dire autre chose que galant homme, homme de bonne conversation, de bonne compagnie.

Historians commonly distinguish, side by side with this, a more bourgeois usage, according to which the term *honnête homme* retained the moral connotations associated with the adjective (as the equivalent of *homme d'honneur*). The following examples from texts of the period illustrate the alternative meaning very clearly:

> Vous êtes un fripon.
> — Monsieur, pardonnez-moi, je suis fort honnête homme.[74]

> La vertu sans argent n'est qu'un meuble inutile:
> L'argent en honnête homme érige un scélérat.[75]

[72] *Ibid.*, I, p. 11.   [73] *Ibid.*, III, pp. 71–2.
[74] Racine, *Les Plaideurs* (1668), lines 410–11.
[75] Boileau, *Épître* v (1674), lines 86–7.

Il n'est rien de plus aisé, quand on est riche, que d'être honnête homme, et c'est quand on est pauvre qu'il est difficile de l'être.[76]

And it is in this sense that it would seem proper to interpret the term when it is used by Molière's characters in certain contexts:

On vous a pris de l'argent?
— Oui coquin; et je m'en vais te pendre, si tu ne me le rends.
— Mon Dieu! ne le maltraitez point. Je vois à sa mine qu'il est honnête homme. (*L'Avare*, V, ii)

Je ferais plus d'état du fils d'un crocheteur qui serait honnête homme, que du fils d'un monarque qui vivrait comme vous. (*D. Juan*, IV, iv)

But by the same token, in the couplet already quoted from *Le Misanthrope*:

Et n'allez point quitter, de quoi que l'on vous somme,
Le nom que dans la Cour vous avez d'honnête homme[77] –

and indeed throughout that play – we may be sure that the terms *honnête, honnête homme* and *honnêteté* express the aristocratic ideas current in the *salon* society in which Alceste and the other characters move. As we have seen, it was in the real-life counterparts of Célimène's *salon* that the most influential section of Molière's audiences was formed; and the *honnête homme* was the male equivalent of the ladies of taste and culture who set the tone for French social life for half a century or more.

Unostentatious and undogmatic the *honnête homme* might be in expressing his opinion, but that opinion was nevertheless confident and authoritative; and this quality – that of the enlightened all-rounder, as distinct from the narrow specialist – is nowhere better characterised than in the following lines of Pascal's, in which the writer draws a distinction between the values of 'le monde' – that is, in this context, the rest of society – and those of 'les gens universels'[78] who represent this social ideal:

On ne passe point dans le monde pour se connaître en vers, si l'on n'a mis l'enseigne de poète, de mathématicien, etc. Mais les gens universels ne veulent point d'enseigne, et ne mettent guère de différence entre le métier de poète et celui de brodeur. Les gens universels ne sont appelés ni poètes, ni géomètres, etc.; mais ils sont tout cela, et juges de tous ceux-là . . . C'est donc une fausse louange qu'on donne à un homme

---

[76] Brueys and Palaprat, *L'Avocat Patelin* (1706), I, xi. [77] See p. 50 above.
[78] Cf. the Italian Renaissance ideal of the 'uomo universale'.

quand on dit de lui, lorsqu'il entre, qu'il est fort habile en poésie et c'est une mauvaise marque, quand on n'a pas recours à un homme quand il s'agit de juger de quelques vers.[79]

The role of the *honnête homme* as critic is a crucial one in the *Critique de l'École des femmes*, in *Les Femmes savantes*, and perhaps above all in Act I of *Le Misanthrope*. More generally, if not always quite so tangibly, the expectations of the urbane, polished society of the *salons* played a vital part in determining the way in which Molière's comedy was to evolve.

One obvious kind of refinement is to be seen in the virtual elimination of all comedy derived from sex and other bodily functions. As we have seen, the courtiers retained a liking for light-hearted farce, but there is a considerable difference between the comic flavour of the early farce *Le Médecin volant*, written for provincial audiences, and that of *Le Médecin malgré lui*, written for the more sophisticated audiences of the capital. In the former play Sganarelle, disguised as a doctor, calls for a sample of the patient's urine, drinks it with relish and complains:

> Quoi? Monsieur Gorgibus, votre fille ne pisse que des gouttes? voilà une pauvre pisseuse que votre fille; je vois bien qu'il faudra que je lui ordonne une potion pissative. (scene iv)

We can easily imagine what the fastidious *honnêtes gens* would have made of that; and *Le Médecin malgré lui*, though it may appear earthy enough when compared with *Le Misanthrope* of the same year, was sufficiently refined to pass muster with the courtiers. Indeed, when Sganarelle is pursuing the Nourrice, attempting to fondle her breasts, he addresses her in a manner which agreeably parodies the metaphorical style of the *précieuses*:

> Nourrice, charmante nourrice, ma médecine est la très-humble esclave de votre nourricerie, et je voudrais bien être le petit poupon fortuné qui tetât le lait de vos bonnes grâces. (II, ii)

An anecdote told by Boursault illustrates well the kind of concession Molière must constantly have had to make in order to please his Paris audiences:

> Dans le comique même, on veut que les obscénités soient enveloppées et Molière, tout Molière qu'il était, s'en aperçut bien dans le *Malade imaginaire* . . . Il y a dans cet ouvrage un Monsieur Fleurant apothicaire, brusque jusqu'à l'insolence, qui vient, une seringue à la main, pour donner un lavement au Malade imaginaire. Un honnête homme, frère de ce prétendu malade . . . , le détourne de le prendre, dont l'apothicaire s'irrite et lui dit toutes les impertinences dont les gens de sa sorte sont

---

[79] *Pensées,* ed. L. Lafuma (Paris, 1951), no. 984.

capables. La première fois que cette comédie fut jouée, l'honnête homme répondait à l'apothicaire: 'Allez, Monsieur, allez, on voit bien que vous avez coutume de ne parler qu'à des culs'. (Pardon, Monseigneur, si ce mot m'échappe; je ne le dis que pour le faire mieux condamner.) Tous les auditeurs qui étaient à la première représentation s'en indignèrent, au lieu qu'on fut ravi à la seconde d'entendre: 'Allez, Monsieur, allez, on voit bien que vous n'avez pas coutume de parler à des visages.' C'est dire la même chose et la dire plus finement.[80]

And of course, Boursault is quite right (if we can accept the truth of his story): in its revised form the phrase is not only more 'refined', but also more subtly comic, in that it calls for participation on the part of the spectator or reader, who has to fill in the missing term ('cul') between the syringe and 'des visages'. By the same token, a passage like Orgon's description of his relations with Tartuffe:

> Je vois qu'il reprend tout, et qu'à ma femme même
> Il prend, pour mon honneur, un intérêt extrême;
> Il m'avertit des gens qui lui font les yeux doux,
> Et plus que moi six fois il s'en montre jaloux (lines 301–4)

with its oblique hint of possible marital misfortune, also represents a subtler form of comedy than the overt references to the traditional cuckold's horns in *Le Cocu imaginaire* and other early plays. A comparison with Shakespeare is very instructive in this respect: whereas the English dramatist chose to season nearly all his writing – not only in his comedies – with broad sexual jokes or frank sexual imagery, Molière's plays are singularly lacking in this type of humour. If we compare them, for instance, with the gross obscenities of the farces that have survived under the name of Tabarin, we should perhaps be grateful to the taste of the *honnêtes gens* for having helped to form a comic style that was vigorous without being crude, and which did not need to rely for its effects on subject-matter with a limited appeal.

More generally, in the same way that the taste of the *salons* led to the elimination of sexual and scatological invention, it was also responsible for the attenuation of other forms of fantasy. The positive criteria on which critical taste was founded are well characterised by Q. M. Hope in his book *Saint-Évremond: The honnête homme as Critic* as 'la finesse', 'la raison', 'le bon sens' and 'le naturel' – while 'le caprice', 'la fantaisie' and 'l'imagination' were correspondingly devalued.[81] Similarly, in an excellent essay on the classical aesthetic, L. F. Benedetto writes:

---

[80] *Lettres nouvelles* (1709), quoted Mongrédien (ed.), *Recueil*, p. 433.
[81] (Bloomington, Ind., 1962), ch. vi.

The ethic of the *honnête homme* coincides in more than one respect with the classical aesthetic . . . The ideals both of ancient literature and of the *honnête homme* proclaimed the same virtues: measure, restraint over the individual *moi*, the subordination of the self to society, universality, a strong rationalistic tendency, the union of solid substance and elegant correctness . . . Under the banner of *honnêteté* . . . seventeenth-century French literature realised its characteristic mixture of truth and beauty. And it is perhaps because it wanted to remain *honnête* that this literature remained literature and did not become poetry.[82]

The effects can be seen by comparing Corneille's early plays with those written later, in which it would be difficult to find exuberant imagery such as the following:

> Sire, mon père est mort: mes yeux ont vu son sang
> Couler à gros bouillons de son généreux flanc,
> Ce sang qui tant de fois garantit vos murailles,
> Ce sang qui tant de fois vous gagna des batailles,
> Ce sang qui, tout sorti, fume encor de courroux
> De se voir répandu pour d'autres que pour vous . . .[83]

– or by contrasting the 'récit de Théramène' in Racine's *Phèdre* (1677) with the corresponding account of Hippolyte's death in earlier French plays on the same subject. And so with Molière too: the imagination, as well as the gross sensuality, to be found in the early farces is modified, to satisfy the criterion of the *honnête homme*: 'ne quid nimis':

> Le rire trop marqué, celui du comique 'bas', ne convient pas aux esprits distingués; mais le sublime . . . les ennuie: la comédie moliéresque se définit justement par l'exclusion des extrêmes: ni Turlupin, ni Lysidas.[84]

On the other hand, it is important not to falsify the picture by suggesting that the quality of Molière's comedy was determined entirely by obedience to the critical taste of the *salons*, and overlooking the playwright's own distinctive contribution. It was common for historians of the eighteenth and nineteenth centuries to play down the importance of the farcical, *gaulois*, theatrical side of Molière's comedy, and to concentrate exclusively on its more refined literary aspects; while more recently there has been a tendency, in reaction against that, to stress the former at the expense of the latter. The

[82] 'The Legend of French Classicism', *French Classicism: A Critical Miscellany*, ed. J. Brody (Englewood Cliffs, N.J., 1966), p. 147.
[83] *Le Cid* (1637), lines 665–70.
[84] J. Morel, 'Médiocrité et perfection dans la France du xviie siècle', *Revue d'Histoire Littéraire de la France*, LXIX (1969), 447.

complete Molière, however, is the sum of two contrasting components, imagination and *bon sens*, the *gaulois* and the *honnête*: the mature
playwright was formed by the combined influences of the *salon* and
the practical theatre.

(vi) The player versus the gentlemen[85]

Twentieth-century students of Molière do not always find it easy to
appreciate the incongruity, the incompatibility even, that existed in
his day between the acting profession and the concept of *honnêteté*, if
we define the term strictly. We are aware, of course, that actors were
in some sense a class apart. They were subject to the grave ecclesiastical sanction of excommunication, and we have some idea of what
that involved in terms of civil liberties; but when we read anecdotes of
the cordial relations Molière enjoyed with certain courtiers at Versailles, we may be tempted to imagine that such relationships were on
a footing of something like equality. In our own meritocratic society
we see nothing incongruous in the thought of the illustrious dames
and knights, and even the occasional peer, who continue to tread the
boards in the exercise of an honoured profession; but for Molière's
contemporaries there were certain boundaries that could never be
crossed. 'Le fameux Molière mourut vendredi dernier . . . qui, à sa
profession près, était un assez honnête homme': so runs the comment
of an obscure, but no doubt representative, contemporary;[86] while
another contemporary source attributes to Boileau the observation
that 'Molière récitait en comédien sur le théâtre, mais il parlait en
honnête homme, avait tous les sentiments d'un honnête homme; en
un mot, il n'avait rien contre lui que sa profession.'[87] It is true that the
more sympathetic a writer is known to have been to the theatre – and
the further removed from Court circles – the less need seems to have
been felt for such reservations. The playwright Palaprat, for instance,
evidently did not see the two terms as incompatible:

[85] It should be explained for the benefit of a younger generation of readers (or of readers
not brought up in a cricket-playing environment) that until 1963 a prominent fixture
in the British cricket calendar was the Gentlemen versus Players match, in which a
team of amateurs was opposed to a team of professionals. The implications of
professional dedication on the one hand, and of fastidious amateurism on the other,
seemed to apply so well to the relationship I have tried to define between Molière
and an important part of his audience, that I ventured to adopt this phrase as my
heading.

[86] P. Taisant, quoted Mongrédien (ed.), *Recueil*, p. 455.

[87] Monchesnay, *Bolaeana*, quoted *ibid.*, p. 428.

Ce grand comédien, et mille fois encore plus grand auteur, vivait d'une étroite familiarité avec les Italiens parce qu'ils étaient bons acteurs et fort honnêtes gens.[88]

Nor, it appears, did Chappuzeau, the theatre historian, writing in the year following Molière's death:

> Outre les grandes qualités nécessaires au poète et à l'acteur, il possédait celles qui font l'honnête homme. Il était généreux et bon ami, civil et honorable en toutes ses actions, modeste à recevoir les éloges qu'on lui donnait, savant sans le vouloir paraître, et d'une conversation si douce et si aisée que les premiers de la Cour et de la Ville étaient ravis de l'entretenir.[89]

It is interesting to see his formula being repeated and developed by La Grange, in the Preface to the 1682 edition of Molière's works:

> Il se fit remarquer à la cour pour un homme civil et honnête, ne se prévalant point de son mérite et de son crédit, s'accommodant à l'humeur de ceux avec qui il était obligé de vivre, ayant l'âme belle, libérale: en un mot, possédant et exerçant toutes les qualités d'un parfaitement honnête homme.[90]

It is surely significant, though, that whereas both Chappuzeau and La Grange credit Molière with the 'qualities' necessary to the *honnête homme*, neither writer calls him an *honnête homme* outright. And their seventeenth-century readers would have drawn a clear distinction between 'un parfaitement honnête homme' and an 'honnête homme parfait'; they would have seen the former as tending towards what La Grange calls 'un homme civil et honnête': an acknowledgement of moral worth rather than of social acceptability.

In other words, however admirable the personal qualities they recognised in him, it looks as though most of these writers found it difficult, if not impossible, to admit Molière to the exclusive fraternity of the *honnêtes gens*. For even if contemporary definitions are not adamant on the score of social rank (in fact, Méré warns us that the Court is never the best place to look for the true *honnête homme*,[91] nevertheless breeding, if not gentle birth, was an indispensable attri-

---

[88] *Oeuvres* (1712), I, Preface; quoted *ibid.*, p. 792.
[89] *Le Théâtre français* (1674); quoted *ibid.*, p. 501.
[90] Molière, *Oeuvres*, ed. Despois and Mesnard, I, xv.
[91] 'Il est bon de se souvenir que cette Cour qu'on prend pour modèle est une affluence de toute sorte de gens; que les uns ne font que passer, que les autres n'en sont que depuis peu, et que la plupart quoiqu'ils y soient nés ne sont pas à imiter', *Oeuvres*, II, pp. 111.

bute. Grimarest is another who seems careful not to bestow the title of
honnête homme on Molière. He too grants him the necessary qualities:

> Molière, né avec des moeurs droites, et dont les manières étaient simples
> et naturelles, souffrait impatiemment le Courtisan empressé, flatteur,
> médisant, inquiet, incommode, faux ami.[92]

He appears nevertheless to judge his social position from the uncompromising point of view of the King and Court:

> C'était un homme de probité, et qui avait des sentiments peu communs
> parmi les personnes de sa naissance.[93]

And even so, the biographer was to find himself sharply criticised by
the anonymous author of the *Lettre critique* for misrepresenting
Molière's social status in his very title:

> C'était un comédien, c'est-à-dire un homme d'une profession ignoble, à
> qui la qualité de Monsieur ne convient nullement . . . En vérité, il
> répugne en ouvrant ce livre, de lire: *La Vie de Monsieur de Molière*.[94]

It is true that Molière was honoured by the King, and had friendly
relations with members of the Court; but he was a *comédien*, a common
player. And if his profession put him beyond the pale in the eyes of
those who equated *honnêteté* with breeding, it was also an obstacle in
another, subtler sense for any who, though perhaps more tolerant on
that score, looked on *honnêteté* as a highly demanding way of life. From
the picture we have built up of the *honnête homme* as defined by Méré or
Saint-Évremond, one thing is abundantly clear: the *honnête homme* is
an amateur, to whom any suggestion of professionalism is abhorrent.
In this strictest, most exclusive sense, the *honnêtes gens* were spectators
rather than participants – or at any rate, 'gentlemen' rather than
'players'; and we can be sure that Molière, who was nothing if not a
professional in every inch of his body, wanted nothing to do with the
sort of social distinction that excluded any possibility of professional
pride in a job well done. Not for him the aspirations of a Boileau or a
Racine, ready to welcome Court office as historiographer royal as a
release from the humble profession of man of letters; there is a story,
apparently first put about early in the eighteenth century, of Molière
himself being prepared to sell his birthright for a mess of the
Academy's pottage:

> Molière était désigné pour remplir la première place vacante à
> l'Académie française; la compagnie s'était arrangée au sujet de sa

[92] *La Vie de M. de Molière*, p. 53.   [93] *Ibid.*, p. 122.   [94] Cf. *ibid.*, p. 133.

profession. Molière n'aurait plus joué que dans les rôles du haut comique, mais sa mort précipitée le priva d'une place bien méritée et l'Académie d'un sujet si digne de la remplir.[95]

But everything we know about Molière: his professional conscience, his feeling of solidarity with his colleagues, and above all the intimate relationship between the man of letters and the *farceur* in him, suggests that this anecdote could never have been based on fact. For Molière never ceased to be a *farceur*: he may have been 'le premier farceur de France', as Somaize grudgingly calls him,[96] but he was still a *farceur*; and this wholly professional man of the theatre, this *farceur*, was as much an outsider to the exclusive club of the *honnêtes gens* as Corneille had been twenty years earlier, preaching the stern aristocratic ideal of the 'éthique de la gloire' from the comfort of his middle-class lawyer's study.

If we lower our sights a little, however, and look at the more day-to-day connotations of the term *honnête homme* in the usage of the time, there is no difficulty in recognising the central importance in Molière's theatre of those qualities which, as we have seen, contemporaries readily attributed to him, and which he, as a playwright, embodied in a series of sympathetic characters running through most of his mature plays. These are the virtues of generosity, fair-mindedness, level-headedness and dependability, together with an integrity of character which rounds out the personality into an admirable whole. The characters displaying these qualities, the Aristes, Chrysaldes, Cléantes and Béraldes of Molière's world, no doubt sometimes fall short of the fastidious standard set by a Méré or a Saint-Évremond; and the 'honnête homme de la pièce' may not always be an *honnête homme tout court*, judged by the most exacting criteria. Yet the way of life practised by these characters, and the principles they proclaim, stamp them as exponents of the same positive ethical system of *honnêteté*, even if they do not possess the social cachet of its most celebrated ambassadors.

In fact, Molière's works do contain two examples of the *honnête homme* in courtly, rather than in bourgeois, guise. One of these is Clitandre of *Les Femmes savantes*, who moves in the same *salon* world as Trissotin, but whose polished manners and good breeding make the necessary contrast with the pedantry, affectation and selfishness of the latter. The other is Philinte, Alceste's self-effacing companion,

[95] Cizeron-Rival, *Récréations littéraires* (1765), quoted Mongrédien (ed.), *Recueil*, p. 797.
[96] See epigraph to Chapter 1 above; and cf. Somaize, *Dictionnaire*, ed. Livet, II, p. 45.

who has always tended to have rather a bad press.[97] For far too long
Philinte has been considered in a purely negative light, as an unin-
teresting foil to the dynamic Alceste: even Jacques Guicharnaud, in
his otherwise excellent interpretation of *Le Misanthrope*, writes of
'l'inhumaine absence de Philinte'.[98] However, as Merlin Thomas has
demonstrated, subsidiary status in dramatic terms should not be
equated with lack of personality;[99] and Philinte surely represents a
very positive social ideal. But what distinguishes Philinte and Clitandre from the other *honnêtes gens* in Molière's world – the breeding and
bon ton necessitated by the setting of the plays in which they appear – is
less important than what they have in common with this larger group
of characters. The attitude to life represented by Molière's *honnêtes
gens* has often been written off as over-cautious and conservative, and
the phrase 'the golden mean' has acquired in this connection a
thoroughly pejorative interpretation. The play Faguet makes with
the notion of safe, prudent mediocrity on the part of Molière's
bourgeois *raisonneurs*, compared with the adventurous spirit shown
by the *précieuses*, the *femmes savantes*, or Monsieur Jourdain, is
notorious:[100] it corresponds to Rousseau's view of Philinte. But this is
an absurd aberration of critical judgement: there can be no doubt that
the function of Molière's *honnêtes gens* is to illustrate a norm of civilised
and socially acceptable behaviour against which the behaviour of the
comic characters can be measured. Measured – and at the same time
judged: for it is difficult to accept the critical view which asks us to
suspend our 'judgement' on Molière's characters in the name of a
more abstract, impersonal, comic effect; and the term 'judgement'
seems to be equally appropriate whether we prefer to stress the
satirical, or the purely comic, aspect of his writing. We may prefer not
to say that the behaviour of one group of characters is 'right' and that
of another group 'wrong'; but if we say that the behaviour of the
second group is 'laughable', or 'comic', we are still making a judgement – even if only an unconscious one – by the reflex action of our
laughter, inasmuch as we relate this behaviour to the standard set by
the actions and reactions of those in the other group.

And not only are the members of the latter group – the 'normal'

[97] For Rousseau's celebrated commentary on him, see below, p. 144.
[98] *Molière: une aventure théâtrale* (Paris, 1963), p. 371.
[99] 'Philinte and Éliante', *Molière: Stage and Study: Essays in honour of W. G. Moore*, ed.
   W. D. Howarth and Merlin Thomas (Oxford, 1973), pp. 73–92.
[100] *Rousseau contre Molière* (Paris, 1912), pp. 228ff.

characters of Molière's world – identified unambiguously with the *honnêtes gens* of the world outside (taking the term in its relatively broad acceptation), but his comic heroes too are themselves defined by reference to the same notion of *honnêteté*. When Dorante, Molière's spokesman in *La Critique de l'École des femmes* (and that is surely one play in which the use of the word 'spokesman' is not out of place) says: 'Il n'est pas incompatible qu'une personne soit ridicule en de certaines choses et honnête homme en d'autres' (scene vi), he is certainly using the expression in a much wider sense than that given to it by Méré, but it refers nevertheless to a concept that was by no means empty of meaning for Molière's contemporaries. From Arnolphe onwards – even if this does not apply to the earlier, more caricatural figures, the Sganarelles of *Le Cocu imaginaire* and *L'École des maris* – his heroes are drawn from the same world as the genuine *honnêtes gens*, the brothers-in-law or friends of the family whose function is to expose the folly of their ways. There is never any question of the comic figures themselves qualifying as *honnêtes gens*: their folly is too pronounced for that. But perhaps we might call them 'honnêtes gens manqués': they are given enough of a rudimentary *état civil*, their personalities are sufficiently rounded, for us to guess what they would each be like without their comic foible or obsession.

The two elements in the make-up of Molière's comic characters, identified in the phrase 'ridicule en de certaines choses et honnête homme en d'autres', can thus be seen to relate to the two aspects of their creator's personality: his private life as a man of the world mixing with courtiers and *honnêtes gens*, and his professional activity as an actor–playwright. His plays reflected many of the values to which his audience of *honnêtes gens* would subscribe; but he was a *farceur* by origin, and deliberately chose to remain a *farceur*. And even when the broader effects of farce are eliminated from his mature comedy, Molière the *farceur* continues to demand from his audience an aesthetic response which offers a real challenge to the *honnêtes gens*.

The nature of this challenge, and the hesitation of the audience to whom it was addressed, are made quite clear in the *Critique de l'École des femmes*. 'C'est une étrange entreprise', says Dorante, 'que celle de faire rire les honnêtes gens' (scene vi). Why, we may ask, should it be an 'étrange entreprise'? Which *honnêtes gens* did Molière have in mind, and why did they find a play like *L'École des femmes* disconcerting? The context would seem to suggest that the phrase refers to Molière's ideal audience, those spectators whose appreciation he particularly valued;

but the text of the *Critique* offers no further clue to their identity, beyond the claim put forward both by Climène the *précieuse* and by Lysidas the Court poet to represent that enlightened body: this fact, and the setting of the play in a society *salon*, perhaps reinforce the view that Molière is here using the term in its more exclusive aristocratic sense. However, there is another text which complements the one just quoted, and which appears to provide rather more help in identifying and characterising this category of 'difficult' spectators. The opening scene of *L'Impromptu de Versailles* contains the following passage, spoken by Molière himself:

> Pensez-vous que ce soit une petite affaire que d'exposer quelque chose de comique devant une assemblée comme celle-ci, que d'entreprendre de faire rire des personnes qui nous impriment du respect et ne rient que quand ils veulent?

What Molière is concerned about here, like his spokesman Dorante in the *Critique*, is, we may be sure, the reception of his plays at the hands of the cultured, educated spectators with a keen sense of their own dignity. And there is plenty of contemporary evidence that to members of this élite, the *honnêtes gens* 'qui nous impriment du respect', laughter was rather suspect, and that reluctance to join in the laughter of a theatre audience was regarded as a mark of superiority. It is true that Dorante's picture of the behaviour of such spectators, in the nobleman 'sur le théâtre' with his indignant cries of 'Ris donc, parterre, ris donc!', is a thoroughly satirical one: such spectators, like the Marquis in the same scene (scene v) with his scorn for 'les continuels éclats de rire que le parterre y fait', are no doubt not genuine *honnêtes gens* in Molière's eyes, but a crude imitation of the real thing. Nevertheless, their behaviour in this respect was modelled on the most impeccable examples.

Méré, for instance, makes it quite clear throughout his various essays on *honnêteté* that his ideal gentleman is not easily moved to laughter:

> Ne vaut-il pas mieux s'ennuyer en honnête homme, que de se divertir comme un sot?[101]

Not that all laughter is necessarily ruled out:

> Une plaisanterie étudiée ou mal prise a ce qu'elle mérite, quand on la rejette, ou qu'on s'en moque. Il faut que'elle soit naturelle et propre au

[101] *Oeuvres*, III, p. 169.

sujet; qu'elle soit noble, honnête et galante, et je ne trouve rien de plus agréable, que de railler de la sorte.[102]

But even at Court, where frivolity is all too fashionable, the superior pleasures of serious conversation are appreciated:

> La plaisanterie est fort à la mode, mais on s'épuise à rire comme à dire des choses plaisantes; et quoiqu'on ne pense guère à la cour qu'à se divertir, je prends garde que les plus disposés à la joie sont quelquefois bien aises d'écouter quelqu'un qui parle et qui décide sérieusement de tout ce qu'on lui demande, quand il sait donner des raisons choisies, épurées, de facile intelligence, et qui ne lassent point.[103]

And Méré's considered advice seems to be that *honnêteté* and laughter do not go well together, and that the profession of joker is best left to others:

> Aussi je conseille aux honnêtes gens du monde, et principalement aux dames de bon air, de songer plus à plaire qu'à faire rire, parce que beaucoup de choses font rire, qu'on n'aime point, mais tout ce qui plaît, se fait aimer.[104]

These texts, of course, all refer to the place of laughter in polite social intercourse, not to the public display of laughter in the theatre. But they can be matched with texts from other authors of the period, which suggest that Méré's *honnête homme* was in the habit of taking his prejudices to the theatre with him; there is plenty of evidence that the *honnêtes gens* at the theatre were just as fastidious as they were in the *salon*. Boileau's strictures on *Les Fourberies de Scapin*[105] are not merely to be interpreted, I think, as a condemnation of physical action on the stage, but of laughter as something beneath the dignity of the *honnête homme*; such, at least, is evidently the opinion attributed to Boileau by his Boswell in the following passage:

> Une des lectures qui faisait le plus de plaisir à Monsieur Despréaux, c'était celle de Térence. C'était un auteur, disait-il, dont toutes les expressions vont au coeur; il ne cherche point à faire rire, ce qu'affectent surtout les autres comiques; il ne s'étudie qu'à dire des choses raisonnables, et tous ses termes sont dans la nature, qu'il peint toujours admirablement . . . Enfin, disait-il, il est étonnant que ce poète ayant écrit après Plaute, ce Plaute si cher à la multitude eût été effacé par un concurrent qui avait pris la route la moins sûre pour plaire: car ce peuple romain . . . voulait rire à quelque prix que ce fût; et voilà qui rendait Térence plus merveilleux, d'avoir accommodé le peuple à lui, sans s'accommoder au peuple: et par là, disait Monsieur Despréaux, Térence

---

[102] *Ibid.*   [103] *Oeuvres*, II, p. 104.   [104] *Oeuvres*, III, p. 171.   [105] See p. 13 above.

a l'avantage sur Molière, qui certainement est un peintre d'après nature, mais non pas si parfait que Térence, puisque Molière dérogeait souvent à son génie noble par des plaisanteries grossières qu'il hasardait en faveur de la multitude, au lieu qu'il ne faut avoir en vue que les honnêtes gens.[106]

An author who makes a similar contrast between the *honnêtes gens* and the *rieurs* is Donneau de Visé, giving advance publicity to one of his own plays in his journal *Le Mercure Galant*:

Les honnêtes gens n'y trouveront pas moins à se divertir que ceux qui veulent rire sans relâche; et qui souvent, après avoir ri, ne trouvent point de sens dans l'économie d'une pièce, parce qu'ils ne veulent rien entendre de sérieux qui établisse le sujet.[107]

An earlier text (from the period of *L'École des femmes*, and possibly also by Donneau de Visé) goes a good deal further in opposing laughter to good taste:

[Molière] veut encore nous persuader, pour rendre sa cause bonne, que les Français n'aiment qu'à rire; mais il fait voir par là qu'il les estime peu, puisqu'il ne les croit pas capables de goûter les belles choses.[108]

The phrase finds an echo in La Bruyère's aphorism, which leaves Méré's counsel of moderation far behind:

Il n'est pas ordinaire que celui qui fait rire se fasse estimer.[109]

However, while the last two quotations are quite categorical, and condemn laughter as uncompromisingly as Bossuet or any church-man, it is true that some of the other passages quoted do make a distinction between moderate and immoderate laughter. La Bruyère himself says elsewhere: 'Je doute . . . que le ris excessif convienne aux hommes',[110] and this was a distinction made in the context of 'le comique du théâtre' by a number of writers who sought thereby to reconcile laughter with *honnêteté*. Donneau de Visé's expression 'rire dans l'âme' no doubt provides the most memorable formulation:

[Les pièces] de cette nature me semblent plus divertissantes encore que l'on y rie moins haut; et je crois qu'elles divertissent davantage, qu'elles attachent, et qu'elles font continuellement rire dans l'âme.[111]

[106] Monchesnay, *Bolaeana*, quoted Mongrédien (ed.), *Recueil*, pp. 48–50.
[107] *Trois Comédies*, ed. P. Mélèse (Paris, 1940), pp. xxvii–xxviii.
[108] *Lettres sur les affaires du théâtre* in *La Querelle de l'École des femmes*, ed. Mongrédien, II, pp. 307.
[109] 'De la société et de la conversation', para. 2.   [110] 'De l'homme', para. 37.
[111] *Lettre sur le Misanthrope* in Molière, *Oeuvres*, ed. Despois and Mesnard, V, p. 440.

But similar formulas were constantly being produced, throughout the classical period. Boileau's remark to Racine on the subject of *L'Avare*, for instance, is quoted elsewhere.[112] Somewhat later, Fontenelle compares 'des ris immodérés et stupides' with 'un sourire spirituel', and congratulates Destouches, in welcoming him to the Academy, on:

> Une espèce de comique qui ne cherche point à exciter bassement un rire immodéré dans une multitude grossière, mais qui élève cette multitude, presque malgré elle-même, à rire finement et avec esprit.[113]

And later still we find Voltaire congratulating himself, in the Preface to *L'Écossaise* (1760), on the fact that 'l'honnête homme y sourit de ce sourire de l'âme, préférable aux rires de la bouche'.

Now, clearly it would be absurd to maintain that the distinction between 'rire' and 'rire dans l'âme' is a wholly imaginary one, or that it is impossible to distinguish between moderate and immoderate laughter. But is it a difference of kind, or a difference of degree? It is clearly arguable that it is merely one of degree; and that writers who claimed to see a categorical difference between 'rire' on the one hand and 'rire dans l'âme', 'le rire intérieur' or 'sourire' on the other, were often begging the question by using the latter formula to refer to something quite unconnected with laughter. This emerges clearly enough from another passage of the *Bolaeana*:

> Monsieur Despréaux . . . me disait qu'il y avait deux sortes de rire, l'un qui vient de surprise, et l'autre qui réjouit l'âme intérieurement, et fait rire plus efficacement, parce qu'il est fondé sur la raison. Car, disait-il, l'effet naturel de la raison est de plaire, et quand vous voyez sur le théâtre une action qui se suit, et des caractères heureusement représentés, vous ne sauriez vous défendre d'applaudir, si ce n'est pas par des éclats de rire violents, au moins par une satisfaction que vous sentez au-dedans de vous-même. Or les bouffonneries qui excitent la risée ont véritablement quelque mérite; mais quand on les oppose au plaisir que produit un caractère naturel et bien touché, c'est un bâtard auprès d'un enfant légitime.[114]

The 'satisfaction' or 'pleasure' Boileau refers to here may well form part of our total response to comic drama; but these specific reactions are surely the way in which we respond, not to the *comic* but to the *dramatic* elements that help to constitute this art form, either of which

---

[112] See epigraph to Chapter 6.
[113] Destouches, *Oeuvres dramatiques* (Paris, 1774), x, p. 290.
[114] Monchesnay, *Bolaeana*, quoted Mongrédien (ed.), *Recueil*, pp. 86–8.

may exist in almost complete independence of the other.[115] Corneille's comedies, for instance, had asked for no more than 'pleasure' and 'satisfaction' on the spectator's part;[116] but in Molière's own case, such reactions are only part of the response he looks for from his audience. This is true even of *Le Misanthrope*, and Donneau de Visé's formula surely acknowledges as much. For although de Visé elsewhere talks disparagingly of genuinely comic writing, the passage from his *Lettre sur le Misanthrope* makes it clear that by 'rire dans l'âme' he means something that is still recognisable as a kind of laughter; indeed, he explicitly congratulates Molière on having succeeded in this play in reconciling laughter and *honnêteté*:

> Voilà, Monsieur, ce que je pense de la comédie du *Misanthrope amoureux*, que je trouve d'autant plus admirable, que le héros en est le plaisant sans être trop ridicule, et qu'il fait rire les honnêtes gens sans dire des plaisanteries froides et basses, comme on l'a accoutumé de voir dans les pièces comiques.[117]

And in this connection it is surely right to see Philinte, the embodiment of *honnêteté* on stage, as giving pointers to the *honnêtes gens* in the audience as to how they should react to Alceste. He is cast in the role of spectator – but more specifically, he is an *amused* spectator; and the lines he addresses to Alceste in the opening scene:

> Je vous dirai tout franc que cette maladie,
> Partout où vous allez, donne la comédie,
> Et qu'un si grand courroux contre les moeurs du temps
> Vous tourne en ridicule auprès de bien des gens (lines 105–8)

together with other references in the same scene to the laughter Alceste's behaviour causes among his friends, seem to be clear indications of the way in which Molière wants us to react to his *atrabilaire amoureux*.

When we turn to the group of major comedies, set in a bourgeois milieu, that were produced during the last four or five years of the playwright's life, we can see that in every play the social standing of the characters is of considerable importance. This is emphasised by

---

[115] This point is made more fully in the Introduction to *Comic Drama: The European Heritage*, ed. W. D. Howarth (London, 1978).

[116] Such a view has been persuasively challenged, as regards *Mélite*, by M. S. Poole ('A Re-reading of Corneille's *Mélite*', *The Classical Tradition in French Literature, Essays presented to R. C. Knight* (London, 1977), pp. 49–60); though it holds good for the comedies written immediately after *Mélite* in the 1630s.

[117] In Molière, *Oeuvres*, ed. Despois and Mesnard, v, p. 440.

the interior decoration, the furniture, and the domestic equipment of a comfortable bourgeois household: a tangible representation of respectability which we may be sure helped the *honnêtes gens* in the audience to identify with the admirable sentiments of a Cléante, an Ariste or a Béralde. There is evidence that in *Les Femmes savantes* at least, Molière deliberately set himself to write the sort of 'grande comédie' that would particularly appeal to the *honnêtes gens*; and the polished verse, the wit, the intellectual level of the conversation, all combine with the portrayal of a well-appointed domestic interior and with the example set by the *raisonneur* and the idealised young courtier, to provide the harmonious whole that would satisfy even the most difficult of spectators. But even in this play, the *farceur* is never absent for long. Bélise is a delightfully extravagant caricature of a *visionnaire*; Chrysale is another in the long line of Sganarelle types played by Molière himself; while Philaminte herself – played by a male actor, Hubert – is a constant reminder of the domineering wives of the farces.

There were certain concessions, then, that Molière may have been prepared to make to the taste of the cultured élite among his audience; and as regards the literary tone, or flavour, of his comedy, their influence was no doubt all to the good. But the really essential concession was one that he was not prepared to make. He was a *farceur*, and it was his business to make people laugh. Dorante's defence of 'les pièces comiques' in the *Critique*:

> Je trouve qu'il est bien plus aisé de se guinder sur de grands sentiments, de braver en vers la fortune, accuser les destins, et dire des injures aux dieux, que d'entrer comme il faut dans le ridicule des hommes, et de rendre agréablement sur le théâtre les défauts de tout le monde . . . (scene vi)

stands as Molière's own proud assertion of the validity of the kind of entertainment he was offering his public. Between the player – the actor–dramatist, seeking out the folly and absurdity of human nature in order to offer it up to the critical laughter of his audience – and the gentlemen – those serious-minded, self-important spectators 'qui nous impriment du respect et ne rient que quand ils veulent' – no compromise was possible. The incompatibility of the two philosophies seems to me to be remarkably well rendered in this fragment of dialogue from a very different source:

> 'The wisest and the best of men, nay, the wisest and best of their actions, may be rendered ridiculous by a person whose first object in life is a joke.'

'Certainly', replied Elizabeth, 'there are such people, but I hope I am not one of them. I hope I never ridicule what is wise or good. Follies and nonsense, whims and inconsistencies do divert me, I own, and I laugh at them whenever I can.'[118]

The proud, aristocratic Mr Darcy could well serve as spokesman for the *honnêtes gens* at their most exclusive; and by the same token Elizabeth Bennett, Jane Austen's favourite heroine, does more than represent her creator's own views here: what she says could serve as a defence of every comic writer – be he novelist or playwright, poet or *farceur* – against the mistrust or the disdain that the exercise of his craft has so often aroused in those who pride themselves on superior taste or judgement.

For this is not merely a seventeenth-century phenomenon. The agelasts, as Meredith calls those who refuse to laugh,[119] are always with us; and Paul Valéry is an excellent example from our own century. Not only did he display a marked hostility towards Molière's comedy:

> Il a donné, par quelques chefs-d'oeuvre, une autorité dont on peut s'émerveiller aux choses les plus vulgaires. Il a mis les rieurs, c'est-à-dire la moyenne, contre l'exception ou plutôt il s'est mis soi-même avec cette moyenne –

but he also showed a rooted distrust of the role of laughter in aesthetic experience. 'Le rire', he wrote, 'est un réflexe qui tient du vomissement et du tremblement'; and it is said that a visit to the cinema to see Chaplin in *The Gold Rush* so upset him that he never again set foot inside a cinema.[120] How much more humane and understanding is Alain's comment on the nature of comedy. When we laugh at Molière's comic heroes, if we accept Alain's view, we are not abrogating our intellectual faculties: on the contrary, we are making use of our critical intelligence in the service of an ideal of civilised social behaviour: 'Ce jugement par le rire marque le plus haut pouvoir de l'esprit.'[121] This view would have been a long way from obtaining universal acceptance in Molière's own time, but at last – and this is the playwright's triumphant achievement – it has prevailed in the twentieth century. In this sense we can say that the player has finally defeated the gentlemen.

[118] *Pride and Prejudice*, ch. xi.
[119] See *An Essay on Comedy and the Uses of the Comic Spirit* (1877), p. 9.
[120] See W. N. Ince, 'Valéry on Molière: An Intellectual out of Humour', *Modern Language Review*, LX (1965), 41–7.
[121] *Propos de littérature* (Paris, 1934), pp. 109–10.

3

Comic Drama Before Molière

Le paysan ou l'ivrogne fournit quelques scènes à un farceur; il n'entre
qu'à peine dans le vrai comique.

(La Bruyère)[1]

(i) Theory

What kind of play was it, in the years preceding Molière's return to
Paris, that best reflected the taste of these urbane, undemonstrative
theatregoers? The *marquis*, as we have seen, had a penchant for the
crude humour of the *turlupinade*; the Court in general seems to have
fancied visual spectacle and the composite entertainment of the *ballet
de cour*; what of the *honnête homme* in the *salons*, conscious of his
dignity, his good breeding, and his superior taste?

It goes without saying that tragedy was likely to satisfy such
spectators better than comedy, especially tragedy as represented by
Pierre Corneille's contributions to that genre, from *Horace* (1640)
onwards: tragedy, that is, purged of the excesses of the baroque
period, the extravagances of style and subject-matter that still
marked plays like Rotrou's *Hercule mourant* (1634) or Corneille's own
Médée (1635). Tragedy had become 'raisonnable', and the muted
heroics of a play like *Nicomède* (1651) were exactly calculated to appeal
to an audience of *honnêtes gens*. In comedy too, Corneille's early group
of plays had anticipated, and came nearest to satisfying, those criteria
to which Saint-Évremond for instance, in his essay on contemporary
comedy, gives prominence: 'la régularité', 'la vraisemblance', 'la
délicatesse', 'le bon sens'; while in the same author's companion
essay, 'De la comédie italienne', it is equally easy to see him expressing the views of the *honnêtes gens* when he writes admiringly of the
Italians' acting technique, but deplores the poor taste of *commedia
dell'arte* dialogue: 'ce sont d'excellents comédiens, qui ont de fort
méchantes comédies'.[2]

[1] *Caractères*, 'Des ouvrages de l'esprit', para. 52.
[2] *Oeuvres choisies*, ed. Hippeau, pp. 190–3, 197.

Corneille's own definition of comedy is contained in the 1660 *Examen* to his first play *Mélite* (probably performed in 1629):

> La nouveauté de ce genre de comédie, dont il n'y a point d'exemple en aucune langue, et le style naïf qui faisait une peinture de la conversation des honnêtes gens, furent sans doute cause de ce bonheur surprenant, qui fit alors tant de bruit. On n'avait jamais vu jusque-là que la comédie fît rire sans personnages ridicules, tels que les valets bouffons, les parasites, les capitans, les docteurs, etc. Celle-ci faisait son effet par l'humeur enjouée de gens d'une condition au-dessus de ceux qu'on voit dans les comédies de Plaute et de Térence, qui n'étaient que des marchands.

This text is important, I think, less as the author's comment on what he had tried to achieve thirty years earlier, than as an attempt to define the theoretical ideal of the educated playgoers of 1660: in the formula 'une peinture de la conversation des honnêtes gens', I believe we have an accurate indication of what many contemporary spectators must have looked for in a comedy.

From a historical point of view, such a theoretical ideal is in the mainstream of comic theory going back, via the French and Italian Renaissance theorists, to Donatus and other commentators of the Middle Ages, and ultimately to their sources in the ancient world. Cicero's 'imitatio vitae, speculum consuetudinis, et imago veritatis'; Diomedes' 'privatae civilisque fortunae sine periculo vitae comprehensio'; Scaliger's 'poema dramaticum, negotiosum, exitu laetum, stylo populari':[3] these definitions led the way for numerous others along the same lines – and according to this body of traditional classical theory, comedy was defined in the first place by the social level of its protagonists, the familiar nature of its language, and its happy ending. Not by the fact that it aimed to arouse laughter: those theorists who embody this specific aesthetic purpose in their definitions are in a minority; and for the century before Molière comedy was seen by the overwhelming majority of theoreticians as an imitative genre whose object was to give pleasure by the faithful representation of reality, not to make audiences laugh by its caricatural distortion. That was the province of farce, not of comedy; and there are many texts in which the contrast is emphatically made between comedy as a respectable literary genre and farce as its bastard relation. The imaginative extravagance of mid-century burlesque is attacked by Balzac on similar grounds:

[3] See H. W. Lawton (ed.), *Handbook of French Renaissance Dramatic Theory* (Manchester, 1949).

Ne saurait-on rire en bon français et en style raisonnable . . .? Pour ne
rien dire de pis de cette sorte de raillerie, elle sent plus la comédie que la
conversation, et plus la farce que la comédie. Ce n'est pas railler en
honnête homme.[4]

And it is interesting to see Corneille, looking back in 1660 on his first
play, deploring as a concession to popular taste precisely that feature
of *Mélite* that we should recognise as most overtly comic: the inventive
fantasy of the sequence in which Éraste, thinking he is responsible for
the deaths of Tircis and Mélite, goes temporarily out of his mind, and
imagining he is in Hades, addresses his friends as mythological
figures.

This theoretical debate about the nature of comedy – as realistic
imitation, or as caricatural distortion, of reality – underlies the critical debate that Molière portrays for us in *La Critique de l'École des
femmes*. We know from the other plays and pamphlets in 'la Guerre
comique' that Molière was accused by contemporaries of blurring the
boundaries between comedy and farce – or to put it in seventeenth-
century terms, 'détruire la belle comédie', a genre which is defined as
follows:

J'entends par la belle comédie, ces pièces qui sont des tableaux des
passions, galamment touchés, où l'on remarque de beaux sentiments, où
l'on voit des moralités judicieusement répandues, où, enfin, l'on trouve
de quoi s'instruire et se divertir agréablement. Je mets en ce rang les
chefs-d'oeuvre du grand Ariste [Corneille], dont je ne prends que le
Menteur pour l'opposer à tout le misérable comique de Zoïle [Molière].[5]

In Molière's own play, the absurdity of the purist position adopted by
his critics is brought out by the semantic paradox that enables
Lysidas to claim that Arnolphe's behaviour in *L'École des femmes*, Act
IV, scene iv, is too *comique* to deserve a place in a *comédie*:

Et ce Monsieur de la Souche enfin, qu'on nous fait un homme d'esprit, et
qui paraît si sérieux en tant d'endroits, ne descend-il point dans quelque
chose de trop comique et de trop outré au cinquième acte, lorsqu'il
explique à Agnès la violence de son amour, avec ces roulements d'yeux
extravagants, ces soupirs ridicules, et ces larmes niaises qui font rire tout
le monde? (scene vi)

For Molière, on the contrary, laughter – and hence the caricatural

---

[4] *Entretien* xxxviii (1657), quoted P. Kohler, *L'Esprit classique et la comédie* (Paris, 1925),
p. 185.
[5] Robinet, *Le Panégyrique de l'École des femmes*, scene v, in *La Querelle de l'École des femmes*,
ed. Mongrédien, i, pp. 204–5.

exaggeration of character in order to make his audience laugh – was of the essence of comedy; and Dorante of the *Critique* quite clearly represents his author's view of the more enlightened *honnête homme*, defending this concept against the pedant Lysidas and against all those cultured playgoers who might be tempted to take his side: those who stood on their dignity and refused to laugh, and those who found Molière's newly-defined formula for comedy an uncomfortable and provocative novelty.

(ii) Practice

There was, of course, an appreciable difference between theory and practice. As in the sixteenth century, when comedies with a considerable admixture of extravagant comic writing were being composed at the same time (and not infrequently by the same authors) as the theoretical works which insisted on a strict separation between comedy and farce, so too in the seventeenth century the practical theatre seldom conformed to the theoretical ideal of the purists. Even Corneille, 'celui qui avait substitué aux bouffons les honnêtes gens',[6] did not remain wedded to the formula of the realistic comedy of manners; and if Bray's phrase applies well enough to the plays of the early 1630s, from *Mélite* to *La Place Royale* (1635), both *L'Illusion comique* (1636) and *Le Menteur* (1643), generally considered to be Corneille's masterpiece in the field of comedy, rely on a generous measure of fantasy and verbal invention for a comic effect that is very different from that produced by 'la conversation des honnêtes gens'.

L'Illusion comique was thoroughly of its time: the baroque imagination, skilfully manipulating various levels of reality, created what Corneille himself called 'un étrange monstre' of a play,[7] while the central character, Matamore, inhabits a fantasy world of the theatre quite out of touch with reality. The most extravagantly larger-than-life of all the braggart soldiers descended from Plautus' Pyrgopolinices, Matamore illustrates better than any other character of the time those 'personnages ridicules' on which the *Examen* to *Mélite* was later to pour scorn. *Le Menteur*, despite its Spanish inspiration, is certainly nearer to comedy of manners; but into a framework that approximates to the setting of *La Galerie du Palais* or *La Place Royale* Corneille has placed a central character of a very different

---

[6] R. Bray, *La Formation de la doctrine classique en France* (Paris, 1951), p. 334.
[7] Dedicatory letter to *L'Illusion comique*.

provenance. Dorante is a compulsive mythomaniac for whom the truth is never interesting enough, and whose fertile imagination constantly invents ever more extravagant fictions; and it is the conflict between his fantasy world and the 'real' world around him that keeps the plot going. Whereas his counterpart in Alarcón's play *La Verdad sospechosa* is punished for his failing, Dorante is presented in a wholly sympathetic light, and we connive at his peccadilloes in the interests of pure entertainment.

R. Guichemerre, in the conclusion to his study of the mid-century period, writes:

> La comédie des années 1640–60 nous semble avoir été essentiellement une comédie de la fantaisie et du jeu. Fantaisie dans l'invention de situations piquantes ou romanesques: les Espagnols lui en offraient de nombreux modèles, mais nos écrivains ont raffiné encore en ingéniosité sur ceux qu'ils imitaient . . . Fantaisie aussi dans la création de personnages ahurissants ou grotesques: les fantoches de la comédie italienne prennent des proportions épiques . . . Fantaisie enfin dans le jeu verbal . . .: il n'est guère de forme de jonglerie verbale qui ne se rencontre dans les pièces de cette époque.[8]

This was the period when Spanish influence was at its height. Besides Corneille in *Le Menteur* and *La Suite du Menteur*, Rotrou and d'Ouville led the way round about 1640, and were followed by prolific writers of comedy such as Scarron, Boisrobert and Thomas Corneille. Plots, which were complicated and ingenious, were based, at any rate in their original sources, on the social conditions peculiar to Spain: the cloistered existence led by unmarried women drives them and their lovers to extreme lengths – elopements, abductions – to circumvent the vigilance of fathers or brothers who embody the fanatical Spanish concept of honour. Together with the plot-interest, suspense and relief of tension offered by these *comédies d'intrigue* went the comic relief provided by the French counterparts of the Spanish *gracioso*. This established role was distinguished from the various Italian *emplois* of the valet by his cowardice, his gluttony, his self-centredness: altogether, to quote Guichemerre, he was 'un assez grossier personnage'.[9] Jodelet, the most celebrated comic actor of the period, acclimatised on the French stage this distinctive Spanish type – though it would no doubt be wrong to attribute everything in Jodelet's case to foreign influences: he had begun by playing farce at

---

[8] *La Comédie avant Molière, 1640–1660* (Paris, 1972), p. 393.
[9] *Ibid.*, p. 182.

the Théâtre du Marais, and one authority claims that 'il doit autant à la farce française qu'à la comédie espagnole'.[10] Jodelet's success at the Marais, in the plays of d'Ouville, Corneille and Scarron, was so great that the actor Villiers of the rival theatre, the Hôtel de Bourgogne, began to imitate him in the role of Philipin in a similar series of plays. With reference to the most successful of all these plays, Scarron's *Dom Japhet d'Arménie*, first played at the Hôtel de Bourgogne in 1646–7 with Philipin in the title role, Lancaster conjectures that it was also played at the Marais by Jodelet;[11] and it was also to be performed by Molière's troupe regularly up to 1665. What the Jodelet plays, and *Dom Japhet*, offered the playgoers of the 1640s and 1650s was a lively, eventful plot with disguises, mistaken identities and all the stock *péripéties* of romanesque comedy; and as light relief, in counterpoint as it were to the romanesque plot, buffoonery and verbal comedy of an entertaining sort from the Jodelet–Philipin figure. The particular form of verbal comedy that was developed with such success by Scarron and his contemporaries was the burlesque, in which great play is made of archaisms, neologisms, and incongruous contrasts of stylistic register, together with inventive rhymes and all the traditional comic procedures of repetition, accumulation and so forth:

> Holà ho, Foucaral!
> Dom Roc Zurducaci! Dom Zapata Pascal!
> – Ou Pascal Zapata: car il n'importe guère
> Que Pascal soit devant ou Pascal soit derrière.
> Holà! mes gens! mon train! ô les doubles coquins,
> Les gredins, les bourreaux, les traîtres, les faquins!
> Sachent tous mes valets que ma bonté se lasse;
> Sachent les malheureux qu'aujourd'hui je les casse.[12]

But the two elements, the dramatic and the comic, remained quite distinct. This is true of Scarron in *Dom Japhet*:

> En somme, Scarron n'arrive pas à résoudre la dualité qui caractérise la comédie de son temps: événements et comique se juxtaposent, mais ne sont pas intimement unis en un tout homogène; même animé et orchestré par Jodelet, le comique demeure, si j'ose dire, un comique en contreplaqué.[13]

[10] C. Cosnier, 'Jodelet: un acteur du xviie siècle devenu un type', *Revue d'Histoire Littéraire de la France*, LXII (1962), 332.   [11] *History*, II, ii, p. 465.
[12] *Dom Japhet d'Arménie*, lines 343–50. See the edition by R. Garapon (Paris, 1967), pp. xixff., and his *La Fantaisie verbale et le comique dans le théâtre français* (Paris, 1957), pp. 190ff.   [13] *Dom Japhet d'Arménie*, ed. Garapon, p. xiii.

It is also true of plays like *Les Visionnaires* by Desmarets de Saint-Sorlin (1637), written to a different formula, but one in which the comic effects are still the product of the author's inventive fantasy, only tenuously related to the real world, and in which the dramatic structure merely serves to hold together a series of virtuoso *exercices de style*. Thus Hespérie 'qui croit que chacun l'aime' is at once less well rooted in a plausible plot and more extravagantly conceived than Molière's Bélise, for whom she serves as an obvious source:

> Cet amant s'est pâmé dès l'heure qu'il m'a vue;
> De quels traits, ma beauté, le ciel t'a-t-il pourvue?
> En sortant du logis je ne puis faire un pas
> Que mes yeux aussitôt ne causent un trépas.
> Pour moi je ne sais plus quel conseil je dois suivre:
> Le monde va périr, si l'on me laisse vivre . . . (lines 217–22)

Around the middle of the century, then, five-act verse comedy was well established in practice, with a supporting body of theoretical writing to satisfy the *érudits*. And although Corneille's early style, which offered a refined portrait of the manners and the conversation of men and women of polite society, had given way to more imaginative – and more amusing – kinds of play owing much more to fantasy than to observed reality, what had appeared in the 1640s and 1650s was equally far removed from Molière's wholly individual fusion of comedy of character with lifelike portrayal of manners, the whole fully integrated into the dramatic structure of his plays.

Yet Molière's highly original formula took some time to perfect. To begin with, as we have seen, he wrote lightweight farces, borrowing from the native French and the Italian traditions. *L'Étourdi* and *Dépit amoureux*, his first five-act comedies, were very much in the manner of mid-century plays written in imitation of Italian and Spanish models; while *Les Précieuses ridicules* and *Sganarelle* are still one-acters, on the borderline between farce and comedy, comedy of character being tied in the former to the flimsiest of story-lines, and in the latter to an involved plot whose stylised complexities add greatly to the charm of the play. Imitation of Terence in the three-act *École des maris* brings Molière within an ace of the full realisation of his successful formula; and *L'École des femmes*, in 1662, takes us the whole way in a five-act comedy in which plot, theme and comic effects are completely integrated, and all stem from Arnolphe's folly. As his jealous rivals recognised at once, Molière's new play was altogether more ambitious than its predecessors. By its form – the five-act verse medium devoted to the most polished literary drama – it demanded to be taken seriously by the spectators who prided themselves on their literary judgement; it retained enough of the flavour of Corneille's early plays to be considered an example of comedy of manners; while with its theme, women's education and the challenge to male supremacy, it focused provocatively on an important topical question.

The Mascarille plays had done none of these things. *L'Étourdi* was very much in the spirit of mid-century comedy, defined by its theatricality rather than by imitation of life; while even *Les Précieuses ridicules*, if it did present social comment, did so principally through the amusing antics of a pair of licensed buffoons. Sganarelle of *Le Cocu imaginaire* had broken new ground, experimentally: ground that was to be consolidated by his namesake in *L'École des maris*. But he was still imperfectly related to the real world; and it is Arnolphe, with his *état civil* as Monsieur de la Souche, who takes the really decisive step.

This is what makes *L'École des femmes* such an important landmark in Molière's brief career as a playwright. There, and in the attendant *Critique,* he is consciously challenging the critical prejudices of the educated, cultured spectator whose preference was for the dignity of tragedy and the 'pièce sérieuse', as well as those of the empty-headed young fop who merely wanted frivolous entertainment. He is also, of course, defending himself against the attacks of jealous rivals. As Robert Garapon writes, after the success of Molière's first plays in Paris it had still been possible for his opponents to dismiss him as a *farceur*:

> Tous ceux qu'offusque sa réussite se font un malin plaisir de le réduire à l'état d'histrion spécialisé dans la bouffonnerie mais incapable de faire valoir les ouvrages vraiment dignes de ce nom, comme des tragédies. C'est là un bon moyen de se débarrasser du gêneur, en le reléguant dans un petit canton de ce que nous appellerions aujourd'hui l'infra-littérature.[14]

Firing off salvoes on the one hand against Lysidas and Climène, on the other against the Marquis, Dorante the enlightened *honnête homme* defends a conception of comedy at once more vigorous and theatrical than Corneille's genteel conversation-pieces, and at the same time more 'natural' and lifelike than the Italian *commedia* or Scarron's burlesque comedies. Scene vi of the *Critique* is not only Molière's defence against the specific attacks that *L'École des femmes* had

---

[14] *Le Dernier Molière, des 'Fourberies de Scapin' au 'Malade imaginaire'* (Paris, 1977), pp. 20–1.

attracted from rival actors and playwrights, the *précieuses* and the *marquis*. More positively, and quite unambiguously, it presents his *profession de foi* as a dramatist: his faith in a new kind of comic drama in which the literary and the theatrical, the cultured and the popular, *la comédie* and *le comique* were to be fused together – fused together, and animated by a comic vision peculiar to Molière himself.[15]

[15] Cf. G. Lanson, 'Molière et la farce', *Revue de Paris* (May 1901), pp. 129–53.

PART II

The plays

4

The legacy of farce

Pour ne pas crever de faim, il a fini par accepter de s'écrire des rôles comiques: Molière malgré lui.

(Jacques Charon)[1]

(i) From Mascarille to Scapin

Mascarille, in *L'Étourdi*, is the *meneur du jeu*. All the action of the play is inspired by him – and deliberately inspired: this is the difference between the Mascarille and the Sganarelle types. For whereas in the case of *L'École des femmes* or *Tartuffe*, for instance, one could say that the whole of the action is 'inspired' by Arnolphe's obsession with marital misfortune, or by Orgon's infatuation with the impostor, that happens in spite of the characters themselves; they live in a complacent world of their own where all is well, and they are consequently at the receiving end of the stratagems engineered by others. But Mascarille is the prince of plotters, the 'fourbum imperator'; indeed, he is nothing but this. *L'Étourdi* is set in Sicily, but the place is no more than a two-dimensional backdrop, a conventional, fantasy Mediterranean setting to which Molière was to return for *Le Sicilien* and *Les Fourberies de Scapin*; no more real, but no less appropriate to these fast-moving theatrical entertainments than are the Forest of Arden, or the Courts of Roussillon or Navarre, to the leisured *marivaudage* of Shakespeare's lovers. The plot lacks the intricate structure of the Italian *commedia*; or rather, the customary involved relationship of two young couples, kept apart by the opposition of parents or guardians, here serves as a flimsy framework for a series of episodes in which Mascarille's ingenious schemes to further his master's love-affair are regularly frustrated by Lélie's own thoughtlessness, impetuosity and inability to keep pace with his valet's fertile imagination. It is the ability to think, rather than to move, quickly that distinguishes Mascarille: unlike the Sganarelle of *Le Médecin volant*, his agility is mental, not physical. Such

---

[1] *Moi, un comédien*, p. 95.

figures are endowed, moreover, with a preternatural capacity for leadership: whether it is other servants, gullible old men, or his master Lélie, the rest of the characters all submit without demur to Mascarille's forceful personality.

Commenting on this relationship, critics have used the metaphor of a puppeteer with his marionettes, of a master of ceremonies, or of the playwright himself, controlling the creatures of his imagination. There is in *L'Étourdi* something of the theatricality of the baroque age. This is seen in its pure state in *L'Illusion comique*, where a showman-figure, the magician Alcandre, acting as the dramatist's *alter ego*, conjures up a parade of shadows on the 'television-screen', as it were, of the play within a play, in order to demonstrate the full range of styles and effects of which the theatre of 1636 was capable; and other plays of the 1630s by Gougenot and Scudéry exploit, though less brilliantly, a similar formula.[2] In Molière's theatre this unashamed virtuosity is seen most clearly in *Les Fâcheux*, which, as we have seen, is nothing more than a parade of eccentrics. *L'Étourdi*, by contrast, is nearer to *Le Menteur*, in that a more conventional plot is made in both plays to serve as a showcase. In Corneille's comedy, this is for a series of brilliant *exercices de style* by means of which, like Billy Liar in our own day, Dorante mystifies the other characters, and entertains the audience, with ever taller stories; in Molière's play it is for an equally inventive series of variants on a single comic device, the clever scheme which has the opposite effect from that intended. Lélie, who so predictably no less than ten times frustrates Mascarille's best intentions, is just as two-dimensional as his wholly theatrical valet: both are created and controlled by the needs of this mechanical contrivance. There is nothing here that could be called 'comic vision': if *L'Étourdi* is a perfect illustration of Bergson's thesis, that we laugh when we see 'du mécanique plaqué sur du vivant' – that is, human beings behaving with a predictable, machine-like regularity[3] – there is as yet none of the social reference, none of the reflective, revealing comment on human nature by which Molière tempers the over-rigid application of such techniques in his later comedies. At this early stage, comedy merely consists in the imposing of agreeably artificial patterns on life.

Between *L'Étourdi* and *Les Fourberies de Scapin* Molière created a

---

[2] See Gougenot, *La Comédie des comédiens* (1632–3), ed. D. Shaw (Exeter, 1974); Scudéry, *La Comédie des comédiens* (c. 1633), ed. J. Crow (Exeter, 1975).
[3] *Le Rire* (1899) (Paris, 1946), p. 29.

number of *valets rusés*. Mascarille himself reappears in *Dépit amoureux*, where his manner is so subdued that he is hardly recognisable; and in *Les Précieuses ridicules*, where the generalised features of the original type have largely given way to those peculiar to this specific variation:

> J'ai un certain valet, nommé Mascarille, qui passe, au sentiment de beaucoup de gens, pour une manière de bel esprit; car il n'y a rien à meilleur marché que le bel esprit maintenant. C'est un extravagant, qui s'est mis dans la tête de vouloir faire l'homme de condition. Il se pique ordinairement de galanterie et de vers, et dédaigne les autres valets, jusqu'à les appeler brutaux. (scene i)

The valet's deception, as the bogus 'Marquis de Mascarille', of the gullible *précieuses* is in any case inspired by his master, and this last Mascarille, though a *fourbe*, is a long way from the 'fourbum imperator' of *L'Étourdi*.

Insofar as La Flèche, Cléante's valet in *L'Avare*, has traditional antecedents, he seems to come in a direct line from Plautus, and to owe nothing to Italian intermediaries. Like Strobilus in the *Aulularia*, he does steal the miser's casket; but apart from that he takes no initiative, and his main function is to act as his master's confidant and counsellor, in a manner very different from that of the self-assertive Mascarille. He is, indeed, acceptable as the stage equivalent of the real-life French servant that his name suggests – though when he quotes Rabelais to Cléante (II, i), he puts a strain on even this interpretation.

A group of three other valets are much more recognisably Italian in inspiration – Hali of *Le Sicilien*, Sbrigani of *Monsieur de Pourceaugnac*, and Covielle of *Le Bourgeois gentilhomme* – before the type achieves its perfection in the central figure of *Les Fourberies de Scapin*. Needless to say, the Oriental-sounding name of Hali means no more in terms of local colour than the fact that the play in which he appears is supposedly set in Sicily: once more, as with *L'Étourdi*, what Molière was trying to do was to suggest a suitably exotic, or escapist, setting for a light-hearted, colourful entertainment. But this play is a slight one-acter; and although Hali is in the main line of a recognisable tradition when he proclaims:

> Non: le courroux du point d'honneur me prend; il ne sera pas dit qu'on triomphe de mon adresse; ma qualité de fourbe s'indigne de tous ces obstacles, et je prétends faire éclater les talents que j'ai eus du Ciel (scene v)

it is actually Adraste, his master, who comes up with the plan to pass himself off as a painter in order to gain access to his beloved and outwit her jealous guardian.

Sbrigani is quite the most active of these Italianate valets in the years leading up to *Les Fourberies de Scapin*: indeed, he is so ruthless in the defence of his master's interests that critics with a moralistic bias have seen *Monsieur de Pourceaugnac*, with *George Dandin*, as one of Molière's 'black' comedies, and have condemned the humiliation of Pourceaugnac as incompatible with the comic spirit. It is no doubt true that if one were to view the play with this sort of seriousness, one's moral sense might well be disturbed by the gratuitous and systematic persecution of the well-meaning provincial from Limoges, harmless except in that he is Éraste's rival for the hand of Julie. But Pourceaugnac is no more to be taken seriously than, for instance, the Géronte of Regnard's *Légataire universel*, duped and swindled by the ingenious Crispin for his master's benefit and to our great delight. The two plays are in fact quite similar, a major part of the comedy in each instance depending on a parade of characters in disguise: in Molière's play we have a pair of provincial women, accompanied by children, each claiming to be Pourceaugnac's wife; Pourceaugnac himself disguised as a woman in order to escape the *archers*; and bogus *suisses* and an *exempt* who see through his disguise. Set this in the framework of a *comédie-ballet*, and it would seem impossible to take a high moral line about any issues involved; at most one might reflect on the taste of courtiers (the play was first performed at Chambord) and Parisians, for whom the discomfiture of the gullible Limousin provided an easy laugh.

Le Bourgeois gentilhomme also, of course, plays up to the prejudices of the courtiers; but it is not dominated to anything like the same extent by a scheming valet. Covielle has the right sort of pedigree – his is in fact the only authentic Italian valet's name before Scapin[4] – but far from being a *meneur du jeu*, he does not appear until the end of Act III. True, from then on he plays a major part, and it is he who master-minds Monsieur Jourdain's burlesque elevation to the dignity of Mamamouchi. Altogether, however, a play like *Le Bourgeois gentil-homme* is poles apart from *L'Étourdi*, in that the dramatic focus is very firmly on the gullible dupe, no longer on the *fourbe*.

[4] In other words Coviello, like Scappino, was an established servant role in the *commedia*. Sbrigani, like Mascarille (and Sganarelle, for that matter), has a name which, though it suggests a meaning in Italian, is invented.

The key to the shift of focus is no doubt to be seen in the fact that none of these valets we have been considering since the Mascarille of *Les Précieuses ridicules* was played by Molière himself, who played instead Dom Pèdre, Harpagon, Pourceaugnac and Monsieur Jourdain: in each case the dupe. In *Les Fourberies de Scapin*, however, he made a brilliant return to the earlier kind of Italianate roles. And Scapin not only calls for the commanding stage presence of Mascarille, the 'fourbum imperator', but also demands the physical agility of the first Sganarelle of *Le Médecin volant*, a remarkable versatility of styles and accents, and a tremendous amount of sheer stamina: the part is said, on the authority of those in the acting profession, to be one of the most exhausting in the French repertoire.[5] But while certain modern writers have marvelled at the agility the 49-year-old actor must have shown,[6] Robert Garapon has recently suggested that there may well lie the reason for what he sees as a 'demi-échec':

> C'est Molière qui jouait Scapin; or avait-il encore la force physique de jouer ce rôle? . . . Le personnage de Scapin implique non seulement la mobilité du meneur de jeu, mais l'agilité du danseur . . . On peut se demander si, pour le représenter sur la scène, Molière n'a pas été trahi par ses forces. On expliquerait ainsi qu'il n'ait pas été tenté, au cours des vingt mois qui lui restaient à vivre, d'en appeler de la première sentence du public: le rôle était trop éprouvant pour lui.[7]

However, although the play had only eighteen performances between 24 May and 19 July 1671, and was not revived until after Molière's death, its takings averaged 417 *l.*, compared with an average of 361 *l.* for the same number of performances of various plays between the reopening on 10 April and 24 May, and with an average of 421 *l.* for four performances of *Le Bourgeois gentilhomme* in July of the same year. In addition, *Les Fourberies de Scapin* was evidently taken off not because of any lack of success, but to make way for *Psyché*, for which the Palais-Royal had been adapted during the Easter closure, and which had been in rehearsal since early June.

Moreover, to speak of *Les Fourberies* as a failure, or even as a 'demi-échec', hardly tallies with such comments from contemporaries as have been preserved. According to Robinet's rhymed *gazette*:

---

[5] See *Les Fourberies de Scapin*, ed. J. T. Stoker (London, 1971), p. 12. The most distinguished of modern Scapins, Robert Hirsch, is said to have lost two kilos every time he played the part (Charon, *Moi, un comédien*, p. 121).
[6] See Stoker (previous note).   [7] *Le Dernier Molière*, pp. 41–2.

On ne parle que d'un Scapin,
Qui surpasse défunt l'Espiègle[8]
(Sur qui tout bon enfant se règle)
Par ses ruses et petits tours
Qui ne sont pas de tous les jours . . .[9]

Boileau, of course, made *Les Fourberies* the subject of his well-known reservations about Molière's comedy;[10] but Grimarest takes pains to correct the impression that this might give of the public's reaction:

Tout le monde sait combien les bons juges et les gens de goût se récrièrent contre ces deux pièces (*Les Fourberies de Scapin* and *La Comtesse d'Escarbagnas*). Mais le peuple, pour qui Molière avait eu intention de les faire, les vit en foule, et avec plaisir.[11]

There is no doubt that to spectators of the time most conscious of the established hierarchy of literary forms and styles, three acts in prose ranked a good deal lower than five acts in verse; and although *Les Fourberies de Scapin* now stands quite high among Molière's plays in terms of total number of performances since the creation of the Comédie-Française in 1680,[12] the play cannot be said to have met with universal approval until the twentieth century, when the sort of prejudice discussed in Chapter 2 section vi had more or less disappeared.

The aesthetic prejudice was linked, it would seem, to misgivings about *Les Fourberies* and other plays on moral grounds: the sort of consideration we have touched on in connection with *Monsieur de Pourceaugnac*. The nineteenth-century critic Moland writes of Scapin in severe terms as a 'repris de justice et démoralisateur de la jeunesse';[13] and P. Brisson, writing in 1942, detects in the very perfection of Scapin's accomplishments a threat to established moral values: 'Certaines violences de fourberie durcissent son visage. Il y a du vrai coquin, du démagogue et de l'émeutier possible en lui. Sa batte d'Arlequin pourrait un jour prendre le poids d'une trique. Son nom sonne beaucoup moins clair que celui de Mascarille.'[14] But such considerations surely never enter into the reactions of an audience in the theatre. From the very opening of the play, with its patterned dialogue:

---

[8] i.e. Till Eulenspiegel.   [9] Quoted Mongrédien (ed.), *Recueil*, p. 390.
[10] See above, p. 13.   [11] *La Vie de M. de Molière*, p. 115.
[12] In ninth place, with 1260 performances up to 1970. *Tartuffe* at this date led with 2751 performances, and 15 plays totalled over 1000 each.
[13] Quoted by Stoker, p. 15.   [14] *Molière: sa vie dans ses oeuvres* (Paris, 1942), p. 264.

— Tu viens, Silvestre, d'apprendre au port que mon père revient?
— Oui.
— Qu'il arrive ce matin même?
— Ce matin même.
— Et qu'il revient dans la résolution de me marier?
— Oui.
— Avec une fille du Seigneur Géronte?
— Du Seigneur Géronte.
— Et que cette fille est mandée de Tarente ici pour cela?
— Oui.
— Et tu tiens ces nouvelles de mon oncle?
— De votre oncle.
— A qui mon père les a mandées par une lettre?
— Par une lettre.
— Et cet oncle, dis-tu, sait toutes nos affaires.
— Toutes nos affaires . . .

followed by the arrival of Scapin, who introduces himself with a self-portrait:

> A vous dire la vérité, il y a peu de choses qui me soient impossibles, quand je m'en veux mêler. J'ai sans doute reçu du Ciel un génie assez beau pour toutes les fabriques de ces gentilesses d'esprit, de ces galan-teries ingénieuses à qui le vulgaire ignorant donne le nom de fourberies; et je puis dire sans vanité, qu'on n'a guère vu d'homme qui fût plus habile ouvrier de ressorts et d'intrigues; qui ait acquis plus de gloire que moi dans ce noble métier . . . (I, ii)

it is perfectly obvious that we are in the unreal world of the theatre. As Scapin instructs the other characters, drills them, rehearses them, exults in his own superior intelligence, and carries out his personal vengeance on the poor Géronte, the whole is a sustained virtuoso performance that has little to do with real life, and everything to do with the art of comedy: the playwright's invention, the skill of the actor, and the delight of an audience who connive at Scapin's rogueries without a thought that any moral issues might be involved. With Scapin, as with Mascarille, the analogy of the comic dramatist's creative activity comes naturally to mind. He has the fertile imagin-ation, and something of the verbal facility, of Corneille's Dorante, as in the scene in which he extorts money from Géronte with the circum-stantial anecdote of his son's capture by pirates who have demanded a ransom (though it is worth remarking that the *comic* effect of this scene (II, vii) – unlike for instance that of *Le Menteur* II, v – depends almost entirely on the reactions of the old miser, with his repeated interjection 'Que diable allait-il faire dans cette galère?'). And the

93

equally celebrated scene in which he persuades the frightened Géronte to hide in the sack, then conducts a dialogue with his imaginary pursuers, impersonating in turn a stage Gascon, a stage Swiss, and 'plusieurs personnes ensemble' before beating his helpless prisoner, is a tribute to the valet's brilliant extemporisation as well as to his physical agility.

This is a play quite without moral values, and in which there is no trace of a moral lesson.[15] Even the traditional convention, on which most comedies from Plautus to Beaumarchais were based, that age and authority are always in the wrong, and youth is always right – a convention which in any case is too hackneyed to have any real social implications[16] – even that is disproved by the dénouement, when Scapin's tricks are shown to have been a gratuitous charade, without effect within the microcosm of the play itself. What brings about the outcome is yet another variant on the recognition-scene: here a double recognition, by which the young men are discovered to be already married to the girls their fathers had chosen for them. As Silvestre remarks: 'Le hasard a fait ce que la prudence des pères avait délibéré' (III, viii).

Altogether, *Les Fourberies de Scapin* is one of the outstanding examples of the innumerable comedies, ancient and modern, that were written to the time-honoured formula according to which 'the spontaneous loves of the young, traversed by the old, are aided and abetted by the servants'.[17] Here, in Molière's hands, with its patterned structure (two pairs of lovers, two fathers . . .), the overall simplicity of the plot and the theatricality of its constituent episodes, the formula acquires a self-sufficient dynamism as generator of an inspired dramatic action. Indeed, from a structural point of view this play is in many ways (whatever Boileau may have thought to the contrary) perhaps the most strictly classical comedy in Molière's whole theatre.

This traditional plot-formula is not confined in Molière's theatre to

---

[15] I do not find Garapon's attempt to define a 'philosophie de Scapin' very convincing: 'Mascarille n'était qu'un valet de comédie. Scapin est beaucoup plus: à de brefs instants, on le soupçonne d'être le porte-parole de son auteur, et c'est par là sans doute que s'explique le mieux la secrète mais évidente parenté qui l'unit au Figaro de Beaumarchais' (*Le Dernier Molière*, p. 89).

[16] *Pace* K. Waterson, *Molière et l'autorité: structures sociales, structures comiques* (Lexington, Ky, 1976), for whom *Les Fourberies de Scapin* represents 'le triomphe définitif du prolétaire' (p. 66).

[17] See E. J. H. Greene, *Menander to Marivaux: The History of a Comic Structure* (Edmonton, Alberta, 1977); and my review of that book, *French Studies*, XXXIV (1980), 232–3.

the plays we have been considering, such as *L'Étourdi* and *Les Fourberies de Scapin*: it is also to be found in the series of comedies built round a Sganarelle-type central figure. Here, however, the focus shifts. The marriage of one or more young couples, though still normally retained as a convenient way of rounding off the play, becomes a very minor feature; and it is no longer a scheming valet supporting the lovers, but the father or guardian providing the obstacle to their marriage, who claims the lion's share of the dramatic interest. And most important of all, this opponent-figure is no longer the purely functional character of theatrical tradition, but is developed with comic insight and human understanding.

(ii) Sganarelle

The scheming valet, from Mascarille to Scapin, is easy to define – indeed, commonly defines himself – by means of simple, positive formulas often tending towards hyperbole:

> — Je sais que ton esprit, en intrigues fertile,
> N'a jamais rien trouvé qui lui fût difficile,
> Qu'on te peut appeler le roi des serviteurs,
> Et qu'en toute la terre . . . (*Étourdi*, lines 15–17)

> — Après ce rare exploit, je veux que l'on s'apprête
> A me peindre en héros un laurier sur la tête,
> Et qu'au bas du portrait on mette en lettres d'or:
> *Vivat Mascarillus, fourbum imperator!* (*ibid.*, lines 791–4)

— A vous dire la vérité, il y a peu de choses qui me soient impossibles . . . (*Fourberies*, I, ii)[18]

He knows his own strengths, as he understands the weaknesses of others, with complete accuracy; and his judgement is not clouded either by over-confidence or by false modesty.

From the beginning, however, the Sganarelle type of character is given these missing human qualities. What he thinks, and says, of himself does not correspond to what we, the audience, see of him in action; and this is one of the principal means by which the type acquires that extra depth which produces the impression of a 'three-dimensional' character. The result may be less brilliant, in terms of spectacle, than the self-consciously theatrical art of the scene, for

[18] For the quotation of this passage in full, see p. 93.

instance, in which Scapin coaches Silvestre in the role of braggart
soldier that he is to assume in order to intimidate Argante:

> Attends. Tiens-toi un peu. Enfonce ton bonnet en méchant garçon.
> Campe-toi sur un pied. Mets la main au côté. Fais les yeux furibonds.
> Marche un peu en roi de théâtre. Voilà qui est bien. Suis-moi. J'ai des
> secrets pour déguiser ton visage et ta voix. (I, v)

Compared with this, the sixty-eight-line soliloquy in *Le Cocu imaginaire*
in which Sganarelle reveals his true nature may appear to exemplify a
static, verbose, over-literary kind of dramatic writing. It is true that
the speech does possess a specific quality of literary parody, in that
Sganarelle's vacillation between bombastic challenge to the 'larron
d'honneur' who he thinks has cuckolded him, and a more realistic
appraisal of his own lack of prowess as a fighter, is an obvious take-off
of the self-analytical dialectics of the Cornelian hero at moments of
crisis, even down to echoes of the grand manner of tragedy in a phrase
like 'courir au trépas', the rhyme 'offense/vengeance', or the line:

> Montrons notre courage à venger notre honte. (line 414)

But Sganarelle's half-conscious awareness of his limitations:

> Je hais de tout mon coeur les esprits colériques,
> Et porte grand amour aux hommes pacifiques;
> Je ne suis point battant, de peur d'être battu,
> Et l'humeur débonnaire est ma grande vertu (lines 421–4)

and his prudent formulation:

> . . . Quant à moi, je trouve, ayant tout compassé,
> Qu'il vaut mieux être encor cocu que trépassé (lines 435–6)

are in the final analysis less revealing than the highly comic climax of
the closing lines of the soliloquy. There, the full measure of the
character's cowardice emerges quite unconsciously under the cover of
a blusteringly aggressive posture:

> Je me sens là pourtant remuer une bile
> Qui veut me conseiller quelque action virile;
> Oui, le courroux me prend; c'est trop être poltron:
> Je veux résolument me venger du larron.
> Déjà pour commencer, dans l'ardeur qui m'enflamme,
> Je vais dire partout qu'il couche avec ma femme.
>
> (lines 469–74)

It would be a mistake, though, to regard this kind of dramatic writing, in which the comic figure naïvely betrays his real motives in spite of himself, as literary rather than theatrical in character. Rather, in the range of expression of mood and feeling that it allows the actor to exploit, we should recognise a marvellous vehicle for Molière's own interpretative talents. In La Neufvillenaine's commentary on the scene, it is notable that he does not separate praise of Molière the author from that of Molière the actor; he calls on painters as well as orators – 'le pinceau' and 'la plume' – to come to his help in trying to do justice to the scene, and writes:

> Jamais il ne se vit rien de plus beau, jamais rien de mieux joué, et jamais vers ne furent si généralement estimés. Sganarelle joue seul cette scène, repassant dans son esprit tout ce que l'on peut dire d'un cocu et les raisons pour lesquelles il ne s'en doit pas mettre en peine, [et] s'en démêle si bien, que son raisonnement pourrait en un besoin consoler ceux qui sont de ce nombre.[19]

And it is clear that when, as La Neufvillenaine reports, Paris audiences called scene xvii 'la belle scène', this was not a judgement that sacrificed theatrical to literary qualities.

As we have seen, one of the most distinctive characteristics of the Sganarelle figures, from *Le Cocu imaginaire* onwards, is their solipsistic isolation from their surroundings.[20] They are in this world, but not of it: they inhabit the universe of their own private fancy. Variations on this type will recur in almost every play throughout the rest of Molière's career, and for that reason the one-act comedy of 1660 has a very special significance.

The play in which this first Sganarelle of the series makes his appearance is an interesting combination of features from the Italian and the French traditions. The plot is Italianate in its complication, its rapidity, its artificial balance and symmetry; a pointer to which is to be seen in the fact that although this is a one-act play, the plot needs a longer summary than many of Molière's full-length comedies. Suffice it to say that each of the four principal characters is led to believe, by various combinations of circumstantial evidence, that his or her partner is unfaithful. Célie thinks her fiancé Lélie is cooling in his affections, and in her distress faints, dropping his portrait. Sganarelle comes to her help, and his wife, observing him holding the swooning Célie in his arms, jumps to conclusions. She picks up the

---

[19] Molière, *Oeuvres*, ed. Despois and Mesnard, II, pp. 197, 201.
[20] See pp. 26ff. above.

portrait, and Sganarelle, subsequently observing her with it, thinks she must be having an affair with Lélie, the subject of the portrait. Lélie, returning from a journey, and finding his own portrait in the hands of Sganarelle, thinks Célie must have married the latter in his absence, and given her husband the portrait of the man she had jilted; while Célie soon follows suit, and thinks Lélie has deserted her for Sganarelle's wife . . . All this is slick, entertaining, *commedia*-type farce; and the fact that the psychological verisimilitude is non-existent, and the behaviour of the characters is almost entirely mechanical and predictable, seldom detracts in any way from the success of this kind of fast-moving situation comedy.

In any case, in *Le Cocu imaginaire*, although the behaviour of three of the characters is mechanical, and governed by the farcical pattern that the plot imposes on their actions, it soon becomes evident that the fourth member of the quartet, Sganarelle himself, has rather more to offer. Whereas the *jeune premier* and *jeune première* with the traditional Italianate names are conventional two-dimensional marionettes – and whereas Sganarelle's wife is a purely functional character, anonymous but for the designation 'la femme de Sganarelle' – Sganarelle has something about him that makes us regard him at once as a genuine *character*: still a caricature, a type, but with that extra dimension that confers dramatic 'reality'. He is obviously the sort of character to whom things happen, and who is given to reflecting on what life has in store for him, and on the cautious attitude it is proper to adopt in the face of the ups and downs of an unfriendly fate. In other words, he already displays in embryo the characteristics which link not only the series of six Sganarelles that span the years 1660 to 1666, but also those more fully developed comic heroes that Molière the playwright was to create for Molière the actor, from Arnolphe in 1662 right through to Argan in the last months of his life. Though Sganarelle is still a clown, he is a clown with a difference; and we see in him not the puppet's mechanical response to a series of contrived situations, but the repeated expression of some inner compulsion. Whereas the misunderstandings of the other characters – especially those of Lélie and Célie – are fortuitous and temporary, Sganarelle's reflect his obsessional view of the world around him, in particular his view of marriage. It is a view that represents the longstanding popular mythology of the mediaeval farces and *fabliaux*; and in our own day the music-hall comedian and television comic have continued to find it a rich source of material.

That Molière was able successfully to combine elements from the different traditions of the French farce and the Italian *commedia* was due to a stroke of considerable originality. For a character like Le Barbouillé had faced a real threat, and had been well and truly tricked by his wife: his world really was that of the cynical *farceurs*, who showed little respect for the institution of marriage. But although Sganarelle is obviously related to the traditional *mal-marié*, he is not in fact a cuckold: he is a *cocu imaginaire*, and the threat to his honour is a product of his own fantasy. And while Lélie and Célie are quite ready at the end to be disabused by the Suivante and to forget their temporary estrangement, Sganarelle greets the dénouement with characteristic scepticism. Though his closing address to the audience takes the traditional form of a reassuring moral, it is clear from the last couplet that he does not really believe in it himself:

> A-t-on mieux cru jamais être cocu que moi?
> Vous voyez qu'en ce fait la plus forte apparence
> Peut jeter dans l'esprit une fausse créance.
> De cet exemple-ci ressouvenez-vous bien;
> Et, quand vous verriez tout, ne croyez jamais rien.

It is not difficult to interpret the last line, in the light of what has gone before, as meaning: 'Et quand vous sauriez tout, n'en dites jamais rien': the prudent man, even if he sees what is going on, finds it better not to complain. A modern editor of the play comments, quite rightly, I think, on Sganarelle's 'manque de mesure, dont il n'est pas près de se corriger'.[21] In this, he again prefigures Molière's more celebrated comic characters, Arnolphe, Orgon, Alceste, Harpagon, Monsieur Jourdain, Argan: each of them displays to the very end the obsession or *idée fixe* which colours his outlook on life. It is a characteristic of Molière's heroes that they are never 'converted': in every case the dénouement, far from curing them of their folly, merely confirms them in it. If this is no more than hinted at in the case of this first Sganarelle, nevertheless we can already see Molière moving in the direction he was later to follow with such success. Similarly, Sganarelle's soliloquy in scene xvii looks forward to important soliloquies by, for instance, Arnolphe, Harpagon and Argan. These produce a variety of comic effects, but what they all have in common is that they serve to reveal the degree to which the comic hero is absorbed by his *idée fixe*, the extent of his isolation in the world of his own imagination.

[21] *Oeuvres complètes*, ed. Jouanny, I, p. 898.

The remaining plays in which the Sganarelle figure appears under his original name were all performed during the period 1661–6. The first of these, *L'École des maris*, goes together with *Le Cocu imaginaire* and *L'École des femmes* to form a group of plays closely related both from the point of view of theme and because of the striking resemblance between the central characters: Arnolphe shares with the two Sganarelles the same fundamental distrust of women and fear of conjugal misfortune, together with a highly developed sensual urge. *Le Mariage forcé*, a one-act play of 1664, contains a very similar character, who in spite of the same distrust of the female sex, is moved to marry a coquette much younger than himself, who will all too evidently subject him to the fate that the first Sganarelle of the series had imagined for himself. Perhaps the following passage from this play, spoken by Sganarelle before his eyes have been opened to his fiancée's true nature, shows better than any other text the possessive nature of the sensual desire that animates these characters:

> Hé bien, ma belle, c'est maintenant que nous allons être heureux l'un et l'autre. Vous ne serez plus en droit de me rien refuser; et je pourrai faire avec vous tout ce qu'il me plaira, sans que personne s'en scandalise. Vous allez être à moi depuis la tête jusqu'aux pieds, et je serai maître de tout: de vos petits yeux éveillés, de votre petit nez fripon, de vos lèvres appétissantes, de vos oreilles amoureuses, de votre petit menton joli, de vos petits tétons rondelets, de votre . . . Enfin, toute votre personne sera à ma discrétion, et je serai à même, pour vous caresser comme je voudrai. (scene ii)

In a similar vein, we have already seen the last of the half-dozen Sganarelles, the central character of *Le Médecin malgré lui*, compensating for the traditional misfortune of having a shrew of a wife by flirting with the buxom Nourrice:

> Peste! le joli meuble que voilà! Ah! Nourrice, charmante Nourrice, ma médecine est la très-humble esclave de votre nourricerie, et je voudrais bien être le petit poupon fortuné qui tétât le lait de vos bonnes grâces. (II, ii)

The other two Sganarelles are seen in a different context. One of them, in *L'Amour médecin*, is a bourgeois *père de famille*, just as authoritarian towards his family as Arnolphe towards his prospective bride – or as Orgon or Argan will later be in their relationships with their daughters. The other, the best-known Sganarelle of them all, servant to the hero of *Dom Juan*, is shown neither as a lover nor as a father. However, he epitomises, even more memorably than his namesakes, the same anti-heroic qualities of cowardly caution and credulity, together with an egotism that is expressed as complacent self-esteem when things are going well, and as self-righteous indignation when they turn against him. It would be impossible to claim that in the half-dozen Sganarelles we are presented with repeated appearances of an identical character; but if they are distinct characters, they all have a strong family likeness. Naïve self-importance, self-esteem, self-indulgence, and a gullibility that makes them the ready prey of the trickery and knavery of others: this is a composite 'profile' not only of the six Sganarelles, but of the great gallery of Molière's major characters from Arnolphe to Argan.

As long as he continues to bear the name Sganarelle, this figure, in spite of his obvious potential for further development as a rounded comic character, remains rooted in his origins in popular theatre. Only the first two plays of the series, *Le Cocu imaginaire* and *L'École des maris*, are in verse; and generally speaking there seems to be, in the other four Sganarelle plays, something of a return towards the character's farcical origins. The homeliness of the language, the crudity of some of the *jeux de scène*, and the caricatural nature of many of the figures surrounding the hero, combine to make the comic impact of this group of plays a good deal less sophisticated than that of, for instance, *L'École des femmes*, which pre-dates them, and in which we can already recognise the flavour of 'la haute comédie'. But the more sophisticated tone of this and other comedies should not make us lose sight of the affinity of Molière's mature comic creations with the simpler Sganarelle figures. Let us examine briefly one or two features of the 'family likeness' between them.

First of all, the relationships with the opposite sex. Arnolphe offers the fullest exploration of the psychology of Molière's comic heroes from this point of view. He is the domineering upholder of marital inequality:

> Du côté de la barbe est la toute-puissance (line 700)

– ready to threaten Agnès, the bride-to-be whom he has honoured with his choice, quite literally with hell-fire if she strays from the path of duty. But it is clear that his bullying and blustering derive from a sense of inferiority and hence of insecurity, particularly *vis-à-vis* women with education, culture and wit. This is why Arnolphe has had Agnès brought up in almost total ignorance:

> Dans ses meubles, dût-elle en avoir de l'envie,
> Il ne faut écritoire, encre, papier, ni plumes:
> Le mari doit, dans les bonnes coutumes,
> Écrire tout ce qui s'écrit chez lui. (lines 780–3)

However, at the same time, the sensual, possessive desire that we have seen in Sganarelle is still present in these more fully developed characters. Arnolphe is no exception, and another of his maxims makes this clear:

> Celle qu'un lien honnête
> Fait entrer au lit d'autrui
> Doit se mettre dans la tête,
> Malgré le train d'aujourd'hui,
> Que l'homme qui la prend, ne la prend que pour lui. (lines 747–51)

Although the others do not perhaps express themselves quite so brutally, their love is of the same earthy nature. They are nearly all made vulnerable by their desire, and exposed to the same traditional humiliation. Harpagon, an elderly widower, wants to marry again and is ready to make a fool of himself; Argan has remarried, and as we see, has already made a fool of himself; Dandin is evidently about to be cuckolded, and takes a most desperate view of his future:

> Lorsqu'on a, comme moi, épousé une méchante femme, le meilleur parti qu'on puisse prendre, c'est de s'aller jeter dans l'eau la tête la première (III, viii)

– while Monsieur Jourdain is ready to desert his wife and commit all sorts of extravagances for the favours of his 'belle marquise'. Only Orgon, in *Tartuffe*, seems to have had the good fortune, in his second marriage, to find a wife sensible and good-humoured enough to achieve a reasonable *modus vivendi* with her egocentric husband; but he, like Jourdain, Harpagon or Argan, is the complete domestic tyrant where his daughter is concerned, perfectly willing to sacrifice her happiness to his own authority, and trying to delude himself that he is acting in her best interests:

> Cet hymen de tous biens comblera vos désirs,
> Il sera tout confit en douceurs et plaisirs.
> Ensemble vous vivrez, dans vos ardeurs fidèles,
> Comme deux vrais enfants, comme deux tourterelles. (lines 531–4)

Their attitude towards women, then, is that they should be subject to paternal authority before marriage, and to a husband's authority afterwards. A common enough male attitude in the seventeenth century, no doubt; but in their case, it is only part of a more general self-esteem and self-importance. For instance, an essential reason for Orgon's addiction to a rigorous form of religion, based on prohibitions and penalties, is that it strengthens his despotic hold on his family. And exactly the same thing can be said of Harpagon's avarice, Argan's hypochondria, or Jourdain's social ambition: each of these obsessions helps to set up the paterfamilias as the tyrannical ruler of a little empire, with its ritual and obsessive cult keeping the other members of the family, his subjects, in their proper place. It is worth adding that in *Les Femmes savantes*, in which the dominant obsession is this time transferred to a woman, we are shown a matriarchal empire every bit as tyrannical, with the henpecked husband as its most obvious victim.

And what about the hero of *Le Misanthrope* in this connection? Although the 'family likeness' may be a good deal more subtle in his case, it is still discernible. To begin with, he betrays the same choleric disposition as Arnolphe, Orgon, Argan and the others.

> Ah! vous êtes dévot, et vous vous emportez!

says Dorine to her master Orgon (*Tar.*, line 552); and Argan has a similar outburst of temper in Act I of *Le Malade*, which nearly makes him genuinely ill. Jourdain behaves in the same way, and so does Harpagon. In Alceste's case, this choleric disposition is explicitly related to the current physiological theory of the dominant humours: Alceste's misanthropy is due to his 'bilious' temperament, which makes him prone to ungovernable outbursts of temper. Hence the violence of his language, his oaths, the extravagance of his attacks on Célimène: the text contains no fewer than eleven passages indicating such outbursts. And if Alceste is obviously not to be identified at all points with the cowardly, gullible Sganarelle, none of Molière's comic heroes better illustrates the alienation of the 'Sganarelle type' from the world he lives in, his retreat into a fantasy world of his own in which he is right and the rest of humanity are wrong. When Philinte attempts to reason with him:

> Je vous dirai tout franc que cette maladie,
> Partout où vous allez, donne la comédie,
> Et qu'un si grand courroux contre les moeurs du temps
> Vous tourne en ridicule auprès de bien des gens

he bursts out in reply:

> Tant mieux, morbleu! tant mieux, c'est ce que je demande;
> Ce m'est un fort bon signe, et ma joie en est grande:
> Tous les hommes me sont à tel point odieux,
> Que je serais fâché d'être sage à leurs yeux. (lines 105–12)

The comparison between Alceste and Don Quixote is one that has often been made: Molière's hero is the same sort of crusading idealist as Cervantes', and if his targets are more real than windmills or flocks of sheep, nevertheless he endows them with an importance wholly out of proportion to their real identity. What are no more than the conventions and the compromises on which any civilised society depends become in Alceste's eyes the blackest examples of treachery and deceit. And finally, like the other characters we have been considering, Alceste refuses to learn from his experience; at the end of the play, far from coming to terms with the real world, he retreats further into his own world of fantasy:

> Trahi de toutes parts, accablé d'injustices,
> Je vais sortir d'un gouffre où triomphent les vices,
> Et chercher sur la terre un endroit écarté
> Où d'être homme d'honneur on ait la liberté. (lines 1803–6)

We must be careful, of course, not to take this identification of Molière's comic heroes with a prototype from a farce tradition too far. One recent writer, stressing these affinities, observes critically that 'Une longue tradition, scolaire dans son esprit comme dans ses origines, veut que l'on étudie le théâtre de Molière comme une collection de pièces ayant chacune son sens et sa valeur propres; chaque comédie tend à devenir l'unité d'explication idéale.'[22] But this is far from being just an interpretation imposed on Molière's theatre by academic custom: it corresponds to our factual experience. The plays *are* separate entities, and each is experienced as such on stage; and though it is easier for the reader to make cross-references from one play to another than it is for the spectator, nevertheless even in reading Molière we remain conscious of the separate context established by each new play. Indeed, there is every reason to suggest that the habit of ignoring such contextual differences, and of treating an author's whole output as if it were a single unit, is an aberration of recent academic criticism – one from which Racine, in particular, has suffered considerably. On the other hand, we must concede that there is one feature in Molière's case that does strongly reinforce the impression of a common identity linking all these roles, and that helps

[22] Pelous, 'Les Métamorphoses de Sganarelle', 821.

to give a real permanence to the Sganarelle figure – or at least, that must have produced this effect on the original spectators, for it is something a reader can be aware of only by a constant effort of the imagination. This is the fact that Molière himself played all these parts: from Sganarelle to Argan, these roles were all conceived as a vehicle for a gifted actor's highly personal talents.

That these talents were above all those of a *comic* actor goes without saying. Molière was trained in the farce tradition; he was much influenced by Scaramouche; and the gestures and grimaces that contemporaries commented on in early plays like *Sganarelle* or *L'École des femmes* no doubt stayed with him as his stock in trade throughout his career. It is not only the farcical 'business' of the master chasing the servant with a stick, of Orgon hiding under the table, of Argan pretending to be dead, that reminds us of the continuity from the early farces onwards; there are also constant reminders in the psychological rigidity of the central characters, in their outbursts of temper, in echoes from one play to another that are suggested by such lines as:

Allons, ferme, mon coeur, point de faiblesse humaine
(*Tar.*, line 1293)

or:

Je ne suis point bon, et je suis méchant quand je veux.
(*Mal. imag.*, I, v)

All these features stamp each comic hero as yet another manifestation of Molière the *farceur* in a new variation on the role of Sganarelle – just as his physical appearance must have done, with the characteristic moustache and the unfashionable costume some years behind the time.

In giving way to Sganarelle, Mascarille not only enabled Molière to follow his real bent as an actor, but also made way for the most fruitful collaboration between actor and playwright, as the simple figure of farce developed into the masterly creations of the mature comedies. There have been other comic actors who have left as great a name as Molière, just as there have been other writers of comedy whose purely literary gifts may have been as great. But no writer of comedy, before or since his day, has brought to the writing of comedy Molière's unique experience and sense of theatre. And if the works of Molière the playwright are the surest tribute to Molière the actor, it was the requirements of the actor in the role of Sganarelle that inspired the most notable achievements of the comic dramatist.

5

Comedy and character

Pouvez-vous ne pas avouer que c'est dans Plaute et dans Térence que
Molière a appris les plus grandes finesses de son art?

(Boileau)[1]

(i) Plautus, Terence and Molière

Nearly all the elements of modern Western drama can be traced back
to the theatre of the ancient world. This is more obviously true of
tragedy than of comedy, since the various forms assumed by comedy
in the modern theatre have been more closely related to the specific
societies in which it has flourished; nevertheless it is perfectly proper
to look back to the drama of antiquity for the antecedents of Molière's
comédie de caractère. In the first place, the notion of character comedy
already existed in germ in the ancient world; while in more general
terms, the literary comedy of the seventeenth century, which provided the formal framework for Molière's own personal contribution
to the development of the genre, can clearly be seen to descend from
Greek and Latin sources. Let us try to see what Molière's contemporaries may have had in mind in comparing him, as they frequently did,
with the playwrights of classical antiquity.

In practice, of course, this meant Plautus and Terence. Of the
Greeks, Aristophanes was little known, and his appeal was only to the
select few: the first complete translation into French seems not to have
been produced until the eighteenth century, and Mme M. Delcourt,
after noting the occasional bookish adaptation at the time of the
Pléiade, comments categorically that 'Aristophane n'a eu aucune
influence sur la littérature vivante.'[2] As for Menander, until the
discovery of more substantial survivals in our own day, first-hand

[1] Letter to Perrault (1700) (quoted Mongrédien (ed.), *Recueil*, p. 741).
[2] *La Tradition des comiques anciens en France avant Molière* (Liège, 1934), p. 5. The terminal
date of that study excludes Racine's *Les Plaideurs* (1668); but this was a play by an
exceptionally well-qualified Hellenist, and in no way invalidates the general conclusion about Aristophanes' lack of influence.

knowledge of his comedies could not possibly have been other than fragmentary, and any hypothetical influence must be sought through the intermediary of Latin comedy. When a writer like La Fontaine (in the Preface to his *L'Eunuque*) acknowledges Menander as his ultimate source, paying homage to 'ces noms illustres de Térence et de Ménandre', this is no more than an empty formula designed to confer additional prestige on his play.

It has been a commonplace of literary criticism since the Renaissance to contrast Plautus' robust vigour with the elegance and refinement of Terence. So widespread has this approach been among critics and historians that it is tempting to see Plautus and Terence as providing the two elements – on the one hand the vigorous sense of *le comique*, on the other the literary polish and the refinement – that were to combine to form Molière's characteristic manner. But such a view needs to be treated with caution: there may be an appreciable difference in tone between Plautine and Terentian comedy, but that does not necessarily indicate a fundamental difference in the two authors' attitudes to the nature of comic drama. Both imitate the same kind of models in Greek New Comedy, and both seem to regard comedy as the mirror of life. If Plautus' mirror appears sometimes to be a distorting mirror, giving us an amused and slightly mocking reflection compared with Terence's, can this really be attributed to a fundamental difference of creative principle, or is it rather a question of the selection and emphasis of details within a framework of 'imitative' comedy based on an attitude to plot and character essentially the same as Terence's? The contrast between the two dramatists does not provide a valid parallel with the French genres of *farce* and *comédie* as they existed before Molière; for if the distinction between *comédie* and *farce* really does depend (as has been suggested above) on a fundamental difference of aesthetic principle, then it would seem – despite the opinion of G. Norwood, for whom 'the work of Terence is high comedy, that of Plautus mostly farce'[3] – that both authors wrote fundamentally the same sort of comedy.

Plautus may be more amusing than Terence, but for the most part the *comique* is incidental to the characterisation: it either takes the form of verbal comedy (witty or impudent sallies by the servants), or of complications of plot involving such devices as mistaken identity, which figures so largely in the *Menaechmi* and the *Amphitruo*. As for his

---

[3] *Plautus and Terence* (London, 1932), p. 3.

characters, they are mostly like Terence's: purely functional types, even if not quite so colourless; in the occasional instances in which character is exploited for comic purposes, that again remains incidental to the main conduct of the plot: there is no systematic and sustained integration of the comic and the dramatic elements by means of the handling of character.

The debt of modern comedy to that of Plautus and Terence has been variously assessed by different critics, but it seems to be generally agreed that, inasmuch as Plautus' characterisation is more lively and distinctive than that of the more uniform Terence, playwrights have more often gone to Plautus for plots, and for suggestions of characters, whereas they have preferred to imitate the style and tone of Terence, who can therefore with justice be considered the forerunner of modern comedy of manners. But when we come to enquire into the relationship between the Latin dramatists and the particular kind of comedy we associate with Molière, it seems that any direct influence, particularly in the case of Terence, must have been considerably attenuated by Molière's debt to other traditions. The author of a thesis on Molière and Terence, Miss K. E. Wheatley, attempts to show that the latter's influence steered Molière in the direction of 'realistic' comedy,[4] away from a more extravagant, imaginative form of dramatic art; however, her comparison between the doctrine of the 'speculum vitae' elaborated by Donatus in his commentary on Terence and the arguments put forward by Dorante in the *Critique de l'École des femmes* is far from convincing. For to single out, as she does, Dorante's 'peindre d'après nature'[5] is to overlook the distinction – on which Molière insists in this scene, at any rate by implication – between *la comédie* and *le comique*, and to ignore the role of character in Molière's comedy. Whilst the form of comedy created by Corneille and his contemporaries in the 1630s had acknowledged the aim of holding up a mirror to nature, Molière was to react against that some twenty years later by introducing into the framework of 'la comédie littéraire' his own distinctive *vis comica* based on exaggeration and caricature. In fact Terence's influence, even more clearly than Plautus', can be reduced to a few borrowings of plot.

It is possible, however, to detect here and there in Latin comedy, and more particularly in Plautus, an approach to character that offers at least a certain affinity with Molière's practice. It must be said that

<hr />

[4] *Molière and Terence* (Austin, Texas), 1931. The subtitle of Miss Wheatley's book is *A Study in Molière's Realism*. [5] *Ibid.*, p. 117.

modern scholars have been far from unanimous in assessing the role of character in Plautus; though one play that is picked out by G. E. Duckworth (in a group in which 'the major emphasis of the playwright appears to be the portrayal of character and customs'),[6] P. Lejay (among 'comédies psychologiques')[7] and G. Michaut[8] is the *Aulularia*. The opinion of Michaut, as a distinguished Molière scholar, naturally has a particular interest in this connection, and must command respect. Not only does he come to the same conclusion as Lejay, that the term *comédie de caractère* has little validity in relation to Plautus' theatre, but the *Aulularia* is the only play whose possible claim to this title he is prepared to consider. He analyses it in some detail as 'le commencement d'une comédie de caractère et l'ébauche d'une peinture de l'avarice';[9] and his comparison of Plautus' characterisation with that of Molière in *L'Avare* provides a useful starting-point for discussion of this problem.

The Prologue, spoken by Euclio's household god, characterises the poverty and avarice of the master of the house, and reveals ·the existence of a pot of gold which Euclio has found and guards jealously. He beats his servant because he suspects her of spying on him; and when Megadorus asks for the hand of his daughter in marriage, Euclio suspects him too of having ulterior motives. The wedding is arranged, and cooks arrive to prepare the banquet (at Megadorus' expense); they too are accused of thieving intentions. Euclio removes the gold to a place of safety, and buries it; but he is observed, and the gold is stolen by Strabilo, servant to Lyconides, Megadorus' nephew, who has ravished Euclio's daughter and wants to marry her. Euclio discovers that the gold is missing, and laments frantically; in the following scene he talks at cross-purposes with Lyconides, who confesses to having wronged him (by seducing his daughter; Euclio can think only of the theft of his gold). The end of the play is missing, but it appears that Lyconides returns the gold stolen by his servant, and that Euclio relents, possibly under the influence of his household god, and gives the couple the pot of gold as a wedding-present. Michaut comments as follows:

> Le dieu Lare nous l'a dit: Euclion est avare par hérédité et succombe au vice de sa famille . . . Seulement, dans tout le reste de la pièce, cette avarice n'est pas mise en pleine lumière . . . Toute l'action de la comédie latine, au lieu de dépendre d'un caractère, tourne autour de la marmite

---

[6] *The Nature of Roman Comedy* (Princeton, N.J., 1952), pp. 142–3.
[7] *Plaute* (Paris, 1925), p. 250.   [8] *Plaute* (Paris, 1920), II, p. 149.   [9] *Ibid.*

surveillée, cachée, convoitée, dérobée et enfin restituée: c'est la situation qui est dépeinte plutôt que le vice.[10]

Although his conclusion:

> L'*Aululaire* n'a que les apparences d'une comédie de caractère. Et ce qui prouve bien que Plaute ne s'est pas proposé d'aussi hautes ambitions, c'est que l'*Aululaire* est seule de son genre parmi ses pièces. Jamais plus nous n'en trouverons aucune qui ait des airs de grande comédie; jamais plus nous n'aurons à nous demander s'il n'a pas voulu personnifier et comme incorporer en un type un défaut humain, une passion maîtresse. Les plus importantes de ses oeuvres ne s'élèvent pas au-dessus de la comédie de moeurs[11]

is somewhat weakened by his insistence on an outmoded 'hierarchy' of genres, and although he is concerned above all with the psychology rather than with the *comique* of the characters of Euclio and Harpagon, nevertheless his comparison goes a long way towards explaining the essential difference between Molière's character comedy and those examples of the comic theatre of the ancient world which appear to have most in common with it. As Michaut says, the portrayal of Euclio's avarice is not sustained: the most effective characterisation is at second hand, by means of other characters' description of him; moreover, it is given too rational a basis. One senses, therefore, a certain contradiction between the rather crude exaggeration of the passage in which we are told that Euclio goes to bed with a bag over his mouth so as not to lose any breath while he is asleep, or that he brings his nail-clippings home from the barber's because he cannot bear to waste them,[12] and the perfectly plausible explanation of his avarice, namely that he is a desperately poor man, in whom excessively careful ways have quite naturally become habitual. In a sense, Euclio's embodiment of the abstract vice of avarice and his manoeuverings to protect the pot of gold are almost independent of each other; if they had been more completely integrated, one can imagine the comic character much nearer to Molière's formula – the obsessively careful man who persists in behaving in a miserly manner even when he has become rich – that Plautus might have created.

The most extravagant creation of Plautus' whole theatre is Pyrgopolynices of the *Miles Gloriosus*: this ancestor of the long line of braggart warriors to be found in Renaissance Italy and seventeenth-century France is conceived as a caricature from start to finish. Once again, if we look at the place of Pyrgopolynices in the plot of the *Miles*,

[10] *Ibid.*, pp. 149–50.   [11] *Ibid.*, p. 151.   [12] Lines 302–3, 311–13.

we must agree that he is hardly the mainspring of the action: the play is quite properly listed by Duckworth among the 'comedies of guileful deception', and the plot is a complicated imbroglio centring round the intrigues of the scheming servant Palaestrio. Nevertheless, the fact that the play was named after this character – Plautus' titles most often serve a sort of mnemonic purpose, and where they do not indicate the central 'pivot' character, they usually pick out either an important material object, or else an episodic character striking enough to be memorable in his own right – does at least suggest that he was regarded as the most interesting in the play, even if his role is almost entirely passive.

The construction of the *Miles Gloriosus* is unusual, in that the traditional Prologue is postponed until the beginning of Act II, the first act being devoted to the comic portrayal of the braggart soldier by means of his own boasting and the blatant flattery of his parasite; but after filling the whole of Act I, Pyrgopolynices does not reappear until Act IV. Acts II and III are relatively colourless: they might well come from any of the comedies in which the ruses of a crafty servant provide the main interest. It would no doubt be technically incorrect to call Pyrgopolynices an episodic character; Duckworth's assessment of the soldier's role is quite accurate:

> Character studies as such are rare in Roman comedy. In many plays, however, even when the plot seems motivated largely by coincidence or trickery, the characters have a decisive influence upon the course of the action; e.g., in the *Miles* the pretense that Periplectomenus has a wife madly in love with the soldier succeeds only because the soldier has a conceited and lecherous nature.[13]

However, he remains very much the stock victim of the conventional intrigue, and one could wish that Plautus had related the whole of the plot more specifically to the foible of his extravagant character.

Plautus' braggart soldier falls short of being a rounded comic 'character', too, because the delineation of the type he represents remains so crude and unsubtle. The lack of subtlety is emphasised, curiously enough, by the way in which another character from the same play is presented: the role of Periplectomenus, which is not intended to produce a marked comic effect, but rather indicates the tendency of Plautus as well as Terence to offer a mirror of the normal and typical. What is striking about the portrayal of Periplectomenus – particularly in the long passage (lines 627–764),

[13] *The Nature of Roman Comedy*, p. 146.

dramatically an hors-d'oeuvre, in which he gives a somewhat prosy apologia of the life of the genial old bachelor – is precisely the sureness of psychological touch, the attention to detail. If this scene amuses us, it is not because of any caricatural quality in the self-portrait itself, but because of its wordiness and the reactions of the impatient listeners. Pyrgopolynices, then, is certainly comic, but is only the rudimentary sketch of a dramatic 'character'; while Periplectomenus, although a rounded, convincing character, is not at all comic: as Lejay suggests, he is 'plutôt un "caractère" de Théophraste'.[14] Neither, taken separately, provides a prototype for seventeenth-century *comédie de caractère*; but it is the combination of these two kinds of characterisation at Molière's hands that produces the formula for that genre, and their juxtaposition in the *Miles Gloriosus* certainly gives that play a place apart if we are considering the antecedents of Molière's comedy in the comedy of antiquity.

The play of Terence's which it is most profitable to examine in this light is the *Adelphi*, which like the *Aulularia* provides an acknowledged source for one of Molière's comedies. The detailed relationship between the *Adelphi* and *L'École des maris* is by no means as close as that between the *Aulularia* and *L'Avare*,[15] but there is a sufficiently close resemblance of basic theme for a comparison with Molière's play to enable one to see how different were the Latin playwright's objectives. In the *Adelphi*, Demea has handed over the education of his elder son Aeschinus to his easygoing bachelor brother Micio, while he himself has brought up his younger son Ctesipho according to the strictest principles. When it is learned that Aeschinus has abducted a slave-girl, Demea complains that this is the deplorable result of his lax upbringing; but it turns out that the girl is Ctesipho's mistress, and that Aeschinus has only been acting on his brother's behalf: he himself wants to marry a girl he has seduced. Demea is half converted: he acknowledges that his own excessive strictness has had undesirable consequences, but by pretending to go to the other extreme he shows up the faults of Micio's excessive indulgence. For once, the intriguing servants play little part in the plot, which is throughout closely related to the contrasting characters of Demea and Micio. Like others of Terence's plays, this is a didactic comedy,

[14] *Plaute*, p. 123.
[15] More immediate sources for *L'École des maris* are in any case to be found in Hurtado de Mendoza's *El marido hace mujer* and in one of Boccaccio's tales (*Decameron*, III, 3). See *L'École des maris*, ed. P. H. Nurse (London, 1959), pp. x–xii.

and at any rate part of the author's purpose is to make us reflect on the attitudes of the two brothers. For the greater part of the play, it seems that we are being invited to criticise the repressive system practised by Demea, and to agree with Micio when he argues for tolerance and restraint; but in the last act Demea certainly appears to turn the tables on his brother, and the outcome of this confrontation between their two systems remains inconclusive.

Sganarelle and Ariste, the brothers in *L'École des maris,* are the guardians respectively of Isabelle and Léonor, and despite the difference in age which separates them from their wards, they wish to marry them. Ariste has allowed Léonor full liberty, while Sganarelle has brought up Isabelle with the strictness shown by Demea to Ctesipho. Playing on Sganarelle's blind vanity, Isabelle makes him unwittingly carry messages to her lover, Valère; and when Sganarelle, persuaded that Valère is about to seduce Léonor, insists on disclosing the affair as a lesson to his brother, he finds that he has been tricked, and that Valère is closeted with Isabelle. The young lovers marry, while Léonor remains willing to marry Ariste. In this play we know quite clearly where we stand: there is never any doubt that *L'École des maris* is a study of Sganarelle's folly. But it is far from being a passive study; the various incidents of the plot are all related to the theme of the play: Sganarelle appears in twenty of the twenty-three scenes, and the details of the plot derive from the foible of the central character himself. Basically similar though the material is, therefore, to that provided by Terence, it receives quite a different emphasis at Molière's hands.

It was in connection with *L'École des maris* that La Fontaine congratulated Molière in 1661 on having reintroduced into French comedy 'le bon goût et l'air de Térence';[16] and the editors of the posthumous edition of Molière's plays published in 1682 were similarly to write:

L'inclination qu'il avait pour la poésie le fit s'appliquer à lire les poètes avec un soin tout particulier: il les possédait parfaitement, et surtout Térence; il l'avait choisi comme le plus excellent modèle qu'il eût à se proposer, et jamais personne ne l'imita si bien qu'il a fait.[17]

But this view of Molière's comedy – like that of twentieth-century critics such as Miss Wheatley – manifestly neglects the most characteristic and essential feature of the playwright's mature comedy,

[16] *Lettre à Mauxcroix,* quoted in Molière, *Oeuvres,* ed. Despois and Mesnard.
[17] *Oeuvres* (Paris, 1682), I, p. iv.

namely the remarkable integration of *comique,* character and action. The *Adelphi,* it is true (though this is not the case with Terence's other comedies), shows action dependent to a high degree upon character, and Terence's characterisation is in general more subtle and psychologically more convincing than that of Plautus; nevertheless, Terence's comedy was capable of providing a model for Molière only insofar as the latter's purpose was the faithful reproduction of ordinary life on stage. But this applies (*pace* Miss Wheatley) merely to the outward form, the more or less conventional literary vehicle, that Molière chose to adopt for his comedy: it takes no account of the distinctive aesthetic response that Molière aimed to arouse in his spectators, or of the wholly original dramaturgy by which he sought to achieve this. The *peinture des moeurs* in Molière's comedy is no more than a background to the imaginative portrayal of an extravagant character; and though such characters are more readily to be found in Plautus than in Terence, both the manner in which Molière conceived of character in dramatic terms, and the techniques he used to exploit it for comic effect, show that in the essentials of his craft he was completely independent of both masters of Latin comedy.

(ii) Seventeenth-century attitudes to character

It is easier to form a clear, and no doubt a more accurate, idea of the connotations of the label *comédie* for Molière's contemporaries than it is to form a similar idea of what the term *caractère* may have conveyed to the seventeenth-century Frenchman. Attitudes to character are likely to have been less coherent and less explicit than opinions on the nature of comedy, except in the case of professional psychologists and physiologists, who were inevitably in a class apart from the imaginative writers of the age, and were hardly representative of the reading or the playgoing public. On the other hand, it is self-evident that all creative writers must to some extent reflect the general habits of thought of their public, and that they will be subject to some of the same intellectual limitations as other contemporary minds.[18]

The seventeenth century witnessed the last fling, as it were, of the schematic a priori systems of physiology and psychology inherited from the mediaeval scholastic tradition. If Descartes's *Traité des pas-*

[18] See J. B. Bamborough, *The Little World of Man* (London, 1952), pp. 9–11. The purpose of the book is to relate Shakespeare's characterisation to the 'psychology' current at the time when Shakespeare was writing.

sions de l'âme (1649) and the *Discours sur les passions de l'amour* attributed to Pascal (*c.* 1653) are happily exempt from the more pedantic absurdities of that tradition, we must not forget that Descartes and Pascal were progressive thinkers in the vanguard of the attack, which was to continue into the eighteenth century, on the legacy of the schoolmen. Marin Cureau de la Chambre (1594–1669), one of the earliest members both of the Académie Française and of the Académie des Sciences, and personal physician to Louis XIV, is a more typical guide to contemporary habits of thought; witness the following passage, in which this author develops the principle that man is by nature 'chaud et sec' whilst woman is 'froide et humide':

> Nous pouvons dire sur le principe que nous avons établi que la femme est *froide* et *humide* pour la fin que la Nature s'est proposée, et que parce qu'elle est froide il faut qu'elle soit faible et ensuite timide, pusillanime, soupçonneuse, défiante, rusée, dissimulée, flatteuse, menteuse, aisée à offenser, vindicative, cruelle en ses vengeances, injuste, avare, ingrate, superstitieuse. Et parce qu'elle est humide il faut aussi qu'elle soit mobile, légère, infidèle, impatiente, facile à persuader, pitoyable, babillarde.[19]

In particular, Cureau de la Chambre was a noted physiognomist, and his major work, *L'Art de connaître les hommes* (1659), is a study of physiognomy and of similar pseudo-sciences which can help to 'apprendre à chacun à se connaître lui-même, en quoi consiste le haut point de la sagesse, et à connaître les autres, qui est le chef-d'oeuvre de la prudence'. In both this book and a preliminary essay, *Les Caractères des passions* (1640), he is concerned to relate the psychological phenomenon to its hidden physical cause on the one hand, and to its external manifestation on the other. The system of physiology still favoured at this time was that of the humours, derived from Hippocrates and Galen, and fossilised into the rigid abstractions of the scholastic tradition. Ideally, the human personality was formed by a properly proportioned mixture of the four fluids of the body: blood, phlegm, choler (or yellow bile) and melancholy (or black bile). An excess of any one fluid produced a sanguine, a phlegmatic, a choleric, or a melancholic temperament; and 'tempéraments mixtes' were the products of every possible combination of dominant humours, duly enumerated. Each temperament not only corresponded to an arbitrary and abstract combination of the elements fire, air, earth and water (thus, for instance, the sanguine temperament was 'chaud et

[19] *L'Art de connaître les hommes* (Paris, 1695), p. 49.

humide', while the melancholic was 'sec et froid'), but was also equipped with a comprehensive range of physical attributes: 'the choleric man, for example, was not only quick to anger but yellow-faced, lean, hairy, proud, ambitious, revengeful and shrewd'.[20]

The various passions are enumerated according to well-established scholastic categories:

> Les passions mixtes les plus considérables sont: la honte, l'impudence, la pitié, l'indignation, l'envie, l'émulation, la jalousie, le repentir, l'étonnement. Car la honte est un mélange de la douleur et de la crainte que donne l'infamie. L'impudence se fait du plaisir et de la hardiesse qu'on a de faire des choses déshonnêtes.[21]

And the same tradition lies behind this passage, where Cureau de la Chambre defines the particular sense in which he proposes to use the term *caractère*:

> C'est donc une chose certaine, que le corps s'altère et se change quand l'âme s'émeut, et que celle-ci ne fait presque point d'actions qu'elle ne lui en imprime les marques, que l'on peut appeler caractères, puisqu'ils en ont les effets, et qu'ils en portent l'image et la figure.[22]

Character, for Cureau, is thus the external manifestation of a person's psychological make-up, which in turn is determined by his physical constitution; and we may be sure that a similar assumption underlies dictionary definitions of the time such as Furetière's 'Il n'y a point de passion qui n'ait son caractère particulier.'[23]

Just as the theoretical basis for seventeenth-century attitudes to character had hardly changed from the one that was prevalent in the ancient world, so the literary expression given to this notion of character by Theophrastus or Terence still provided a model for seventeenth-century writers. Terence, through the medium of his modern commentators, was a not unimportant influence on French *moraliste* writing in the seventeenth century; while Theophrastus, with his rigid, schematic interpretation of character, was imitated in English by Joseph Hall in 1608, Hall's *Characters* being in turn trans-lated into French – first in 1610, and then again (by Urbain Chev-

---

[20] *Encyclopaedia Britannica* (15th edition, 1976), s.v. 'Humour'. See also R. Doranlo, *La Médecine au xviie siècle: Marin Cureau de la Chambre* (Paris, 1939), pp. 66ff.; J. Lévy-Valensi, *La Médecine et les médecins français au xviie siècle* (Paris, 1933), pp. 12ff.; M. Raynaud, *Les Médecins au temps de Molière* (Paris, 1862), ch. vii; and Bamborough, *The Little World of Man*, pp. 57ff., 89ff.

[21] Cureau de la Chambre, *Les Caractères des passions* (Paris, 1640) 'Avis au Lecteur'.

[22] *Ibid.*, p. 3.   [23] *Dictionnaire universel* (1690) (Geneva, 1970), s.v. 'caractère'.

reau) in 1646.[24] When La Bruyère in due course published his translation of Theophrastus in 1688, as the basis of his own *Caractères*, he was criticised by contemporaries because his portraits, unlike Theophrastus' systematic illustrations of abstract a priori definitions, were built up by the accumulation of details observed from the contemporary scene:

> Théophraste a traité la chose d'un air plus philosophe: il n'a envisagé que l'universel; vous êtes plus descendu dans le particulier. Vous avez fait vos portraits d'après nature. Théophraste n'a fait les siens que sur une idée générale. Vos portraits ressemblent à certaines personnes, et souvent on les devine. Ceux de Théophraste ne ressemblent qu'à l'homme. Cela est cause qu'ils ressembleront toujours. Mais il est à craindre que les vôtres ne perdent quelque chose de ce vif et de ce brillant qu'on y remarque, quand on ne pourra plus les comparer avec ceux sur qui vous les avez tirés.[25]

The attitude to 'character' represented here (however perfidiously) by Charpentier was still illustrated in practice at the end of the century, for instance by one Brillon, who styled himself 'le Théophraste moderne', and whose *Nouveaux Caractères sur les moeurs*[26] are much nearer to the manner of the Greek *moraliste*; or by Du Puy, whose *Caractères et portraits critiques sur les moeurs*[27] exhibits a strong physical determinism. Moreover, similar attitudes continued to underlie characterisation in comic drama well into the eighteenth century. For countless uninspired 'hautes comédies', nominally written in imitation of Molière's *comédie de caractère*, in fact owed their origin to a priori notions of character going back to Theophrastus; and when the authors of such plays lamented – as they were already doing soon after Molière's death – that the author of *Le Misanthrope* had pre-empted them and 'taken all the characters', this itself was evidence of their over-schematic, abstract approach.

How important for the study of Molière's comedy are these classical concepts of character, and the physiological theory of the humours on which they were based? And how does Molière's kind of character comedy relate in this respect to English comedy of humours? The theory of the humours has traditionally been regarded as fundamental to an understanding of Jonson in particular, and to English

---

[24] See H. G. Hall, 'Molière, Chevreau's *École du sage*, and Joseph Hall's *Characters*', *French Studies*, XXIX (1975), 398–410.

[25] Charpentier, Doyen of the Académie Française, in reply to La Bruyère's 'Discours de réception'; quoted by P. Richard, *La Bruyère et ses Caractères* (Paris, 1946), pp. 138–9.

[26] Paris, 1700.   [27] Paris, 1695.

comedy in general through to Congreve;[28] though it has more recently been argued that in spite of what he writes in the Prologue to *Every Man out of his Humour*, Jonson was less concerned with the physically determined 'humours', or inborn temperaments, that have always been associated with his name, than with 'pseudo-humours', or acquired characteristics.[29] According to this reassessment of the English tradition, comic characterisation, instead of depending on physiologically determined conditions (in the sense in which Hamlet's melancholy is a 'humour'), should rather be seen as based on 'assiduously cultivated affectations and eccentricities'.[30]

Specific references to the humours in Molière's plays are rare, but by no means insignificant. On the one hand, there is the burlesque diagnosis by the bogus doctor Sganarelle in *Le Médecin volant*:

> Oui, ce grand médecin, au chapitre qu'il a fait de la nature des animaux, dit . . . cent belles choses; et comme les humeurs qui ont de la connexité ont beaucoup de rapport; car, par exemple, comme la mélancolie est ennemie de la joie, et que la bile qui se répand par le corps nous fait devenir jaunes, et qu'il n'est rien plus contraire à la santé que la maladie, nous pouvons dire avec ce grand homme, que votre fille est fort malade.
>
> (scene v)

This is hardly designed to inspire confidence in the classical theory, any more than the jargon uttered so glibly by the Premier Médecin in *Monsieur de Pourceaugnac*:

> Je l'appelle mélancolie hypocondriaque, pour la distinguer des deux autres; car le célèbre Galien établit doctement à son ordinaire trois espèces de cette maladie que nous nommons mélancolie, ainsi appelée non-seulement par les Latins, mais encore par les Grecs, ce qui est bien à remarquer pour notre affaire; la première, qui vient du propre vice du cerveau; la seconde, qui vient de tout le sang, fait et rendu atrabilaire; la troisième, appelée hypocondriaque, qui est la nôtre, laquelle procède du vice de quelque partie du bas-ventre et de la région inférieure, mais particulièrement de la rate, dont la chaleur et l'inflammation porte au cerveau de notre malade beaucoup de fuligines épaisses et crasses, dont la vapeur noire et maligne cause dépravation aux fonctions de la faculté princesse, et fait la maladie dont, par notre raisonnement, il est manifestement atteint et convaincu. (I, viii)

---

[28] For a clear statement of this traditional view, see J. Palmer, *Ben Jonson* (London, 1934), ch. ii.

[29] Cf. H. L. Snuggs, 'The Comic Humours: A New Interpretation', *PMLA*, LXVII (1947), 114–22.

[30] Snuggs, 'The Comic Humours', 116. And cf. Congreve: 'Affectation is generally mistaken for humour' (quoted by Snuggs, *ibid.*).

On the other hand, the physiology of the humours quite clearly provides a basis for the characterisation in *Le Misanthrope*; the projected subtitle 'L'Atrabilaire amoureux' points unambiguously to the physical cause of Alceste's misanthropy, as do references in the text of the play by the hero himself:

> ... la cour et la ville
> Ne m'offrent rien qu'objets à m'échauffer la bile:
> J'entre en une humeur noire, en un chagrin profond ... (lines 89–91)

or by Philinte:

> Mon flegme est philosophe autant que votre bile. (line 166)

This certainly seems to indicate that Molière (like his audiences, we may surmise) accepted the general principles of temperamental determinism along the lines of the theory of dominant humours, even if he was prepared to make fun of its detailed mechanistic application as elaborated by the more reactionary doctors of his day. *Le Misanthrope* provides, alongside the portrait of Alceste, several examples of characterisation based on 'pseudo-humours': the courtiers Oronte, Acaste and Clitandre are nothing if not an accumulation of 'assiduously cultivated affectations'.[31] On the other hand, it does appear that Alceste's character is based on a genuine 'humour', and that in that respect he is nearer to Hamlet (to return to our English examples) than to the eccentrics and the fops of Jonson's comedy of humours; and moreover that Arnolphe, Harpagon, Argan – indeed, all the manifestations of the Sganarelle type – are similarly rooted in an a priori concept of character as the product of physical determinants. However, if Molière's characterisation does relate in this way to the classical theory of character, he translates theory into practice in a manner very different from that of Theophrastus – and of his own successors in the field of character comedy. In plays like *Le Distrait*, *Le Glorieux*, or *Le Méchant*,[32] the abstract type remains in evidence throughout, governing the central character's whole behaviour; with Molière, on the other hand, even if the theoretical abstraction provides the skeleton, this is fleshed out with the particularising detail

---

[31] Similarly, Célimène's portraits, which can certainly be interpreted as valid evidence of the interest taken in 'character' by the *habitués* of the *salons* (and therefore by an influential section of Molière's spectators), are built up by the accumulation of observed details.

[32] By Regnard (1697), Destouches (1732), and Gresset (1745). As further evidence of the schematic exploitation of abstractions in eighteenth-century comedy, cf. for instance the large number of plays on the theme of *le jaloux*.

that comes from acute observation, so that like all the greatest comic creations, Molière's characters are at one and the same time type and individual.

(iii) 'Ridicule en de certaines choses et honnête homme en d'autres'

At first sight, Molière hardly seems to have committed himself to a conscious and coherent theory of comedy: of the other major comic dramatists of the classical period in France, Corneille, Dancourt, Destouches, Voltaire and Beaumarchais all left a more substantial and explicit commentary on their work. Molière seldom accompanied the published text of his plays with a preface, and the prefaces he did publish are either circumstantial and anecdotal in nature (*Les Fâcheux, L'École des femmes*) or vehicles for special pleading (*Les Précieuses ridicules, Tartuffe*). On the other hand, the Preface to *L'École des femmes* serves as advance publicity for 'une dissertation que j'ai faite en dialogue . . . je ne mets point dans cette préface ce qu'on verra dans la *Critique* . . .'. Fortunately, the *Critique* not only fulfils the specific requirement of a self-justificatory argument 'qui réponde aux censeurs et rende raison de mon ouvrage': scene vi in particular goes far beyond the immediate context of the 'Guerre comique', and suggests a convincing theoretical basis for a new and distinctive form of comedy.

It is usual to call this 'comédie de caractère'; but as we have seen, Molière's character comedy differs from that of his predecessors – and of many of his successors – in that the central character, from whose folly or eccentricity the incidents of the comic plot derive, is no longer the flat, two-dimensional abstraction produced by a priori characterology, but a 'rounded' figure possessing the extra dimension of truth to life that only detailed observation of reality can give. The formula 'ridicule en de certaines choses et honnête homme en d'autres' – so simple in appearance, yet so far-reaching in its suggestion of a wholly original approach to comic characterisation – emerges as the reply to a two-pronged attack on *L'École des femmes* by Lysidas the poet-critic. First of all:

> Arnolphe ne donne-t-il pas trop librement son argent à Horace? Et puisque c'est le personnage ridicule de la pièce fallait-il lui faire faire l'action d'un honnête homme? (scene vi)

And conversely:

Ce Monsieur de La Souche enfin, qu'on nous fait un homme d'esprit, et qui paraît si sérieux en tant d'endroits, ne descend-il point dans quelque chose de trop comique et de trop outré au cinquième acte, lorsqu'il explique à Agnès la violence de son amour, avec ces roulements d'yeux extravagants, ces soupirs, et ces larmes niaises qui font rire tout le monde? (*ibid.*)

In other words Lysidas, voicing, no doubt, the typical criticism of the time, based on conventional theories of comedy, appears to be saying that Molière ought to make up his mind what sort of play he is writing. Is Arnolphe a pasteboard abstraction such as would have been appropriate to the burlesque comedy of Scarron or Jodelet, or is he a convincingly lifelike portrait, suitable to 'une peinture de la conversation des honnêtes gens'? Is he meant to make the spectators laugh, or to arouse their sympathetic interest? In the eyes of the purist, Arnolphe does not fit into the framework of previously-established genres. He is too 'comic' to be the hero of a refined literary comedy, but equally, there are features of his make-up which do not belong to the extravagant, caricatural characterisation proper to burlesque or to farce. Dorante's reply, rebutting the charge of inconsistency in Arnolphe's character, at the same time points the way forward to Molière's other memorable comic creations. Arnolphe is so possessed by an obsessive fear of being made a cuckold that he is driven to the most extravagant behaviour; yet he is a much more rounded portrayal of a credible bourgeois character than the Sganarelles of *Le Cocu imaginaire* or *L'École des maris* had been; and the same is true of Orgon, Alceste, Harpagon, Monsieur Jourdain or Argan: in every case the caricatural portrayal of folly – the 'type' of the Miser, the Misanthrope, and so on according to classical tradition – has been turned into the lifelike portrait of an individual with an identifiable place in the social world of seventeenth-century France. The comic hero has become a man of the world, a respectable member of society, he is recognisable as one of ourselves; but he has a comic foible, or obsession, which makes him the dupe of others and the object of our laughter. When Sganarelle ceases to be called Sganarelle and becomes Arnolphe, Orgon or Monsieur Jourdain he does not cease to be absurd; but he has acquired an extra dimension, and we do not find it impossible to imagine what Arnolphe would have been like without his obsession with marital misfortune, Orgon without his infatuation for Tartuffe, or Jourdain without his ridiculous compulsion to ape the nobility.

How does Molière set about giving his characters this extra dimension which turns them from farcical stereotypes into rounded comic heroes? To begin with, the literary framework has something to do with it. It is an interesting fact that having – as we may well consider – perfected the polished five-act verse-form in *Le Misanthrope*, Molière was to write only two more plays, *Tartuffe* and *Les Femmes savantes*, in this form which enjoyed such special prestige. Nevertheless, not only these plays, but also the prose *L'Avare*, *Le Bourgeois gentilhomme* and *Le Malade imaginaire*, as well as three-act plays like *George Dandin* and *Monsieur de Pourceaugnac*, illustrate a general tendency towards refinement of vocabulary and general literary polish, compared with farces like *Le Mariage forcé* or *Le Médecin malgré lui*; and this is certainly one factor that helps to narrow the gap between the later versions of the Sganarelle figure and the *honnêtes gens* in Molière's audience. But a more important factor, perhaps, is the tangible relationship between the hero and material aspects of the society of his day. Even though these characters remain alienated in one sense from the world about them, in another sense they are credible representatives of the world in which they are situated. They are given a more substantial *état civil*; we know something of their past lives, of their family situation, of their opinions on various matters, of their social and economic standing. An excellent example of this (apart from the more immediately obvious cases of Orgon, Alceste or Monsieur Jourdain) is George Dandin in the play of that name. Here, a character showing very strong affinities with the *mal-marié* of the farce tradition is given a contemporary identity as a wealthy peasant farmer who, in order to further his social ambition, has married the daughter of an impoverished nobleman; and husband, wife and parents-in-law each fit into a precisely delineated niche in the social hierarchy. Arnolphe provides another good illustration of the way in which Molière's characters are given social roots, for he has acquired a quite separate identity as Monsieur de la Souche; and while this might suggest an artificial division between the comic type (Arnolphe) and the individual with a social identity (Monsieur de la Souche), in practice the effect is to endow Arnolphe with greater credibility as a 'real' character.

Again, the good opinion of other characters, themselves respected by the audience, helps to establish the social acceptability of the central figure. Chrysalde's friendship for Arnolphe, Cléante's for Orgon, Philinte's affectionate regard for Alceste – and perhaps even more notably in Alceste's case the high opinion Éliante has of him:

Et la sincérité dont son âme se pique
A quelque chose en soi de noble et d'héroïque.
C'est une vertu rare au siècle d'aujourd'hui,
Et je la voudrais voir partout comme chez lui (lines 1165–8)

– such relationships play an important part in providing the necessary credentials for Molière's comic heroes.

There is one way in which this 'rounding' of Molière's characters in terms of social identity is effected that is often overlooked because we take it for granted. Previous writers of comedy had observed the convention, dating from the theatre of the ancient world, according to which the social life of the characters portrayed, their arguing, bargaining, quarrelling and love-making, had all been carried on in the open street. Even Corneille's comedies, in spite of their claim to realism, had adhered to the same convention; and Molière had kept to it for nearly all his early plays: most of the half-dozen Sganarelle plays, for instance, take place out of doors, and so does *L'École des femmes*. But in certain early plays he had found it necessary, for reasons of particular verisimilitude, to adopt an interior setting: *Les Précieuses ridicules* was set indoors in order, no doubt, to emphasise the play's satirical effect, while *La Critique de l'École des femmes* and *L'Impromptu de Versailles*, as conversation-pieces, had both necessitated a similar move. And as a development from these modest beginnings, when Sganarelle stopped being a simple farcical stereotype and began to acquire a social identity, he went indoors. Plays like *Tartuffe*, *L'Avare*, *Les Femmes savantes* and *Le Bourgeois gentilhomme* gain enormously from this development, while it could be said that *Le Misanthrope* positively depends on it: the tapestries and furnishings of Célimène's *salon* are really as indispensable to the flavour of the play as Oronte's sonnet or the affected dress of the *petits marquis*.

These are all moves in the direction of an urbane comedy of manners, of which the verse comedies no doubt provide the most polished examples, but which is also illustrated in plays like *L'Avare* or *Le Bourgeois gentilhomme*. And the effect of these various changes of style, structure and setting must surely have been to bring the imaginative world of Molière's comedy within the grasp of a cultured audience. Not only do the so-called 'raisonneurs' more or less explicitly represent the standards and values of the *honnêtes gens*, but the comic heroes themselves belong to the same social milieu: if they are not *honnêtes gens*, they are 'honnêtes gens manqués'.

The formula 'ridicule en de certaines choses et honnête homme en d'autres', vital as it is as a key to Molière's comic creation, must not be thought of as fixed and invariable. The *dosage* of the 'ridicule' and the 'honnête', of extravagant fantasy and sober observation, in fact varies quite considerably from play to play. Argan and Monsieur Jourdain may perhaps seem to us to be situated at one end of the spectrum of Molière's great characters, as the most obviously caricatural roles with a strong comic impact on the spectator; with Orgon, George Dandin and Harpagon, as with Arnolphe, the attachments to the real world are more consistently in evidence, and the element of fantasy correspondingly reduced; while Alceste, at the other extreme, illustrates such a subtle fusion of 'ridicule' and 'honnête' that the critical interpretation of this character will no doubt always be the subject of debate. But it is not only the atrabilious hero of *Le Misanthrope* who poses this sort of problem, even if his is an extreme case: Goethe's view of *L'Avare* as 'in the highest sense tragic',[33] as well as nineteenth-century interpretations of the characters of Arnolphe, Orgon or George Dandin can be set beside the Alceste of Rousseau and of the Romantic generation, as indications of the enigmatic quality possessed by these characters whose folly is attenuated by their *honnêteté*.

As twentieth-century readers or spectators, we may be perfectly well disposed to accept this blend of fantasy and realism; it may well seem to us the natural counterpart, in the technique of Molière the creative writer, of an acting style which combined the complementary features of comic extravagance and truth to life.[34] But the original audience – or at any rate their more articulate and influential members – were more difficult to satisfy. 'C'est une étrange entreprise que celle de faire rire les honnêtes gens': Molière was well aware of the challenge he was offering to contemporary prejudices; and the record shows that the *honnêtes gens* of the 1660s were not without their counterparts in the eighteenth and nineteenth centuries.[35]

---

[33] To Eckermann, 12 May 1825.

[34] On the one hand, there is the evidence of La Neufvillenaine and others which we have already quoted; on the other, Molière's own description in the *Critique* of the way he played Arnolphe in Act V of *L'École des femmes*: 'ces roulements d'yeux extravagants, ces soupirs, et ces larmes niaises qui font rire tout le monde' – invaluable as an indication both of the playwright's intentions and of the actor's manner.

[35] See M. Descotes, *Les Grands Rôles du théâtre de Molière* (Paris, 1960); and *Molière et sa fortune littéraire* (Bordeaux, 1970).

6

Laughter and 'le rire dans l'âme'

Je vous estime trop pour croire que vous n'y ayez pas ri, du moins
intérieurement.

(Boileau (to Racine, discussing L'Avare))[1]

(i) From 'Le Cocu imaginaire' to 'Le Malade imaginaire'

It is merely a chronological accident that the title of what is in many
ways the most important of Molière's early plays, the first in which
the Sganarelle figure takes over from Mascarille, should find an echo
in the title of what proved to be the playwright's last work; but for all
that the coincidence remains richly suggestive. To quote Albert
Thibaudet:

> Il est très remarquable que cette période de la comédie de Molière, qui
> fait presque la totalité de sa carrière, commence avec le *Cocu imaginaire* et
> finisse avec le *Malade imaginaire*. L'épithète pourrait s'appliquer à toutes
> les manifestations de Sganarelle: l'imaginaire, au lieu que Mascarille
> était l'imaginatif.[2]

Having made this point, Thibaudet goes on to propose a series of
subtitles: 'Arnolphe, ou le Mari imaginaire'; 'Jourdain, ou l'Homme
de qualité imaginaire'; 'Orgon, ou le Dévot imaginaire'; 'Chrysale, ou
le Courageux imaginaire'; 'Alceste, ou l'Honnête homme imaginaire'. While the last of these suggestions undoubtedly contains much
more controversial implications than the others, I imagine few readers would want to quarrel with Thibaudet's general proposition. Not
only the first Sganarelle and Argan, but the whole series of major
comic heroes who come in between, are *imaginaires*:[3] their behaviour is
governed not by empirical reactions to the real world in which they
live, but by the preconceived notions, the intellectual abstractions,

---

[1] Monchesnay, *Bolaeana*, quoted Mongrédien (ed.), *Recueil*, p. 105.
[2] 'Molière et la critique', *Revue de Paris*, xxxvii, 6 (1930), 386.
[3] *Imaginaire*: 'qui n'est que dans l'imagination', Richelet, *Dictionnaire français* (1680); 'qui n'est que dans l'imagination, et n'est point réel', *Dictionnaire de l'Académie* (1694).

which they constantly substitute for the direct experience of reality. Molière's typical comic characters live in a self-imposed isolation from the world around them, a solipsistic universe of their own creating. They are *aliénés,* if not in the clinical, pathological sense, at any rate in a sense that can be seen to have a definite connection with this technical use of the term. La Bruyère has a striking portrait of a courtier appointed to an important office, whose new dignity has, as we say, 'gone to his head' (the phrase is a revealing one):

> Voyez . . . comme il plie sous le poids de son bonheur, quel air froid et sérieux il conserve pour ceux qui ne sont plus ses égaux: il ne leur répond pas, il ne les voit pas; les embrassements et les caresses des grands, qu'il ne voit plus de si loin, achèvent de lui nuire; il se déconcerte, il s'étourdit; c'est une courte aliénation.[4]

This is a graphic picture of a *temporary* 'aliénation': the condition of Molière's comic figures, on the other hand, is of a more long-term nature, and in some cases we are evidently to regard it as incurable. Their minds are dominated by an obsession which colours their whole thinking, rendering them just as oblivious as La Bruyère's courtier to the established conventions of social intercourse:

> Quel avantage a-t-on qu'un homme vous caresse,
> Vous jure amitié, foi, zèle, estime, tendresse,
> Et vous fasse de vous un éloge éclatant,
> Lorsqu'au premier faquin il court en faire autant?
> Non, non, il n'est point d'âme un peu bien située
> Qui veuille d'une estime ainsi prostituée;
> Et la plus glorieuse a des régals peu chers,
> Dès qu'on voit qu'on nous mêle avec tout l'univers:
> Sur quelque préférence une estime se fonde,
> Et c'est n'estimer rien qu'estimer tout le monde.
> Puisque vous y donnez, dans ces vices du temps,
> Morbleu! vous n'êtes pas pour être de mes gens;
> Je refuse d'un coeur la vaste complaisance
> Qui ne fait de mérite aucune différence;
> Je veux qu'on me distingue; et pour le trancher net,
> L'ami du genre humain n'est point du tout mon fait
>
> (Mis., lines 49–64)

and even to the ordinary relationships of family life:

> Ne me répliquez pas davantage, ma fille sera marquise en dépit de tout le monde; et si vous me mettez en colère, je la ferai duchesse. (*B. gent.*, III, xii)

---

[4] *Caractères*, 'De la cour', para. 50.

The imaginary world inhabited by these characters, though a projection of their private fantasies and obsessions, is not always a model of the ideal world as they would like it to be. On the contrary: Sganarelle and his successors are essentially weak characters, and if the obsession with conjugal misfortune of Sganarelle the *cocu imaginaire* is shown to have little foundation in fact, that of George Dandin, for instance, seems to be much more likely to prove well founded. But more commonly, the world of the imagination in which they live – and which they seek to impose on others – is the weak character's protective device by which he compensates for the imperfections of the real world. The authoritative system of Sganarelle in *L'École des maris*; Arnolphe's picture of society in which 'Du côté de la barbe est la toute-puissance', and where:

> . . . ce que le soldat, dans son devoir instruit,
> Montre d'obéissance au chef qui le conduit,
> Le valet à son maître, un enfant à son père,
> A son supérieur le moindre petit frère,
> N'approche point encore de la docilité,
> Et de l'obéissance, et de l'humilité,
> Et du profond respect, où la femme doit être
> Pour son mari, son chef, son seigneur et son maître;
> (*É. des f.*, lines 700, 705–12)

and similarly Alceste's ideal programme:

> Plus on aime quelqu'un, moins il faut qu'on le flatte;
> A ne rien pardonner le pur amour éclate;
> Et je bannirais, moi, tous ces lâches amants
> Que je verrais soumis à tous mes sentiments,
> Et dont, à tous propos, les molles complaisances
> Donneraient de l'encens à mes extravagances
> (*Mis.*, lines 701–6)

like his final ultimatum to Célimène:

> . . . Pourvu que votre coeur veuille donner les mains
> Au dessein que j'ai fait de fuir tous les humains,
> Et que dans mon désert, où j'ai fait voeu de vivre,
> Vous soyez, sans tarder, résolue à me suivre
> (*ibid.*, lines 1761–4)

are all attempts by a male lover, conscious that he lacks the psychological advantages of social graces, wit and polish, to reduce the odds against him by dictating courtship and marriage on his own chosen terms.

127

Elsewhere, as has often been observed, the Sganarelle figure seems to depend on his restructured image of the society in which he lives, the better to dominate his family with the petty authority of a domestic tyrant. However completely Orgon may himself be controlled by Tartuffe, it certainly suits his authoritarian view of family life (again, the attitude of a weak man lacking in self-confidence?) to be able to say of his pious protégé:

> Enfin le Ciel chez moi me le fit retirer,
> Et depuis ce temps-là tout semble y prospérer.
> Je vois qu'il reprend tout, et qu'à ma femme même
> Il prend, pour mon honneur, un intérêt extrême;
> Il m'avertit des gens qui lui font les yeux doux,
> Et plus que moi six fois il s'en montre jaloux.
>
> *(Tar.*, lines 299–304)

Argan similarly exploits his hypochondria:

> . . . me voyant infirme et malade comme je suis, je veux me faire un gendre et des alliés médecins, afin de m'appuyer de bons secours contre ma maladie, d'avoir dans ma famille les sources des remèdes qui me sont nécessaires et d'être à même des consultations et des ordonnances.
>
> *(Mal. imag.*, I, v)

Philaminte, a no less striking example of matriarchal despotism, makes a virtually identical use of the intellectual pretensions around which her life revolves, in order to bolster up her power over Henriette and keep Chrysale in his place:

> Ce Monsieur Trissotin dont on nous fait un crime,
> Et qui n'a pas l'honneur d'être dans votre estime,
> Est celui que je prends pour l'époux qu'il lui faut,
> Et je sais mieux que vous juger de ce qu'il vaut;
> La contestation est ici superflue,
> Et de tout point chez moi l'affaire est résolue.
>
> *(F. sav.*, lines 631–6)

Whether the 'aliénation' of the central figure is to be explained as due to his instinct for self-preservation or for self-assertion; whether – as in Alceste's case – it is explicitly related to physiological determinants; or whether – as appears to be the case with Harpagon – it is a more gratuitous phenomenon, the course it takes follows a similar pattern: hypertrophy of the mental processes in one imaginative area produces quite literally an unbalanced mind, as the obsession dominates all the character's thinking. A simple instance of this is Harpagon's 'Les beaux yeux de ma cassette!' (*L'Avare*, V, iii). No matter that this dialogue of two speakers at cross purposes is already to be found in the *Aulularia*: Molière has thoroughly assimilated it, and it serves as a marvellously effective illustration of the character's total preoccupation with money, which closes his mind to everything else. Orgon's 'Et Tartuffe?' – 'Le pauvre homme!', with which he punctuates Dorine's attempts to tell him of his wife's illness (*Tar.*, lines 231–58); Jourdain's instructions to the astonished Dorimène:

—Un peu plus loin, Madame.
—Comment?
—Un pas, s'il vous plaît.
—Quoi donc?
—Reculez un peu, pour la troisième; (*B. gent.*, III, xvi)

and Argan's terror at the impressive-sounding list of diseases with which he has been cursed by Monsieur Purgon:

> Je n'en puis plus. Je sens déjà que la médecine se venge... Vous voyez, mon frère, les étranges maladies dont il m'a menacé ... Il dit que je deviendrai incurable avant qu'il soit quatre jours (*Mal. imag.*, III, vi)

all of these justly celebrated passages likewise epitomise the character's complete absorption by his *idée fixe*, so that he is no longer 'on the same wavelength' as his interlocutor.

The folly of the central character cries out to be exploited by others. 'Le principal thème du comique de Molière', writes V. Vedel, 'est le jeu entre la sottise et la ruse';[5] and in terms of plot we can distinguish two kinds of 'ruse'. In the first place, many of Molière's *imaginaires* are the ready victims of charlatans and impostors, whose activities help to exteriorise for dramatic purposes, and in a way might be said to symbolise, the former's obsessions: not only in the obvious case of Orgon exploited by Tartuffe, but in a whole range of other examples, from Magdelon and Cathos hoodwinked by Mascarille and Jodelet to Jourdain the 'vache à lait' of Dorante, the *femmes savantes* taken in by Trissotin, and Argan playing into the hands of his doctors and apothecaries as well as of his second wife. This is the most intimate, and no doubt the most creative, sort of relationship between *folie* and *fourberie*; though quite often, Molière's plot requires the presence of what one might call on the one hand the reluctant, and on the other, the benevolent, *fourbe*. The former, admittedly working in his or her own interests, nevertheless has the moral approval of the audience:

---

[5] *Deux Classiques français vus par un critique étranger: Corneille et son temps; Molière* (Paris, 1935), p. 476.

Isabelle of *L'École des maris,* outwitting her jealous guardian Sganarelle, or Cléonte and Covielle, humouring the folly of Monsieur Jourdain; while the latter employs deception quite disinterestedly, in order to rescue the *imaginaires* from the worst consequences of their folly: Ariste, for instance, with his device for showing up Trissotin's mercenary motives, or Béralde and Toinette opening Argan's eyes to the perfidy of Béline. In all these cases 'la ruse', while it takes advantage of the vulnerability of the self-centred *imagination,* is used in a very traditional way to thwart the plans of the parent or guardian, and to promote the interests of the sympathetic young lovers.

There are two important cases, however, in which no *fourbe* appears. In neither *L'École des femmes* nor *Le Misanthrope* did Molière need to have recourse to this ancient plot device, and the temperamental foibles of Arnolphe and Alceste respectively are sufficient on their own to keep the plot going. It is true that the plot of *L'École des femmes* has often been criticised on the score of artificiality: the repeated confidences of Horace in Arnolphe whom he does not know as Monsieur de la Souche, together with the highly contrived nature of the dénouement, fail to satisfy those who set a high premium on naturalism in drama; while *Le Misanthrope* has conversely sometimes been found lacking in incident. What these complementary criticisms show is that Molière's attitude towards plot was remarkably eclectic: if in most of his plays he was content to cast his comedy in a traditional mould, with a conventional logical relationship between plot and dénouement, in *L'École des femmes* he played fast and loose with the convention, and produced something like a parody of the traditional form, while *Le Misanthrope,* at the other extreme, approaches the 'slice of life' with a minimum of artificial contrivance. And in both cases the plot, such as it is, derives in a completely satisfactory way from the central character of the play: it is noteworthy that *L'École des femmes* and *Le Misanthrope* share the structural feature of a long introductory dialogue in which the personality of the comic hero on whom the plot will depend is fully explored before the action gets under way.

If Molière's *imaginaires* are rich in plot potential, they are also a fertile source of comic effect. The comic possibilities of a character existing in a fantasy world, more or less cut off from reality, are obvious enough; yet it is worth observing that the contrast between reality and the private world of an *imaginaire* is not necessarily of itself comic: everything depends on the way in which the contrast is presented, and on the standpoint that the spectator or reader is encouraged to adopt. Let us take as a case in point Don Quixote, perhaps the best known of all the *imaginaires* in European literature. It seems inconceivable that Cervantes, in creating his knight-errant hero, was not inviting his readers to share the point of view of the narrator, for whom Quixote's extravagant fantasies are a source of good-humoured mockery. But if we compare the treatment of a similar theme in *Madame Bovary* – where Emma's reading during her formative years at the convent plays very much the same role as Quixote's immersion in the romances of chivalry – we see at once that the author's point of view is by no means as obvious as that of Cervantes, but that it certainly seems to be quite different. In the modern novel (and in the modern theatre, too: see for instance Crommelynck's *Le Cocu magnifique* (1920), with its evocatively moliéresque title) we can seldom automatically assume that re-assuring identity of outlook between the author and his public, based on the acceptance of the social norms, on which classical comedy depends. It is partly, perhaps, a question of realism of setting – the detail in which Flaubert presents Emma's life helps us to see the world in which she lives through her eyes – but even more it is a question of post-Romantic attitudes to the human personality. Whereas Voltaire's Pangloss, for instance, is still an *imaginaire* in the classical tradition, from Rousseau onwards we have been encouraged not to laugh at, or to judge, the eccentric or nonconformist individual, but to understand him. As the twentieth-century playwright Lenormand wrote of his own practice: 'I wanted to have done with the classical conception of man . . . I submitted the Cartesian hero, whose motives are entirely lucid, to the dissolving influences which emanate from his subconscious mind.'[6]

While such considerations are very relevant indeed to the Romantic and post-Romantic interpretations of Molière's comedy, they do not affect the moral and psychological outlook of the dramatist himself, and of the spectators for whom he wrote. If the *imaginaire* was a kind of *aliéné*, whose obsessions cut him off from normal social and intellectual contact with his fellows, this made him an ideal subject for a type of comedy that took for granted the basic premise of Cartesian psychology, that 'le bon sens' was a universal common denominator, and that departures from this common-sense norm could quite properly be judged, if not corrected, by the comic process.

[6] Quoted by D. Knowles, *French Drama of the Inter-War Years* (London, 1967), p. 91.

In particular, the tendency on the part of those obsessed with an *idée fixe* to behave in an automatic, mechanical manner is a perfect illustration of Bergson's theory of laughter, according to which 'les attitudes, gestes et mouvements du corps humain sont risibles dans l'exacte mesure où ce corps nous fait penser à une simple mécanique'.[7] Bergson's theory of 'du mécanique plaqué sur du vivant'[8] has not been without its critics, who have maintained that to reduce all the sources of laughter, even in a literary or theatrical context, to this single formula is excessively restrictive; but it is nonetheless true that if it is applied to Molière's character comedy, Bergson's formula fits it remarkably well.

The rigidity, and mechanical repetition, of physical gesture is the basis of the circus clown's technique; a corresponding automatism in the mental attitudes of Molière's *imaginaires* finds expression most obviously, perhaps, in the repetition of a revealing phrase. Orgon's 'Et Tartuffe?' — 'Le pauvre homme!' has already been quoted; similar examples are to be found in Harpagon's 'Sans dot' with which he three times in quick succession cuts short Valère's attempts to put forward more reasonable attitudes towards his daughter's marriage (*L'Avare*, I, v); and in the 'Que diable allait-il faire dans cette galère?' with which Géronte no fewer than six times betrays the miserly attitude that makes it so hard for him to surrender the money needed for his son's 'ransom' (*Fourberies*, II, vii). A more subtle illustration is provided by the scene (*Mis.*, I, ii) in which Alceste three times parries Oronte's invitation to criticise his sonnet 'avec sincérité' with a 'Je ne dis pas cela; mais . . .': more subtle, because what Alceste's phrase reveals is not the obstinate single-mindedness of some of Molière's *imaginaire* characters, but the impossibility of reconciling his principle of plain speaking with the courtesies of polite social intercourse. He does try to make such a compromise – but very awkwardly; and the evasive formula betrays at the same time his desire to avoid a confrontation, and his inability to carry this out.

Elsewhere, the *idée fixe* of the central character may be portrayed by means of a looser, and more flexible, kind of verbal repetition. This can result in an irregular sequence of phrases linked thematically in the course of a single scene, or else in the recurrence in more than one scene, as a sort of leitmotif, of words and phrases expressive of the character's obsession. A good illustration of the more compact ver-

[7] *Le Rire*, p. 22.   [8] *Ibid.*, p. 29.

sion of this technique, which produces a powerful cumulative effect, is scene iv of *Les Précieuses ridicules*, where almost every time Magdelon and Cathos open their mouths, their speech is liberally strewn with examples of *précieux* jargon:

—ce que vous dites là est du dernier bourgeois . . .

—il ne se peut rien de plus marchand que ce procédé . . .

—des gens qui sont tout à fait incongrus en galanterie . . .

—Quelle frugalité d'ajustement et quelle sécheresse de conversation!

—une oreille un peu délicate pâtit furieusement à entendre prononcer ces mots-là.

The comic effect derives partly from the extravagance of such vocabulary – but partly, too, from the fact that it is used in such an undiscriminating way, indeed almost mechanically, by the two girls. The opening scenes of *La Comtesse d'Escarbagnas* use a very similar cumulative technique to make clear to the spectator the Comtesse's absurd self-importance. Here the terms are not in themselves extravagant, and the comic effect consists in the frequency with which the character introduces, as it were compulsively, references to 'mon laquais', 'mon écuyer', 'mon suisse' (scenes ii to iv). In *Le Bourgeois gentilhomme*, the exposition depends on a rather different technique, whereby very close verbal echoes, dispersed over a number of scenes, produce a leitmotif effect which in this case helps to establish the nature, and the extent, of Monsieur Jourdain's infatuation with the gentry:

—Je me fais habiller aujourd'hui comme les gens de qualité . . . (I, ii)

—Est-ce que les gens de qualité apprennent aussi la musique? (*ibid.*)

—Est-ce que les gens de qualité en ont [sc. des concerts de musique]? (II, i)

—Les personnes de qualité portent les fleurs en enbas? (II, v)

If we leave these examples of the ways in which the behaviour of Molière's *imaginaires* is exploited for purposes of verbal comedy, and turn now to other aspects of the playwright's comic technique, a parallel can clearly be seen in the character whose compulsive behaviour gives rise to a series of situations, all of them variations on the same basic incident. We have already looked briefly at the plot of *Sganarelle ou le Cocu imaginaire*, in which we laugh at the mechanical effect produced by a succession of scenes in which all four characters repeatedly misinterpret the evidence of their eyes, and conclude that their partners are being unfaithful; however, as we have seen, it is only in the case of Sganarelle himself that such a conclusion depends on a characteristic, temperamental jealousy: as far as the others are concerned, the comic misunderstandings are accidental, and their effects temporary. This is a comedy of situation largely independent of character. But if we turn to the play which followed *Sganarelle – Dom Garcie de Navarre, ou le Prince jaloux* – we find a five-act play whose entire plot is built on a series of incidents in which the central character's jealousy leads him to misinterpret what he sees, and to accuse Done Elvire time and again of being unfaithful to him.

Dom Garcie de Navarre was not a successful play; indeed, it stands out in Molière's career as one of the very few failures. The accepted explanation for this used to be that the play represented a last attempt on the part of a frustrated actor who still hoped for success in serious drama,[9] to provide a heroic, or even a tragic,[10] role for himself. However, as I have suggested elsewhere,[11] the plot-pattern of this play is very much that of a comedy, even if the heroic tone of the alexandrines, and the sentimental jargon which composes much of the dialogue, remind one of Corneille (especially, perhaps, of the 'comédie héroïque' *Don Sanche d'Aragon* of 1649) rather than of Molière's own verse style in, say, *Sganarelle ou le Cocu imaginaire*. P. A. Chapman, among others, suggests that Molière was trying to fit a romantic hero into a comic plot:

> Molière was here attempting to create for himself a heroic role. Don Garcie is valorous on the battlefield, submissive before his mistress, endowed with those qualities of high-minded generosity which Corneille and his successors had led audiences to look for in a hero. Yet when Molière tries to get this figure into the plot which he has chosen, what does happen? It is somewhat as if, in an Italian comedy, a mask were put upon the figure of the lover. A 'character' is drawn, with a single, dominant, invincible trait, which is jealousy.[12]

But I think such a view of the play rests on a mistaken assumption, that Molière set out to create a 'hero' who should arouse admiration, not a 'character' whose jealous obsession should impose a comic pattern on the play. In fact, it would be more reasonable to suggest that if there is a certain incongruity between character and plot in

[9] 'L'acteur ambitionnait encore les lauriers tragiques', Vedel, *Deux Classiques*, p. 292.
[10] Brisson, *Molière*, p. 67, writes of Molière's lack of success 'dans un rôle tragique'.
[11] See Chapter 1, note 13.
[12] *The Spirit of Molière: An Interpretation* (Princeton, 1940), p. 141.

Dom Garcie, that is because Molière was trying to fit a comic character into a romantic plot, not the other way round. The plot is romantic, heroic or romanesque in such features as the presence of the *traître* Dom Lope, who plays *vis-à-vis* Garcie the role of Shakespeare's Iago; the echoes of affairs of state, wars and conspiracies which recur throughout the play; and the part played by coincidence and disguise in some of the scenes in which Garcie's jealousy is revealed. One can see why Thibaudet comments, 'Dans *Don Garcie* les causes occasionnelles de la jalousie viennent toujours du dehors, sont amenées par des coïncidences extraordinaires comme les "étourderies" de Lélie, et rendraient aussi bien jaloux l'homme le plus confiant.'[13] Yet on the other hand, however romanesque in character, these incidents are all linked by Garcie's temperamental failing. No fewer than five times he offends, having vowed he will never repeat his offence: indeed, on the first occasion (I, iii), he is in the middle of his declaration that he is a changed man, when the arrival of a letter addressed to Elvire makes him stop short, once more a prey to jealous suspicions. Elvire, observing this, remarks on what is in effect a temporary 'aliénation':

> A ces regards qu'il jette,
> Vois-je pas que déjà cet écrit l'inquiète?
> Prodigieux effet de son tempérament!
>   . . . Il me semble
> Que vous me répondez d'un ton fort altéré;
> Je vous vois tout à coup le visage égaré:
> Ce changement soudain a lieu de me surprendre;
> D'où peut-il provenir? le pourrait-on apprendre?
> — D'un mal qui tout à coup vient d'attaquer mon coeur. (327–37)

And when she offers him the letter to read, as proof of her innocence, her exhortation:

> Ah! prince faible! Hé bien! par cet écrit
> Guérissez-le, ce mal: il n'est que dans l'esprit (lines 341–2)

makes it abundantly clear that Dom Garcie, like Molière's other *imaginaires*, lives in a mental world remote from reality. This contrast between the real and the illusory is emphasised through each of the five acts as the Prince, in spite of his protestations, repeatedly puts more faith in the misleading evidence of his eyes, interpreted in the light of his jealous obsession, than in the assurances of the woman he loves. However, there is a final touch of the romanesque. Instead of

[13] 'Molière et la critique', 387.

having to pay the full penalty of his folly like those other jealous *imaginaires* Arnolphe and Alceste, Garcie is pardoned yet again, and the play ends on an optimistic note of reconciliation.

In other words, the marriage between character and plot in *Dom Garcie de Navarre* may have been only imperfectly achieved; but I think there can be no doubt that in the mind of his creator Dom Garcie belonged to the series of *inadaptés* which starts with the Sganarelle of *Le Cocu imaginaire*, even if his social pedigree appears to set him apart from the half-dozen characters who still bear that name. 'Arnolphe et Alceste', says Thibaudet, 'sont d'autres Garcie dévorés par la jalousie'[14] – and it is as a first draft for these later, more complex, adaptations of the simple Sganarelle that Dom Garcie, 'le prince jaloux', offers most interest to the student of Molière.

(ii) Dom Garcie into Alceste

Whether or not Dom Garcie is 'ridicule en de certaines choses', he is certainly 'honnête homme en d'autres'. His reputation, his bearing, the esteem of other characters combine to stamp him as a chivalrous soldier-prince, an ornament of the court of Léon. The elevation of the style, with its 'heroic' vocabulary and its high degree of abstraction, also contributes to this impression, which is no doubt the principal reason for the inability, or unwillingness, of readers of the play to recognise Garcie as one of Molière's *imaginaires*. If we accept that *Dom Garcie de Navarre* does suffer from a certain contradiction between subject and setting, let us see how Molière has resolved that contradiction in his later plays.

As a study of the dramatic (perhaps we should not beg the question by saying the *comic*) effects of jealousy, *Dom Garcie de Navarre* belongs to an important group of Molière's plays. As its title suggests, *La Jalousie du Barbouillé* shows a very early interest in the theme; and the Barbouillé figure is diversified in the Sganarelles of *Le Cocu imaginaire* and of *Le Mariage forcé*, before reaching its fullest development in George Dandin. Despite his family likeness to the other Sganarelles, the central character of *L'École des maris*, as we see him, is too complacent to be jealous; though it might be said that the dénouement of that play not only saves Isabelle from marriage to a tyrannical husband, but also rescues Sganarelle himself from the certain torments of jealousy

14 *Ibid.*

after marriage. (His namesake of *Le Mariage forcé*, whose eyes are similarly opened before marriage to what will happen if he marries a woman who does not love him, is nevertheless compelled by his fiancée's family to go through with the match.) There remain three major plays, in addition to *George Dandin*, in which the hero's jealousy is a principal plot-motif: *L'École des femmes, Le Misanthrope* and *Amphitryon*.

It is significant that these four plays all figure prominently among those of Molière's works which pose problems of critical interpretation; in each of these four cases, moreover, the problem concerns the relationship between those aspects of the central character that we may conveniently call, using Molière's own terms, the 'ridicule' and the 'honnête'. It appears to be much easier for spectators and readers to recognise comic folly in the social aspirations of a Jourdain, in the intellectual pretensions of the *femmes savantes*, or in the hypochondria of an Argan, than to see sexual jealousy as a similar source of comic effect. Yet it was precisely apropos of Arnolphe that Molière chose to specify his intentions: Dorante's formula from scene vi of the *Critique*, and Lysidas's description in the same scene of the manner in which Molière, as actor, played the crucial scene with Agnès at the climax of the play, provide us with invaluable evidence of the playwright's conception of the role of Arnolphe.

It may well appear to us that the way in which Arnolphe has been characterised leaves little room for ambiguity. Agnès's innocence, and the obnoxious, inhuman nature of her guardian's ideas on marriage which have led him to refuse her all education:

Épouser une sotte est pour n'être point sot (line 82)

are abundantly evident, it would seem. But if on the one hand G. Michaut, for instance, can dismiss him as 'odieux',[15] on the other hand there is ample testimony to an interpretative tradition, well established in the nineteenth century both in the theatre and on the printed page, which saw Arnolphe as a noble, admirable character, 'très digne d'estime, très digne d'affection',[16] pathetic (if not tragic) in the manner in which he suffers at the hands of 'une fine mouche qui s'entend parfaitement à duper son jaloux sans en avoir l'air et qui

[15] *Pascal, Molière, Musset: Essais de critique et de psychologie* (Paris, 1942), p. 169.
[16] Gustave Planche, *Revue des Deux Mondes* (1856), quoted by Descotes, *Les Grands Rôles*, p. 30.

pratique déjà à ravir les charmantes roueries en usage chez les amoureux'.[17]

How is it that the same role can give rise to two such contradictory interpretations? Does Molière's text really leave this enormous amount of discretion to the individual director, actor or critic? To begin with, certain interpreters have had such a strong subjective, or doctrinaire, approach to Molière that they have been quite unable to let the text speak for itself: this was certainly the case with many readers and spectators of the Romantic generation, who projected their own neurotic phobias onto the playwright and his characters. Seeing themselves as sensitive sufferers in a harsh and hostile world, they created their own Molière, exploited by Court and society and shamelessly deceived by his wife. As Maurice Descotes puts it, 'Pour que leur image de Molière fût parfaite, les Romantiques avaient besoin, si l'on peut dire, d'un Molière cocu, ou tout au moins ravagé par la jalousie. Cette triste situation était la condition même de son génie.'[18] This distorted view of Molière's life carried with it a similar bias in the interpretation of his characters: of such among them, at any rate, as could be seen as the expression of his own unhappiness. And that he should have created a series of figures 'ravagés par la jalousie' was naturally taken to be a further indication of what he himself suffered:

> Les tortures de la jalousie peuvent avoir fait sortir Othello et Alceste tout armés du poignard et de l'épée, des fronts divins de Shakespeare et de Molière.[19]

The more obviously farcical *jaloux*, from Le Barbouillé to the Sganarelle of *Le Cocu imaginaire*, hardly lend themselves to this sort of identification with their creator. But from *Dom Garcie* onwards, every *jaloux* who is also an *honnête homme* was commonly seen by the Romantics – and is still sometimes seen – as the melancholy reflection of an unhappy playwright's bitter disillusionment with marriage and the opposite sex. And while a large part of this critical bias can be explained by subjective, a priori attitudes on the part of the critics concerned, it must be conceded that Molière's distinctive formula, setting the comic folly of his characters in a framework of more sympathetic features, inevitably leaves room for a genuine divergence

[17] G. d'Heylli, *Journal intime de la Comédie-Française* (1853), quoted Descotes, *Les Grands Rôles*, p. 50.
[18] *Molière et sa fortune littéraire* (Bordeaux, 1970), p. 84.
[19] Vigny, *De Mlle Sedaine* (1841), quoted *ibid*.

of opinion in some cases, even among those who are willing to let the text speak for itself.

In the case of Arnolphe, these sympathetic features can readily be identified: his generosity towards Horace (cited by Lysidas in the *Critique*); the 'man of the world' side to his character, which has resulted in the esteem of Chrysalde and others; and his assumption of a new life-style as Monsieur de la Souche. In other words, Arnolphe is presented (if less fully than Orgon or Monsieur Jourdain) as a rich bourgeois with a recognisable niche in contemporary French society. What makes him at the same time comic is not the simple fact of his alienation from the world around him, deriving from his obsession, which could equally well be a subject for pathos, or even tragedy – Othello could after all be said to suffer from the same alienation – but the way in which this is given dramatic expression.

The setting of the play is by no means irrelevant in this connection. The action of *L'École des femmes* takes place out of doors: we are asked to accept a stylised comic convention stretching back to the theatre of the Romans. Moreover, the structure of the play includes an equally stylised dénouement; the patterned *comique* of the scene with the Notaire, who for over twenty lines carries on a conversation with Arnolphe, who is talking to himself, unaware of the other's presence; and the knockabout farce of the scenes with Alain and Georgette. On the other hand, it is not simply a case of a rounded, credible character being made to appear ridiculous by the dramatic context into which he is put, reducing what would otherwise be serious drama to the level of broad comedy or farce. Much more important still are the ways in which Arnolphe himself constantly undercuts the serious, sympathetic aspects of his personality. First of all, by the sort of comic incongruity which J. D. Hubert has well analysed,[20] the contrast in stylistic register between some of the soliloquies in which the character comments on his repeated discomfiture, and charts the progress of his growing jealousy:

> Car enfin de mon coeur le trouble impérieux
> N'eût pu se renfermer tout entier à ses yeux;
> Il eût fait éclater l'ennui qui me dévore . . .
> Éloignement fatal! Voyage malheureux! (lines 373–5, 385)

> Ciel! que mon coeur pâtit! (line 406)

[20] 'L'École des femmes, tragédie burlesque?', *Revue des Sciences Humaines*, XCVII (1960), 41–52.

> Quoi, l'astre qui s'obstine à me désespérer
> Ne me donnera pas le temps de respirer? (lines 1182–3)

and the earthy vigour of his language elsewhere:

> Sans cesse nuit et jour je te caresserai,
> Je te bouchonnerai, baiserai, mangerai. (lines 1594–5)

Of all Molière's plays, *L'École des femmes* contains by far the largest proportion of soliloquies: Arnolphe speaks nearly two hundred lines alone, well over a tenth of the total text. This feature helps to establish an obvious stylistic link with tragedy, but it is important to distinguish what sort of stylistic link it is. In fact, it stamps the play as a 'tragédie burlesque', to use Hubert's label.[21] The bourgeois setting, the close relationship with a pair of oafish servants, the crudity of the character's own utterances when his feelings get the better of him:

> Ouf! Je ne puis parler, tant je suis prévenu,
> Je suffoque, et voudrais me pouvoir mettre nu (lines 393–4)

all make Arnolphe's high-flown appeals to the destiny that is persecuting him sound very much like a comic pose. In any case, what he invokes as his 'astre', the symbol of an ineluctable tragic fate, is clearly shown to be something much more down-to-earth: not the tragic character's noble destiny, but a wholly comic blend of trivial chance and temperamental folly.

Hubert is right to emphasise the 'diversité de tons' which characterises the language of this play: 'Les souffrances d'Arnolphe, d'autant plus qu'elles s'expriment souvent dans le vocabulaire de la tragédie, se caractérisent par leur discontinuité, par leur isolement: elles ont beau être réelles et parfaitement justifiées par les événements, elles semblent toujours déplacées et saugrenues.'[22] This is no mere stylistic virtuosity on the author's part, but something intimately related to the central character of the *imaginaire* in his lack of permanent contact with reality. The elevated style of Arnolphe's 'heroic' soliloquies and other similar passages reflects not only his solipsistic retreat into a fantasy world but also his vanity and pretentiousness, of which the most eloquent proof, for contemporary spectators, would no doubt be the 'C'est assez. / Je suis maître, je parle: allez, obéissez' (lines 641–2), a literal repetition of lines 1867–8 of Corneille's *Sertorius*,

---

[21] Or more accurately, perhaps, an example of the mock-heroic, as found in Boileau's *Le Lutrin* or Pope's *Rape of the Lock*. Cf. the distinction drawn by Boileau in the 'Au Lecteur' to his poem.   [22] '*L'École des femmes*', 43.

where the imperious words were spoken not by a humble bourgeois, but by one of Rome's most distinguished generals.[23]

Like the Sganarelle of the earlier *École*, Arnolphe is rendered vulnerable by his self-centred vanity. The plot is an excellent illustration of the *trompeur trompé* mechanism, as all Arnolphe's precautions recoil against him. *L'École des femmes* could well be called, like Scarron's short story which provided one of Molière's sources, 'La Précaution inutile'; but unlike Scarron or Dorimon,[24] Molière makes much more of this formula than mere romanesque situation comedy. The repeated reversals of fortune do derive from a series of coincidences – but also, more fundamentally, from the character of Arnolphe; and the play thus possesses that moral sense that is implicit in all Molière's great comedies. Arnolphe's obsession not only frustrates Agnès's natural development but also clashes with his own instincts – and whereas a mere outline of the plot might suggest that *L'École des femmes* is solely concerned with the traditional opposition between jealous guardian and young lovers, the *comic* structure of the play depends also on the conflict between 'le mécanique' and 'le vivant' in Arnolphe himself. The same prudence which has led Arnolphe to choose a four-year-old child as his future bride, and to bring her up in complete ignorance as a guarantee of her fidelity, ought also to dictate that once his plan has miscarried – when he discovers that Agnès loves Horace – he should abandon it (and perhaps begin his experiment all over again?); instead, he now loves the girl so much himself that he will try any expedient to keep her, on her terms if he can no longer have her on his:

> Tout comme tu voudras tu pourras te conduire;
> Je ne m'explique point, et cela c'est tout dire. (lines 1596–7)

The 'maximes du mariage', the dread of being made a cuckold, have gone by the board: he is desperate to possess Agnès, even if this now means sharing her with another man. For J. Arnavon, and not a few other commentators, this scene, with its humiliating capitulation, is pathetic, not comic. 'Le ton de la comédie est largement dépassé', Arnavon writes; 'L'effet comique . . . est ici secondaire. Ce qui

---

[23] The play had been performed some ten months earlier at the Marais. Of all the plays by authors other than Molière himself, *Sertorius* was the one most frequently performed by Molière's company.

[24] Dorimon's comedy *L'Ecole des cocus, ou la Précaution inutile* (1660–1; see the edition by H. G. Hall, *Australian Journal of French Studies*, IX (1972), 117–47) probably suggested the formula for the titles of *L'École des maris* and *L'École des femmes*.

compte, c'est le trouble de cette âme ravagée, dévastée, scalpée pour ainsi dire.'[25] But the reader can too easily be tempted to take an individual scene in isolation from its dramatic context; and it is essential when we read this scene to remember the context Molière has provided for it in the theatre. We are faced at this point with a character who has been built up through four acts as a consistently comic *imaginaire*, and we cannot suddenly begin to look at him as a pathetic figure. Far from being an interruption of the *comique* of the play, Act V scene iv is the climax of the comic portrayal of the central character.[26]

The first four acts thus serve to establish a point of view. There is no room here for the detailed line-by-line analysis which alone could demonstrate how this point of view is slowly but surely created, in the case of *L'École des femmes* above all by the long opening scene; but at the end of that scene there can be little doubt that any open-minded spectator who has let the text speak for itself will be on the side of one of the protagonists, and against the other. When we talk about 'taking sides' in relation to Molière's characters, it is something that involves not so much distinguishing between moral right on one side and moral wrong on the other, as being persuaded to choose between one character's acceptance of human nature as it is, with all its imperfections, and another character's attempt to impose an artificial model of behaviour, fashioned in the mind of a doctrinaire idealist. Some readers or spectators, as we have seen, are able to achieve a subjective identification with the eccentric individualist who tries to mould the world to his own pattern; but most of us are empiricists, and experience less difficulty in accepting the world as we find it. So that at the end of the long introductory scene of *L'École des femmes*, when the two characters part, each with an aside to the audience in which he expresses his opinion of the other:

> *Chrys.* Ma foi, je le tiens fou de toutes les manières.
> *Arn.* Il est un peu blessé sur certaines matières (lines 195–6)

it is to be expected that the normal spectator, if he has been properly attentive to the course of their conversation, will have no hesitation about which judgement he endorses. In fact, the function of Chrysalde, and of the other so-called 'raisonneurs' in Molière's theatre, far from acting as the author's mouthpiece in order to indoctrinate the

---

[25] *L'École des femmes de Molière* (Paris, 1939), pp. 297, 314.
[26] For a more detailed analysis, see my edition of the play (Oxford, 1963), pp. xv–xix.

spectator, is to represent a common denominator of the values and attitudes to be found among the audience.

If Molière's blend of the 'ridicule' and the 'honnête' gives rise to certain problems of interpretation with regard to Arnolphe, the case of Alceste poses problems of quite a different order; and it may well seem as though in *Le Misanthrope* the balance of sympathetic and extravagant elements in the main character is so delicately poised that any increase in the former would tip the scales decisively in favour of the 'honnête' and make it quite impossible to sustain a comic interpretation. For some distinguished commentators, indeed, such a tipping of the scales has already taken place. And yet, if we take a close and careful look at Act I scene i of *Le Misanthrope*, does it not produce very much the same effect as the corresponding scene in *L'École des femmes*? From the opening lines, the dynamic exchanges between the choleric Alceste and the urbane Philinte almost force the spectator to take sides. It is certainly difficult to remain detached and objective; and the common run of spectators surely find themselves siding with the representative of normal civilised behaviour: finding the dogmatic, intolerant Alceste somewhat lacking by the standards of civility and *savoir-faire*, they submit him to the critical judgement of their laughter.

When Alceste's intemperate outburst:

> Morbleu! c'est une chose indigne, lâche, infâme,
> De s'abaisser ainsi jusqu'à trahir son âme;
> Et si, par un malheur, j'en avais fait autant,
> Je m'irais, de regret, pendre tout à l'instant

is countered by Philinte with perfect equanimity:

> Je ne vois pas, pour moi, que le cas soit pendable,
> Et je vous supplierai d'avoir pour agréable
> Que je me fasse un peu grâce sur votre arrêt
> Et ne me pende pas pour cela, s'il vous plaît; (lines 25–32)

or when Philinte's friendly warning:

> Je vous dirai tout franc que cette maladie,
> Partout où vous allez, donne la comédie,
> Et qu'un si grand courroux contre les moeurs du temps
> Vous tourne en ridicule auprès de bien des gens

is rejected out of hand by the *atrabilaire* Alceste:

Tant mieux, morbleu! tant mieux, c'est ce que je demande;
Ce m'est un fort bon signe, et ma joie en est grande:
Tous les hommes me sont à tel point odieux,
Que je serais fâché d'être sage à leurs yeux (lines 105–12)

– this is interpreted by Rousseau, for instance, as evidence of Alceste's
incorruptible virtue, and of Philinte's 'coupable complaisance':[27]

Ce Philinte est le sage de la pièce; un de ces honnêtes gens du grand
monde, dont les maximes ressemblent beaucoup à celles des fripons; de
ces gens si doux, si modérés, qui trouvent toujours que tout va bien,
parce qu'ils ont intérêt que rien n'aille mieux; qui sont toujours contents
de tout le monde, parce qu'ils ne se soucient de personne; qui, autour
d'une bonne table, soutiennent qu'il n'est pas vrai que le peuple ait faim;
qui, le gousset bien garni, trouvent fort mauvais qu'on déclame en faveur
des pauvres; qui, de leur maison bien fermée, verraient voler, piller,
égorger, massacrer tout le genre humain sans se plaindre: attendu que
Dieu les a doués d'une douceur très méritoire à supporter les malheurs
d'autrui.[28]

To the unbiased reader, such an interpretation is a travesty of the
scene as Molière wrote it, and tells us much more about Rousseau
than it does about Molière's play. But similar, though perhaps less
extreme, views of what Alceste and Philinte respectively represent are
not uncommon in our own day;[29] and on the whole, Philinte has
generally had an unfavourable reception.[30] To the spectator or reader
who allows Molière's text to speak for itself, however, it would seem
difficult not to conclude that Act I scene i of *Le Misanthrope* deliberately probes the hollowness of Alceste's 'sincérité', and demonstrates
unambiguously that his pretended idealism, which is far from disin-
terested:

Je veux qu'on me distingue; et pour le trancher net,
L'ami du genre humain n'est point du tout mon fait (lines 63–4)

rests on the same self-centred basis as Arnolphe's initial com-
placency.

Is Alceste an *honnête homme*, as Rousseau and others maintain,[31] or is

[27] *Lettre à M. d'Alembert*, ed. M. Fuchs (Lille–Geneva, 1948), p. 50.
[28] *Ibid.*, pp. 51–2.
[29] See for instance the exchange of views on this subject between J. Arnavon and
G. Michaut in Michaut, *Pascal, Molière, Musset*, pp. 160–76.
[30] But cf. Thomas, 'Philinte and Éliante', and see above, p. 67.
[31] For a modern expression of this view, cf. M. Gutwirth: 'Alceste est un *honnête homme*: il
ne tient ni à se passer des hommes ni à les supprimer. Il veut vivre avec eux dans la
bonne foi, la franchise, la décence. Il veut pouvoir les estimer. . .', *Molière ou
l'invention comique* (Paris, 1966), p. 189.

he Thibaudet's 'honnête homme imaginaire'? If we look again, first at the opening scene with Philinte, and then at scene ii with Oronte, we may observe that these scenes not only portray the obvious incompatibility between Alceste and the society he lives in – the incongruity between a thoroughgoing individualist and a society of courtiers, if not of *honnêtes gens* – but that there is another source of comedy interwoven with this, in that Alceste himself clearly aspires to be regarded as an *honnête homme,* and a somewhat subtler comic effect derives from his attempts to adapt his unsociable temperament to a sophisticated code of social behaviour. In both cases – Alceste's attempts to conform, and the explosive outbursts in which he rejects conformity – a genuinely exemplary figure provides the necessary contrast: that of Philinte, and behind him the urbane, aristocratic ethic that he represents.

The traits of character and behaviour that separate Alceste from the *honnêtes gens* may seem more obvious at first sight than his attempts to conform to their way of life. He is irritable and quick-tempered, he knows no moderation, he pretends to a stiff, austere form of virtue that seems just as archaic by comparison with the manners of his age – Philinte refers to 'Cette grande raideur des vertus des vieux âges' (line 153) – as does his manner of dress by comparison with the elegant fashions of his day. However, as T. E. Lawrenson has recently shown, it is quite likely that 'l'homme aux rubans verts', far from representing the fashions of a generation long past, wishes to indicate, by choosing for his ribbons a colour very much in vogue, a desire to be sartorially abreast of his times. It is true that Alceste scoffs at certain extravagances of current fashion, illustrated by Clitandre's 'vaste rhingrave' and 'grands canons'; but his own way of dressing – both the ribbons themselves and their colour, if Lawrenson is right – seems to signify at any rate a desire to be thought to dress with taste.[32] If something went wrong – and that Célimène should characterise him as 'l'homme aux rubans verts' suggests that all was not quite right with Alceste's wardrobe – it may well be that the knowledgeable spectator, aware of the discrepancy between wish and fulfilment, would appreciate all the better the solecism of the green ribbons.

I think it can be shown that a similar solecism underlies Alceste's behaviour in ethical matters. All the time he is contravening in

---

[32] 'The Wearing o' the Green: Yet Another Look at "L'homme aux rubans verts"' in Howarth and Thomas (eds.), *Molière: Stage and Study,* pp. 163–9.

various ways the code of *honnêteté*, he is forever proclaiming, implicitly if not explicitly, his wish to be considered an *honnête homme*. And the explicit references themselves are numerous enough; indeed, one could claim with some justice that the whole of Act I scene i constitutes a debate on the nature of *honnêteté*. It is clear that what Alceste means by an *honnête homme* is not precisely the sort of *honnête homme* that Philinte represents: if we take E. Livet's definition 'L'honnête homme . . . c'était l'homme du monde homme de bien',[33] then one would have to say that the proportions of the two components vary, and that for Alceste the 'homme de bien' is more prominent, while for Philinte it is the 'homme du monde'. But if this is quite evidently the case when Alceste uses the term 'homme d'honneur' (lines 16, 35) or when he uses the superlative 'le plus honnête homme' (line 140), the difference is by no means so striking in line 48, where by implication he appears to enrol himself among the *honnêtes gens* according to the standard usage of the day. If in this opening scene, then, it is a somewhat idiosyncratic version of the concept of *honnêteté* that Alceste is defending, nevertheless in a larger sense he too is defining his ideal code of gentlemanly behaviour within this particular society to which both men belong. But although he seems to subscribe to a code of behaviour not unlike that of Philinte (and we shall see more evidence of this in Act I scene ii), his lack of restraint, his atrabilious temperament, his refusal to believe in the realities of human nature, constantly give the lie to his ability to put his principles into practice; so that one might be tempted to modify Dorine's admonition to Orgon, and to comment: 'Vous êtes honnête homme, et vous vous emportez!'

Like so many of Molière's other *imaginaires*, Alceste is a misfit, a nonconformist who is incapable of learning the rules of the social game. His exclamation 'Je veux qu'on me distingue' can nevertheless be construed as a keen desire to belong to that élite of *honnêtes gens* whose merit won them universal recognition: one has only to read Méré's *Discours* to be struck by a similar craving for distinction – expressed, of course, a good deal less ingenuously. Like the true *honnête homme*, Alceste needs the society of other men in order to satisfy his craving; but the logic of his absolutism is such that the only place where he would be able to practise his peculiar brand of *honnêteté* proves to be

> . . . un endroit écarté
> Où d'être homme d'honneur on ait la liberté. (lines 1805–6)

[33] *Lexique de la langue de Molière* (3 vols., Paris, 1895–7).

When we turn from theory to practice, and look for the implementation of Alceste's ideas on *honnêteté*, it is the 'scène du sonnet' that offers the most striking example. The particular feature of *honnêteté* that is in question here had been clearly defined by Pascal:

> C'est une fausse louange qu'on donne à un homme quand on dit de lui, lorsqu'il entre, qu'il est fort habile en poésie et c'est une mauvaise marque, quand on n'a pas recours à un homme quand il s'agit de juger de quelques vers.[34]

The *honnête homme* is a cultured amateur, of whose taste there is no room for doubt; and an unmistakable line of demarcation separates him from the professional man of letters. Not only does Oronte's initial approach to Alceste:

> Enfin je suis à vous de toutes les manières;
> Et comme votre esprit a de grandes lumières,
> Je viens, pour commencer entre nous ce beau noeud,
> Vous montrer un sonnet que j'ai fait depuis peu,
> Et savoir s'il est bon qu'au public je l'expose (lines 293–7)

enable us to situate Act I scene ii in this precise context, but the latter's replies make it quite clear that he too takes for granted the same sort of distinction between the *honnête homme* and the poet that Saint-Évremond, for instance, expresses in the following passage:

> La poésie demande un génie particulier, qui ne s'accommode pas trop avec le bon sens. Tantôt c'est le langage des dieux, tantôt c'est le langage des fous, rarement celui d'un honnête homme . . . Ce n'est pas qu'il n'y ait quelque chose de galant à faire agréablement des vers; mais il faut que nous soyons bien maîtres de notre génie; autrement l'esprit est possédé de je ne sais quoi d'étranger qui ne lui permet pas de disposer assez facilement de lui-même.[35]

In his capacity as a would-be *honnête homme*, Alceste advises the aspiring author in remarkably similar terms. 'Il faut qu'un galant homme', he says (and here, as often, the term *galant homme* should be taken as synonymous with *honnête homme*):

> Il faut qu'un galant homme ait toujours grand empire
> Sur les démangeaisons qui nous prennent d'écrire. (lines 345–6)

The desire to see oneself in print 'a gâté de fort honnêtes gens' (line 360), and he earnestly pleads with Oronte:

---

[34] *Pensées*, ed. Lafuma, no. 984.
[35] 'Sur la poésie', in *Oeuvres*, ed. R. de Planhol (Paris, 1927), I.

> Croyez-moi, résistez à vos tentations,
> Dérobez au public ces occupations;
> Et n'allez point quitter, de quoi que l'on vous somme,
> Le nom que, dans la Cour, vous avez d'honnête homme,
> Pour prendre, de la main d'un avide imprimeur,
> Celui de ridicule et misérable auteur. (lines 367–72)

His comic evasions (comic, because Oronte has begged him to give his opinion with the same 'sincérité' that he has so fervently preached to Philinte in the opening scene), his

> . . . un jour, à quelqu'un, dont je tairai le nom,
> Je disais . . . , (lines 343–4)

his thrice-repeated 'Je ne dis pas cela': all these are notable concessions to the conciliatory spirit of genuine *honnêteté*. But it is not difficult to guess, from the tone of his asides to Philinte, that Alceste will not be able to sustain his role for very long. And indeed, when his self-control breaks down, giving way to the outburst we are expecting, he not only abandons any attempt at the civility required of the *honnête homme,* but goes to the other extreme, and displays all the obstinacy and self-importance that are associated with the pedant, whom the *honnêtes gens* regarded as their pet aversion.

The question is often asked: did Molière prefer, and expect his audience to prefer, Oronte's sonnet or Alceste's 'vieille chanson'? But such a question is really irrelevant, for if the dramatic context presents the sonnet in an absurd light (as it must obviously do, with Oronte's fatuously self-satisfied delivery), it also makes Alceste and his song look ridiculous. Alceste is ridiculous because he proves unable to maintain the pose of the *honnête homme,* whose tact and diplomacy enable him to deal with awkward situations; and in abandoning this pose he exhibits a complete lack of proportion, magnifying a trifle into an issue of moral significance:

> Ce style figuré, dont on fait vanité,
> Sort du bon caractère et de la vérité;
> Ce n'est que jeu de mots, qu'affectation pure,
> Et ce n'est point ainsi que parle la nature.
> Le méchant goût du siècle, en cela, me fait peur . . . (lines 385–9)

The intrinsic merits, or defects, of the 'vieille chanson' are therefore less important than the use Alceste makes of it, to support an attitude that, by contrast not just with the stance adopted by Philinte but also

148

with his own initial pose, can only be described as pompous and pedantic.[36]

Of the three parallel subthemes by which the principal theme of *la sincérité* is explored – *poésie*, *procès* and *passion* – the first reveals most clearly the comic disparity between Alceste's so-called 'honnêteté' (he says himself in line 1511, referring to his conduct towards Oronte, that all he has done is to treat him 'avec honnêteté') and the behaviour of the genuine *honnêtes gens*. The second is treated less fully, and here it is less a question of Alceste attempting, but failing, to live up to the code of *honnêteté* than of his rejecting that code, as expounded by Philinte, in favour of his own highly individual sense of honour. Here, then, the 'homme de bien' definitely predominates over the 'homme du monde' – but it is a most idiosyncratic conception of the 'homme de bien' that is displayed by Alceste, whose uncompromising absolutism makes him incapable of distinguishing between abstract principles of justice and the customary judicial procedures. When in reply to Philinte's question:

> Mais qui voulez-vous donc qui pour vous sollicite? –

a reasonable query, in which it would surely be wrong to see any suggestion of corrupt practices[37] – he retorts:

> Qui je veux? La raison, mon bon droit, l'équité, (lines 186–7)

he places himself in clear-cut opposition to the common-sense pragmatism of the *honnêtes gens*, for whom Philinte's phlegmatic

> Je prends tout doucement les hommes comme ils sont (line 163)

could well serve as the motto. With regard to his lawsuit, even Alceste himself is lucid enough to realise that he lacks the philosophical temperament that would enable him, like Philinte, to bear the vicissitudes of fortune:

> Je me verrai trahir, mettre en pièces, voler,
> Sans que je sois . . . Morbleu! je ne veux point parler,
> Tant ce raisonnement est plein d'impertinence. (lines 179–81)

---

[36] If my contention that we find both Alceste and Oronte comic in this scene seems to contradict the view advanced elsewhere, that most comic scenes involve 'laughing with' as well as 'laughing at', I would suggest that the role played by Philinte here is not unimportant in this respect. Philinte is evidently enjoying the confrontation, and doing his best to help it along (lines 319–38). We 'laugh with' Philinte: his attitude here seems designed to guide the audience's reaction.

[37] See Michaut, *Pascal, Molière, Musset*, pp. 166–7.

And when he admits:

> Je n'ai point sur ma langue un assez grand empire;
> De ce que je dirais je ne répondrais pas,
> Et je me jetterais cent choses sur les bras, (lines 1574–6)

he acknowledges that self-control, a quality so essential to the *honnête homme*, does not form part of his make-up.

The encounter with Arsinoé provides a similar test of the hero's 'honnêteté'. At first, her flattery, like Oronte's, is met with the unassuming modesty of the *honnête homme* who eschews all ostentation. Both Oronte and Arsinoé, in seeking him out, are satisfying that 'soif de distinction' to which Alceste has confessed in the opening scene; his initial response in both cases is consistent with the self-deprecating modesty of the genuine *honnête homme*.

> Monsieur, c'est trop d'honneur que vous me voulez faire

he says in one case (line 287); and in the other:

> Moi, Madame! Et sur quoi pourrais-je en rien prétendre?
> Quel service à l'État est-ce qu'on m'a vu rendre?
> Qu'ai-je fait, s'il vous plaît, de si brillant de soi,
> Pour me plaindre à la cour qu'on ne fait rien pour moi? (lines 1053–6)

And even when he mentions what he evidently regards as his most distinctive quality, this takes the form of a modest disclaimer of which even such an authority as Méré would no doubt have approved. He says to Oronte:

> . . . j'ai le défaut
> D'être un peu plus sincère, en cela, qu'il ne faut (lines 299–300)

and to Arsinoé:

> Le Ciel ne m'a point fait, en me donnant le jour,
> Une âme compatible avec l'air de la cour;
> Je ne me trouve point les vertus nécessaires
> Pour y bien réussir et faire mes affaires.
> Être franc et sincère est mon plus grand talent;
> Je ne sais point jouer les hommes en parlant;
> Et qui n'a pas le don de cacher ce qu'il pense
> Doit faire en ce pays fort peu de résidence. (lines 1083–90)

With Arsinoé, as with Oronte, he is able to maintain this courtier's manner just so long as his pose as an *honnête homme* is not directly challenged; to begin with, he even appears to be able to respond to her insinuations about Célimène's behaviour in a spirit of magnanimity and detachment:

> Mais, en disant cela, songez-vous, je vous prie,
> Que cette personne est, Madame, votre amie? (lines 1195–6)

But by the end of the scene he has begun to weaken:

> ... sur ce sujet quoi que l'on nous expose,
> Les doutes sont fâcheux plus que toute autre chose;
> Et je voudrais, pour moi, qu'on ne me fît savoir
> Que ce qu'avec clarté l'on peut me faire voir. (lines 1121–4)

And by the time Act IV opens, Arsinoé having in the meantime shown him Célimène's letter, his 'honnêteté' has already given way to the fundamental egoism of the character. It is Alceste's egoism that dictates the proposal of marriage to Éliante in IV, ii; it is his egoism that provokes the impassioned outbursts against Célimène in IV, iii. Indeed, from beginning to end of Act IV Alceste abandons all pretence of acting as an *honnête homme*; as so often happens with Molière's *imaginaires*, his love proves to be the crucial test of his assumed personality: the precarious mask of his 'honnêteté' slips aside, revealing the self-centred character beneath.

Both the fact that Célimène later proves to be guilty in some degree towards Alceste, and the much-discussed problem of the extent of her guilt, are of secondary importance here; neither of these considerations affects the essential development, by means of which the *honnête homme imaginaire* is revealed as a self-seeking individualist incapable of adapting himself to the conventions of the society in which he lives. Though in parenthesis, Jacques Guicharnaud is surely right to argue for an interpretation which at least leaves Célimène's objective guilt a matter of doubt:

> Répétons-le: faire de Célimène une menteuse, une trompeuse systémati-que, c'est réduire la pièce à un élégant vaudeville sur le 'pré-cocuage'. Accepter Célimène sur parole, comme nous croyons honnête de le faire ...

– an extremely interesting choice of epithet, in the context of our present enquiry; for it is precisely in his failure to give Célimène the benefit of the doubt that Alceste betrays his inability to sustain his pose as an *honnête homme* –

> ... c'est révéler la richesse de la pièce, sur le plan de l'intuition moliéresque aussi bien que sur celui de la prise de conscience de l'impasse comique.[38]

[38] *Molière: une aventure théâtrale*, p. 515.

151

Of all Molière's major scenes, Act IV scene iii is the one which most needs to be set firmly in the dramatic context provided by the structure of the play. It is no doubt tempting to consider it in isolation as a brilliant *tour de force*, a masterpiece of psychological comedy; and when this is done, it is perhaps not surprising that it should often be looked at through Alceste's own eyes. But Alceste's relationship with Célimène cannot be put into a compartment by itself: it is intimately bound up with the whole complex of his attitudes to the world around him; and to treat it on its own, as something detached from the rest of the play, is to falsify the picture Molière so carefully built up. Act IV scene iii not only brings this relationship to crisis-point, but is also the climax of the dramatic analysis of the central themes of *sincérité* and *honnêteté*. It is surely no accident that Alceste comes to his energetic denunciation of Célimène's 'treachery' fresh from having himself just offered marriage to Éliante. Without giving Célimène a hearing, his wounded vanity is prepared to take instant revenge; and his declaration to Éliante comically juxtaposes the 'ardeur si constante' that Célimène has betrayed, with :

> les sincères voeux,
> . . . le profond amour, les soins respectueux,
> Les devoirs empressés et l'assidu service
> Dont ce coeur va vous faire un ardent sacrifice. (lines 1250, 1255–8)

It is impossible to say why Molière should have decided to reuse material from *Dom Garcie de Navarre* when he came to write *Le Misanthrope*. Other instances of the playwright's borrowing from himself are rare and fragmentary, so that the repetition of some sixty or seventy lines, either wholly or in part, from an earlier play, stands out as unique in his work. Two reflections seem to impose themselves. First, that there must have existed in Molière's mind a certain resemblance between the heroes of the two plays; and since the borrowed passages all concern the nature of Garcie's love for Elvire and the extravagances to which his jealousy constantly drives him, it seems legitimate to read the same passages as evidence of a similar extravagance on Alceste's part. And second, that the heroic vocabulary and elevated style which were appropriate to a play whose plot mixes matters of state with affairs of the heart, and in which Elvire has to contend not only with Garcie's jealous suspicions, but also with the political enmity of the usurper Mauregat, are absurdly incongruous in the everyday setting of a Paris *salon*. If we look at the opening exchanges of Act IV scene iii:

O Ciel! de mes transports puis-je être ici le maître?
—Ouais! quel est donc le trouble où je vous vois paraître?
Et que me veulent dire, et ces soupirs poussés,
Et ces sombres regards que sur moi vous lancez?
—Que toutes les horreurs dont une âme est capable
A vos déloyautés n'ont rien de comparable;
Que le sort, les démons, et le Ciel en courroux
N'ont jamais rien produit de si méchant que vous.
—Voilà certainement des douceurs que j'admire.
—Ah! ne plaisantez point, il n'est pas temps de rire.
Rougissez bien plutôt, vous en avez raison;
Et j'ai de sûrs témoins de votre trahison . . . (lines 1277–88)

it is almost as if the two characters are speaking lines from different plays. What we have said above about the verbal comedy deriving from a contrast of stylistic registers in *L'École des femmes* applies even more clearly here.[39] To take one detailed example: analysis of Alceste's characteristic vocabulary reveals a score of instances in which he uses the words *trahir, traître* or *trahison*. Only two of these instances suggest a colourful colloquial use, analogous to his forceful oaths of Act I scene i;[40] for the rest (especially if we add the occasional term like *noirceur, outrage, perfidie*), we can distinguish a consistent thematic use of the sort of language that would have excited no comment in a contemporary tragedy, but which is hardly appropriate to the 'conversation des honnêtes gens'. As J. D. Hubert comments:

> The point is that Molière wished to put in the mouth of his misanthrope the most intensely dramatic speech available, abounding in heroic and even tragic overtones. That the words did not quite fit the hero's situation probably suited the playwright's purpose, for the discrepancy between speech and action drives home the fact that Alceste is really living in an imaginary world, quite unrelated at times to his surroundings. Thus the chief value of his intensely dramatic speech stems from its irrelevance. It reveals Alceste in his true light as a mock-heroic character who vainly attempts to transform the banalities of Parisian salons into momentous, anachronistic adventures.[41]

[39] The editors of the Grands Écrivains edition (*Oeuvres*, ed. Despois and Mesnard) comment (Vol. ii, p. 302) on the line 'Mon astre me disait ce que j'avais à craindre' (*D. Garcie*, line 1281, *Mis.*, line 1294): 'Cet *astre* cependant, dans la bouche de ce prince romanesque. . ., paraît plus naturel que dans celle d'Alceste.' Moreover, as the same footnote points out, in *Dom Garcie* Elvire too uses similar imagery; not so Célimène, however.

[40] Oronte uses the verb quite differently, in a figurative sense typical of *précieux* hyperbole (line 303); only Arisinoé (line 1110) uses it in the same way as Alceste, but she can be presumed to be adopting his idiom in telling him of Célimène's 'betrayal' of his love.

[41] *Molière and the Comedy of Intellect* (Berkeley, Cal., 1962), p. 146. See also H. G. Hall's

Célimène's other lovers, when they in their turn are also 'betrayed' by her (V, iv), express their feelings in ordinary, banal terms: it would be quite out of character for Acaste, Clitandre or Oronte to invoke his 'astre' or his tragic fate. And by the same token, the couplet spoken by Alceste at the end of the play as he goes off to seek his 'endroit écarté':

> Trahi de toutes parts, accablé d'injustices,
> Je vais sortir d'un gouffre où triomphent les vices (lines 1803–4)

– a couplet which in a different context might well suggest a poignant and pathetic conclusion – loses a good deal of its poignancy when it is seen as the culmination of the incongruous heroics by which the character constantly seeks to over-dramatise his situation.[42]

This comic exposure of Alceste's character through the flavour of his speech is not the only link with *L'École des femmes*. There is the same intimate relationship between character and action; and just as Arnolphe's desire for Agnès proves stronger than his doctrinaire principles, so too Alceste's 'sincérité' fails to stand up to the test of his love for Célimène. Not only do Alceste's blustering heroics make a comic contrast with Célimène's cool self-control; he allows himself to be manoeuvred into a position in which he explicitly abandons the principles he has so vehemently proclaimed, and pleads with Célimène to deceive him:

> Rendez-moi, s'il se peut, ce billet innocent:
> A vous prêter les mains ma tendresse consent;
> Efforcez-vous ici de paraître fidèle,
> Et je m'efforcerai, moi, de vous croire telle. (lines 1387–90)

'Être' has given way to 'paraître'; and this abdication of all Alceste has stood for up to now is neatly underlined by Célimène's reply:

> Allez, vous êtes fou, dans vos transports jaloux,
> Et ne méritez pas l'amour qu'on a pour vous.
> Je voudrais bien savoir qui pourrait me contraindre
> A descendre, pour vous, aux bassesses de feindre,
> Et pourquoi, si mon coeur penchait d'autre côté,
> Je ne le dirais pas avec sincérité. (lines 1391–6)

excellent article 'The Literary Context of Molière's *Le Misanthrope*', *Studi Francesi*, XIV (1970), 29–38.

[42] Indeed, Alceste's persistent self-dramatisation, combined with the friendly concern shown by Philinte in the closing couplet of the play, suggest that instead of departing for his 'désert', Alceste will probably remain in Parisian society, and that it may not be long before he is paying court to Célimène again.

'Sincérité' has passed over to her side, and it is now Alceste who is guilty of the 'bassesses de feindre': a remarkably effective reversal of fortune, which depends entirely on the misanthropist's character. Like Arnolphe's, Alceste's principles prove to be only skin-deep, and they are totally discarded in this desperate, instinctive attempt to win Célimène – or at any rate, to have her on her terms if he can no longer have her on his own.

The declaration of the 'extreme' quality of his love, with which this crucial scene ends:

> Ah! rien n'est comparable à mon amour extrême;
> Et dans l'ardeur qu'il a de se montrer à tous,
> Il va jusqu'à former des souhaits contre vous.
> Oui, je voudrais qu'aucun ne vous trouvât aimable,
> Que vous fussiez réduite en un sort misérable,
> Que le Ciel, en naissant, ne vous eût donné rien,
> Que vous n'eussiez ni rang, ni naissance, ni bien,
> Afin que de mon coeur l'éclatant sacrifice
> Vous pût d'un pareil sort réparer l'injustice,
> Et que j'eusse la joie et la gloire, en ce jour,
> De vous voir tenir tout des mains de mon amour (lines 1422–32)

is the final proof, if proof were needed, of the *imaginaire* world that Alceste inhabits. We may take it, perhaps, as a subconscious acknowledgement that he, like Arnolphe, cannot hold his own in a free exchange on equal terms with a clever, sophisticated woman of the world. Arnolphe has sought to redress the balance in his case by educating his child-bride in complete ignorance from her earliest years; Alceste compensates by creating a mental image of an outcast from society, despised by her fellows, who would owe everything to the magnanimity of her noble lover. But however hard we may try to discover a credible psychological urge behind such a fantasy, it needs only Célimène's matter-of-fact comment:

> C'est me vouloir du bien d'une étrange manière! (line 1433)

to show up this would-be Pygmalion in all his comic absurdity.

However, for all his absurdity, Alceste has always been the most sympathetic of Molière's heroes. Even if we leave out of account the very subjective judgements of Rousseau and the Romantics, or the moralising interpretation of a Beaumarchais, for whom *Le Misanthrope* was evidently a sombre *drame bourgeois*:

Quand Molière a bien humilié la coquette ou coquine du *Misanthrope*, par la lecture publique de ses lettres à tous ses amants, il la laisse avilie sous les coups qu'il lui a portés; il a raison: qu'en ferait-il? Vicieuse par goût et par choix, veuve aguerrie, femme de cour, sans aucune excuse d'erreur, et fléau d'un fort honnête homme, il l'abandonne à nos mépris, et telle est sa moralité[43]

– it is still true that for a great many commentators on the play, the 'honnête' side of Alceste's character is so pronounced as to make them turn a blind eye to his laughable features. La Harpe was not far from the mark when he wrote, addressing Molière:

Le prodige de ton art est d'avoir montré le Misanthrope de manière qu'il n'y a personne, excepté le méchant, qui ne voulût être Alceste avec ses ridicules.[44]

Aglaé, the wife of Anouilh's Alceste-like hero, the Général of *L'Hurluberlu*, seems to express a somewhat similar view when she says to her husband:

C'est aussi, un peu, pour votre rigueur grondeuse que je vous ai aimé, par réaction. A douze ans, j'étais amoureuse d'Alceste en classe de français![45]

If the balance so carefully created by Molière between the 'honnête homme' and the 'ridicule' in Alceste no longer works for some twentieth-century readers and spectators, this is no doubt partly because of the differences between the social and moral climate in which Molière's play is set, and that of our own day; as Jules Lemaître wrote, some eighty years ago: 'Alceste ne peut plus être pour nous ce qu'il était pour les gens du dix-septième siècle.'[46] In each of the areas in which Alceste is at odds with the world around him: his refusal to comply with normal judicial procedure and solicit his judges; his views on fashions in courtiers' dress; his literary taste, preferring a simple old-fashioned song to the *poésie galante* of his own day; and his professed intention to live away from Paris and the Court, in a remote country property – on all of these points, either our views have moved much closer to Alceste's, or else we are prepared to interpret Alceste's views in the light of modern attitudes and to give him the benefit of any doubt. This has not prevented the most clear-sighted of modern

[43] Preface to *Le Mariage de Figaro* (1784).
[44] Quoted by M. Wagner, *Molière and the Age of the Enlightenment*, Studies on Voltaire and the Eighteenth Century, cxii (Banbury, 1973), p. 212.
[45] *L'Hurluberlu, ou le Réactionnaire amoureux* (Paris, 1959), p. 130.
[46] *Impressions de théâtre* (Paris, c. 1900), i, p. 37.

moliéristes[47] from recognising that Alceste's most basic intellectual attitudes – his intolerance, his egocentricity – do not depend on such changes in fashion brought about by social history; but it is surely the case that many neo-Romantics of the 1980s, like their predecessors of the 1830s, find it possible, by a somewhat selective reading of Molière's text, to create an Alceste in their own image.

In fact, there is plenty of evidence of a similar bias among the play's first spectators. The best known of seventeenth-century commentaries on *Le Misanthrope*, on the other hand, recording as it does the reactions of an audience of *honnêtes gens* to the portrait of a would-be *honnête homme* on stage, does full justice to the balance the playwright surely sought to achieve:

> Voilà, Monsieur, ce que je pense de la comédie du Misanthrope amoureux, que je trouve d'autant plus admirable, que le héros en est le plaisant sans être trop ridicule, et qu'il fait rire les honnêtes gens sans dire des plaisanteries fades et basses, comme l'on a accoutumé de voir dans les pièces comiques. Celles de cette nature me semblent plus divertissantes, encore que l'on y rie moins haut; et je crois qu'elles divertissent davantage, qu'elles attachent, et qu'elles font continuellement rire dans l'âme. Le Misanthrope, malgré sa folie, si l'on peut ainsi appeler son humeur, a le caractère d'un honnête homme.[48]

Donneau de Visé's paragraph is a triumphant vindication of the formula outlined in the *Critique de l'École des femmes*. Identification with Alceste's sympathetic qualities should not be so strong as to make us close our eyes to his 'folie'; while our critical recognition of his faults leaves room, if not for admiration, at least for understanding. The result – what de Visé so felicitously calls 'rire dans l'âme' – is neither the punitive, hostile laughter of satire nor the detached, gratuitous laughter of farce, but that rare reflective laughter which is alone capable of producing comedy's equivalent of the tragic catharsis.[49]

(iii) 'Visionnaires' and 'femmes savantes'

Despite the very favourable opinions recorded by Donneau de Visé and other contemporaries, *Le Misanthrope* was far from being the most successful of Molière's plays in his lifetime, even if it was by no means

---

[47] Cf. the quotations from Michaut, Thibaudet and Guicharnaud above.
[48] 'Lettre sur le Misanthrope', in Molière, *Oeuvres*, ed. Despois and Mesnard, v, p. 440.
[49] An earlier version of the foregoing analysis of *Le Misanthrope* was published as 'Alceste, ou l'honnête homme imaginaire', *Revue de l'Histoire du Théâtre* (1974), 93–8.

the initial failure that has sometimes been claimed. It is perhaps for this reason that during the second half of his Paris career Molière produced fewer five-act verse comedies than in the years leading up to *Le Misanthrope*: if we exclude *Tartuffe*, of which a five-act version probably existed before 1666, and *Psyché*, of which Molière was only part-author, we are indeed left with a single play, *Les Femmes savantes* (1672), written in the form to which subsequent critical opinion has attached such a special prestige.[50]

There is an interesting piece of contemporary evidence which suggests that Molière intended *Les Femmes savantes* to occupy a particularly important place among his works; Donneau de Visé's review of the play in the *Mercure Galant* begins:

> Le fameux Molière ne nous a point trompés dans l'espérance qu'il nous avait donnée il y a tantôt quatre ans de faire représenter au Palais-Royal une pièce comique de sa façon qui fût tout à fait achevée.[51]

While opinions may differ as to the precise implications of the term 'achevée', a recent editor expresses the general view when he interprets it as follows: 'Molière seems to have meant *Les Femmes savantes* as his masterpiece and to have given it more attention than any other play.'[52] Indeed, from the point of view of form the new play can be seen to follow on directly from *Le Misanthrope*, with an equally far-reaching elimination of physical action and farcical comedy (the only vestige of this, the clumsy lackey Lépine in III, ii, corresponds to Alceste's servant Du Bois in Act IV scene iv of *Le Misanthrope*) and a comparable abstraction and intellectualisation of the dialogue. On the other hand, if we look at the way in which Molière has exploited the essential comic formula, *Les Femmes savantes* seems to have more in common with *Le Bourgeois gentilhomme* or *Le Malade imaginaire*, and to illustrate a certain retreat from the originality of *Le Misanthrope* towards something safer because more conventional.

Neither Chrysale nor the *femmes savantes* make anything like the same intimate appeal to the spectator's sympathy as Alceste, or even Arnolphe. We preserve the necessary critical detachment for our reaction to be predictable, and this play has attracted few of the

---

[50] That this esteem was shared by Molière's contemporaries is suggested by the following mention in the Preface by La Grange to the 1682 edition of the playwright's works: '[Ces pièces] qu'on estime les meilleures, comme le *Misanthrope*, le *Tartuffe*, les *Femmes savantes* etc., sont des chefs-d'oeuvre qu'on ne saurait jamais assez admirer.'   [51] Quoted Mongrédien (ed.), *Recueil*, p. 408.
[52] *Les Femmes savantes*, ed. H. G. Hall (London, 1974), p. 7.

problems of interpretation posed by its distinguished predecessors. Its theme, of course, bears a close relationship to that of the *Précieuses ridicules*, updated to take account of more topical aspects of the movement for feminine emancipation. Linguistic refinement is still one of the preoccupations of the new generation of 'learned ladies' (cf. their project for a literary academy, among whose tasks will be the freeing of French vocabulary from 'ces syllabes sales/Qui dans les plus beaux mots produisent des scandales', lines 913–4); but it has now been joined by Descartes's cosmology ('J'aime ses tourbillons' – 'Moi, ses mondes tombants', (line 884)) and a general interest in physical sciences as a fashionable pursuit. There is no doubt that the learned ladies – Philaminte and Armande, at any rate – are intellectually on a very different level from Magdelon and Cathos, the foolish provincials; but they are comic for very much the same reason. Their total dedication to the life of the mind shows them up as *imaginaires*, incapable of meeting ordinary inhabitants of the real world on any common ground. It is not really a question of whether a woman should aspire higher than the kitchen sink: Chrysale's

> Nos pères sur ce point étaient gens bien sensés,
> Qui disaient qu'une femme en sait toujours assez,
> Quand la capacité de son esprit se hausse
> A connaître un pourpoint d'avec un haut-de-chausse (lines 577–80)

is an equally limited point of view which hardly commends itself to the audience, and Clitandre's well-known passage presents a much more balanced view of a woman's activities:

> Je consens qu'une femme ait des clartés de tout,
> Mais je ne lui veux point la passion choquante
> De se rendre savante afin d'être savante;
> Et j'aime que souvent aux questions qu'on fait,
> Elle sache ignorer les choses qu'elle sait . . . (lines 218ff.)[53]

Rather, it is that Philaminte, her sister-in-law and her elder daughter are so completely undiscriminating in their pursuit of knowledge that this produces in them a preconditioned, mechanical response to every situation; in other words, like Orgon, Monsieur Jourdain or Argan,

[53] It is interesting to compare Clitandre's lines with the following passage written by Mlle de Scudéry: 'Encore que je voulusse que les femmes sussent plus de choses qu'elles n'en savent pour l'ordinaire, je ne veux pourtant jamais qu'elles agissent ni qu'elles parlent en savantes' (from *Le Grand Cyrus*, in Somaize, *Dictionnaire*, ed. Livet, II, p. 373).

they consistently display the automatism of Bergson's 'mécanique plaqué sur le vivant'.

However, if their characterisation lacks the subtlety that makes Alceste, for instance, so sympathetic, the three *femmes savantes* have been sufficiently rounded to appear quite credible in human terms; and to appreciate this, it will perhaps be useful to look first of all at Bélise, who, as we have seen,[54] is modelled on Desmarets's Hespérie. This character and her two sisters, as well as the four potential suitors for their hands, are two-dimensional caricatures. As Desmarets's title indicates, they are *visionnaires*, that is to say each inhabits his own private fantasy world. The element of plot is negligible: the play is simply a parade of eccentrics; and the dialogue is a true *dialogue de sourds*, as each character gives free rein to his particular brand of folly. One of the lovers is Artabaze, the *capitan*, whose long soliloquy opens the play:

> Je suis l'amour du Ciel, et l'effroi de la terre;
> L'ennemi de la paix, la foudre de la guerre;
> Des dames le désir, des maris la terreur,
> Et je traîne avec moi le carnage et l'horreur.
> Le Dieu Mars m'engendra d'une fière Amazone,
> Et je suçai le lait d'une affreuse lionne.
> On parle des travaux d'Hercule encore enfant,
> Qu'il fut de deux serpents au berceau triomphant:
> Mais me fut-il égal, puisque par un caprice,
> Étant las de téter j'étranglai ma nourrice?

Hespérie is cast in a similar mould, and indeed, her speeches are a variant on an almost identical theme, with the same hyperbole and extravagant imagery recurring:

> Dieux! que je suis à craindre! est-il rien sous les cieux
> Au genre des humains plus fatal que mes yeux?
> Quand je fus mise au jour, la Nature peu fine
> Pensant faire un chef-d'oeuvre avançait sa ruine.
> On compterait plutôt les feuilles des forêts,
> Les sablons de la mer, les épis de Cérès,
> Les fleurs dont au printemps la terre se couronne,
> Les glaçons de l'hiver, les raisins de l'automne,
> Et les feux qui des nuits assistent le flambeau,
> Que le nombre d'amants que j'ai mis au tombeau.
>
> (lines 223–32)

Compared with a character of this sort, who is no more than the development of a gratuitous literary conceit, Bélise represents a

---

[54] Above, p. 82.

masterpiece of restraint. Molière has created a character, moreover, whose folly at every point receives genuinely *dramatic* expression. Bélise may not be essential to the basic plot of *Les Femmes savantes*, if that is defined as the rivalry between Clitandre and Trissotin for the hand of Henriette; but insofar as she does relate to it, with her constant assumption that Clitandre's declared love for Henriette disguises his real love for herself, this produces dramatic interest as well as comic effect. When Hespérie (lines 435ff.) lists the names of imaginary lovers – Lysis, Erylas, Lycidas, Périandre, Corylas and Tirsis – it is to report their death, madness, serious illness or projected acts of violence. When Bélise produces a similar list, the tone is by contrast one of understatement, and the passage is credible in human terms as well as being delightfully comic:

> On est faite d'un air je pense à pouvoir dire
> Qu'on n'a pas pour un coeur soumis à son empire;
> Et Dorante, Damis, Cléonte et Lycidas
> Peuvent bien faire voir qu'on a quelques appas.
> —Ces gens vous aiment?
>   —Oui, de toute leur puissance.
> —Ils vous l'ont dit?
>   —Aucun n'a pris cette licence;
> Ils m'ont su révérer si fort jusqu'à ce jour,
> Qu'ils ne m'ont jamais dit un mot de leur amour;
> Mais pour m'offrir leur coeur et vouer leur service,
> Les muets truchements ont tous fait leur office. (lines 375–84)

Bélise is not just an old maid, whose active imagination compensates for her sexual frustration; she is also engaged in the philological and scientific activities of her sister-in-law's *salon*: which at once makes her a richer character with more varied human interest, even though the expression given to her intellectual interests shows her to be the most foolish of the *femmes savantes*.

Armande's character shows more psychological complexity, and even if she is the least attractive – and the least comic – of the three,[55] she is the easiest to believe in. As well as providing her own variation on the theme of women's learning, with her adopted pose of the ascetic who scorns 'la partie animale / Dont l'appétit grossier aux bêtes nous ravale' (lines 47–8), she also constitutes an essential

[55] 'Il ne fait pas de doute que, des trois femmes savantes, [Armande] est la plus odieuse à Molière, dans sa prétention à refuser les lois de la nature. Bélise n'est que grotesque; Philaminte est insupportable; mais Armande, avec ses dédains, sa sécheresse, est la négation de toute féminité', Descotes, *Les Grands Rôles*, p. 234.

element of the plot, as the tangible obstacle to the marriage of the young lovers.

The analysis of the role of Philaminte presents a certain problem. On the one hand, there is surely a real dignity in her character, which is shown in the nature of her intellectual aspirations, as well as in the philosophical way in which she faces up to apparent adversity in Act V. Yet in the original production of *Les Femmes savantes* Philaminte was played by a male actor, Hubert, and – at any rate at first sight – that would seem to suggest the world of pantomime dames and *Charley's Aunt*. But twentieth-century readers are at something of a disadvantage here. We do not know how the spectators of 1672 reacted to that aspect of the role, though from such evidence as is available it seems to have been an established convention in the comic theatre of the period, due no doubt to the unwillingness of young and attractive actresses to accept such thankless roles. If we look at the other roles played by Hubert *en travesti*, Madame Pernelle is obviously an unsympathetic figure of fun, but Madame Jourdain on the other hand is sensible and sympathetic; and to take an example from an earlier comedy, Discret's *Alizon* (1637), Antoine Adam can write of the courtship between the elderly Karolu and the eponymous heroine, played by a man: 'ces deux amoureux grisonnants sont touchants, et non ridicules'.[56] In the case of Philaminte, of course, subsequent productions failed to follow the precedent set in 1672;[57] but the fact that the role was originally played by a man cannot be ignored when one is discussing the 'rounding' of the characters in *Les Femmes savantes*, even if the precise implications are not easy to determine.[58]

As regards the role played by Molière himself, it is not difficult to see how Chrysale fits into the series of characters which evolved from the early Sganarelle. Though he has gone up in the world – the label 'bon bourgeois' indicates a comfortable social standing – he is still the same weak, timid character, and his is the most fully-developed portrait of a henpecked husband in the whole of Molière. But once again, he is far from being a pure caricature, and the vacillations of this character who constantly puts his domestic peace before his

[56] *Histoire*, I, p. 560; and see Plate VIII.   [57] Descotes, *Les Grands Rôles*, p. 233.
[58] 'On n'est pas forcé de conclure que Molière voulait faire jouer Philaminte en grosse charge. Il suffisait que le personnage fût d'un caractère un peu masculin. Il y a lieu de penser que, dans un genre de travestissement qu'Hubert avait le don de rendre suffisamment vraisemblable, il savait garder la mesure', Molière, *Oeuvres*, ed. Despois and Mesnard, IX, p. 49.

principles, and who backs down from any confrontation with his dragon of a wife – 'C'est à vous que je parle, ma soeur' (line 558) – remain completely credible.

In a recent critical study which deals with the closing years of Molière's career, Robert Garapon seeks to bring out the affinity of *Les Femmes savantes* not with the 'hautes comédies' of the middle 1660s, but with the group of plays produced from *Les Fourberies de Scapin* onwards: 'Sa conception de la comédie s'est assez sensiblement modifiée à partir de l'*Avare* et tout particulièrement dans les dernières années de sa vie . . . le poète semble bien avoir renoncé, en 1672–1673, à la règle de la séparation des genres.'[59] As we have already suggested, *Le Misanthrope* represents the extreme development of Molière's conception of character comedy; and no play written after 1666 was to offer the blend of *comique* and sympathetic interest that we find in Alceste. In this respect, M. Garapon is quite right to talk of a 'retour au comique' in what were to be the last years of the playwright's life;[60] and the variations on the *imaginaire* character we are presented with in *Les Femmes savantes* certainly seem closer in their comic inspiration to the heroes of *Le Bourgeois gentilhomme* and *Le Malade imaginaire* than to the *atrabilaire amoureux* of 1666. But to go further, and to claim to see a similar affinity of structure and dramaturgical technique with the *comédies-ballets* of this final period, seems misguided. The comic extravagances of the learned ladies stop well short of the fantasy that animates both Jourdain and Argan, and that finds its 'objective correlative' in the burlesque initiation-ceremonies which put a final seal on the folly of those two characters; and when Garapon, analysing *Les Femmes savantes*, talks of 'une structure apparentée à la comédie-ballet',[61] he is surely misusing critical terminology. When he says of Act III of the play that 'les figures de ballet, dans les paroles comme dans les gestes, se succèdent les unes aux autres presque sans interruption au long de ces quatre cents vers',[62] he means that stylistic features such as repetition, symmetry and stichomythia abound, and that the reading of Trissotin's two poems, as well as the quarrel between the two pedants, are conceived as patterned 'performances'. Such devices, however, recur throughout Molière's comedy, and it seems reasonable to assume that for most spectators or readers the resemblance, structural as well as thematic, between Act III, scenes ii and iii of *Les Femmes savantes* and Act I

[59] *Le Dernier Molière*, p. 192.   [60] *Ibid.*, p. 226.
[61] *Ibid.*, p. 193.   [62] *Ibid.*, p. 218.

163

scene ii of *Le Misanthrope* would be far more relevant than any comparison with the *comédies-ballets* – though both Oronte's reading of his sonnet and the subsequent quarrel with Alceste could well lend themselves to the same sort of stylistic analysis.

The fact is rather that style and structure combine with theme and characterisation to produce the effect of polished literary comedy that was to give this play its special cachet. And as has been suggested above,[63] in any assessment of this kind of comedy of manners the part played by costume and setting must not be underestimated. As regards dress, the costume worn by Molière as Chrysale helps to situate the play in the milieu of the rich bourgeoisie:

> Justaucorps et haut-de-chausses de velours noir et ramage à fond aurore, la veste de gaze violette et or, garnie de boutons, un cordon d'or, jarretières, aiguillettes et gants[64]

while the furnishings appropriate to this setting – the ideal set may perhaps be imagined as bringing to life the atmosphere of a bourgeois interior by Abraham Bosse[65] – would reinforce the precise social reference of much of the dialogue. As for the form of this dialogue, there is all the difference in the world between the prose of most of the late plays and the stylised alexandrines of *Les Femmes savantes* – a verse-form which not only accommodates the stichomythia and other verbal patterns of Act III scene ii, but also provides an admirable vehicle for the dialectical exchanges of the opening scene. It is the interplay of all these various features that makes Molière's penultimate play 'une pièce. . . tout à fait achevée'.

(iv) The 'Lettre sur l'Imposteur'

The foregoing pages on the evolution of Molière's comedy show the playwright's practice to be wholly in keeping with the ideas expressed in the most important text in which the nature of his comedy is discussed. This is the *Critique de l'École des femmes*; for however simple the ideas formulated there by Dorante may be, there is no doubt that they are both far-reaching and highly original. Of the other texts to which Molière put his name, none compares with scene vi of the *Critique* as providing the guidelines of a new type of character comedy: the Prefaces to the *Précieuses ridicules* and to *Les Fâcheux* are occasional

---

[63] p. 123.
[64] Inventory taken on Molière's death, Mongrédien (ed.), *Recueil*, p. 408.
[65] Plate VII.

pieces, concerned to present a particular play in the best possible light, and even the Preface to *Tartuffe*, though a more substantial text, is the work of an author very much on the defensive, fighting to preserve the right to perform his most successful, as well as his most controversial, play.

There remains, however, one text to which some Molière specialists have been prepared to attach a considerable importance as an expression of the playwright's views on the nature of comedy: the anonymous *Lettre sur la comédie de l'Imposteur* of 1667. Although perhaps only a few scholars would positively ascribe its authorship to Molière himself,[66] it is generally accepted as being from the pen of someone closely associated with him.[67] In one respect, the *Lettre* is quite invaluable to students of Molière: the first, descriptive or narrative, half provides a remarkably detailed account of the 1667 version of *Tartuffe*, and is the basis for much of the informed speculation about the way in which the original play of 1664 developed into the definitive version of 1669. The status, and the value, of the more analytical part are, however, more open to doubt; and although the second half of the *Lettre* devotes a number of pages to analysing the comic process, the result is in my view too verbose and repetitive to be readily acceptable as a persuasive first-hand expression of Molière's theoretical ideas. The author of the *Lettre* begins this second section with a definition of 'le ridicule', which is 'une des plus sublimes matières de la véritable morale', and of the way in which we respond to it:

> Le ridicule est donc la forme extérieure et sensible que la providence de la nature a attachée à tout ce qui est déraisonnable, pour nous en faire apercevoir, et nous obliger à le fuir. Pour connaître ce ridicule, il faut connaître la raison dont il signifie le défaut, et voir en quoi elle consiste. Son caractère n'est autre, dans le fond, que la convenance, et sa marque sensible, la bienséance, c'est-à-dire le fameux *quod decet* des anciens: de sorte que la bienséance est, à l'égard de la convenance, ce que les Platoniciens disent que la beauté est à l'égard de la bonté, c'est-à-dire qu'elle en est la fleur, le dehors, le corps et l'apparence extérieure; que la bienséance est la raison apparente, et que la convenance est la raison essentielle. De là vient que ce qui sied bien est toujours fondé sur quelque raison de convenance, comme l'indécence sur quelque disconvenance, c'est-à-dire le ridicule sur quelque manque de raison.[68]

---

[66] But cf. e.g. McBride, *The Sceptical Vision of Molière* (London, 1977), p. 8.

[67] The name of Donneau de Visé has perhaps received most support, see e.g. R. Robert, 'Des Commentaires de première main sur les chefs-d'oeuvre les plus discutés de Molière', *Revue des Sciences Humaines*, xxx (1956), 27–32.

[68] *Oeuvres*, ed. Despois and Mesnard, IV, p. 560.

The views adumbrated here are strikingly similar to those expressed by Pascal in the *Lettres provinciales*. On the one hand, the implied definition of the comic as the perception of incongruity ('la disconvenance') echoes a passage in the eleventh *Provinciale* where, discussing certain examples of Jesuit casuistry, Pascal writes:

> Lorsqu'on entend ces décisions et autres semblables, il est impossible que cette surprise ne fasse rire, parce que rien n'y porte davantage qu'une disproportion surprenante entre ce qu'on entend et ce qu'on voit[69]

– and both could be said to look forward to modern 'intellectualist' theories of laughter such as that formulated by Arthur Koestler in *Insight and Outlook*.[70] On the other hand, the statement that 'comme la raison produit dans l'âme une joie mêlée d'estime, le ridicule y produit une joie mêlée de mépris'[71] is even closer to the following passage from the same text of Pascal's:

> Comme les vérités chrétiennes sont dignes d'amour et de respect, les erreurs qui leur sont contraires sont dignes de mépris et de haine, parce qu'il y a deux choses dans les vérités de notre religion: une beauté divine, qui les rend aimables, et une sainte majesté, qui les rend vénérables; et qu'il y a aussi deux choses dans les erreurs: l'impiété, qui les rend horribles, et l'impertinence, qui les rend ridicules.[72]

In both of the latter cases the emphasis is very strongly on the moral, or corrective, function of the comic process: a much more restrictive definition. And it is this aspect of the comic which preoccupies the author of the *Lettre* in the remainder of the text, where he is concerned to demonstrate that because the 'galanterie' affected by Tartuffe (or Panulphe, as this character is called in the 1667 version) in his attempt to seduce Elmire is incongruous, and therefore ridiculous, in the person of a pious man, it will serve to warn prospective victims of real-life *faux dévots* who may similarly seek to seduce under a mask of piety. It is hardly surprising, of course, that this should be the emphasis of the *Lettre*: Molière's play was still subject to an ecclesiastical ban in 1667, and the author of this text – whether Molière himself or (as seems more likely) an ally such as Donneau de Visé – was naturally concerned to counter allegations of immorality and impiety.

But such an approach, which automatically links the intellectual perception of the absurd with a corrective, satirical or didactic pur-

[69] Ed. H. F. Stewart (Manchester, 1920), p. 125.   [70] London, 1949.
[71] p. 559.   [72] p. 122.

pose, does impose a misleading limitation on the interpretation of Molière's theatre. It may be more appropriate to *Tartuffe* than to most of the other plays – but even here, it is noteworthy that the analysis given in the *Lettre* concentrates on Panulphe himself to the exclusion of Orgon, who as an object of 'le ridicule' is not only much more characteristic of Molière's comic method but also more central to the play. And in the case of Orgon, the link between the 'intellectual' and the 'moral' aspects of the comic process is surely a good deal subtler than that claimed for Panulphe in the *Lettre sur l'Imposteur*.

We have no means of knowing what course Molière's career as a playwright might have followed if he had not died at the early age of fifty-one. Grimarest seems to suggest a further series of *comédies de caractère* – he cites one projected title, *L' Extravagant*[73] – but that is no doubt just as speculative as Garapon's concept of a new pattern in Molière's comic writing from 1671 onwards. It is impossible even to know to what extent Molière thought, like later interpreters of his work, in terms of a hierarchy of genres, with the five-act verse plays like *Le Misanthrope*, *Tartuffe* and *Les Femmes savantes* representing the peak of his achievement. On the other hand, although he left no fully worked-out statement of his views on the moral, or corrective, function of comedy, I think we can be sure that he was as fully alive as any of his contemporaries to the relationship between satire and other kinds of comic writing. It is this relationship that we shall examine in our next chapter.

<hr>

[73] *La Vie de M. de Molière*, pp. 104–5.

7
From Satire to Comedy of Ideas

The satirist is a stern moralist, castigating the vices of his time and place.
(T. S. Eliot)[1]

Le lendemain il y eut une comédie nouvelle qu'un comédien que l'on appelle Molière a fait [sic]; c'est un homme qui a autant d'esprit que l'on en peut avoir et qui, à l'exemple des anciens, dans toutes ses comédies, se moque de tous les vices de son siècle.
(Le Duc d'Enghien)[2]

(i) 'La satire honnête et permise'?

When Molière himself uses the term *la satire*, it seldom has such a specific meaning as is commonly attached to it in modern critical practice. For instance, in citing Arnolphe's extravagant behaviour in Act V of *L'École des femmes* as an example of 'la satire des amants',[3] he appears to be suggesting a target for satirical writing so broad that satire ceases to be distinguishable from other forms of comic writing: the definition there implied is entirely lacking in that specific local and temporal reference for which we normally look. For if satire is to be identified as a distinct literary mode, this surely depends on the fact that unlike other kinds of comic invention, it requires a recognisable point of reference in the real world, to which the play, poem or novel is related in a particular way.

The peculiar relationship of the satirist to the world in which he lives is acknowledged by La Bruyère when he writes:

Un homme né chrétien et Français se trouve contraint dans la satire; les grands sujets lui sont défendus: il les entame quelquefois, et se détourne ensuite sur de petites choses, qu'il relève par la beauté de son génie et son style.[4]

The constraints imposed on the seventeenth-century writer — by

---

[1] Introduction to Johnson's *London and the Vanity of Human Wishes* (London, 1930) (quoted A. Pollard, *Satire* (London, 1970), p. 50).
[2] Quoted Mongrédien (ed.), *Recueil*, p. 246.
[3] *Critique*, scene vi.   [4] *Caractères*, XIV, para. 65.

considerations of taste as well as by fear of censorship – are particularly relevant when we come to study Molière as a satirist. It could hardly be maintained, if one thinks of *Tartuffe* or *Dom Juan*, that Molière avoided La Bruyère's 'grands sujets'; but the latter's comment helps us to appreciate the courage – or the foolhardiness – involved in putting on these provocative plays. Even if we look at the early plays, written before 1664, we can see that the playwright did not always play safe, and was not afraid to run the risk, right from the beginning of his Paris career, of antagonising groups of influential spectators. And it was the banding together of some of these spectators, roused by Molière's satire, with his professional rivals at the Hôtel de Bourgogne that produced the 'Guerre comique', or 'Querelle de l'École des femmes', in 1663.

For from an early date there can be distinguished, alongside the farces, or the pure comedies of Italianate inspiration, a parallel series of plays much more closely related by their theme and setting to the real world of Paris and the Court in which Molière's spectators lived. Although the imaginative fantasy of *La Jalousie du Barbouillé* and *Le Médecin volant* carries on into later plays like *Sganarelle* or *Le Mariage forcé*, it is perhaps not without significance that *Les Précieuses ridicules*, as the first new play to be written for Paris audiences after the company's return to the capital, should deal in a provocative way with an aspect of contemporary manners; in this respect it was followed by *Les Fâcheux*, and both the *Critique* and the *Impromptu* contain an important satirical element. Moreover, if one looks at the series *Sganarelle – L'École des maris – L'École des femmes*, the increase in realism of setting from one play to the next brings with it, if not quite the same sort of satirical reference as is contained in *Les Précieuses ridicules* or *Les Fâcheux*, at least a notable increase in topicality and (to use a fashionable term) 'relevance'. As a result, we can see how *L'École des femmes* acted as a catalyst, and brought about an alliance of those hostile forces that had previously remained separate.

The Preface to *Les Précieuses ridicules*, for all its brevity, makes an interesting statement about Molière's views on satire. 'Cette comédie', it declares, 'se tient partout dans les bornes de la satire honnête et permise'; and the playwright goes on to say that the object of his satirical attack is not 'les véritables précieuses' but 'de mauvais singes, qui méritent d'être bernés': imitators who stand in the same relationship to the real thing as do 'le docteur de la comédie' and 'le capitan' to 'les véritables savants et les vrais braves'. There appears to be a certain ambiguity here. On the one hand, the distinction drawn between 'les véritables précieuses' and 'les ridicules qui les imitent mal' suggests that Magdelon and Cathos possessed an identifiable counterpart in real life: that the leading luminaries of preciosity did have their shallow and vulgar imitators. On the other hand, the reference to 'le docteur' and 'le capitan' would appear to imply that 'la satire honnête et permise' is not really satire as we know it at all, but the innocuous exercise of the playwright's imagination, since these two traditional roles had long since lost any satirical force they might once have had. What this means in practice, I think, is that a play like *Les Précieuses ridicules* does contain a genuine satirical element, but that the angle of the satirist's vision is so broad, and such a large dose of fantasy has entered into the creation of the two foolish girls, that it can hardly be regarded as satire with a real cutting edge.

Of course, it has often been argued that this is a very conventional disclaimer; that the distinction between 'true' and 'false' preciosity is an imaginary one; and that the text of the play contains specific references which suggest that the target of the satire included Mlle de Scudéry herself, the high priestess of preciosity, as well as her less discriminating acolytes. However, the nature of such references needs further analysis. The most crucial is the sequence in scene iv where the two girls are attempting to justify their rejection of their suitors on the grounds that their courtship had been too brisk, and that they proceeded to an offer of marriage without going through the elaborate rigmarole prescribed by the romanesque novels of the day. When Gorgibus protests that this seems to him a very proper way to go about it, Magdelon replies:

> Mon Dieu, que, si tout le monde vous ressemblait, un roman serait bientôt fini! La belle chose que ce serait si d'abord Cyrus épousait Mandane, et qu'Aronce de plain-pied fût marié à Clélie!

And she is backed up by her cousin, with further reference to Madeleine de Scudéry's novel *Clélie*:

> En effet, mon oncle, ma cousine donne dans le vrai de la chose. Le moyen de bien recevoir des gens qui sont tout à fait incongrus en galanterie? Je m'en vais gager qu'ils n'ont jamais vu la Carte de Tendre, et que Billets-Doux, Petits-Soins, Billets-Galants et Jolis-Vers sont des terres inconnues pour eux.

These two passages stand out quite clearly from the rest of the scene, in which the *précieuses* reproduce the sort of affectation of speech and manner that can frequently be documented as authentic, it is true, but which cannot be pinned down to the same sort of precisely identifiable source. Such specific references have led commentators on the play to assert that Mlle de Scudéry herself must have been the target of Molière's satire; but I think we need to look a little more closely at the nature of the comedy at this point. There is surely an important difference between the *précieux* mannerisms and affectations of speech on the one hand, and on the other, the attempt on the part of these two characters to base courtship and marriage on models taken from literature. Magdelon and Cathos are the first examples of Molière's *imaginaires*: they have lost the ability to distinguish between the real world they live in and the imaginary world of romanesque fiction, and the primary object of our laughter is the folly of the girls themselves, who are content to live their lives according to second-hand formulas. Only at a secondary level, if at all, do we laugh at the *précieux* novels themselves and at their author: it is not the novelist, but her readers, who are shown to be absurd. Satire *is* present in *Les Précieuses ridicules*, and it operates through the *précieuses* themselves insofar as we are able to regard them as a class of person, to be found in French society of the time, who had similarly lost the capacity to discriminate between wit and folly, and whose life was similarly controlled by *idées reçues*. It also operates, of course, through Mascarille and Jodelet, to the extent that their assumed role as courtiers caricatures real contemporary affectation.

And here there can be little doubt. Magdelon and Cathos, whether or not they stand for a contemporary class of provincial hanger-on to the *précieux* culture, certainly represent a more permanent and universal kind of folly – and are to that extent comic, rather than satirical, portraits; but Mascarille, as a conscious and deliberate mimic of contemporary Court fashions of dress, speech and behaviour, fulfils an unambiguously satirical role. In fact, Molière was to keep up a running attack for several years on the *marquis*, that social type of the 1660s who was in many ways the precursor of the *petits-maîtres*, or fops, ridiculed by Dancourt, Dufresny and other satirists among the next generation of playwrights. Mascarille, with his extravagant costume and exhibitionist manners, was to be followed by the satire of affected courtiers in *Les Fâcheux*: we have already quoted from that play[5] the opening portrait of an importunate theatregoer. The fact that this person remains anonymous, and that it is Éraste who is addressed as

[5] Above, p. 36.

'Marquis', should not mislead us: the unnamed *fâcheux* certainly belongs to the class of courtier whom Molière labelled for convenience 'marquis' or 'petits marquis', and whom he chose to ridicule time and again. The 'Remercîment au Roi', an occasional poem of a hundred lines in which he expresses his thanks to the King in 1663 for the grant of a pension, contains an equally satirical picture of this kind of foppish young courtier, as the poet instructs his muse:

> Et vous ferez votre cour beaucoup mieux,
> Lorsqu'en marquis vous serez travestie.
> Vous savez ce qu'il faut pour paraître marquis;
> N'oubliez rien de l'air ni des habits:
> Arborez un chapeau chargé de trente plumes
> Sur une perruque de prix;
> Que le rabat soit des plus grands volumes,
> Et le pourpoint des plus petits . . .[6]

The *Critique de l'École des femmes* presents three targets of Molière's satire. But whereas Lysidas, the pedantic man of letters, is treated with evident respect (and it is his argument with Dorante in scene vi which, relating as it does particular points to general aesthetic principles, demonstrates the serious purpose of the play), neither the *précieuse* nor the *marquis* is shown much quarter. Climène's criticisms of *L'École des femmes* amount to nothing more than denunciation by empty hyperbole, while the Marquis is established as a brainless 'turlupin',[7] whose reiterated slogans such as 'Tarte à la crème!' merely reflect a fashionable prejudice. This was very direct, and very effective, satire; and it is not surprising that the *Critique* was soon followed by a counter-attack. In spite of the title of Donneau de Visé's *Réponse à l'Impromptu de Versailles*, its polemical inspiration is betrayed by its subtitle . . . *ou la Vengeance des marquis*.[8]

Le Misanthrope shows that even as late as 1666 Molière had not

---

[6] The 'Remercîment' is reproduced in Vol. III of the *Oeuvres*, ed. Despois and Mesnard.

[7] The word *turelupin* or *tirelupin* existed before the seventeenth century, but *turlupin*, *turlupinade* took their meaning in Molière's time from the actor Henri Legrand, or Belleville, of the Hôtel de Bourgogne (d. 1637), whose stage name was Turlupin, and whose speciality was to 'faire rire par de méchantes pointes ou équivoques' (Furetière, *Dictionnaire universel*). Molière's association of the terms with the *marquis* was so effective that the nickname became established, and courtiers were even ready to call each other 'turlupin': 'Il leur donne sujet de se rire les uns des autres et s'appeler entre eux Turlupins, comme ils font à la Cour depuis qu'Élomire a joué sa *Critique*' (Donneau de Visé, *Zélinde*, scene viii).

[8] This one-act play is reproduced in Mongrédien (ed.), *La Querelle de l'École des femmes*, Vol. II.

relented in his satirical attack on this social type. Both directly, as in Acaste's complacent self-appraisal:

> Parbleu! je ne vois pas, lorsque je m'examine,
> Où prendre aucun sujet d'avoir l'âme chagrine.
> J'ai du bien, je suis jeune, et sors d'une maison
> Qui se peut dire noble avec quelque raison;
> Et je crois, par le rang que me donne ma race,
> Qu'il est fort peu d'emplois dont je ne sois en passe.
> Pour le coeur, dont sur tout nous devons faire cas,
> On sait, sans vanité, que je n'en manque pas,
> Et l'on m'a vu pousser, dans le monde, une affaire
> D'une assez vigoureuse et gaillarde manière.
> Pour de l'esprit, j'en ai sans doute, et du bon goût
> A juger sans étude et raisonner de tout,
> A faire aux nouveautés, dont je suis idolâtre,
> Figure de savant sur les bancs du théâtre,
> Y décider en chef, et faire du fracas
> A tous les beaux endroits qui méritent des has (lines 781–96)

and indirectly, in Alceste's portrait of Clitandre:

> Mais au moins dites-moi, Madame, par quel sort
> Votre Clitandre a l'heur de vous plaire si fort?
> Sur quel fonds de mérite et de vertu sublime
> Appuyez-vous en lui l'honneur de votre estime?
> Est-ce par l'ongle long qu'il porte au petit doigt
> Qu'il s'est acquis chez vous l'estime où l'on le voit?
> Vous êtes-vous rendue, avec tout le beau monde,
> Au mérite éclatant de sa perruque blonde?
> Sont-ce ses grands canons qui vous le font aimer?
> L'amas de ses rubans a-t-il su vous charmer?
> Est-ce par les appas de sa vaste rhingrave
> Qu'il a gagné votre âme en faisant votre esclave?
> Ou sa façon de rire et son ton de fausset
> Ont-ils de vous toucher su trouver le secret? (lines 475–88)

the 'petits marquis' are pilloried for precisely the same faults that had been so faithfully copied by Mascarille: extravagance in dress, with a proliferation of ribbons and lace, and vanity and self-centredness in behaviour. The reason for Molière's satirical campaign against the *marquis* remains obscure. It may be that some incident at Court – a slight, or rebuff – motivated the original attack; or it may be that the choice of subject for *Les Précieuses ridicules* was due, in the case of both the *marquis* and the *précieuses,* to an ambitious dramatist's desire to make his comedy topical and provocative. If so – if this first appearance of a satirical element in his comedy was offensive rather than defensive in character – there is little doubt that it succeeded in its aim, and that it was at least partly by provoking the hostility of certain social groups that Molière got himself talked about, and established himself so quickly as the leading dramatist of his day.

On the other hand, I think it can be said of these early encounters with the *précieuses* and the *marquis* that Molière's writing remains within the bounds of 'la satire honnête et permise', and that what Uranie says of *L'École des femmes*:

> Ces sortes de satires tombent directement sur les moeurs, et ne frappent les personnes que par réflexion. N'allons point nous appliquer nous-mêmes les traits d'une censure générale; et profitons de la leçon, si nous pouvons, sans faire semblant qu'on parle à nous. Toutes les peintures ridicules qu'on expose sur les théâtres doivent être regardées sans chagrin de tout le monde. Ce sont miroirs publics, où il ne faut jamais témoigner qu'on se voie; et c'est se taxer hautement d'un défaut, que se scandaliser qu'on le reprenne (*Critique*, scene vi)

can be applied without too much strain to *Les Précieuses ridicules* and other early plays. Such satirical portraits as there are either contain a large measure of comic invention (as with Mascarille in *Les Précieuses,* or the importunate spectator in *Les Fâcheux*); or else (as in the case of Climène, the *précieuse* of the *Critique*, who is much nearer to being a real-life portrait) are built up from traits presumably drawn from observation of a broad social group, and not identifiable with individual models. We are told that Lysidas of the *Critique* may have been intended to represent Donneau de Visé, but the fact that Boursault was prepared to recognise himself in the character suggests that Lysidas too is likely to have been conceived in more general terms.

There are of course cases in Molière's theatre of a more personal kind of satire, satire of a quite unambiguous character. The first example is the caricatural imitation of Montfleury and his colleagues at the Hôtel de Bourgogne in scene i of the *Impromptu de Versailles*. Far from being a biting personal lampoon,[9] this passage is really remarkably good-natured, especially if one considers the form that Montfleury's reprisal took, when he accused Molière 'd'avoir épousé la fille, et d'avoir autrefois couché avec la mère'.[10] If these were the weapons his jealous rivals were prepared to use against him, one can only admire Molière's moderation as a polemicist.

[9] *Lampoon*: 'a personal satire in writing; low censure' (Chambers); 'a virulent or scurrilous satire upon an individual' (*Shorter O.E.D.*).
[10] See Racine's letter (November 1663), quoted Mongrédien (ed.), *Recueil*, p. 195.

The best-known example of a personal satire in Molière's theatre is no doubt *Les Femmes savantes*, where Trissotin and Vadius represent the *salon* poet Cotin and the grammarian Ménage. The *Mercure Galant* professed itself unable to believe that 'un homme qui est souvent parmi les premières personnes de la Cour et que Mademoiselle honore du nom de son ami' [i.e. the Abbé Cotin] 'puisse être cru l'objet d'une si sanglante satire';[11] but the facts speak for themselves. Madame de Sévigné refers to the play shortly before the first performance as 'Tricotin'; Cotin and Ménage had had a public quarrel some years earlier, and Ménage himself was later to confess that that provided the source for the quarrel in Act III of the play; and, most convincing of all, both the sonnet and the epigram recited by Trissotin are to be found in Cotin's *Oeuvres galantes*, published in 1663. This time, there is clear evidence that Molière's satirical attack was not unprovoked: Cotin had long been hostile to Molière and to Boileau, and in particular had apparently preached against *Tartuffe*. (The unfortunate Ménage, on the other hand, seems to have done little to deserve his fate, and to have been included by association.) Boileau's response to Cotin was fairly traditional, and no doubt fairly innocuous: it consisted of unflattering references in the *Satires*;[12] but Molière's pointed lampooning of the two pedants in a flesh-and-blood impersonation on the stage was more unusual, and much more effective. Trissotin is shown up as a bad poet, a shallow flatterer, and a character quite lacking in integrity; and Gaston Hall is fully justified in remarking, in his edition of *Les Femmes savantes*:

> The satire of Cotin and Ménage through Trissotin and Vadius introduces personal satire on a scale unprecedented in Molière's theatre, a return to a Greek concept of comedy traditionally played down in Renaissance dramatic theory. In this respect Molière is closer to Aristophanes' satire of the living Socrates as a pedant and fool than to the impersonal satire defended ten years earlier by Molière's spokesman in *La Critique de l'École des femmes*.[13]

(ii) Marriage à la mode

If we adopt the restrictive definition of satire proposed above, the comedy deriving from Molière's treatment of conjugal relationships

---

[11] 25 May 1672, quoted Mongrédien (ed.), *Recueil*, p. 409.
[12] See especially *Satire* IX. Molière makes capital out of this by putting the following exchange into the mouths of his two pedants at the height of their quarrel:
— Oui, oui, je te renvoie à l'auteur des *Satires*.
— Je t'y renvoie aussi. (lines 1026–7)   [13] p. 64.

can be termed satirical, if at all, only where it seems to throw a critical light on features of the particular society in which the playwright and his audiences lived. Judged by this criterion, not only are plays like *Sganarelle* or *Le Mariage forcé* quite devoid of satirical implications, but genuine satire makes a minimal contribution to plays like *L'École des maris* or *L'École des femmes*. In a number of his plays, Molière is content to treat marriage in the same way as it had been treated in the farces and the *fabliaux*: as a battle of wits between the two partners; and if plays like the two *Écoles* do incidentally make the audience reflect on the attitudes that are proper in those about to marry, this is done in the manner of a comedy of ideas, not by satirising specifically seventeenth-century attitudes. There are two plays, however, which deal more searchingly with the marriage relationship; and each in its own way is much more closely related to a specific social background.

Comparing *George Dandin* with *La Jalousie du Barbouillé*, of which it is a reworking in three acts, one notices straightaway the introduction of a new theme, that of misalliance. Le Barbouillé had been a simple *mal-marié*; but Dandin's opening soliloquy ascribes *his* marital misfortunes to his folly in marrying a 'demoiselle'. He himself is a 'paysan' (a modern editor uses the term 'bourgeois campagnard' to define his status);[14] and in exchanging his wealth for the 'gentilhommerie' of his in-laws he had made a very bad bargain, for he is constantly browbeaten by Angélique and her parents, and he is on the point of being cuckolded. His rival, Clitandre, is a conventional enough figure, a seventeenth-century equivalent of Emma Bovary's Rodolphe; but in the case of the parents-in-law, Molière has been at pains to give quite a precise indication of their social position. Monsieur le Baron de Sotenville and his wife (née Prudoterie) represent, *vis-à-vis* George Dandin, a formidable force of privilege, experience, and ruthless instinct for self-preservation. They may have been forced into a bargain themselves in order to replenish their coffers, but they are not prepared to make any further concessions, and their parvenu son-in-law is tolerated only so long as he toes the line:

> Apprenez, s'il vous plaît, que ce n'est pas à vous à vous servir de ce mot-là avec une personne de ma condition; que tout notre gendre que vous soyez, il y a grande différence de vous à nous, et que vous devez vous connaître. (I, iv)

Clitandre, however, they recognise as one of themselves; and when

---

[14] *Oeuvres complètes*, ed. Jouanny, II, p. 893.

M. de Sotenville offers him a day's hunting, as they part after their first meeting, this automatic civility from one gentleman to another helps as much as anything else to mark Dandin as an outsider. From a strictly dramaturgical point of view, as the opponents of Dandin, the Sotenvilles occupy a position of strength, if not of invulnerability. At the same time, the spectator is invited to look at them in a rather different light; and in terms of the social satire contained in the play, these proud, self-important provincial nobles are almost as ridiculous as the peasant parvenu. The names Sotenville and Prudoterie are richly evocative, and even though their characterisation may seem to us only mildly caricatural, this would have been enough for an audience of courtiers, confident in their superior *savoir-faire* and sure of their own *quartiers de noblesse,* to be able to look down on these provincial squireens. With their use of the jargon, and the stylised attitudes, of fossilised family pride:

—Jour de Dieu! je l'étranglerais de mes propres mains, s'il fallait qu'elle forlignât de l'honnêteté de sa mère.
—Corbleu! je lui passerais mon épée au travers du corps, à elle et au galant, si elle avait forfait à son honneur (*ibid.*)

the Sotenville couple provide a sort of counterpart to the *précieuses ridicules,* the doctors or the pedants whom Molière elsewhere satirises by concentrating on the rigid attitudes and the jargon of a class or a profession. The difference is that elsewhere the satirical exposure of the affectations and the poses of a Trissotin or a Purgon is matched by their defeat in dramatic terms. Even in *Le Bourgeois gentilhomme,* the aristocratic couple who are making a good living for themselves out of Monsieur Jourdain's obsession are finally exposed and rendered powerless; but the Sotenvilles are allowed to retain their position of immunity. The final victory of characters who have been shown in an unsympathetic light puts *George Dandin* in a unique position among Molière's comedies; though it seems not unlikely that the original three-act version of *Tartuffe* may have had a similar ending, with the impostor in a position of triumph. The defeat or discomfiture of characters who have been shown in a critical light is part of the comfortable happy ending we look for in comedy; here, the rules of the game appear to have been broken, and this is one of the features that help to make *George Dandin* a somewhat disturbing play.

Not the least interesting character, from the point of view of the topical relevance of the play, is Angélique. She can hardly be called sympathetic, but of all the protagonists, she is the one who is allowed to express her feelings most seriously and sensibly. If one considers the kind of real-life situation that is implied in *George Dandin,* the parvenu husband is not the only victim: his wife is obviously another. And at least Dandin has entered into the marriage willingly and with his eyes open; Angélique, on the other hand, was never consulted: she was sold by her parents to someone who was prepared to pay good money. So, whatever we may think of her duplicity, her rejoinder when Dandin reminds her of her marriage-vow commands our respect:

> Moi? Je ne vous l'ai point donnée de bon coeur, et vous me l'avez arrachée. M'avez-vous, avant le mariage, demandé mon consentement, et si je voulais bien de vous? Vous n'avez consulté, pour cela, que mon père et ma mère; ce sont eux proprement qui vous ont épousé, et c'est pourquoi vous ferez bien de vous plaindre toujours à eux des torts que l'on pourra vous faire. Pour moi, qui ne vous ai point dit de vous marier avec moi, et que vous avez prise sans consulter mes sentiments, je prétends n'être point obligée à me soumettre en esclave à vos volontés; et je veux jouir, s'il vous plaît, de quelque nombre de beaux jours que m'offre la jeunesse, prendre les douces libertés que l'âge me permet, voir un peu le beau monde, et goûter le plaisir de m'ouïr dire des douceurs. Préparez-vous-y, pour votre punition, et rendez grâces au Ciel de ce que je ne suis pas capable de quelque chose de pis. (II, ii)

It faces the facts of life, and challenges accepted ideas about arranged marriages. In the same scene, her *cri de coeur*:

> Je vous déclare que mon dessein n'est pas de renoncer au monde, et de m'enterrer toute vive dans un mari

echoes the feminist aspirations of her *précieuse* sisters, protesting against the harsh realities of marriage – quite a striking echo if one thinks of this complaint of a character from the Abbé de Pure's novel *La Précieuse*:

> On se prévaut de ma jeunesse et de mon obéissance, et on m'enterre, ou plutôt m'ensevelit toute vive dans le lit du fils d'Évandre.[15]

The confrontation between Dandin and Angélique is Molière's most sustained examination of what for many women were the realities of contemporary marriage. There are many other plays, of course, in which the plot raises the question of a young girl's being forced into marriage against her wishes; and normally the dramatic sympathies aroused coincide with the intellectual support commanded by the

---

[15] Ed. E. Magne (Paris, 1939), I, p. 280.

expression of enlightened ideas on marriage. With Angélique, however, this is not so, and the fact that a serious critique of the arranged
marriage is put into the mouth of a character who has alienated our
sympathy is another factor that helps to create the moral ambiguity of
this unusual play.

Nevertheless, however strong its topical implications, *George
Dandin* is firmly rooted in the farce tradition. The dramatic structure
could not be simpler: each of the three acts presents the same pattern
of events, as Dandin first learns from Lubin that Angélique and
Clitandre plan to deceive him, then confronts his parents-in-law with
his infallible proof of Angélique's guilt, only to find she has managed
to turn the tables on him. And Dandin himself, in spite of the
contemporary sociological reference, is still the *mal-marié* of popular
literature: as a recent writer expresses it, he is 'a member of an ancient
club'.[16] Modern criticism, and recent productions like that of Roger
Planchon in the late 1960s, have stressed the play's social realism,
and read into it a sombre message; the hero's closing soliloquy in
particular seems to have lent itself to such an interpretation:

> . . . lorsqu'on a, comme moi, épousé une méchante femme, le meilleur
> parti qu'on puisse prendre, c'est de s'aller jeter dans l'eau la tête la
> première.

But we should not forget that *George Dandin* was written for performance at Versailles, as part of the 'Grand Divertissement royal'; it was
immediately followed by a sequence in which, to Lulli's music,
shepherds singing of love are challenged by another group singing the
praises of Bacchus; as Mrs Crow suggests, the Court audience 'was
left with the impression that George Dandin would in the event
drown his sorrows only in wine'.[17] Even when the play was transferred to the Palais-Royal, and deprived of the framework of a royal
'divertissement', it is difficult to imagine Molière's spectators
identifying themselves, like Planchon's ideal audience, with the self-
inflicted sufferings of a country bumpkin; and Robinet's verdict is
surely a much better reflection of a contemporary audience's reaction:

> . . . un sujet archi-comique,
> Auquel rirait le plus stoïque,
> Vraiment, malgré-bongré ses dents,
> Tant sont plaisants les incidents.[18]

[16] Joan Crow, 'Reflections on *George Dandin*' in Howarth and Thomas (eds.), *Molière:
Stage and Study*, pp. 3–12 (p. 9). [17] *Ibid.*, p. 6. [18] Mongrédien (ed.), *Recueil*, p. 314.

For Molière's audience of courtiers and *honnêtes gens*, then, both the parvenu Dandin and his conceited in-laws the Sotenvilles represented classes of 'outsiders' who could be mocked from the safe, complacent vantage-point of 'la Cour et la Ville'. *Amphitryon*, however, which was performed at the Palais-Royal in the same year, 1668, must have made more disturbing viewing for some of its first spectators.

At first sight, *Amphitryon* seems to be of all Molière's plays the one with the smallest degree of topical relevance. Molière followed Rotrou in adapting Plautus, and though not quite such a close copy as his predecessor's *Les Sosies* (1636), his play is faithful to the Latin original as regards its setting in the ancient world and many details of its plot;[19] this is especially true of the role of Sosie, played by Molière himself. It is when we come to look more closely at the themes suggested by the Amphitryon legend that the originality and the provocative implications of Molière's treatment become apparent.

Not that Molière exploits the tragic, or even the pathetic, implications of the ancient myth: on the contrary. It is well known that it inspired tragedies, as well as Plautus' 'tragicomoedia', in antiquity,[20] and among modern versions, Kleist's 'comedy after Molière' of 1807 is a kind of Romantic tragedy, representing in Alkmene the dignity of the human condition; but in Molière's version the playwright has been content to present both Alcmène and Amphitryon as sympathetic – neither ridiculous nor pathetic – victims of the inexplicable series of events that disturbs their marital harmony, before restoring that harmony with the conventional happy ending. At least, that is the reading of the play that seems to make most sense; I find it difficult to endorse the interpretation of Dr McBride, for instance, who sees Jupiter as a sort of super-Tartuffe and Amphitryon, deceived by him, by implication as the equivalent of Orgon, whose 'dogmatic attitude to the opinions of others is easily recognizable as that of the Molière *imaginaire*' – or, like Dom Garcie, 'perpetually mastered by his jealous temperament, which is not easily given to forgiveness and forgetfulness'.[21] I see no evidence in the text that Amphitryon is *temperamentally* jealous, or that he lives in the solipsistic world of the typical *imaginaire*. Suddenly faced with the bewildering contradictions produced by Jupiter's appearance as his double, and Alcmène's

[19] Jacques Scherer calls the play 'cette aventure aussi dépaysante pour la conscience commune qu'aujourd'hui les anticipations de la science-fiction', 'Dualités d'*Amphitryon*' in Howarth and Thomas (eds.), *Molière: Stage and Study*, pp. 185–97 (p. 196).
[20] For a succinct review of earlier versions, see Scherer, *ibid*.
[21] *The Sceptical Vision of Molière*, pp. 163ff., 181, 185.

insistence that she has remained faithful when she has obviously spent the night with someone other than himself, Amphitryon becomes a sort of Everyman, confronted by the challenge of the supernatural. Dr McBride makes interesting play with the Cartesian notion of a 'mauvais génie' sent to test the human reason (a stage in the development of Descartes's method of systematic doubt, leading to the final certainty of his 'cogito ergo sum'). According to McBride, Amphitryon is at fault – and comically at fault – in affirming a certainty of his own identity that is purely subjective, and in not recognising the possibility of an alternative explanation of the evidence. But it is Sosie who is richly comic in his abject surrender of his identity to Mercure; Amphitryon's bewildered, but brave, re-action to the challenge from Jupiter commands our respect: if we are amused at his situation, we feel too much of a sympathetic involvement for our laughter to be unchecked.

Moreover, to interpret the play in terms of a metaphysical enquiry into the nature of human identity represents a misguided intrusion of twentieth-century preoccupations into an area where they do not belong.[22] If *Amphitryon* did have certain disturbing qualities for its first spectators, this was not because of any metaphysical content. We must imagine the spectators of 1668 reacting with pleasure, in the first place, to the immediate visual attraction of the 'comedy of errors', introduced and rounded off by a modest display of machine effects,[23] and to the unusual refinement of Molière's *vers libres*: all of this – the interplay of reality and illusion, in a suitably unworldly setting – reminds us that no absolute dividing line can be drawn, chronologically or thematically, between 'baroque' and 'high classicism'. But in addition, the triangular relationship between Alcmène, Amphitryon and Jupiter, as presented by Molière, must have given spectators food for thought. Molière's originality is to have focused, in two passages at least, not so much on the contrast between the human and the divine attributes of the two male members of this triangle, as on the opposition between husband and lover. Alcmène is exceptional in seventeenth-century terms, Mercure remarks in the Prologue, in that the only possible way for a lover to prevail has been for Jupiter to impersonate her husband:

---

[22] See L. Gossman, *Men and Masks: A Study of Molière* (Baltimore, 1963), ch. i, as well as McBride, *ibid.*
[23] Modest, because the Palais-Royal had only very limited resources for machine effects. It was to be re-equipped for the production of *Psyché* in 1671.

> . . .près de maint objet chéri,
> Pareil déguisement serait pour ne rien faire,
> Et ce n'est pas partout un bon moyen de plaire
> Que la figure d'un mari. (72–5)

When Jupiter is taking his leave, he tries hard to get Alcmène to admit that it was the lover, not the husband, in the 'Amphitryon' with whom she has spent the night, whom she will remember with particular affection; and again in Act II, scene vi, he seeks to blame the husband in him for the quarrel that had developed in scene ii. But Alcmène will accept no such distinction. She says in the first instance:

> Amphitryon, en vérité,
> Vous vous moquez de tenir ce langage,
> Et j'aurais peur qu'on ne vous crût pas sage,
> Si de quelqu'un vous étiez écouté, (lines 608–11)

and in the second:

> Ah! toutes ces subtilités
> N'ont que des excuses frivoles,
> Et pour les esprits irrités
> Ce sont des contretemps que de telles paroles. (lines 327–30)

She speaks, of course, as a faithful wife who has no reason to suspect that husband and lover are not one and the same person; but all the same, to a contemporary audience such a contrast must have had a very obvious reference, beyond the immediate context, to the *précieux* debate on marriage, 'honnête amitié' and the delights to be found in extra-marital affairs. As a contribution to this debate the role of Alcmène, as a wife who remains loyal to her marriage vow and her husband's love, makes an uncompromising stand against contemporary fashion in the beau monde, where the notion of conjugal love tended to be more than a little devalued; and in his conception of this role Molière takes a significant step towards the marvellous creation of Giraudoux.

However, if in one respect Alcmène represents the ideal of conjugal fidelity, the dénouement of the play forces us to look at things in another light. Jupiter has had his way with her, and from his point of view his ruse has succeeded: Alcmène has been established, however briefly, as the favourite of the king of the gods. And here a much more difficult question of topical application comes in. For to courtiers and cultured Parisians who kept up with current production in literature and the arts, the figure of Jupiter must have been a transparent allegory for that of Louis XIV. P. Römer, in his study of *Amphitryon*, quotes an impressive array of texts from the poets of the time, echoing La Fontaine who declared as early as 1661 that 'Jupiter et Louis, c'est le même'; and with reference to the visual arts, concludes that in the painting of the period it became 'almost a commonplace' to depict the King in the guise of the ruler of Olympus.[24] Authors of *ballets de cour* were especially fond of this particular allegory; and among the ballets in which the King himself danced was the *Ballet royal de l'Impatience* of 1661 in which he had appeared as Jupiter, disguised in order to seduce a mortal, and had recited the following verses by Benserade:

> Je descends vers l'objet qui seul me peut charmer,
> Et même j'y descends, non sans quelque surprise
> Qu'à dessein de me faire aimer
> Il faille que je me déguise.
>
> Les mortels ne sauraient, quand je traite avec eux,
> Souffrir de ma splendeur qu'une légère trace;
> Et mon éclat trop lumineux
> Les éblouit et m'embarrasse.
>
> Devant une beauté je cache finement
> Cette pompe divine où mon être se fonde;
> Et l'on me prendrait seulement
> Pour le premier homme du monde.[25]

In the light of such evidence, the question is not whether spectators of Molière's play would make this identification of Jupiter with their monarch – but rather, what conclusions they can be expected to have drawn from it. The problem is that the interpretation which imposes itself hardly squares with the apologia for chastity and conjugal fidelity in Alcmène. For whether or not the King's liaison with Mme de Montespan was public knowledge at this time,[26] the adulation of the godlike ruler as a being above the moral law:

> Lorsque dans un haut rang on a l'heur de paraître,
> Tout ce qu'on fait est toujours bel et bon;
> Et suivant ce qu'on peut être,
> Les choses changent de nom (lines 128–31)

is never questioned, from the Prologue right through to the final *éclaircissement*. And if one does take into account the real-life implications in terms of the public misfortunes of the Marquis de Montes-

---

[24] *Molières 'Amphitryon' und sein gesellschaftlicher Hintergrund* (Bonn, 1967), pp. 95, 98.
[25] Quoted *ibid.*, p. 99.   [26] *Ibid.*, pp. 40–6, 61–73.

pan (however different his own position may have been from that of Amphitryon, and however different his wife's response from that of Alcmène), the cynicism of the finale becomes clear enough:

> Un partage avec Jupiter
> N'a rien du tout qui déshonore;
> Et sans doute il ne peut être que glorieux
> De se voir le rival du souverain des Dieux. (lines 1896–1901)

It is true that Sosie's wry aside: 'Le Seigneur Jupiter sait dorer la pilule' (line 1913), and his final intervention, which prevents Naucratès from congratulating Amphitryon on his good fortune, seem to close the play on a note of apparent realism:

> Messieurs, voulez-vous bien suivre mon sentiment?
> Ne vous embarquez nullement
> Dans ces douceurs congratulantes:
> C'est un mauvais embarquement,
> Et d'une et d'autre part, pour un tel compliment,
> Les phrases sont embarrassantes. (lines 1928–33)

But can we really believe that Molière is inviting his spectators to dissociate themselves from the chorus of conventional adulation, so widespread in the literature and the visual arts of the time? Such temerity on the part of a humble *comédien*, however well established he may have been in the King's service, is quite unthinkable. Sosie's viewpoint is that of an outsider; it does not challenge the more worldly-wise view of the courtiers; and painful though it may be for most of us today to discover Molière in the servile role of a sycophantic Court poet, that was evidently the price that had to be paid from time to time for the support on which he and his company depended. Although one need not accept Michelet's view that the play must have been written at the King's command, his commentary does, I think, deserve assent in more general terms:

> La chose était barbare; elle navrait la Reine et la Vallière, et Madame de Montausier, M. de Montespan, tant d'autres. Molière n'eût pas fait de lui-même cette cruelle exécution. Il y déplore sa servitude. Que peut Molière-Sosie? Il sert et servira. Car il n'a que son maître, et contre lui toute la cour.[27]

In short, I find this an uncomfortable play on a disturbing subject. The 'pilule' remains, 'dorée' or not; and it is difficult not to see Amphitryon, within the play, as the sympathetic victim of a cruel

---

[27] Quoted *ibid.*, p. 43.

hoax, while his analogue in real life is the complaisant husband, humiliated by being sacrificed to the pleasures of the Sun King. How much more humane is the dénouement Giraudoux chose for his *Amphitryon 38*, where his Alcmème wins Jupiter over so that the events of the night are veiled in oblivion to their human participants. There, myth remains myth, with no uncomfortable application to the world of reality.

(iii) Molière and the doctors

Looked at from one point of view, Molière's satire of medicine and the medical profession follows the predictable lines of a well-defined comic tradition; yet it is in that same field that we find one of the most striking cases in his theatre of satire in the form of the personal lampoon, while in several plays we are reminded of topical controversies on important issues.

Satirical comedy at the expense of the learned professions had a long history in the European theatre, and the *dottore*, or pedant, was a common figure both of the *commedia erudita* and *commedia dell'arte*, and the French comedy derived from these sources.[28] The relation between the *dottore* of Italian tradition and the equally pedantic medical doctor can easily be recognised when the latter is seen dazzling and browbeating ordinary people with his display of learning, taking refuge in the obscurity of the Latin tongue, and dogmatically insisting on the infallibility of his art, with much reference to the authority of Galen and Hippocrates. For the most part, fantasy contributes so largely to such caricatures that if they can be called satirical, it is only in the most general terms; and when Molière borrowed from this tradition in some of his early provincial farces, it was very much in the same spirit. Sganarelle of *Le Médecin volant* is a pure figure of fun, and in the farcical context of that play it would be difficult to see any marked satirical force even in such remarks as 'Il ne faut pas qu'elle s'amuse à se laisser mourir sans l'ordonnance du médecin' (scene iv).[29]

It was some time after he returned to Paris before Molière again turned his attention towards the doctors. The *docteurs* Pancrace and Marphurius of *Le Mariage forcé* of 1664 are pedantic philosophers, not

[28] See A. Gill, 'The "Doctor in the farce" and Molière', *French Studies*, II (1948), 101–28; R. Guichemerre, *La Comédie avant Molière*, pp. 159ff.
[29] This joke recurs in both *L'Amour médecin* (II, ii) and *Le Médecin malgré lui* (II, iv).

docteurs en médecine; and although the two comic types traditionally had certain traits in common – for instance, Le Barbouillé had said of Le Docteur: 'A cause qu'il est vêtu comme un médecin, j'ai cru qu'il lui fallait parler d'argent' (*Jalousie*, scene ii) – it was not until the following year, 1665, that Molière brought on to the Paris stage a character dressed in the tall hat and long black gown that constituted – in theatrical idiom, at any rate – the insignia of the medical profession. Even then, the character in question is the Sganarelle of *Dom Juan*, who is no more a 'real' doctor than his namesake in *Le Médecin volant* had been. At the beginning of Act III of *Dom Juan* Sganarelle and his master have changed clothes in order to escape pursuit: Sganarelle is dressed as a doctor, and the act opens with a sequence of traditional jokes about medicine. Fantasy predominates, but this does not prevent the introduction of a specific reference of considerable topicality:

> *Sganarelle*: Cependant vous voyez depuis un temps que le vin émétique fait bruire ses fuseaux. Ses miracles ont converti les plus incrédules esprits; et il n'y a pas trois semaines que j'en ai vu, moi qui vous parle, un effet merveilleux.
> *D. Juan*: Et quel?
> *Sgan.*: Il y avait un homme qui depuis six jours était à l'agonie. On ne savait plus que lui ordonner, et tous les remèdes ne faisaient rien; on s'avisa à la fin de lui donner de l'émétique.
> *D. Juan*: Il réchappa?
> *Sgan.*: Non, il mourut.
> *D. Juan*: L'effet est admirable.
> *Sgan.*: Comment! Il y avait six jours entiers qu'il ne pouvait mourir, et cela le fit mourir tout d'un coup. Voulez-vous rien de plus efficace?
> (III, i)

'Emetic wine', a preparation of antimony, had been in use since the early sixteenth century, though it aroused prolonged controversy in France. Banned by the Medical Faculty in 1566 and in 1615, it was to be included in the official pharmaceutical code in 1638; however, the controversy continued until 1666, when the last opposition was overcome and the Faculty registered its approval of the drug. In 1658 the antimony cure had been used in a serious illness of the King's, and that had had a considerable effect on public opinion; hence, Molière's apparent scepticism about the 'miracles' performed by the drug would seem to suggest a certain audacity. Nevertheless, if the passage has a background of topical polemic, its tone is one of light-hearted comic invention.

The same is true of the satire on medicine in *Le Médecin malgré lui* of

1666. Here too, Sganarelle, forced by circumstances to pose as a doctor, finds that it is not difficult to succeed, once one has the robes and a smattering of the jargon:

> On me vient chercher de tous les côtés; et si les choses vont toujours de même, je suis d'avis de m'en tenir, toute ma vie, à la médecine. Je trouve que c'est le métier le meilleur de tous; car soit qu'on fasse bien ou soit qu'on fasse mal, on est toujours payé de même sorte: la méchante besogne ne retombe jamais sur notre dos; et nous taillons, comme il nous plaît, sur l'étoffe où nous travaillons. Un cordonnier, en faisant des souliers, ne saurait gâter un morceau de cuir qu'il n'en paye les pots cassés; mais ici l'on peut gâter un homme sans qu'il en coûte rien. Les bévues ne sont point pour nous; et c'est toujours la faute de celui qui meurt. Enfin le bon de cette profession est qu'il y a parmi les morts une honnêteté, une discrétion la plus grande du monde; et jamais on n'en voit se plaindre du médecin qui l'a tué. (III, i)

There is, it is true, a passing mention of 'une certaine drogue que l'on appelle du vin amétile' (III, iii); other references, too, are capable of conveying a more serious critical comment, such as the threat to bleed someone in perfect health:

> — Mais, Monsieur, voilà une mode que je ne comprends point. Pourquoi s'aller faire saigner quand on n'a point de maladie?
> — Il n'importe, la mode en est salutaire; et comme on boit pour la soif à venir, il faut se faire aussi saigner pour la maladie à venir (II, iv)[30]

or the use of empty tautology to conceal the shortcomings of medical science:

> — . . . Je vous apprends que votre fille est muette.
> — Oui; mais je voudrais bien que vous me puissiez dire d'où cela vient.
> — Il n'est rien plus aisé: cela vient de ce qu'elle a perdu la parole.
> — Fort bien; mais la cause, s'il vous plaît, qui fait qu'elle a perdu la parole?
> — Tous nos meilleurs auteurs vous diront que c'est l'empêchement de l'action de sa langue. (*ibid.*)

But the context of such passages, in this farcical plot about a fake doctor called in to treat a fake illness, is such that their satirical

---

[30] A case in point here is that of the King himself, who was subjected by his doctors throughout his life to a frightening regime of bleeding and purging. Similarly, it has been claimed that Louis XIII was turned by medical intervention from a robust infant into 'a neurotic, unhappy and handicapped adult', E. W. Marvick, 'The Character of Louis XIII: the Role of his Physician', *Journal of Interdisciplinary Studies*, IV, 347–74, quoted by H. G. Hall, 'Molière Satirist of Seventeenth-Century French Medicine: Fact and Fantasy', *Proceedings of the Royal Society of Medicine*, LXX (1977), 425–31.

impact is absolutely minimal: the tone of *Le médecin malgré lui* remains that of good-natured fantasy throughout.

In 1665, however, Molière had written a play which, despite its farcical nature, is also the vehicle for some very pointed personal satire. The essential plot of *L'Amour médecin*, which is not unlike that of *Le Médecin malgré lui* (a young girl feigns illness, and her lover adopts the disguise of a doctor; the pair are able to hoodwink Sganarelle, the father, and the play ends with their marriage) is contained in Acts I and III of the play. The middle act is completely episodic: it contributes nothing to the plot, consisting as it does of a 'consultation' by four doctors who, having been called in to give their opinions on Lucinde's illness, in fact spend their time discussing the affairs of the Faculty, congratulating themselves on preserving their prerogatives, and resisting all innovation as an affront to their profession. There is conclusive evidence from commentators of the time that these four doctors, together with a fifth who arrives at the beginning of Act III and upbraids his colleagues for airing their disagreement in public, were intended as caricatural portrait of eminent contemporary representatives of the Faculty. Their names either correspond to those of their real-life counterparts (Des Fonandrès: Des Fougerais; Filerin: Yvelin) or else indicate their identity by their Greek etymology. Of the four principals one (Tomès) is a fanatical advocate of bleeding; another (Des Fonandrès) is an equally determined partisan of 'le vin émétique'; while the other two are characterised by distinctive impediments of speech. To make the identification more certain, the actors wore masks; and a spectator recorded the effect on the doctors concerned:

> Ce qui faisait encore plus rire, c'est que les masques ressemblaient tellement particulièrement à M. Guénaut, à M. Esprit et à des Fougerais qu'il n'y a personne qui ne les ait pris pour eux. M. Guénaut a traité cela de raillerie. Mais M. Esprit n'en peut rire.[31]

Dr Gaston Hall, in his article on seventeenth-century medicine as a background to Molière's satirical treatment of the subject, suggests that the correct analogy would be with 'the end-of-term review, destined to "take off" but not necessarily to disgrace the butts of satire'.[32] But there is a considerable difference between this comment, for example, from one of Montaigne's essays:

---

[31] Cf. texts quoted in *Recueil*, pp. 245–8.   [32] 'Molière Satirist', 426.

Ce que la fortune, ce que la nature ou quelque autre cause étrangère (desquelles le nombre est infini) produit en nous de bon et de salutaire, c'est le privilège de la médecine de se l'attribuer; tous les heureux succès qui arrivent au patient qui est sous son régime, c'est d'elle qu'il les tient[33]

and the virtually identical remark put into the mouth of Filerin – that is to say Yvelin, a leading doctor at Court:

Mais le plus grand faible des hommes, c'est l'amour qu'ils ont pour la vie; et nous en profitons, nous autres, par notre pompeux galimatias, et savons prendre nos avantages de cette vénération que la peur de mourir leur donne pour notre métier. Conservons-nous donc dans le degré d'estime où leur faiblesse nous a mis, et soyons de concert auprès des malades pour nous attribuer les heureux succès de la maladie, et rejeter sur la nature toutes les bévues de notre art. N'allons point, dis-je, détruire sottement les heureuses préventions d'une erreur qui donne du pain à tant de personnes. (III, i)

By the same token, it is comic, but hardly satirical, when Lisette the *suivante* says:

Il ne faut jamais dire: 'Une telle personne est morte d'une fièvre et d'une fluxion sur la poitrine'; mais: 'Elle est morte de quatre médecins et de deux apothicaires'. (II, i)

However, the satire takes on an unusually sharp edge when Tomès and Des Fonandrès accuse each other at the culmination of their quarrel:

—Souvenez-vous de l'homme que vous fîtes crever ces jours passés.
—Souvenez-vous de la dame que vous avez envoyée en l'autre monde, il y a trois jours. (II, iv)

If it is impossible to do more than guess why Molière should have indulged in this sort of personal lampoon,[34] it is equally difficult to know why he should so quickly have abandoned it. It was not long before he apparently lost interest in the antimony controversy; and although *Le Malade imaginaire* alludes to another important topical controversy (concerning the circulation of the blood), that is done without any hint of a satirical attack on individuals. In the meantime,

---

[33] *Essais*, ii, xxxvii.
[34] Grimarest, following Le Boulanger de Chalussay's *Élomire hypocondre*, suggests that a quarrel between Molière and his landlord (recently shown to have been Daquin, who is portrayed as Tomès in the play) may have provided the motive for writing *L'Amour médecin* (*La Vie de M. de Molière*, pp. 61–2). According to other early biographers, however, Molière was dispossessed by his landlord in retaliation for his satirical attack.

Molière had offered in *Monsieur de Pourceaugnac* – as an episodic element in the parade of comic types referred to in Chapter 4, section i – another parody of a medical consultation:

> A Dieu ne plaise, Monsieur, qu'il me tombe en pensée d'ajouter rien à ce que vous venez de dire! Vous avez si bien discouru sur tous les signes, les symptômes et les causes de la maladie de Monsieur; le raisonnement que vous en avez fait est si docte et si beau, qu'il est impossible qu'il ne soit pas fou, et mélancolique hypocondriaque; et quand il ne le serait pas, il faudrait qu'il le devînt, pour la beauté des choses que vous avez dites, et la justesse du raisonnement que vous avez fait. Oui, Monsieur, vous avez dépeint fort graphiquement, *graphice depinxisti*, tout ce qui appartient à cette maladie: il ne se peut rien de plus doctement, sagement, ingénieusement conçu, pensé, imaginé, que ce que vous avez prononcé au sujet de ce mal, soit pour la diagnose, ou la prognose, ou la thérapie; et il ne me reste rien ici, que de féliciter Monsieur d'être tombé entre vos mains, et de lui dire qu'il est trop heureux d'être fou, pour éprouver l'efficace et la douceur des remèdes que vous avez si judicieusement proposés. (I, viii)

Once again, however, even if the imputation of wordy pedantry combined with ignorance seems to be brought by implication against a whole profession, this falls far short of the satirical passages quoted from *L'Amour médecin*, with their allegations of cynical self-seeking against thinly-disguised individuals. The doctors who appear in *Pourceaugnac* are the products of a light-hearted fantasy: there is no suggestion but that they accept Pourceaugnac as a genuine patient, and they are just as much taken in by Sbrigani as the unfortunate Limousin himself.

Le Malade imaginaire stands out from Molière's other 'doctor' plays in more than one respect. It is the only play in which the subject of medicine is central not only to the plot, but also to the theme: the only one, indeed, that could properly be termed a 'play about medicine'. Moreover, it is the only play to present 'real' doctors dealing with a 'real' patient. What we see elsewhere are fake illnesses, with a bogus doctor who assumes the role in order to favour a clandestine marriage; or else we have bona fide doctors who are presented as lacking the wit to recognise a fake illness when they see one. But Argan's is a very different case; and *Le Malade imaginaire* provokes thought about the relations between doctors and their patients in the real world in a way that none of the other plays sets out to do. Argan is a 'malade imaginaire', it is true: but what does that mean? Put at its simplest, he is a person who lives in his own make-believe world: he is not really ill, any more than Sganarelle is *cocu*. Things are not quite so simple, however. In the case of cuckoldry, one can have recourse to objective evidence: either Sganarelle is *cocu*, or he is not; the facts show that he is not, so we label him a 'cocu imaginaire'. But Argan's state of health can hardly be put to the same sort of objective test. From one point of view, he must be physically fit, and possess an exceptionally sound constitution, in order to withstand all the medicaments of which his opening soliloquy draws up such a formidable list: as Béralde says:

> J'entends, mon frère, que je ne vois point d'homme qui soit moins malade que vous, et que je ne demanderais point une meilleure constitution que la vôtre. (III, iii)

Yet on the other hand, it is hardly possible to disagree with J.-M. Pelous when he writes, 'La maladie d'Argan est en un sens très réelle: ce n'est pas un mal imaginaire, mais une maladie de l'imagination dont le premier et le plus grave symptôme est que celui qui en souffre est persuadé d'être malade.'[35] Of course, seventeenth-century diagnosis of mental illness can scarcely be compared with that of our own day; and the very fact that Molière chose to call his character a 'malade imaginaire' indicates clearly enough, in seventeenth-century terms at any rate, that he is to be taken as being in a different category from the genuinely sick. What, then, of the doctors in *Le Malade imaginaire*? When Toinette tells Argan that he is 'une bonne vache à lait' (I, ii), she uses the same expression that Mme Jourdain had used to her husband (*B. gent.*, III, iv); and the inference might well seem to be that Argan is being consciously 'milked' by unscrupulous doctors in just the same way that Monsieur Jourdain is being duped by Dorante. But M. Pelous argues convincingly that the medical practitioners we see in action here are doing an honest job according to their lights, and in keeping with the current state of medical knowledge:

> Ce serait une erreur de considérer ces médecins comme des ignorants; les raisonnements qu'ils tiennent sur le cas de leur malade sont très cohérents et tout à fait conformes à la pratique médicale de l'époque . . . Il ne fait pas de doute que le cas d'Argan correspond à une affection connue et dûment répertoriée par la médecine traditionnelle du xviie siècle.[36]

If this is so, it would appear that Molière has shifted his ground considerably since *L'Amour médecin*. There, the parody of a medical consultation had revealed four charlatans, deliberately feathering

[35] 'Argan et sa maladie imaginaire', *Marseille*, no. xcv (1973), 179–87 (p. 179).
[36] *Ibid.*, p. 182.

their own nest; here, we have conscientious professional men, pedantic and narrow-minded it may be, but behaving with apparent integrity. In one sense, this is obviously less provocative than the personal lampoon directed against identifiable Court physicians; yet looked at in another light, the satire in *Le Malade imaginaire,* if less vindictive, is much more far-reaching, since the whole profession is now held up to the judgement of our critical laughter.

'Ce ne sont pas les médecins qu'il joue, mais le ridicule de la médecine', says Béralde, speaking of Molière (III, iii); and though that is normally taken as a rather unconvincing disclaimer, I think it can serve as a pointer to the true nature of the satire in the play. For it becomes evident in *Le Malade imaginaire* that Molière's target is no longer individual doctors such as Daquin and his colleagues, or specific cures like 'le vin émétique', but nothing less than medicine itself as a dangerous and unreliable pseudo-science. 'Tout leur art est pure grimace', Dom Juan had said of doctors (III, i); and other characters in previous plays had, as we have seen, expressed a similar scepticism; but the impression normally given by these passing *boutades* is that Molière is exploiting an age-old critical tradition quite light-heartedly for comic purposes. The scene with Béralde, however, is developed at such length that it stands out, like certain scenes in *Tartuffe* or *Dom Juan,* as a dialectical set piece. Argan, on the one hand, represents the orthodox view of medicine as a dogmatic science based on the teaching of Hippocrates and Galen, and practised by initiates who have inherited this long tradition – a tradition that must not be challenged either by doctors or by their patients; whereas Béralde's attitude is that of the empirical thinker for whom the only valid criterion for judging medical science is its utility:

—Mais raisonnons un peu, mon frère. Vous ne croyez donc point à la médecine?
—Non, mon frère, et je ne vois pas que pour son salut il soit nécessaire d'y croire.
—Quoi! vous ne tenez pas véritable une chose établie par tout le monde, et que tous les siècles ont révérée?
—Bien loin de la tenir véritable, je la trouve, entre nous, une des plus grandes folies qui soit parmi les hommes, et, à regarder les choses en philosophe, je ne vois point de plus plaisante mômerie; je ne vois rien de plus ridicule qu'un homme qui se veut mêler d'en guérir un autre.
—Pourquoi ne voulez-vous pas, mon frère, qu'un homme en puisse guérir un autre?
—Par la raison, mon frère, que les ressorts de notre machine sont des mystères, jusques ici, où les hommes ne voient goutte, et que la nature

nous a mis au-devant des yeux des voiles trop épais pour y connaître quelque chose.
—Les médecins ne savent donc rien, à votre compte?
—Si fait, mon frère. Ils savent la plupart de fort belles humanités, savent parler en beau latin, savent nommer en grec toutes les maladies, les définir et les diviser; mais, pour ce qui est de les guérir, c'est ce qu'ils ne savent point du tout.

Moreover, Béralde's stance is not that of the destructive critic. Unlike the other characters Molière uses as mouthpieces for his satire of doctors and of the art of medicine, Béralde has a positive standpoint, a belief in the benign influence of nature as a healing force. In other words he is placed – and we may consider that Molière places himself, to the extent that we are willing to identify the playwright with the opinions of his character – in the main line of post-Renaissance naturalist thought represented in France most notably in Montaigne's *Essais*:

Je laisse faire nature, et présuppose qu'elle se soit pourvue de dents et de griffes, pour se défendre des assauts qui lui viennent, et pour maintenir cette contexture, de quoi elle fuit la dissolution. Je crains, au lieu de l'aller secourir, ainsi comme elle est aux prises bien étroites et bien jointes avec la maladie, qu'on secoure son adversaire au lieu d'elle, et qu'on la recharge de nouveaux affaires.[37]

Similarly, at the climax of the argument in III, iii Béralde elaborates on the naturalist message:

—Mais, enfin, venons au fait. Que faire donc quand on est malade?
—Rien, mon frère.
—Rien?
—Rien. Il ne faut que demeurer en repos. La nature, d'elle-même, quand nous la laissons faire, se tire doucement du désordre où elle est tombée. C'est notre inquiétude, c'est notre impatience qui gâte tout, et presque tous les hommes meurent de leurs remèdes, et non pas de leurs maladies.
—Mais il faut demeurer d'accord, mon frère, qu'on peut aider cette nature par de certaines choses.
—Mon Dieu, mon frère, ce sont pures idées dont nous aimons à nous repaître, et de tout temps il s'est glissé parmi les hommes de belles imaginations que nous venons à croire, parce qu'elles nous flattent, et qu'il serait à souhaiter qu'elles fussent véritables. Lorsqu'un médecin vous parle d'aider, de secourir, de soulager la nature . . . il vous dit justement le roman de la médecine. Mais, quand vous en venez à la vérité et à l'expérience, vous ne trouvez rien de tout cela, et il en est

[37] *Essais*, I, xxiv.

193

comme de ces beaux songes qui ne vous laissent au réveil que le déplaisir
de les avoir crus.

This crucial scene can be compared with other sustained dialectical
exchanges involving Molière's *visionnaire* or *imaginaire* characters.
Whether it be Arnolphe talking with Chrysalde, Alceste with
Philinte, Orgon with Cléante or Armande with Henriette – and
whatever the ostensible subject of their discussion – the underlying
theme is the same. Each of these important scenes consists of a
confrontation between a priori dogmatism and its opposite; between
authoritarian system-building and a common-sense distrust of all
systems; between the urge to force others into restrictive patterns of
behaviour in the name of some intellectual abstraction and the resistance to such coercion in the name of human nature. The close
similarity of theme between *Tartuffe* and *Le Malade imaginaire* is particularly striking; and some light is thrown on Molière's likely intentions in this respect if the latter play is studied in the light of certain
events that immediately preceded its writing.

For it has been plausibly argued that the genesis of Molière's last
play is closely connected with events in the academic world of Paris
round about 1670: the attempt by the Sorbonne authorities to revive
the decree, published by the Parlement de Paris in 1624, which had
forbidden anti-Aristotelian theses on pain of death. The attempt was
unsuccessful, but it shows how strongly the scholastic tradition was
still entrenched in Church and University; and as a reaction from
supporters of 'la nouvelle philosophie', it provoked a satirical rejoinder written by Boileau in the form of his *Arrêt burlesque* (1671), in
which 'la Raison' is banished from the University by a mock decree.
The Preface to this piece, written by Bernier, a disciple of Gassendi,
explicitly links Molière with the enterprise:

> On m'avait dit que le sieur Molière observait toutes les démarches de ces
> messieurs, et qu'il se proposait de démêler toutes leurs intrigues dans
> une comédie qu'il préparait pour le divertissement de la Cour.[38]

Bernier goes on to say that the playwright changed his mind about
writing a direct satire of the reactionary academics; but to quote a
modern editor of the play that he wrote instead, 'it is impossible to
mistake the degree to which *Le Malade imaginaire* was inspired' by
these events.[39]

[38] Quoted in *Le Malade imaginaire*, ed. P. H. Nurse (London, 1965), p. 15.
[39] *Ibid.*

In the light of this evidence it is easy to see that the portrait of the reactionary and obscurantist doctors in Purgon and Diafoirus, and of the narrow scholasticism that governs the teaching of new doctors in the latter's son Thomas, would carry a broader message for the play's first spectators than mere satire of contemporary medical practice. That is there, of course – and the following reference to Thomas by his father:

> Ce qui me plaît en lui, et en quoi il suit mon exemple, c'est qu'il s'attache aveuglément aux opinions de nos anciens, et que jamais il n'a voulu comprendre ni écouter les raisons et les expériences des prétendues découvertes de notre siècle touchant la circulation du sang et autres opinions de même farine (II, v)

tellingly pinpoints the theoretical background to that practice – but the links with academic scholasticism in other fields are clear enough to make Molière's satire a wide-ranging attack on a more important target. If to this broadening of the intellectual range is added the positive contribution made by Béralde's humanist message, the result is a comedy of ideas, or a comedy of values, that transcends by far the limitations of what we normally mean by satire.

(iv) 'Tartuffe': satire or comedy?

In one sense, *Tartuffe* and *Dom Juan* stand together, and apart from the rest of Molière's theatre, as the two plays in which he deliberately provoked a confrontation with the most powerful vested interests of contemporary society: *Tartuffe* was performed freely only after a five-year struggle with ecclesiastical authority, and there is good reason to believe that the disappearance of *Dom Juan* from the repertory after fifteen extremely successful performances was also due to the intervention of the censor.[40]

There is no doubt that in writing *Tartuffe*, Molière was tackling one of La Bruyère's 'grands sujets', and that to write a comedy about religious belief was either a very courageous, or a very foolhardy, thing to do. I deliberately use the phrase 'a comedy about religious belief' rather than 'about hypocrisy', because that is surely the true nature of Molière's provocation in this play. The five-year ban on *Tartuffe*, and what we know of the playwright's difficulties with the Church authorities, have inevitably led scholars to pay too much

---

[40] See R. Robert, 'Le *Don Juan* de Molière a-t-il été interdit?', *Revue des Sciences Humaines*, XXX (1956), 50–3.

attention to the background of contemporary ideas, and to indulge in fruitless speculation about the individuals proposed as models for Tartuffe. Since we do not possess the text of 1664, any deductions we may be led to make about Molière's original intentions must contain some guesswork; but the most prudent interpretation of the evidence, as presented by historians like G. Michaut,[41] H. d'Alméras[42] and F. Baumal,[43] would seem to be that the playwright did not have an individual model in mind, and that none of the individuals named – Desmarets de Saint-Sorlin, Charpy de Sainte-Croix and the Abbé Roquette are those most frequently named – is likely to have served as a 'source vivante'. There is nevertheless one contemporary who may have played a large part in determining the choice of subject. This is the Prince de Conti, the patron and benefactor of Molière's troupe during his years in the provinces, whose protection had come to an abrupt end on his conversion in 1655, when he had become a fanatical opponent of the theatre. Molière clearly chose to believe that Conti's was a feigned conversion, an example of that deliberate self-seeking under a mask of piety that is the common theme of *Tartuffe* and *Dom Juan*; so that as well as offering a real-life illustration of the *grand seigneur méchant homme*, it seems not unlikely that Conti, by his behaviour towards Molière, also provided a stimulus for the writing of *Tartuffe*.

Evidence as to the form and contents of the first *Tartuffe* is tantalisingly contradictory. Did the performance at Versailles on 12 May 1664 consist (for reasons unknown) of three acts of a five-act play, or was the original *Tartuffe* conceived in three acts? In either case, if the spectators of 1664 saw a version which stopped where the present Act III ends – that is, with the dismissal of Damis, and with Tartuffe securely in possession – the dozen lines from line 1172:

> Non, en dépit de tous vous la fréquenterez

to the couplet which closes Act III:

> Le pauvre homme! Allons vite en dresser un écrit,
> Et que puisse l'envie en crever de dépit!

would make an effective ending to a very different play from the one that has come down to us. John Cairncross, however, argues ingeniously that the 1664 *Tartuffe* was a complete version containing

---

[41] *Les Luttes de Molière* (Paris, 1925), pp. 33ff.
[42] *Le Tartuffe de Molière* (Paris, 1928).   [43] *Tartuffe et ses avatars* (Paris, 1925).

Acts I, III and IV of the definitive text – the result being, of course, that such a version would have ended with the unmasking of Tartuffe and the opening of Orgon's eyes, but with the latter being turned out of his house.[44] In the absence of hard evidence, the question must remain undecided; but it is of the utmost importance to remember that in its inspiration and motivation, *Tartuffe* belongs to 1664. We do not know what details of plot and dialogue may have been added between 1664 and 1667, or changed between 1667 and 1669: what can be said with certainty, however, is that the basic conception of the plot, depending on the relationship between the principal characters, was established in 1664. The original inspiration of *Tartuffe* places the play in the first half of Molière's Paris career, at a point at which 'la grande comédie' had not yet assumed pride of place in his theatre, and at which his comic writing was nearer to its origin in popular farce. It has been said that it is fortunate *Tartuffe* was written when it was, and not ten years earlier, when it might have taken the form of a crude farce with the title 'Mascarille fourbe et Sganarelle dévot'.[45] The comment is a fair one: the play has gained immeasurably by being written as a polished five-act comedy of manners; but even in the 1669 text, the essential comic relationship remains that of Mascarille and Sganarelle. These are the 'originals' of Tartuffe and Orgon in the only sense that matters, not Charpy de Sainte-Croix and his host, M. de Patrocle, or any other real-life couple.

Other survivals of the tone and manner of farce can be seen in the 1669 text. The whole role of Madame Pernelle, for instance: the opening scene of the play can be seen as a variant of those episodes of the farces in which the pedant speaks non-stop, preventing other characters from getting a word in;[46] while the fact that Madame Pernelle was played by a male actor, and her beating of Flipote at the end of this scene, suggest a dramatic style completely at variance with the tone of much that follows. And what is one to make of the scene with Orgon under the table? This surely illustrates the sort of imaginative fantasy that belongs to farce, not to a more realistic comedy of manners. It is totally illogical that Orgon should agree to Elmire's invitation to witness something, the very possibility of which he has

---

[44] *New Light on Molière* (Geneva–Paris), 1956.

[45] G. Lanson, 'Molière et la farce', *Revue de Paris* (May 1901), 129–53. (Reprinted in *Essais de méthode, de critique et d'histoire littéraire* (Paris, 1965), pp. 189–210 (p. 206).

[46] The point has been convincingly made by A. Gill in a videotape presentation of the relevant scenes prepared by the University of Glasgow A.V.A. Unit.

just shown himself to be intellectually incapable of accepting; and there must be some degree of incongruity between the subtlety of the dialogue between Tartuffe and Elmire in this scene, and the gross visual effect of the husband under the table. That is, if the scene is properly directed: too many directors attempt a compromise here in the name of realism, covering Orgon with the table-cloth so that he is hidden not only from Tartuffe but also from the audience – whereas the comic effect requires that Orgon remain fully visible, so that he can give a running commentary on the scene by means of mime and gesture. These are the *moyens scéniques* of farce, not of a more sophisticated literary comedy; and an instructive contrast can be drawn between this episode and the dénouement of the play, the point at which, if Molière had been writing entirely in the farce tradition, the discomfiture of the impostor would have been marked by the ritual *coups de bâton*.

The *coups de bâton* that had ended *Les Précieuses ridicules* would not have been out of place in a farcical 'Mascarille fourbe et Sganarelle dévot'; but they have given way to an ending more in keeping with a serious comedy of ideas: the intervention of the Exempt, and the eulogy of 'un prince ennemi de la fraude', are the positive counterpart of the satirical attack on *fausse dévotion* as a real-life phenomenon. Whatever the precise contents of the three-act version of 1664, we may be virtually certain of such a change of emphasis; and a scene like the discussion between Tartuffe and Cléante, which lies outside the relationship between the trickster and his dupe, is likely to have been added during this second phase of the play's evolution.

As for the identification of Tartuffe with a particular sect or party, the very fact that plausible cases have been made out, based on selective use of textual evidence, for making him a Jansenist, a Jesuit, or a member of the Compagnie du Saint-Sacrement, suggests that none of these identifications is exclusive, and that Molière's *faux dévot* wears a composite mask. That Jansenists and Jesuits should each see the other as the object of his satire is hardly surprising; though the lines about 'la direction de l'intention':

> Selon divers besoins, il est une science
> D'étendre les liens de notre conscience,
> Et de rectifier le mal de l'action
> Avec la pureté de notre intention (lines 1489–92)

seem much nearer the bone than any allusions to Jansenist asceticism. As for the Compagnie, that was a secret society, and it seems certain that modern historians know much more about it than contemporaries were in a position to know; this being so, apparent allusions to its activities such as interfering in family life, spying and informing, may well be the result of coincidence. The Panulphe of 1667 and the Tartuffe of 1669 were designed, we may be sure, to represent the lay *directeurs de conscience* who had become so numerous round the middle of the century, but there is no indication that in either form Molière's hypocrite was meant to have a specific affiliation with any sect. When the playwright wrote:

> Les Tartuffes, sous main, ont eu l'adresse de trouver grâce auprès de votre Majesté, et les originaux enfin ont fait supprimer la copie (First Placet)

he was probably expressing his frustation and resentment that churchmen of all sorts should have had access to the royal ear, and that their influence should have prevailed; and the same is surely true of the passage in the Second Placet in which he talks of '[les] célèbres originaux du portrait que je voulais faire': they are 'originaux', or models, of his portrait, not because they are Jesuits, or Jansenists, but because they are – or can be made to appear – hypocrites. In his mild state of persecution-complex, it is hardly to be wondered at that he should identify all his ecclesiastical opponents with hypocrites like Conti, and that he should seek to defend his play by attacking the sincerity of his accusers.

In any case, modern commentators have tended to pay too much attention to the external circumstances of the ban on the play, and perhaps also to Molière's special pleading in its defence. Too little regard has been shown in this respect for the text of the play itself – especially the text as it comes across in the theatre: for here is a case in which the reader, meditating on certain passages in conjunction with Molière's own skilful commentary in the Preface and the Placets, may be led to adopt quite a different emphasis from the one that is imposed on us as spectators. For even the text of the 1669 version as it stands has preserved the fundamental emphasis of our hypothetical 1664 original: the comic focus is firmly on the figure of Orgon, and this comic focus – the contrast between his *imaginaire* view of the world based on subjective fantasy, and the objective reality of the world as it is shown to us – takes precedence over any satirical implications dependent on the material or moral consequences of Tartuffe's ascendency over him. Tartuffe's presence in Orgon's household indeed depends on the latter's fantasy world, of which he represents the tangible objectivisation, no less than Trissotin objectivises the obsession of the *femmes savantes*, Dorante, Dorimène and the various tutors the obsession of Monsieur Jourdain, and Purgon and Diafoirus that of the *malade imaginaire*. The satirical implications of Orgon's infatuation with Tartuffe, and the sinister consequences of the worsening relationships with his own family, remain relatively unstressed: even Damis's expulsion and the threatened expropriation of Orgon himself, while they are important as plot-motifs, are hardly presented in a realistic manner. Molière has preserved the tone of comedy by focusing firmly on the conflict between subjective fantasy and objective reality.

No other comedy of Molière's so insistently explores this conflict, which is here interpreted in terms of the value of visual evidence. The gullible Orgon believes everything he sees, in the contextual field of *dévotion*; the evidence of his eyes is not subject to the critical control of his reason, as we see from his account of his first meeting with Tartuffe:

> Ha! si vous aviez vu comme j'en fis rencontre . . . (lines 281 ff.)[47]

On the other hand, where it is a question of Tartuffe's behaviour towards Elmire, the converse is the case, and the would-be seducer is taken for the pious preserver of family morality:

> Je vois qu'il reprend tout, et qu'à ma femme même
> Il prend, pour mon honneur, un intérêt extrême;
> Il m'avertit des gens qui lui font des yeux doux,
> Et plus que moi six fois il s'en montre jaloux. (lines 301–4)

In other words, ocular evidence has no objective value: it is filtered through a screen of a priori prejudice. Orgon wants to believe in Tartuffe, so he takes his ostentatious piety at its face value, while reinterpreting the evidence of his senses when what he sees would be inconsistent with his preconceived idea. As Tartuffe says, '. . . je l'ai mis au point de voir tout sans rien croire' (line 1526). The verb *voir*, and other semantically related terms, run through the play like a leitmotif, reaching a climax at the point where Orgon, now painfully disabused, attempts to enlighten his mother, who remains subject to a similar error of judgement:

[47] For a detailed commentary on this passage, see W. D. Howarth and C. L. Walton, *Explications: The Technique of French Literary Appreciation* (London, 1971), pp. 59–69.

> Je l'ai vu, dis-je, vu, de mes propres yeux vu,
> Ce qu'on appelle vu; faut-il vous le rabattre
> Aux oreilles cent fois, et crier comme quatre? –

whereupon her reply naively underlines the comic moral of the whole play:

> Mon Dieu, le plus souvent l'apparence déçoit:
> Il ne faut pas toujours juger sur ce qu'on voit. (lines 1676–80)

The much-praised entry of Tartuffe in Act III allows the author to build up an effective picture of his hypocrite before he actually appears; but this is a process which operates at two levels, and it is in the angle of vision between the evidence of the rational, dependable characters and the subjective interpretation that Orgon puts on what he sees that the comedy consists.

Moreover, this focus on the subjective nature of Orgon's judgement is very relevant to any consideration of *Tartuffe* as a play about religion. It is a focus that is often lost sight of – and Molière is surely guilty of misleading his reader. For the question is not, and was not in 1669, whether Tartuffe represents true or false piety. The title of the play, *L'Imposteur*; the stage-direction 'apercevant Dorine' which precedes Tartuffe's marvellous opening couplet:

> Laurent, serrez ma haire avec ma discipline,
> Et priez que toujours le Ciel vous illumine; (lines 853–4)

that other curious stage-direction at line 1487: 'C'est un scélérat qui parle': all of these provide proof, if proof were needed, that Tartuffe is a hypocrite, an impostor, a *faux dévot*; and for Molière to claim that 'les originaux ont fait supprimer la copie' is a clear case of special pleading. *Tartuffe* was objected to by sincere churchmen of all shades of opinion – and surely with every justification; for the real provocation lay not in the portrayal of Tartuffe the obvious hypocrite, but in that of Orgon the genuine believer. Ramon Fernandez asks the searching question: would Orgon be any less comic if Tartuffe himself were a genuine *dévot*?

> Il est vrai que M. Purgon est un convaincu alors que Tartuffe est un hypocrite, mais une comédie qui eût mis en scène un M. Purgon de la religion eût-elle différé sensiblement, *pour la signification comique*, du *Tartuffe* que nous possédons?[48]

There can be only one answer, and it is given by Fernandez. What-

---

[48] *La Vie de Molière* (Paris, 1929), p. 159.

ever the nature of the stimulus – true or false piety on the part of
Tartuffe – Orgon is comic because of his withdrawal into a world
apart; this is due to his own genuine (if misguided) piety, and 'l'isolement chrétien devient le type de l'isolement comique'.[49]

The most provocative passage of the whole play, from the point of
view of Molière's relations with the churchmen of his day, must surely
be lines 273–9:

> Qui suit bien ses leçons goûte une paix profonde,
> Et comme du fumier regarde tout le monde.
> Oui, je deviens tout autre avec son entretien;
> Il m'enseigne à n'avoir affection pour rien,
> De toutes amitiés il détache mon âme;
> Et je verrais mourir frère, enfants, mère et femme,
> Que je m'en soucierais autant que de cela.

When Tartuffe bends the language of *dévotion* to serve his own ends,
Molière is careful to indicate that it is 'un scélérat qui parle'. Here,
however, we have Orgon, who is not a hypocrite but a sincere
believer, expressing an opinion which, for all its revolting inhuman-
ity, is demonstrably close to the letter of an authentic Christian text:
'If any man cometh unto me, and hateth not his own father, and
mother, and wife, and children, and brethren, and sisters, yea, and
his own life also, he cannot be my disciple' (Luke 14.26). It is true that
in his obsessive egoism, Orgon leaves out the phrase 'yea, and his own
life also', which gives the Biblical text its full meaning; but even
though his formula may misrepresent in this way the spirit of Christ's
teaching, the resemblance to the letter is undeniable. Indeed, the
closeness to Luke's 'If any man hate not . . .' is particularly striking if
one compares this with the much milder version of the same passage
given by Matthew: 'He that loveth father or mother more than me is
not worthy of me; and he that loveth son or daughter more than me is
not worthy of me' (10.37). And Molière's audacity at this point is
reinforced, not attenuated, by Cléante's rejoinder:

> Les sentiments humains, mon frère, que voilà! –

not 'What a travesty of Christian doctrine!', but 'What a travesty of
human feeling!' The similarity to the Biblical text passes unchal-
lenged; and though it would be wrong to read too much into Cléante's
single line, it can certainly be construed in its context as putting
forward, by implication, a humanist alternative to the harsh in-

[49] *Ibid.*, pp. 161–2.

humanity of the Christian precept. If we object that the letter of the Biblical text is misleading, and needs to be interpreted before it can be understood, then we are allowing Molière to usurp the functions of the Church by distinguishing between the spirit and the letter; we are accepting the doctrine, which no Catholic churchman of the time could possibly have accepted, that the individual has the duty to exercise his *libre examen* and to interpret the Biblical text in the light of human reason. Such are the implications of this highly provocative passage: implications that go far beyond the distinction between true and false *dévotion* in the person of Tartuffe. We may be broad-minded enough today to reject the view that 'ce n'est point au théâtre à parler de ces matières';[50] but this passage provides abundant justification for any obedient son of the Church in 1669 who thought that Molière had gone much too far.

Is this to be seen as part of the *satirical* message of *Tartuffe*? Only if one takes 'satirical' in the widest possible sense. In such a passage, Molière is not only ridiculing the beliefs of real-life bigots in the society in which he lived; more than that, he is making a forceful statement by comic means about habits of thought common to bigoted thinkers in every age, people who use the authority of Church or political party as the justification for anti-social attitudes or inhuman activities. There may well have been counterparts of Orgon and Madame Pernelle in the France of Molière's day, but that is less important than the permanent relevance of the portrait of the family tyrant who needs the support of textual authority, or the casuistry of a *directeur de conscience*, to provide a basis for his dictatorial behaviour. The comic writing that exposes the warped thinking of such characters is a kind of comedy that goes well beyond the limitations of satire; and perhaps this is what Fernandez had in mind in suggesting that it is impossible to write a play like *Tartuffe* 'sans changer l'ordre intellectuel du monde'.[51]

Certain eighteenth-century thinkers were to deplore the fact that Molière was not able to make a direct attack on the real-life Tartuffes in the Church of his day; to quote Grimm:

Si Molière avait osé faire de son Tartuffe un prêtre qui . . . séduit la femme sous le langage mystique de la religion . . . et parvient à ruiner cette famille de fond en comble; si, bien loin d'être puni à la fin contre toute vraisemblance en vertu de notre pitoyable système dramatique, ce

[50] Molière puts this view into the mouth of his opponents in the Preface to *Tartuffe*.
[51] Quoted in Moore, *Molière: A New Criticism*, p. 23.

fourbe triomphait . . . , alors le *Tartuffe* serait devenu un ouvrage important au public, digne à jamais de servir d'école aux moeurs et d'instruction à une nation éclairée.[52]

Such an anti-clerical satire, if it had been possible in the 1660s, would
no doubt have delighted the eighteenth-century *philosophes*; but a
Tartuffe of that sort would have had far less lasting interest than the
play which after three hundred years not only makes us laugh at
eternal comic types, but also forces us to think about issues of permanent and universal importance. The imposition of an anachronistic
thesis is just as limiting in this respect as the imposition of anachronistic costumes and settings. Both militate against the universality of the
playwright's chosen theme: a universality that is firmly established
by the relationship of the two principal characters. We may not know
the details of Molière's own *mise-en-scène*, but we can be tolerably sure
that while the setting was indicated with a certain degree of realism,
Orgon and Tartuffe on the other hand were portrayed with enough
stylisation to remind the audience that beneath their bourgeois exterior, the pious paterfamilias and his saintly guest were still the
Sganarelle and Mascarille of a longstanding comic tradition.

(v) 'Dom Juan': Molière's black comedy

Dom Juan is recognised today, after centuries of neglect,[53] as an
equally powerful comedy of ideas; but it is a play which fits much less
easily into any accepted pattern. *Tartuffe* is exactly what one would
expect of a play originally conceived in 1664: it is true to the plot-
formula adopted for most of Molière's plays; it is set in the family; it
opposes 'la sottise' and 'la ruse'; and the dénouement, whatever we
may think of the way in which it is brought about, is thoroughly
conventional in that it unites the young lovers and restores family
harmony. *Dom Juan* on the other hand appears to have only the
slightest connections with any other of the playwright's works, and
although one of the protagonists is called Sganarelle, the relationship
between 'sottise' and 'ruse' is here handled in a completely novel way.
Characters and incidents nearly all owe their origin to sources outside

[52] Quoted by M. Wagner, *Molière and the Age of Enlightenment* (Banbury, 1973), p. 132.
[53] When the play was revived after Molière's death, the rhymed adaptation by Thomas
Corneille was preferred, and Molière's text was not played at the Comédie-
Française until 1847. Even then, for the next hundred years productions of *Dom
Juan* were few and mediocre.

Molière's theatre; and although there is a striking similarity of theme with that of *Tartuffe*, the dramatic treatment of this theme could not be more different.

It has been plausibly suggested that the difficulties caused by the reception of *Tartuffe* in the previous year helped to determine Molière's choice of subject for his new play; and it was essentially by introducing the theme of hypocrisy and *fausse dévotion* into the Don Juan legend[54] that the playwright put his own mark on the traditional material. The first Don Juan, in Tirso de Molina's *Burlador de Sevilla*, has something of the character of a mediaeval Everyman, and the play retains at least the vestigial imprint of a morality-play. The hero is a sincere believer, and although he has a prodigious capacity for sowing wild oats, and is ready to commit all sorts of villainy in the process, he has it in him genuinely to reform one day. The message of Tirso's version, then, is that one cannot win salvation after a lifetime of debauchery by a nicely-gauged death-bed repentance: the retribution of Heaven will strike before one is ready, just as Don Juan is borne off to Hell by the agent of divine justice, the statue of the Commander whom he killed while attempting to seduce his daughter. The Italian versions which followed in the middle of the century reflect a much freer intellectual atmosphere: they are the product of a society in which religious indifference could be taken for granted, and Da Ponte's libretto for Mozart's *Don Giovanni* a century later, although not perhaps very close in details of plot, is very near to Cicognini's version in spirit.

There were two French versions before Molière's.[55] Both Dorimon and Villiers seem to have used a lost Italian text as their principal source, but both of these plays show a seriousness of tone, and a serious moral purpose, that is lacking in the surviving Italian versions. Although pagan references are used ('les Dieux', 'le Ciel') instead of Christian terms, so as not to offend the Church, the hero in both plays is a convincing embodiment of the important current of free-thinking which underlay the official orthodoxy and conformism of the Grand Siècle. Not that Dorimon or Villiers is using the Don Juan theme in order to *preach* free-thought; far from it: their heroes

54 The spelling 'Don Juan' is here used to refer to the theme, the legendary character, or versions other than Molière's. 'Dom Juan' refers to Molière's version.
55 Dorimon, *Le Festin de pierre ou le Fils criminel, tragicomédie* (performed Lyon 1658, Paris 1661, published 1659); Villiers, *Le Festin de pierre ou le Fils criminel, tragicomédie* (performed 1659, published 1660).

richly deserve their punishment at the end, and the moral lesson is clear enough. But whereas previous Don Juans had not reflected overmuch, but had tricked, seduced and abandoned their victims in obedience to irresistible sensual impulses, in these French plays the hero for the first time defends his conduct rationally as part of a coherent programme of self-fulfilment. From his origins as a lusty young animal, Don Juan has now become a lucid, amoral intellectual.

With Molière, the transformation is complete. Whatever else his Dom Juan may be, he is hardly, or at any rate not simply, a 'Don Juan' in the conventional sense of the name. It is true that Sganarelle describes him in the opening scene as a consummate womaniser; but priority is given, even in this introductory portrait, to the *libertinage de pensée* of which Dom Juan's *libertinage de moeurs* is only a secondary product:

> Tu vois en Dom Juan, mon maître, le plus grand scélérat que la terre ait jamais porté, un enragé, un chien, un Diable, un Turc, un hérétique, qui ne croit ni Ciel, ni Saint, ni Dieu, ni loup-garou, qui passe cette vie en véritable bête brute, en pourceau d'Épicure, en vrai Sardanapale, ferme l'oreille à toutes les remontrances chrétiennes qu'on lui peut faire, et traite de billevesées tout ce que nous croyons.

Despite the comic accumulation of incongruous items in these charges brought by the simple Sganarelle against his master, we are here given a clear picture at the outset, before Dom Juan himself appears, of a ruthless individualist bent on the satisfaction of his desires as part of a philosophy of life. And when Dom Juan appears, he justifies his life of sexual conquest by an appeal to an intellectual, not a physical, appetite:

> Il n'est rien de si doux que de triompher de la résistance d'une belle personne, et j'ai sur ce sujet l'ambition des conquérants, qui volent perpétuellement de victoire en victoire, et ne peuvent point se résoudre à borner leurs souhaits. Il n'est rien qui puisse arrêter l'impétuosité de mes désirs: je me sens porté à aimer toute la terre; et comme Alexandre, je souhaiterais qu'il y eût d'autres mondes, pour y pouvoir étendre mes conquêtes amoureuses.

Sganarelle's reply to this is significant:

> ... Il semble que vous ayez appris par coeur cela, et vous parlez tout comme un livre. (I, ii)

Indeed, his master's self-justification is proclaimed in the manner of a doctrinaire programme: Don Juan has now become the Man of

Reason. He hoodwinks the peasant girls – as he no doubt fascinated Elvire – by his superior mental powers; and even this simple, stylised episode is an example of seduction by means of intellectual rather than physical charms. At two points in the play there are even touches of the refined, sadistic pleasure one associates with the Lovelaces and the Valmonts of the following century, for whom seduction was to be such a cerebral exercise, rather than with Tirso's hot-blooded Burlador. The first of these comes at the end of Act I, when Dom Juan tells Sganarelle of a new project he has in mind: the seduction of a 'jeune fiancée', whom he has observed with her lover:

> . . . Je ne pus souffrir d'abord de les voir si bien ensemble; le dépit alluma mes désirs, et je me figurai un plaisir extrême à pouvoir troubler leur intelligence, et rompre cet attachement, dont la délicatesse de mon coeur se tenait offensée.

The second occasion comes in Act IV, on the departure of Elvire, who has come in order to plead with Dom Juan to mend his ways and ward off the anger of Heaven. He is not unaffected by the sight of her grief; as he tells Sganarelle:

> Sais-tu bien que j'ai encore senti quelque peu d'émotion pour elle, que j'ai trouvé de l'agrément dans cette nouveauté bizarre, et que son habit négligé, son air languissant et ses larmes ont réveillé en moi quelques petits restes de feu éteint? (IV, vii)

In both of these passages there is a touch of perversity – if not of perversion – which strikes an essentially modern note.

But Dom Juan's relations with women are only part of the picture; and from Act III scene i onwards we are concerned with his intellectual attitudes in a wider sense, as each scene fills in a new aspect of the portrait sketched in its outlines in the opening scene:

> Ce n'est là qu'une ébauche du personnage, et pour en achever le portrait, il faudrait bien d'autres coups de pinceau.

At the beginning of Act III Sganarelle's disguise as a doctor is the pretext for his master's attack on medicine as 'une des grandes erreurs qui soient parmi les hommes'. From that subject they pass to religion, and Dom Juan, pressed by Sganarelle, declares as his articles of faith that 'deux et deux font quatre, et quatre et quatre font huit'. Well attested as the death-bed remark of Maurice, Prince of Orange earlier in the century, this phrase helps to situate Dom Juan in relation to the materialistic scepticism in vogue among the emancipated aristocrats represented by this 'grand seigneur méchant homme'.

Having declared his principles, Dom Juan soon has a chance to give a practical demonstration of his impiety: meeting a poor hermit begging for alms, he says he will give him a *louis d'or* if he will 'swear' (i.e. if he will blaspheme by *forswearing* his Christian faith. Blasphemy was punishable by death in the seventeenth century, and the episode is based on an anecdote told of the Chevalier de Roquelaure, a free-thinking nobleman of the time). The poor man resolutely refuses to deny his God, whereupon Dom Juan gives him the money 'pour l'amour de l'humanité': a formula in which we are meant to see a profane version of the conventional 'pour l'amour de Dieu'. Act III closes with the statue nodding its head in reply to the traditional invitation to supper; even the free-thinking Dom Juan seems to be taken aback by this phenomenon, yet he soon recovers his aplomb, and Act IV opens with him explaining it away on rational grounds:

> C'est une bagatelle, et nous pouvons avoir été trompés par un faux jour, ou surpris de quelque vapeur qui nous ait troublé la vue.

This act is taken up with various encounters, in which Dom Juan displays his individualist ethic by flouting all the normal social conventions. Towards Monsieur Dimanche, a creditor, he uses an effusive show of politeness to get out of paying his bills; towards his father, who exhorts him to remember his obligations as a gentleman, he shows a flippant lack of concern; and when Elvire comes to plead, in the name of her love for him, that he should be mindful of his salvation, her grief-stricken state merely arouses something of his former desire, and on a sudden impulse he tries to prevail on her to stay the night.

In Act V he carries his amoral individualism to new lengths, and proclaims his intention to exploit his fellow-men by systematically hypocritical behaviour. He easily deceives his father by a pretence of genuine conversion, and when Sganarelle congratulates him on his new resolve, he cuts him short and launches into a long tirade on the utility of religious hypocrisy as a weapon in the individual's war against society:

> Aujourd'hui, la profession d'hypocrite a de merveilleux avantages. C'est un art de qui l'imposture est toujours respectée; et quoiqu'on la découvre, on n'ose rien dire contre elle. Tous les autres vices des hommes sont exposés à la censure, et chacun a la liberté de les attaquer hautement; mais l'hypocrisie est un vice privilégié, qui, de sa main, ferme la bouche à tout le monde, et jouit en repos d'une impunité souveraine.
>
> (V, ii)

He claims that religious hypocrites, 'les gens du parti', form a coherent, organised society; and here, too, it is impossible to miss the
reference to the contemporary intellectual climate in France.
Whether these *faux dévots* are meant to be identified with a particular
group such as the Compagnie du Saint-Sacrement is not certain; but
what does seem certain is that Molière is here hitting back at those
authorities, both lay and ecclesiastical, whose pious protests had led
to the banning of *Tartuffe* the year before. History records several
striking cases of noblemen who turned to religion after a life of scandal
– the Prince de Conti has already been referred to in this respect – and
Molière was not alone in seeing the new mask of piety as a cover for
the sort of amoral self-seeking he shows in his hero.

Finally, retribution overtakes Dom Juan, as it does his counterpart
in the other versions. The warnings given by Sganarelle, Dom Louis
and Elvire, and the supernatural phenomenon of the Statue walking
and talking, have failed to have any effect on him; and in the end, as
the Statue comes to claim its victim, he meets death with a constancy
that we must admire, whatever we may think of the life he has led:

> Il ne sera pas dit que, quoi qu'il arrive, je sois capable de me repentir.
>
> (V, v)

From beginning to end of the play, then, we are given a consistent
portrayal of rational man, intellectually self-sufficient, rejecting the
hypothesis of the supernatural and pursuing his individualist ethic
without acknowledging any sanctions from without. This Don Juan is
at every point closely related to the climate of ideas in Molière's own
society; and his characterisation is a product of the dramatist's original creative vision: we are not forced constantly to make a comparison
with preceding versions, but can accept it without any difficulty as
existing in its own right. From one point of view, if we are concerned
with the selection of material, Molière's play really is derivative. He is
quite content to take over characters, relationships, scenes and episodes from his models; and strictly speaking, there is only the scene
with Monsieur Dimanche that has no counterpart at all in earlier
versions. But in taking over these characters, and in borrowing these
episodes, Molière makes them entirely his own. Everything is subor-
dinated to his own conception of the central character, and to the
highly individual development he has given to the relationship between the Don Juan figure and his servant.

Structurally, as we have seen, the play is most unorthodox. It is episodic to a degree, and its sequence of unrelated scenes can literally be seen as filling in – now by discussion with Sganarelle, now by confrontation with others – the character-sketch of the hero outlined at the beginning of the play. The unfamiliar structure no doubt contributed, along with the enigmatic content, to *Dom Juan* being neglected for so long. 'Pièce mal faite, rôle injouable': Maurice Descotes sums up what must have been the consensus of opinion, both theatrical and academic, until well into the twentieth century.[56]

As regards the first of these charges, time has set things right: in a period in which the 'well-made play' itself has tended to be devalued, *Dom Juan* has come into its own. Its lack of coherent plot (for instance, the fact that there is no cross-reference at all between the Elvire scenes, those concerning Dom Louis, and those in which the Statue appears); the abrupt changes of tone; the mixture of spectacle and slapstick, rhetoric and ribaldry: these are no longer counted as defects, but may even be seen as positive virtues; so that since Jouvet's epoch-making production in 1948, *Dom Juan* has never ceased to appeal to producers and their publics. And what of the 'rôle injouable'? Does the character of *Dom Juan* emerge from this bizarre amalgam as a coherent, unified whole? He is certainly one of the most controversial and enigmatic of Molière's characters; and the difficulties of interpretation seem to derive from a quite unusual tension between the comic and the dramatic structures of the play. Normally, in the world of Molière's comedy, the comic and the dramatic processes work together: for instance, Arnolphe is the object of our laughter, and his scheme to marry Agnès is unsuccessful; we laugh at Monsieur Jourdain, and his opposition to Lucile's marriage is rendered harmless. In *Dom Juan*, this is not the case. Not that the comic structure is not strongly in evidence; the play contains several scenes of pure *comique* – those with peasants and with Monsieur Dimanche – and others with a mixture of serious and comic content, the most important of which is Act III scene i, where a comic pattern is imposed on the discussion of a highly serious subject. But in none of these scenes do I find Dom Juan himself a comic character, as some commentators have been able to do.[57] The scenes themselves are richly comic; but, as almost always in the theatre (except perhaps

---

[56] *Les Grands Rôles*, p. 74.
[57] See especially Moore, *Molière: A New Criticism*, pp. 15–16, 93–7; and '*Dom Juan* Reconsidered', *Modern Language Review*, LII (1957), 510–17.

where it is a case of pure verbal comedy), we are laughing *at* one character, and laughing *with* another. And in all these scenes, in my view, we laugh *with* Dom Juan, and *at* his gullible victims. In real life, presumably we do not approve of the seduction of silly girls by a bogus promise of marriage, any more than we do of a nobleman's refusal to pay his debts; but in the theatre the comic process is so powerful that our moral judgement is suspended, and we applaud the hero's cleverness and connive at his duplicity. More important still, in Act III scene i, whether or not we share Dom Juan's views on the unreasonableness of medicine, and whether or not we are ourselves free-thinkers, the comic relationship between the two characters is such that, by laughing with one and at the other, we do temporarily take sides; and there is surely little doubt that for the normal spectator, whether he agrees with such an opinion or not, 'je crois que deux et deux font quatre' is, in theatrical terms, the argument that wins the day.

On the other hand, if we examine the dramatic structure of the play, there is a series of scenes, particularly in the last two acts (though the first meeting with Elvire in Act I, and the 'scène du Pauvre' and scenes with Elvire's brothers in Act III, also come into this category) in which there seems to be no comic content at all, and in which our sympathies are determined by quite a different dramatic process. And so we have the curious case of a central character whose skill and intelligence win our allegiance in a series of comic encounters, but who in a sequence of dramatic scenes at the end of the play becomes more and more odious until he meets a well-deserved punishment. This is the profound effect of the play's lack of unity of tone; and the consequent ambivalence in the audience's reaction to the hero is not the least of the challenges that the play presents to producer and actor.

This ambivalence can perhaps be explained by what we may presume to have been Molière's satirical purpose, the portrayal of the *grand seigneur méchant homme*. Such a portrait had to show the dangerous charm of Dom Juan's real-life counterparts, their success in exploiting in others the prejudices and conventions from which they themselves were free; and precisely because these men were so powerful as a result of their emancipation from the weaknesses of ordinary men and their immunity from the sanctions that are normally observed, Dom Juan cannot be 'cut down to size' by the corrective processes of comedy. His dramatic function is that of the *fourbe*: he is the creator, not the object, of ridicule; and so his punishment has to be part of the dramatic, not the comic, structure of the play.

Whereas *Tartuffe* subordinates satire to comedy of ideas, *Dom Juan* strains uneasily at the very limits of comedy. Both plays, it is true, rely on an arbitrary dénouement of the *deus ex machina* type: Orgon and his family are rescued by the King's unexpected intervention, just as Dom Juan's victims are avenged by the unforeseen action of the Statue. But there is this difference between the two cases. Tartuffe's trickery has been seen through by all the characters of good sense from the beginning of the play, and by the end Orgon himself is disabused; so that even before the Exempt's arrival, the impostor's moral hold over the family has been broken (if at a considerable material cost). Moreover, inasmuch as the comic focus in *Tartuffe* remains firmly on the dupe, not the *fourbe*, Orgon's punishment by the normal corrective processes of comedy is in the final analysis just as important as his last-minute rescue by providential means. There is no such comic compensation in *Dom Juan*: the master's moral hold over his servant can be broken, the *grand seigneur's* contempt for his fellow-men can be punished, only by the most violent means. Whereas the heroes of Tirso and Cicognini are about to be apprehended by human justice when divine punishment strikes, retribution comes to Molière's hero as he is congratulating himself on his complete impunity.

It looks very much as though Molière's dénouement was the product of wishful thinking. Is it too fanciful to see him dispensing poetic justice to his enemies, unassailable in real life behind their barricades of privilege and power? Given his conception of the character of Dom Juan, the dramatist was bound to have recourse to intervention from outside. Whether one regards the dénouement as an artificial *deus ex machina*, or as a convincing manifestation of the divine wrath that a hardened sinner has carned, there is some measure of contradiction between the comic and the dramatic content of the play.[58]

[58] For an ampler treatment of some of these points, see the Introduction to my edition of *Dom Juan*.

8

Comedy and ballet

Le ballet est pour la comédie ce qu'est la mort pour la tragédie: le saut dans l'au-delà, l'accomplissement de la trajectoire, l'élan suivi jusqu'au bout, sans retour, sans réaccommodation factice à l'optique du monde. (R. Fernandez)[1]

(i) The Court entertainments

It would be a mistake to insist too rigidly on the contrast between the plays Molière wrote for Court performance and those which were performed at the Palais-Royal. As we have seen, there was a regular overlap between the two audiences; moreover, the majority of Molière's plays were put on, at one time or another, both at Court and in the capital; and particularly after 1671, when the Palais-Royal was re-equipped for *Psyché*, it was possible to mount elaborate and sophisticated spectacles in Paris as well as at Court. Nevertheless, it is clearly the case that the type of comedy that evolved in response to the taste of the town audience (and in this respect Molière's plays can be compared with those of his contemporaries: Racine's *Les Plaideurs* (1668), for instance, or the comedies of Quinault, Boursault or Hauteroche) differed in certain essential respects from the sort of entertainment that was favoured by King and Court; and Garapon's thesis in *Le Dernier Molière* – that the last phase of the playwright's career is marked by a desire to 'réconcilier en un même divertissement le comique le plus bouffon, quelque chose qui rappelle la danse, et les peintures humaines les plus vraies'[2] – surely blurs a necessary distinction.[3]

---

[1] *La Vie de Molière*, p. 210.   [2] p. 11.

[3] R. W. Herzel seems to be much nearer the mark when he writes of Molière's final years: 'The success of *Psyché*, and the troupe's decision to invest in equipping the theatre for machine plays, had the effect of polarising Molière's scenic practice into two mutually exclusive modes. "Simple" plays that were written from this time on would have a single décor and would not incorporate ballet or musical interludes; plays that did incorporate these attractions would be staged with all the scenic sophistication of which the troupe was now capable', 'The Décor of Molière's Stage: The Testimony of Brissart and Chauveau', *PMLA*, xciii (1978), 950.

The difference can perhaps best be expressed as between one kind of drama in which matter is more important, and another in which greater importance is attached to manner. In the plays Molière wrote for performance at the Palais-Royal (and the same would be true of plays written by rival dramatists for the Hôtel de Bourgogne), he was following, in however personal and original a fashion, conventions of comic drama established before his time in which plot, theme and characterisation are what count; in the art form that was created to cater for the taste of the King and his courtiers, on the other hand, content of this traditional nature was less important than the display of imagination and fantasy in the manner of presentation. The immediate entertainment of the participants as well as their audience; the stylisation of verbal text as lyrical libretto, and the relegation of that libretto to a subordinate place as part of a combined spectacle which depended above all on musical and visual appeal: these made of the *ballet de cour*, as practised at the beginning of Louis XIV's reign, an essentially ephemeral genre, in spite of its long and vigorous history.[4] When Molière entered the King's service as collaborator, alongside the musicians, choreographers and *metteurs-en-scène*, this was the kind of entertainment to which he was expected to contribute. In certain cases, he was content to accept a subordinate role, but in others he developed a degree of integration between framework and content which not only gave a new direction to the royal entertainments, but also produced a distinctive form of dramatic comedy.

The Court entertainments in vogue at the beginning of the young King's reign were the product of a desire to bring all the arts together in a harmonious synthesis; but it is abundantly clear that the narrative, or dramatic, element in this 'Gesamtkunstwerk' was traditionally the weakest, and that the role of the poet was generally confined to providing suitable lyrical support for the composer and the choreographer. When Molière contributed to the *Ballet des Incompatibles* at Montpellier in 1655, there is no reason to suppose that he sought to alter that long-established relationship: such evidence as we have of this entertainment suggests that it fitted squarely into the convention of the *ballet de cour*.[5] Even the festivities organised by Fouquet at Vaux-le-Vicomte in August 1661 were, despite their extravagance and ostentation, quite conventional in character; and as we have seen

[4] See McGowan, *L'Art du ballet de cour*; H. Prunières, *Le Ballet de cour en France avant Benserade et Lulli* (Paris, 1914); Christout, *Le Ballet de cour*.
[5] See *Oeuvres*, ed. Despois and Mesnard, I, pp. 523ff.

in an earlier chapter,[6] it was a chance factor – the shortage of qualified dancers to sustain a succession of *entrées* in the ballet – that gave Molière the chance, in *Les Fâcheux*, to assert the role of the dramatist. The importance of this innovation cannot be too strongly emphasised; however, despite its potential as shown by some of its later developments, *comédie-ballet* in its original form in *Les Fâcheux* was a simple affair, the structure of which was determined by its function. The framework – Éraste's repeated frustration as he is prevented from keeping a rendezvous with Orphise – was capable of accommodating an indefinite number of *entrées*; and the only feature distinguishing *Les Fâcheux* from previous *ballets de cour* is the fact that a proportion of its *entrées* consisted of spoken dialogue, and that these 'straight' dramatic scenes set the theme for what became, in effect, ballet interludes.

After *Les Fâcheux*, Molière's contributions to the royal entertainments show two main lines of development. On the one hand, plays like *La Princesse d'Élide*, *La Pastorale comique* and especially *Psyché* belong to a kind of lyric drama, growing out of the *ballet de cour* and influenced by the earlier pastoral tradition, which was to culminate at the hands of Quinault (one of Molière's collaborators in the writing of *Psyché*) in the operas of the 1670s and 1680s. Such plays were mostly commissioned for important spectacular fêtes at the royal palaces: *La Princesse d'Élide* for the 'Plaisirs de l'Ile enchantée' at Versailles in 1664; *La Pastorale comique* (with the unfinished *Mélicerte*) for the 'Ballet des Muses' organised by Benserade at Saint-Germain in 1666; and *Psyché*, first performed at the Carnival celebrations at the Tuileries in 1671. They are essentially works of collaboration between poet, composer and choreographer; and in spite of their importance – especially in the case of *Psyché*[7] – in the evolution of French opera, they show Molière adapting, and subordinating, his creative talents to the requirements, and the taste, of King and Court to an extent which must set these works apart from any consideration of his achievements as a comic dramatist.

The fact that Molière and his company re-equipped the Palais-Royal, at considerable expense, for the performance of machine-plays, and that *Psyché* was adopted for an unprecedented run of

---

[6] See pp. 43–4.
[7] 'Quant à *Psyché*, . . . c'est l'opéra avant l'opéra, et cette oeuvre résume par avance toutes les qualités qu'on peut exiger du genre', J. Tiersot, *La Musique dans la comédie de Molière* (Paris, 1922), p. 161.

thirty-eight consecutive performances in this new setting, suggests that if the playwright's career had not been cut short so soon afterwards, he may have intended increasingly to exploit the new popularity of lyric drama with his town audiences. It is an intriguing question, to which any answer can only depend on guesswork. What is certain, however, is that if they were hoping to extend their activities in this direction, Molière and his colleagues were reckoning without the ambitions of Lulli.

The celebrated musician, born at Florence in 1632, had come to Paris as a boy; he had soon entered the young King's service, and by his early twenties was in charge of the music for Court entertainments. At first, he had had a close and cordial relationship with Molière, composing the music for no fewer than ten of his plays: the results can be seen not only in the creation of the conventional kind of ballet on mythological subjects, the development of which led to *Psyché*, but also in the collaboration of the 'two Jean-Baptistes' in *Le Bourgeois gentilhomme*. However, the cooperation was soon to come to an abrupt end. In 1669, Colbert had been persuaded to found the Académie de Musique, and the *privilège* for the directorship went to Perrin, an incompetent, second-rate poet and librettist. When Perrin was imprisoned for debts in 1672, Lulli took over the *privilège*; according to one contemporary account, having agreed with Molière that they should make a joint application (which would have been a logical step on Molière's part after the success of *Psyché*), the Florentine went behind his colleague's back and procured it in his own name. The *privilège* carried a monopoly with it, which he immediately set about exploiting quite ruthlessly: an injunction was at once served on the Paris theatres – including Molière's – preventing them from employing an orchestra of more than twelve players, or a chorus of more than six voices. The whole purpose of the re-equipment of the Palais-Royal was thus frustrated, and a breach between Molière and Lulli became inevitable. Although the latter had composed the music for the production of *La Comtesse d'Escarbagnas* at Saint-Germain, when this play was transferred to the Palais-Royal in July 1672 it was accompanied by the music of Charpentier, who was also commissioned to compose the score for *Le Malade imaginaire*. For his part, Lulli continued to perform, and to publish, the works composed in collaboration with Molière without acknowledgement; and his triumph was complete when, on Molière's death, he was able to use his influence with the King to procure the Palais-

Royal as his own theatre. His monopoly was now made even more restrictive, and he was to preside in dictatorial manner over the creation of French opera.

(ii) 'Le Bourgeois gentilhomme' and 'Le Malade imaginaire'

Quite apart from this unfortunate deterioration in Molière's relations with Lulli, the collaboration between the poet–dramatist on the one hand, and composer and choreographer on the other, could in the nature of things hardly be an equal partnership; and as has been seen, there are certainly cases in which Molière was content to defer to the taste of his Court audience and accept the subordinate role which tradition prescribed. However, running parallel to the development of Court entertainment into opera that we have briefly sketched above, there is the second line of development already referred to, one that is much more closely concerned with Molière's evolution as a comic dramatist, for it was the series of *comédies-ballets* that gave a new and original dimension to the genre of literary comedy. In these plays the dramatist assumed the initiative, and succeeded in transforming the traditional Court entertainment into a viable art form defined in the first place by its specifically dramatic character, but of which the musical and spectacular components provided an integral part. Of the plays that come into the category of *comédie-ballet* so defined, two are acknowledged masterpieces: *Le Bourgeois gentilhomme*, the high point both of Molière's work for the Court and of his collaboration with Lulli; and *Le Malade imaginaire*, written in partnership with Charpentier, and (as a result of the breach with Lulli, who retained the King's favour) the first play in which the new formula was addressed directly to a town audience at the Palais-Royal.

None of the previous *comédies-ballets* had shown the same degree of integration of the dramatic and the musical elements: witness the fact that most of these plays were later to appear in the repertory of the Comédie-Française without ballet or musical accompaniment, as straight plays. However, it is possible to trace the evolution of the composite genre, from its rudimentary beginnings in *Les Fâcheux* as a succession of episodic *entrées*, to its full development in *Le Bourgeois gentilhomme* and *Le Malade imaginaire*.

Les Fâcheux was followed by *Le Mariage forcé* (1664), another play with a simple framework, in which Sganarelle's attempt to seek advice on whether or not he should marry provides a pretext for episodic scenes with Géronimo, a neighbour, Pancrace, a *docteur aristotélicien*, Marphurius, a *docteur pyrrhonien*, and a pair of gypsy fortune-tellers.[8] However, this is less of a *pièce à tiroirs* than its predecessor; and a more conventional dramatic shape is given to it by scenes with Dorimène, whose coquetry and extravagant tastes soon make Sganarelle decide that it would be a mistake to marry her, and with her brother, whose challenge to a duel for breach of promise equally quickly persuades him to change his mind again. The play is rounded off by a *mascarade* to celebrate the marriage; and in a final *entrée de ballet* it is suggested that Dorimène has already begun to flirt with masked admirers.

As was implied in an earlier chapter,[9] the plot of *L'Amour médecin* can easily be separated from the *entrées* for which it provides a framework: this applies both to the spoken scenes introducing the Court physicians, and to that in which the quack doctor sings his patter-song, which in turn is followed by a ballet interlude devoted to the same theme. It is true that on its first performance at Versailles in September 1665 the three acts of *L'Amour médecin* were framed by musical scenes; but the opening one is totally independent of Molière's text, and only the closing scene, in which the performers are ostensibly hired by Clitandre as part of the plot to hoodwink Sganarelle, is genuinely incorporated into the dramatic content of the play.

The loosely-linked structure of the *comédie mêlée de chants* takes a step towards fuller integration in *Le Sicilien*, a one-act play composed to provide an appropriate conclusion for the 'Ballet des Muses' at Saint-Germain in January 1667. Here, the serenade, the ballet-scene and the closing *mascarade* are all as essential to the plot as is the scene in which Adraste adopts the disguise of a painter in order to gain access to Isidore. There is no change of mood, and hardly any change of style, between the musical and the non-musical scenes: disguises, serenades and masked entertainments are all taken for granted in the fantasy Mediterranean setting of a play where nothing matters but *galanterie* and the pursuit of pleasure.

From this point of view, *George Dandin* marks a retrograde step. Here, there is absolutely no integration between the play and its

---

[8] It is evident from the published *livret* of the ballet, as danced at the Louvre in January 1664, that these *entries* also included one without dialogue, in which the King himself took the part of a gypsy: 'combinaison bizarre, où le Roi était spectateur de la comédie, et danseur dans le ballet', Molière, *Oeuvres*, ed. Despois and Mesnard, IV, p. 3.
[9] See pp. 188–9.

spectacular framework; and the text is so completely independent of the ballet interludes with which it was staged at Versailles in 1668 that it is difficult to believe that it suffers in any way from being played as a straight play.[10] Style, comic tone and dramatic structure give *George Dandin* much more affinity with the town plays than with the Court entertainments. On the other hand, in both *Monsieur de Pourceaugnac* (performed at Chambord in 1669) and *La Comtesse d'Escarbagnas* (Saint-Germain, 1671) there is a large measure of the gratuitous fantasy that marks pure entertainment, and the plot is in each case designed to accommodate simple *entrées* and interludes of a musical nature alongside the scenes of dialogue that are like so many sketches in the loose framework of a modern revue.

But of all the Court entertainments, none demonstrates the potential of the *comédie-ballet* as a distinct new genre more effectively than *Les Amants magnifiques*. This was written as part of the 'Divertissement royal' staged at Saint-Germain in February 1670; and we are told that the subject of the play was provided by the King himself: the rivalry of two princes, suitors for the hand of the heroine Ériphile, who vie with each other to dazzle her, and the Princess Aristione her mother, with spectacular entertainments. The play opens with a water-pageant offered by Iphicrate, and the *intermède* between Acts II and III consists of a pastoral entertainment given by his rival Timoclès. A venal astrologer, bribed by Iphicrate, arranges the spectacular appearance of a false Venus as a means of furthering the latter's suit; while additional interludes are provided by other characters in an attempt to dispel the melancholy of the young Princess, and the festivities conclude with a representation of the Pythian games. 'Couronnons', says Aristione, 'par ce pompeux spectacle cette merveilleuse journée.' Described baldly in this way, *Les Amants magnifiques* might appear to be no more than a pretext, a framework for a series of spectacles on a grander scale than the normal *entrée de ballet*. However, the plot has much more to offer than this. In the first place, the rivalry between the two princes, and the intervention of the fraudulent astrologer, not only establish the framework, they also create the *theme* of the play: the conflict between illusion, or ephemeral ostentation, and reality, or solid worth. For the outcome is that neither Iphicrate nor Timoclès wins the hand of Ériphile: she marries the soldier Sostrate, who lacks the advantages of birth and fortune, but whose love is returned because, instead of the superficial glamour of spec-

[10] See above, pp. 176–80.

tacle and show, he is able to offer the real assets of military prowess and courage; it is he who saves Aristione when she is attacked by a wild boar, while the romanesque kidnapping that was to be staged by Anaxarque the astrologer so that Iphicrate could 'rescue' the Princess never materialises. The plight of the outsider, Sostrate, apparently without a chance of succeeding, recalls that of the hero of Corneille's *Don Sanche d'Aragon* (1649) – but whereas Corneille had recourse to a thoroughly romanesque device (the dénouement revealing that Sanche was really the Prince of Aragon, and therefore abundantly qualified to marry his princess), Molière allows merit and virtue to reap their own reward; and rather than looking back towards Corneille, Molière's treatment of the relationship between the two lovers looks forward, for their reciprocal affection is handled with a delicate touch which suggests that of Marivaux. The lovers are supported, not by the traditional figure of the valet, but by Clitidas, a *plaisant de cour*. This relatively 'straight' role (played by Molière) also helps to assert the primacy of reason, common sense and the natural order of things, when faced with the vanity and ostentation of the professional courtiers.

The theme of *Les Amants magnifiques*, then, is that of baroque theatricality, consisting of spectacle and illusion, being defeated by simplicity, sincerity and integrity. But paradoxically, the theatricality of the spectacle mounted at Saint-Germain was so consummately successful that the play could be performed only in the most extravagant of Court settings, and was consequently never transferred, like most of Molière's other *comédies-ballets*, to his town theatre at the Palais-Royal.[11]

Only in *Le Bourgeois gentilhomme* and *Le Malade imaginaire* did Molière succeed in marrying the framework of the *comédie-ballet* to the content of character comedy in his own distinctive manner, and on the scale on which it had been developed in major plays such as *Tartuffe* and *Le Misanthrope*. *George Dandin* perhaps reflects an attempt to produce this sort of combination; but there, as we have seen, the comedy of the *mari confondu* had remained quite independent of the ballet framework. For the rest, Molière had either preferred a simple theme which could be treated episodically (as in *Les Fâcheux*, *Le Mariage forcé* or *L'Amour médecin*) or else had chosen – in *Les Amants magnifiques*, the most ambitious of this series to date – the sort of romanesque subject on which he had turned his back after *Dom Garcie*

[11] For an excellent appreciation of this much-neglected play, see J. Guicharnaud, 'Les Trois Niveaux critiques des *Amants magnifiques*', in Howarth and Thomas (eds.), *Molière: Stage and Study*, pp. 21–42.

de Navarre. But *Le Bourgeois gentilhomme* is right in the mainstream of Molière's comedy. Monsieur Jourdain is one of the most memorable of his great *imaginaires*, and the plot of the play is entirely determined by the comic exploration of his dominant obsession. To quote Fernandez: 'Chaque scène du *Bourgeois* est une démonstration, merveilleusement juste et gaie, d'un trait de caractère ou de sentiment, réduit aux lignes essentielles. Et ces lignes sont rendues sensibles par des jeux de théâtre qui annoncent les figures du ballet.'[12] Thus, music and ballet find a place in the scheme of things without any artificial contrivance at all: Jourdain poses as a patron of the arts, and employs a music-master and a dancing-master, so that the Prologue and first *intermède* are a natural extension of the comedy itself. Similarly, his ostentation in dress, and desire to keep up with sartorial fashion, are not only displayed in the scenes with the Maître Tailleur and his helpers, but are also illustrated in the *intermède* following Act II, when 'les quatre garçons tailleurs se réjouissent par une danse'. At the end of Act III the *intermède* is devoted to the entry of the six cooks who have prepared the supper offered by Jourdain to the Marquise Dorimène; and during the supper, in Act IV, the musical entertainment devised by Dorante finds a natural place. Act IV concludes with the most elaborate of the musical contributions, which is so well integrated into the overall conception of the comedy that it is not properly speaking an *intermède* at all, but an essential part of the dramatic structure as the climax of Covielle's stratagem to persuade Monsieur Jourdain to give Lucile in marriage to Cléonte. The latter has already made his entry as 'le fils du Grand Turc', and now, to complete the deception, comes the burlesque ceremony in which the dignity of 'Mamamouchi' is conferred on the unsuspecting Jourdain: a triumphant combination of the spectacular manner of the traditional *ballet de cour* – Lulli not only composed the music and directed the choreography, but also took the part of the Mufti – and the dramatic logic of Molière's character comedy. The macaronic 'Dara dara bastonnara', chanted by the Mufti and his acolytes as they beat their victim, is at once the climax of a splendidly lavish *intermède*[13] and the culmination of the dramatic plot. The duping of the *imaginaire* has now been successfully completed – so successfully that he complacently repeats

[12] *La Vie de Molière*, p. 212.
[13] One contemporary source (d'Arvieux, *Mémoires*, quoted Mongrédien (ed.), *Recueil*, pp. 376–7) suggests that *Le Bourgeois gentilhomme* was built round this ballet, and that the King gave orders for an entertainment 'où l'on pût faire entrer quelque chose des habillements et des manières des Turcs'.

the same phrase to his wife in Act V as proof of his knowledge of the Turkish language – and the threat to the marriage of the young lovers has been effectively neutralised. The closing ballet, at the end of the brief fifth Act, is a self-contained 'Ballet des Nations', presented by Dorante for the entertainment of 'Son Altesse Turque' and the rest of the company: though not linked thematically with the rest of the play, it harmonises well with the festive, celebratory mood of the end of the comedy proper.

A striking feature of *Le Bourgeois gentilhomme* is its serene good humour. There is an inescapable family likeness between Jourdain and the other *imaginaires* of Molière's world, but his folly is treated more charitably by the comic process than is the case, for instance, with Orgon or Harpagon. Above all, the dénouement is not punitive. Jourdain is allowed to retain his self-delusion, and even to believe that his distorted view of the world he lives in has been accepted by others: 'Ah! voilà tout le monde raisonnable' (V, vi). The curtain comes down – or rather, the 'Ballet des Nations' takes over – in a mood of pleasurable satisfaction, with all the characters having achieved what they wanted. It may be a precarious, short-lived euphoria, but the audience is not invited to stay and witness Jourdain's disillusionment as he wakes from his dream world to the cold light of reason and common sense. Realism is kept out: satirical references to the mores of 'la Cour et la Ville' may be there if we want to look for them, but they are toned down by the genial fantasy that pervades the play. Perhaps this means that *Le Bourgeois gentilhomme* belongs to a lower order of comedy than *Tartuffe*, *Le Misanthrope* or *Les Femmes savantes*: plays which represent the 'comedy of ideas' we have defined in an earlier chapter. If this is so, it is still a masterpiece at its own level: a play, moreover, in which Molière has overcome the limitations of a hybrid genre which normally produced ephemeral entertainment, and integrated the arts of music and dance into a version of the character comedy that he had made his own.

Le Malade imaginaire does not communicate the same impression of serenity and good humour. Partly, no doubt, this is due to accidental circumstance: the bitter irony that Molière should himself die, almost on stage, after playing the part of a hypochondriac who asks: 'N'y a-t-il point quelque danger à contrefaire le mort?' has always tended to cast a retrospective *frisson* over the play. But there is a more fundamental reason, inherent in the play itself: for *Le Malade imaginaire* is a comedy of ideas, and beneath the comic fantasy there are serious issues that must give any spectator food for thought. Here, as in *Le Bourgeois gentilhomme*, the dénouement allows the *imaginaire* to retreat into his own fantasy world and cling to the consolation of his illusions; but whereas Jourdain's imaginary world is a sociable place, peopled with hangers-on who flatter his vanity, Argan's 'univers imaginaire' is a lonely, cheerless one, with self-pity as its dominant note. Relationships with their respective families may seem to be similar, but whereas Jourdain's attitude towards his wife and daughter is one of complacent indifference, Argan depends to a much greater extent on those near to him; and one of the principal ways in which his situation changes for the worse during the play is that his eyes are opened to the perfidy of his second wife Béline. Béralde's contribution to the comedy of ideas is a crucial one, of course; and if we compare his role with that of Madame Jourdain, who fulfils roughly the same dramatic function, both what he says and what he does establish him as a much more important character. Where Madame Jourdain represents simple intuitive common sense, Béralde is an articulate spokesman for the humanist critical tradition; and while Madame Jourdain, in breaking up the supper party and putting Dorimène to flight, merely provokes her husband to a show of ill-temper, when Béralde's intervention leads to Monsieur Purgon abandoning his patient, it is as if Argan's very life were in jeopardy.

Despite this increased seriousness, however, *Le Malade imaginaire* is far from being a sombre play. Argan's naïve gullibility, the self-important pedantry of Purgon and Diafoirus, and Toinette's inventive impersonation of an itinerant doctor, constantly relate it to established comic tradition. But more than anything else, perhaps, the comic tone is preserved by the burlesque degree ceremony. Like the 'turquerie' at the end of *Le Bourgeois gentilhomme*, it is an integral part of the conception of the play: the arts of music and dance are called in to enact the apotheosis of Argan's fantasy. Once again, there is no punitive element here: the obstacle to the marriage of Angélique and Cléante is removed, and Argan's folly is rendered harmless, by the most extravagant of pretences, and the mood is one of celebration. Comedy of ideas, satire and comedy of character finally dissolve in the pure entertainment of the macaronic incantations:

> Vivat, vivat, vivat, vivat, cent fois vivat,
> Novus doctor, qui tam bene parlat!
> Mille, mille annis, et manget, et bibat,
> Et seignet, et tuat!

PART III

The aesthetic of comedy

9

The Playwright as Poet

Prose, on the stage, is as artificial as verse: or alternatively, verse can be as natural as prose. (T. S. Eliot)[1]

(i) The prose plays

Tradition has it that when engaged in observing his fellow-men in order to obtain material for his plays, Molière had recourse to the seventeenth-century equivalent of the tape-recorder; he is pictured by Donneau de Visé[2] and others as 'le Contemplateur': seated apart, not participating in the conversation, but recording it on his 'tablets'. However, as many a playwright must have learned from painful experience, to preserve a record of natural speech is one thing: to translate it into dialogue which works in the theatre is a very different task, requiring other gifts besides a sensitive ear; and it is in the qualities of selection and arrangement that enable apparently naturalistic dialogue like that of Beckett or Pinter to 'passer la rampe' that the elusive genius of the comic dramatist consists.

Two of Molière's plays stand out from the rest as conversation-pieces, examples of a style much nearer to genuine stage naturalism than anything else surviving from the seventeenth century; for that matter, they are much more convincing in this respect than any domestic drama of the eighteenth century, despite the ambitious theoretical programme of Diderot and his contemporaries. Even Corneille's 'peinture de la conversation des honnêtes gens' had retained the inevitable stylisation of the verse medium, however unobtrusive the alexandrines of a play like *La Galerie du Palais* may be; but *La Critique de l'École des femmes* on the one hand, as an impression of the conversation in a typical *salon* gathering, and *L'Impromptu de Versailles* on the other, as the record of a work-session between Molière and his colleagues, achieve an appearance of almost total realism in reproducing the convincing flavour of everyday speech. 'Everyday speech' here, however, means in one case the conversation

[1] *Poetry and Drama* (London, 1951), pp. 12–13.   [2] *Zélinde* (1663), scene vi.

of a group of people, several of whom are consciously acting a part, so that diversity is provided by the contrast between the *honnêtes gens* and the *précieuse*, the pedant and the *marquis* (and also by Élise's mischievous imitation of the *précieuse* Climène); and in the other case a dialogue structured on the distinctive pattern of the theatrical rehearsal, diversity being produced here by the quotations in different stylistic registers and the contrast in acting styles. In these two plays, therefore, the dialogue acquires the necessary theatrical quality through the give-and-take of a lively discussion, which achieves variety of tone and pace without sacrificing the appearance of truth to life:

> *Climène*: Hélas! je parle sans affectation.
> *Élise*: On le voit bien, Madame, et que tout est naturel en vous. Vos paroles, le ton de votre voix, vos regards, vos pas, votre action et votre ajustement, ont je ne sais quel air de qualité, qui enchante les gens. Je vous étudie des yeux et des oreilles; et je suis si remplie de vous, que je tâche d'être votre singe, et de vous contrefaire en tout.
> *Cl.*: Vous vous moquez de moi, Madame.
> *Él.*: Pardonnez-moi, Madame. Qui voudrait se moquer de vous?
> *Cl.*: Je ne suis pas un bon modèle, Madame.
> *Él.*: Oh! que si, Madame!
> *Cl.*: Vous me flattez, Madame.
> *Él.*: Point du tout, Madame.
> *Cl.*: Épargnez-moi, s'il vous plaît, Madame.
> *Él.*: Je vous épargne aussi, Madame, et je ne dis pas la moitié de ce que je pense, Madame. (*Critique*, scene iii).

If this is *comic* dialogue, it belongs to the genre of comedy of manners: we laugh – or smile – at this exchange not because Climène is an extravagant product of the playwright's fantasy, but partly because we recognise in her the epitome of a social type, the *précieuse*, as defined by Élise before Climène's arrival, and partly because of the pleasure with which we acknowledge a fragment of dialogue that rings so true.

At the other end of the comic spectrum, however, there is a kind of imaginative writing that owes very little to observation of reality, and almost everything to the dramatist's fantasy. Two passages of this nature come at once to mind, as transcending the contextual requirements of the surrounding dialogue (it is significant that both are virtual monologues); and though neither is totally independent of characterisation, both passages reveal a rare indulgence on Molière's part in the sound of words for their own sake. The better known of the two passages – spoken by the Sganarelle of *Dom Juan*, unsure of himself in spite of his intellectual pretensions – couples verbosity with meaningless *galimatias*:

> O Ciel! qu'entends-je ici? Il ne vous manquait plus que d'être hypocrite pour vous achever de tout point, et voilà le comble des abominations. Monsieur, cette dernière-ci m'emporte et je ne puis m'empêcher de parler. Faites-moi tout ce qu'il vous plaira, battez-moi, assommez-moi de coups, tuez-moi, si vous voulez: il faut que je décharge mon coeur, et qu'en valet fidèle je vous dise ce que je dois. Sachez, Monsieur, que tant va la cruche à l'eau, qu'enfin elle se brise; et comme dit fort bien cet auteur que je ne connais pas, l'homme est en ce monde ainsi que l'oiseau sur la branche; la branche est attachée à l'arbre; qui s'attache à l'arbre, suit de bons préceptes; les bons préceptes valent mieux que les belles paroles; les belles paroles se trouvent à la cour; à la cour sont les courtisans; les courtisans suivent la mode; la mode vient de la fantaisie; la fantaisie est une faculté de l'âme; l'âme est ce qui nous donne la vie; la vie finit par la mort; la mort nous fait penser au Ciel; le Ciel est au-dessus de la terre; la terre n'est point la mer; la mer est sujette aux orages; les orages tourmentent les vaisseaux; les vaisseaux ont besoin d'un bon pilote; un bon pilote a de la prudence; la prudence n'est point dans les jeunes gens; les jeunes gens doivent obéissance aux vieux; les vieux aiment les richesses; les richesses font les riches; les riches ne sont pas pauvres; les pauvres ont de la nécessité; nécessité n'a point de loi; qui n'a point de loi vit en bête brute; et par conséquent, vous serez damné à tous les diables. (V, ii)

In seventeenth-century terms, this is a burlesque parody of the sententious manner of innumerable stage *confidents*: Sganarelle's speech is composed of a string of banal *sententiae*, or maxims. However, the inconsequentiality of his argument gives his speech a modern, almost surrealist quality; it has been compared to Lucky's speech in *Waiting for Godot*, and to 'un beau poème de Jacques Prévert'.[3]

Mostly, however, verbosity on the part of Molière's characters is accompanied by pedantic logic; an early example is this passage spoken by the Docteur of *La Jalousie du Barbouillé*, who has already given evidence of his logic-chopping as well as of his long-windedness:

> Tu me prends donc pour un homme à qui l'argent fait tout faire, pour un homme attaché à l'intérêt, pour une âme mercenaire? Sache, mon ami, que quand tu me donnerais une bourse pleine de pistoles, et que cette bourse serait dans une riche boîte, cette boîte dans un étui précieux, cet étui dans un coffret admirable, ce coffret dans un cabinet curieux, ce cabinet dans une chambre magnifique, cette chambre dans un appartement agréable, cet appartement dans un château pompeux, ce château

---

[3] Jouvet, *Témoignages sur le théâtre*, p. 67.

dans une citadelle incomparable, cette citadelle dans une ville célèbre,
cette ville dans une île fertile, cette île dans une province opulente, cette
province dans une monarchie florissante, cette monarchie dans tout le
monde; et que tu me donnerais le monde où serait cette monarchie
florissante, où serait cette province opulente, où serait cette île fertile, où
serait cette ville célèbre, où serait cette citadelle incomparable, où serait
ce château pompeux, où serait cet appartement agréable, où serait cette
chambre magnifique, où serait ce cabinet curieux, où serait ce coffret
admirable, où serait cet étui précieux, où serait cette riche boîte dans
laquelle serait enfermée la bourse pleine de pistoles, que je me soucierais
aussi peu de ton argent et de toi que de cela. (scene ii)

When the pedant *dottore* of the farces becomes a doctor of medicine,
and his laboured reasoning is enlisted in support of reactionary
scientific and medical learning, the purely satirical effect of the per-
verted logic is still frequently attenuated by the playwright's fantasy,
which endows the satire with a highly imaginative, and therefore
richly comic, quality:

Monsieur, ce n'est pas parce que je suis son père, mais je puis dire que
j'ai sujet d'être content de lui, et que tous ceux qui le voient en parlent
comme d'un garçon qui n'a point de méchanceté. Il n'a jamais eu
l'imagination bien vive, ni ce feu d'esprit qu'on remarque dans quel-
ques-uns; mais c'est par là que j'ai toujours bien auguré de sa judiciaire,
qualité requise pour l'exercice de notre art. Lorsqu'il était petit, il n'a
jamais été ce qu'on appelle mièvre et éveillé. On le voyait toujours doux,
paisible, et taciturne, ne disant jamais mot, et ne jouant jamais à tous ces
petits jeux que l'on nomme enfantins. On eut toutes les peines du monde
à lui apprendre à lire, et il avait neuf ans, qu'il ne connaissait pas encore
ses lettres. 'Bon, disais-je en moi-même, les arbres tardifs sont ceux qui
portent les meilleurs fruits; on grave sur le marbre bien plus malaisément
que sur le sable; mais les choses y sont conservées bien plus longtemps, et
cette lenteur à comprendre, cette pesanteur d'imagination, est la marque
d'un bon jugement à venir' . . .

However, the long tirade, with its incantatory rhythms or its
cumulative rhetorical effects, is not the only kind of prose dialogue in
which Molière's poetic imagination finds expression. Another kind is
evoked in the same scene from *Le Malade imaginaire* (II, v), where
Angélique's suitor Cléante, disguised as her singing-master, is invited
to offer the company a sample of his pupil's accomplishments. What
he produces is defined as:

. . . de la prose cadencée, ou des manières de vers libres, tels que le plaisir
et la nécessité peuvent faire trouver à deux personnes qui disent des
choses d'eux-mêmes, et parlent sur-le-champ.

Cléante's impromptu opera, assisted as it is by musical accompaniment, may perhaps strike us as nearer verse than prose; however, Molière's plays offer other examples of 'prose cadencée' by means of which the dialogue of the prose plays frequently achieves patterns and stylistic effects similar to those we associate more readily with verse.

Among the various kinds of scene calling for exchanges between young lovers, there is one, the *dépit amoureux*, that was such a successful set piece that Molière produced variations on it in a number of his plays. By their nature, such scenes lend themselves to a high degree of stylisation, and in both *Dépit amoureux* and *Tartuffe* this stylisation is of course conveyed through the medium of the alexandrine; nevertheless, the prose of the corresponding scene in *Le Bourgeois gentilhomme* loses nothing by comparison. First of all, an appropriate atmosphere is created by the exalted expression of the lover's chagrin:

> Je fais voir pour une personne toute l'ardeur, et toute la tendresse qu'on peut imaginer; je n'aime rien au monde qu'elle, et je n'ai qu'elle dans l'esprit: elle fait tous mes soins, tous mes désirs, toute ma joie; je ne parle que d'elle, je ne pense qu'à elle, je ne fais des songes que d'elle, je ne respire que par elle, mon coeur vit tout en elle; et voilà de tant d'amitié la digne récompense!

Then a comic deflation is produced by the incongruous juxtaposition of the valet's burlesque sufferings, undercutting those of his master:

> — Peut-on rien voir d'égal, Covielle, à cette perfidie de l'ingrate Lucile?
> — Et à celle, Monsieur, de la pendarde de Nicole?
> — Après tant de sacrifices ardents, de soupirs et de voeux que j'ai faits à ses charmes!
> — Après tant d'assidus hommages, de soins, et de services que je lui ai rendus dans sa cuisine!
> — Tant de larmes que j'ai versées à ses genoux!
> — Tant de seaux d'eau que j'ai tirés au puits pour elle!
> — Tant d'ardeur que j'ai fait paraître à la chérir plus que moi-même!
> — Tant de chaleur que j'ai soufferte à tourner la broche à sa place!

During the quarrel-scene between the lovers themselves, and their equally impetuous reconciliation, the text is economical but expressive; and as the two couples pirouette round each other, their wounded *amour-propre* not wholly concealing the tender affection they feel, the whole sequence is like a verbal ballet. In a different vein, the same is true of Jourdain's encounters with his various tutors in Act I, and with his tailor in Act II: indeed, throughout *Le Bourgeois gentilhomme* one can see how rhythms and speech-patterns have been successfully adapted to varying subject-matter, so that the play is a veritable compendium of the expressive resources of Molière's prose.

Of the other prose plays, *Dom Juan* is surely the one that contains the greatest range of linguistic expression and variety of tone, from the peasant patois of Act II to Elvire's emotional rhetoric, which expresses with dignity and restraint the wounded sensibility of the wife whom Dom Juan has abandoned:

> Je vous ai aimé avec une tendresse extrême; rien au monde ne m'a été si cher que vous; j'ai oublié mon devoir pour vous, j'ai fait toutes choses pour vous; et toute la récompense que je vous demande, c'est de corriger votre vie, et de prévenir votre perte . . . (IV, vi)

While the scene with Monsieur Dimanche no doubt remains fairly near to the tone of a real-life conversation between a *grand seigneur* and his *marchand* (with just the necessary selection and arrangement to produce a comic effect), it can reasonably be assumed that those between Dom Juan and his father are much more influenced by literary convention, and that however formal actual modes of address between father and son may have been in Molière's day, Dom Louis's sententious periods reflect the author's sense of what was needed to arouse the right degree of dramatic sympathy:

> Hélas! que nous savons peu ce que nous faisons quand nous ne laissons pas au Ciel le soin des choses qu'il nous donne, quand nous voulons être plus avisés que lui, et que nous venons à l'importuner par nos souhaits aveugles et nos demandes inconsidérées! J'ai souhaité un fils avec des ardeurs nonpareilles; je l'ai demandé sans relâche avec des transports incroyables; et ce même fils, que j'obtiens en fatiguant le Ciel de voeux, est le chagrin et le supplice de cette même vie dont je croyais qu'il devait être la joie et la consolation . . . (IV, iv)

As for Dom Juan himself, he has no characteristic style, but adapts to circumstances: Act II, scene iv, for instance, in which he attempts the simultaneous seduction of the two peasant girls, is a masterpiece of the 'verbal ballet' technique of rapid, patterned exchanges. However, we have been warned by Sganarelle early in the play that his master talks 'tout comme un livre'; and especially in the scenes with Sganarelle, naturalistic speech gives way to a programmatic, expository manner, as verisimilitude yields to the requirements of theatrical dialectic.

It has often been asked why some of Molière's comedies were written in prose rather than in verse. To contemporaries conscious of an

established hierarchy of genres, it seemed reasonable that trifles like
Les Précieuses ridicules or *Le Médecin malgré lui* should be in prose, but the
notion of a five-act comedy in prose was considered something of a
contradiction in terms, and *Dom Juan* and *L'Avare* both seemed awkward anomalies.[4] It has been suggested that these plays were composed in such a hurry that Molière did not have time to write them in
verse; to quote Voltaire: 'Molière avait écrit son *Avare* en prose pour le
mettre ensuite en vers; mais il parut si bon que les comédiens voulu-
rent le jouer tel qu'il était, et que personne n'osa depuis y toucher.'[5]
This is of course a purely gratuitous supposition, which perhaps tells
us more about Voltaire's own methods of poetic composition than it
does about Molière's. The only piece of tangible evidence that might
be used in support of the claim is the presence, often remarked on, in
Dom Juan of a number of concealed, 'ready-made' alexandrines. Dom
Louis's speech (IV, iv), for instance, contains the following:

> Je suis bien las aussi de vos déportements . . .
> La naissance n'est rien où la vertu n'est pas . . .
> . . . Au contraire, l'éclat
> N'en rejaillit sur vous qu'à votre déshonneur.

But even if one adds all the other half-lines that can be isolated in the
speech, the proportion is hardly surprising; and this feature of
Molière's writing suggests not so much that what we have here is a
prose draft ready for 'translation' into verse, as that in creating a
tirade of such a sententious, rhetorical nature he deliberately chose to
give it a more stylised, cadenced form.

A similar question arises apropos of *Le Sicilien,* a play whose poetic
qualities were recognised by contemporaries, even if not as a subject
for unequivocal praise:

> Généralement parlant, la prose de Molière est ampoulée, poétique,
> remplie d'expressions précieuses et toute pleine de vers. *Le Sicilien,* par
> exemple, est une petite comédie toute tissue de vers non rimées . . .[6]

The 'Grands Écrivains' editors, who examine this aspect of the play
in detail, express a more precise, as well as a more favourable,
appreciation:

[4] Cf. the comments of Grimarest and Robinet quoted in Mongrédien (ed.), *Recueil*,
pp. 317–19.
[5] *Dictionnaire philosophique*, art. 'Art dramatique'. And cf. F. Génin, *Lexique comparé de la
langue de Molière* . . . (1846), s.v. 'Vers blancs': '*L'Avare*, comme plusieurs autres
comédies en prose de Molière, est écrit presque tout entier en vers blancs. Le rythme
et la mesure y sont déjà; il n'y manque plus que la rime.'
[6] *Ménagiana* (1693), quoted in Molière, *Oeuvres*, ed. Despois and Mesnard, VI, p. 213.

> Le style du *Sicilien* est remarquable . . . il s'y mêle à l'agrément comique une sorte de poésie qui semble chanter la romance.[7]

It is as if the fantasy Mediterranean setting stimulated the poet's imagination; and certainly a passage like the following: 'Il fait noir comme dans un four: / le ciel s'est habillé ce soir en Scaramouche, / et je ne vois pas une étoile / qui montre le bout de son nez' (scene i) shows a most felicitous marriage of imagery and rhythm.

'Tout ce qui n'est point prose, est vers; et tout ce qui n'est point vers, est prose': the Maître de Philosophie's celebrated utterance is perhaps, in this context, not quite the self-evident truth that it appears to be. For there are numerous gradations from the naturalistic prose of *L'Impromptu de Versailles* to the alexandrines of *Tartuffe* or *Le Misanthrope*; and not a few of Molière's prose plays were clearly written with a poet's ear for language.[8]

(ii) The verse plays

In the light of what has been said about *Le Sicilien*, it is extremely interesting that that play should immediately have been followed by *Amphitryon*. Molière had previously used *vers libres* in libretti for ballets like the stylised *Pastorale comique* of 1666; and the fact that *Le Sicilien* with its poetic prose, the only new play produced in 1667, was succeeded the next year by *Amphitryon*, a full-length play in *vers libres*, suggests a particular desire to experiment with dramatic language at this stage of the dramatist's career.

Critical opinion has on the whole been very favourably disposed towards the free verse of *Amphitryon*, often to the disadvantage of those plays whose verse-form remains more traditional; it is not easy to disregard the comment of so notable a *moliériste* as Fernandez, when he says:

> Le vers libre, plus souple que l'alexandrin, surtout que l'alexandrin de Molière, se prête aux demi-teintes et décompose minutieusement l'action. La parole suit de près les mouvements du corps et de l'âme.[9]

For my part, although I can appreciate the success with which the irregular form has been used in isolated passages – especially in the much-praised soliloquy by Sosie which opens the play – I cannot see

---

[7] *Ibid.* See also pp. 213–16, 234.
[8] See P. Larthomas, *Le Langage dramatique* (Paris, 1972), *passim*.
[9] *La Vie de Molière*, p. 199.

that the play, taken as a whole, gains by being written in *vers libres*. The combination of the varying lengths of line and the irregular rhyme-pattern is disconcerting to my ear, here just as much as in Corneille's *Agésilas*: it is well suited to the virtuoso effects La Fontaine achieves in his fables, but less so, in my opinion, to *dramatic* verse; and the reason is surely that we are so accustomed to accept the alexandrine couplet as the conventional medium for theatrical dialogue that when we listen to *vers libres* we become too preoccupied with the mechanics of the unfamiliar verse-form. If it is true, as has been suggested,[10] that Molière chose to write in *vers libres* at least partly so as not to seem to be following too closely in the footsteps of Rotrou, I can only say that Boileau is not alone in finding the comparison with *Les Sosies* not wholly to Molière's advantage.[11]

Besides expressing the critic's appreciation of the verse-form of *Amphitryon* itself, Fernandez's remark contains by implication a severe judgement on Molière's handling of the alexandrine: a point of view with a respectable pedigree, since it goes back at least to Fénelon:

> Térence dit en quatre mots, avec la plus élégante simplicité, ce que celui-ci ne dit qu'avec une multitude de métaphores qui approchent du galimatias. J'aime bien mieux sa prose que ses vers. Par exemple, *L'Avare* est moins mal écrit que les pièces qui sont en vers. Il est vrai que la versification française l'a gêné; il est vrai même qu'il a mieux réussi pour les vers dans *Amphitryon*, où il a pris la liberté de faire des vers irréguliers.[12]

It hardly seems necessary to defend Molière against this kind of prejudice: the simplest and most effective defence is that his alexandrines succeed triumphantly in the theatre. The opinion, still often encountered, that Molière wrote 'carelessly' or 'awkwardly' usually overlooks the fact that he was a *dramatic* poet, and that alexandrines that are criticised for their ungainly style may, in their dramatic context, be the apt expression of a character's evasiveness, embarrassment, anger or pedantic self-importance, as the case may be.

Thus, Elmire's embarrassment in her tête-à-tête with Tartuffe is effectively rendered by the hesitation, and self-evident improvisation, conveyed by these lines with their confusing sequence of 'on':

> Et lorsque j'ai voulu moi-même vous forcer
> A refuser l'hymen qu'on venait d'annoncer,

[10] See Molière, *Oeuvres*, ed. Despois and Mesnard, vi, p. 344.
[11] Cf. the passage quoted in Mongrédien (ed.), *Recueil*, pp. 303–4.
[12] *Lettre sur les occupations de l'Académie française* (1714), ch. vii.

Qu'est-ce que cette instance a dû vous faire entendre,
Que l'intérêt qu'en vous on s'avise de prendre,
Et l'ennui qu'on aurait que ce noeud qu'on résout
Vînt partager du moins un coeur que l'on veut tout? (lines 1431–6)[13]

Similarly, when Arsinoé replies to Célimène's insinuations about her age, it is not difficult to interpret the involved expression as due to her indignation:

Ce que de plus que vous on en pourrait avoir
N'est pas un si grand cas pour s'en tant prévaloir. (*Mis.*, lines 987–8)

R. A. Sayce comments that 'les paroles de Célimène sont d'une parfaite netteté, faisant apercevoir un fond de franchise malgré ses coquetteries . . . Les réponses d'Arsinoé, par contre, s'embourbent dans des complications syntaxiques dont on perd aisément le fil.'[14] For Pierre Fortassier, the 'negligent' rhyme 'autrement' – 'indubitablement' (*Mis.*, lines 451–2) is well suited to the pompous self-importance of Alceste's speech:

Oui, je vous tromperais de parler autrement;
Tôt ou tard nous romprons indubitablement.

By the same token the awkward assonance ('sans s'emporter') of line 1359 helps to express the same character's growing unease at the critical point of his crucial scene with Célimène in Act IV:

Non, non, sans s'emporter, prenez un peu souci
De me justifier les termes que voici.[15]

What did Fénelon and others mean by Molière's 'galimatias'? Gustave Rudler, in an excellent paragraph, equates this with the influence of *précieux* style.[16] Especially in the plays set in an upper-class milieu, examples of 'le jargon précieux' abound, and in *Le Misanthrope* it is not only Célimène and her admirers who subscribe to the fashion, but also Alceste himself, as for instance in the typically *précieux* metaphor of his final appeal to Célimène:

Pourvu que votre coeur veuille donner les mains
Au dessein que j'ai fait de fuir tous les humains. (lines 1761–2)

Generally speaking, the language of *Le Misanthrope* is full of linguistic

---

[13] For Sainte-Beuve's comments on these lines, see Molière, *Oeuvres*, ed. Despois and Mesnard, IV, p. 494.
[14] 'Réflexions sur le style comique de Molière', *CAIEF*, XVI (1964), 220–1.
[15] See the whole of his 'Molière poète', *Revue de l'Histoire du Théâtre* (1974), 140–55.
[16] *Le Misanthrope*, ed. G. Rudler (Oxford, 1947), pp. xxxvii–xxxviii.

features characteristic of the *bel usage* of the day, but which have now dated, such as the substitution of 'mon âme', 'mon coeur' for the simple personal pronoun 'je'. In this Molière is being neither more nor less than a man of his time. Ferdinand Brunot comments on this innocuous line from *L'École des femmes*:

> Mais je n'ai point pris foi sur ces méchantes langues (line 472)

'[Il] a beau être de Molière, c'est du galimatias' – even though on the very next page he remarks of Racine: 'Il parle la langue de son temps, voilà tout.'[17] In short, the fact that Célimène speaks in the idiom of a *salon* hostess of the 1660s should not bother us any more than that Dorine, or Martine, express themselves in a manner appropriate to servants:

> A table, au plus haut bout il veut qu'il soit assis;
> Avec joie il l'y voit manger autant que six;
> Les bons morceaux de tout, il fait qu'on les lui cède;
> Et s'il vient à roter, il lui dit: 'Dieu vous aide!' (*Tar.*, lines 191–4)

> Ce n'est point à la femme à prescrire, et je sommes
> Pour céder le dessus en toute chose aux hommes. (*F. sav.*, lines 1641–2)

The test of a playwright's handling of the alexandrine is first, whether his verse is successfully adapted to its particular dramatic context (and appropriate to the speaker); and second, whether he possesses a wide enough range to suit a variety of different contexts. Though perhaps of necessity less extensive in its compass than his prose, Molière's verse spans a really considerable range of tones and dramatic effects. As regards stylistic register, it can be adapted to the pastoral lyricism of *Mélicerte*:

> Ah! Myrtil, prenez garde à ce qu'ici vous faites:
> N'allez point présenter un espoir à mon coeur,
> Qu'il recevrait peut-être avec trop de douceur,
> Et qui, tombant après comme un éclair qui passe,
> Me rendrait plus cruel le coup de ma disgrâce (lines 452–6)

or to the heroic attitudes of *Dom Garcie de Navarre*:

> En vain Léon m'appelle et le trône m'attend:
> La couronne n'a rien à me rendre content,
> Et je n'en veux l'éclat que pour goûter la joie
> D'en couronner l'objet où le Ciel me renvoie,
> Et pouvoir réparer par ces justes tributs
> L'outrage que j'ai fait à ses rares vertus (lines 1766–71)

---

[17] *Histoire de la langue française*, Part IV, *La Langue classique* (Paris, 1924–5), p. 562.

as well as to the mock-heroic parodies of these attitudes that, as we have seen, are characteristic of *L'École des femmes*:

> Quoi? L'astre qui s'obstine à me désespérer
> Ne me donnera pas le temps de respirer? . . . (lines 1182–3)[18]

and of *Le Misanthrope*:

> O Ciel! de mes transports puis-je être ici le maître? . . . (line 1277)[19]

For the most part, however, Molière uses the alexandrine as the conventional stage counterpart of 'la conversation des honnêtes gens'. Contemporary theorists distinguished between 'le style sublime', 'le style médiocre' and 'le style simple':[20] the comic dramatist was naturally expected to adopt the latter, never rising beyond 'le style médiocre'; and the really distinctive feature of 'le style simple' was the comparative rarity of purely decorative figures of speech. The playwright had at his disposal, however, rhetorical devices of a functional character with which he could produce dramatic effects of repetition, antithesis or other kinds of emphasis when required;[21] and since Molière makes more sparing use of such devices than previous dramatists had tended to do, the results are much more striking. Stichomythia, for instance, had evolved during the course of the century from the rigid pattern of which we see a late example in Corneille's *La Suivante*, where one scene (III, ii) consists of forty single-line exchanges between two characters, towards something much more flexible, which often combines the single-line *réplique* with the half-line and the couplet. Though Molière does occasionally use stichomythia merely for ornament (see the opening scenes of *Mélicerte*), this sort of brisk exchange is normally reserved for the climax of an argument. Sometimes it takes the purer form of a brief sequence of single lines, as in the ten-line exchange between Trissotin and Vadius at the height of their quarrel (*F. sav.*, III, iii); more often that of 'stichomythie à forme souple',[22] such as the climax of the sonnet-scene in *Le Misanthrope* (I, ii), where the single-line alternation is broken at one point by the exchange of couplets. One effect that seems to be constant in all arguments or quarrels in stichomythic form is well illustrated by both these passages; it is the character who

---

[18] See above, pp. 139–40.   [19] See above, pp. 152–4.
[20] See B. Lamy, *La Rhétorique, ou l'Art de parler* (Paris, 1675).
[21] For these terms, see P. France, *Racine's Rhetoric* (Oxford, 1965), p. 5.
[22] Cf. J. Scherer, *La Dramaturgie classique* (Paris, 1950), p. 305.

speaks the second line of each shared couplet, and whose rhyme 'caps' the other, who has the better of the encounter:

> *Oronte*: Il me suffit de voir que d'autres en font cas.
> *Alceste*: C'est qu'ils ont l'art de feindre, et moi, je ne l'ai pas.
> *Or.*: Croyez-vous donc avoir tant d'esprit en partage?
> *Al.*: Si je louais vos vers, j'en aurais davantage . . . (lines 421–4)

> *Vadius*: La ballade pourtant charme beaucoup de gens.
> *Trissotin*: Cela n'empêche pas qu'elle ne me déplaise.
> *Vad.*: Elle n'en reste pas pour cela plus mauvaise.
> *Tris.*: Elle a pour les pédants de merveilleux appas.
> *Vad.*: Cependant nous voyons qu'elle ne vous plaît pas . . .
> (lines 1008–12)

Used with discretion, stichomythia is a form of dramatic writing with considerable potential; it is also evidently one in which the metrical pattern and the rhyme-scheme powerfully reinforce any effect that might be produced by a similar passage in prose. The same is true of other forms of patterned dialogue. Éliante's long speech (*Mis.*, II, v), for instance (whatever one may think of the appositeness of this set piece from Lucretius), gains cumulative force from the construction to which theorists of rhetoric give the name 'enumeration'; and that in turn depends for its effect both on rhyme, and on the relationship between the grammatical and the metrical structure of the speech. Éliante is talking of the bias men show in discussing the women they love:

> La pâle est aux jasmins en blancheur comparable;
> La noire à faire peur, une brune adorable;
> La maigre a de la taille et de la liberté;
> La grasse est dans son port pleine de majesté;
> La malpropre sur soi, de peu d'attraits chargée,
> Est mise sous le nom de beauté négligée;
> La géante paraît une déesse aux yeux;
> La naine, un abrégé des merveilles des cieux;
> L'orgueilleuse a le coeur digne d'une couronne;
> La fourbe a de l'esprit; la sotte est toute bonne;
> La trop grande parleuse est d'agréable humeur;
> Et la muette garde une honnête pudeur.
> C'est ainsi qu'un amant dont l'ardeur est extrême
> Aime jusqu'aux défauts des personnes qu'il aime. (lines 717–30)

In another well-known example of patterned dialogue, which comes in Act I of *Tartuffe*, Orgon interrogates Dorine about Tartuffe's state of health while he has been away. It would be difficult to maintain that a successful comic scene in prose could not have been constructed on the basis of the fourfold repetition 'Et Tartuffe?'—'Le pauvre homme!'; but once again, the felicitous combination of rhythm and rhyme underscores the neatness of the dramatist's invention, and helps to make of this passage a memorable comic masterpiece (lines 231–58).

Where Molière's verse dialogue no doubt lacks the flexibility of his prose is in the rendering of quick, lively exchanges between a number of characters. He wisely never attempts anything like the sustained virtuosity we find in Hugo (see for instance *Marion de Lorme, passim*) or Rostand (in *Cyrano de Bergerac*) – one effect of which must in any case be to make it almost impossible for the ear to detect the articulation of the alexandrine – and although there are notable cases in Molière of a completely fractured line:

> Ne vous a-t-il point pris, Agnès, quelque autre chose?
> Ouf!
>   — Hé! il m'a . . .
>   — Quoi?
>   — Pris . . .
>   — Euh!
>   — Le . . .
>   — Plaît-il?
>   — Je n'ose,
> Et vous vous fâcherez peut-être contre moi . . . (*E. des f.*, lines 571–3)

such cases remain exceptional, and normally the effect of his verse dialogue is to confer a certain pattern and rhythm on the shapelessness of ordinary speech.

Molière's handling of rhyme is serviceable rather than showy. For instance, there are few examples of the comic neologism at the rhyming position:

> Tu sais qu'à toi toujours je me suis confiée:
> Fais moi . . .
> — Non, vous serez, ma foi, tartuffiée (*Tar.*, lines 673–4)

which is much more typical of Scarron; and generally speaking, the effects produced by Molière's rhymes depend less on surprise and incongruity – though there are exceptions, and it would probably be true to say that the rhyming in *Sganarelle*, for instance, is more inventive than in the later verse plays – than on the juxtaposition of a pair of terms which possess an evident affinity of some kind. Very often the rhyming words belong to the same grammatical category, as

for instance in the passage in which Tartuffe is trying to seduce
Elmire by a display of casuistry:

> Je puis vous dissiper ces craintes ridicules,
> Madame, et je sais l'art de lever les scrupules.
> Le Ciel défend, de vrai, certains contentements;
> Mais on trouve avec lui des accommodements;
> Selon divers besoins, il est une science
> D'étendre les liens de notre conscience
> Et de rectifier le mal de l'action
> Avec la pureté de notre intention.
> De ces secrets, Madame, on saura vous instruire;
> Vous n'avez seulement qu'à vous laisser conduire.
> Contentez mon désir, et n'ayez point d'effroi:
> Je vous réponds de tout, et prends le mal sur moi. (lines 1485–96)[23]

The final couplet of this speech provides a good illustration of another
distinctive feature of Molière's versification: the technique of 'anticipation', by which the playwright sets up an obvious rhyme, the
second element of which will be foreseen by the alert spectator, as a
means of creating comic, or more commonly dramatic, effect. Here,
Tartuffe's 'sur moi' is given extra emphasis in this way, as the climax
of his casuistical appeal; and a similar effect can be observed in
passages such as the following:

> Et que prétendez-vous qu'une sotte, en un mot. . .
> — Épouser une sotte est pour n'être point sot (*É. des F.*, lines 81–2)

> Quoi? vous ne pouvez pas, voyant comme on vous nomme,
> Vous résoudre une fois à vouloir être un homme? (*F. sav.*, 683–4)

Like Racine, Molière goes against the recommendations of the influential Malherbe in his practice with regard to rhyme: instead of the
striking, out-of-the-way rhyme he deliberately prefers the ordinary
and the obvious, playing on the spectator's sense of anticipation
rather than attempting to surprise him with the unexpected.[24]

Another way in which Molière, as a dramatic poet, shows his
affinity with Racine is in the flexibility he can give to his alexandrine
by the handling of the caesura, the subsidiary *coupes*, and enjambe-
ment. A passage like the following shows how far Molière's verse
dialogue is from the stereotype of the 'end-stopped' alexandrine with

[23] Cf. e.g. *Mis.*, lines 145ff.
[24] See W. D. Howarth, 'Some Thoughts on the Function of Rhyme in French Classical
Tragedy', *The Equilibrium of Wit: Essays presented to Odette de Mourgues*, ed. P. J. Bayley
and D. G. Coleman (Lexington, Ky) (1982), pp. 150–65.

a heavily articulated caesura, as advocated by Malherbe (and frequently practised by Corneille):

> Monsieur, cette matière est toujours délicate,
> Et sur le bel esprit nous aimons qu'on nous flatte.
> Mais un jour, à quelqu'un, dont je tairai le nom,
> Je disais, en voyant des vers de sa façon,
> Qu'il faut qu'un galant homme ait toujours grand empire
> Sur les démangeaisons qui nous prennent d'écrire;
> Qu'il doit tenir la bride aux grands empressements
> Qu'on a de faire éclat de tels amusements;
> Et que, par la chaleur de montrer ses ouvrages,
> On s'expose à jouer de mauvais personnages. (*Mis.*, lines 341–50)

Finally, a word about inversion. Modern commentators, following nineteenth-century theorists such as Hugo or Banville, sometimes tend to regard inversion as an awkward *pis aller*, to which poets of an earlier period resorted only because they were unable to reconcile the normal grammatical requirements of the sentence with the metrical requirements of the alexandrine. In fact, inversion is capable of producing a real positive effect, by turning a banal prose sentence into something with a recognisable poetic quality. If one compares lines like the following:

> De la chose lui-même il m'a fait un récit (*Étourdi*, line 938)

> A vous prêter les mains ma tendresse consent (*Mis.*, line 1388)

> De toutes amitiés il détache mon âme (*Tar.*, line 277)

> Croyez-vous pour vos yeux sa passion si forte,
> Et qu'en son coeur pour moi toute flamme soit morte?
> (*F. sav.*, lines 111–12)

with their equivalent in normal word-order it can be seen how in each case the inversion, by giving the significant terms a particular emphasis, produces a dramatic impact that would otherwise be lacking.[25]

Some of Molière's contemporaries – La Bruyère, Fénelon – were inclined to dismiss his talents as a poet; though if we may believe the well-known anecdote about his advice to the King, Boileau was more discerning.[26] On the whole, later generations have been more appreciative of the qualities of Molière's verse. 'Jamais phrase, de vers ou de prose', says Gustave Rudler of *Le Misanthrope*, 'n'a serré de plus près l'allure de la pensée ou du sentiment.'[27] And Victor Hugo

---

[25] Cf. J. B. Ratermanis, 'L'Inversion et la structure de l'alexandrin', *French Studies*, VI (1952), 58–66.   [26] See above, p. 13.   [27] *Le Misanthrope*, ed. Rudler, p. xl.

himself, that forthright critic of neo-classical verse drama, makes it abundantly clear that his strictures on the seventeenth-century alexandrine do not apply to Molière:

> Pour se convaincre du peu d'obstacles que la nature de notre poésie oppose à la libre expression de tout ce qui est vrai, ce n'est peut-être pas dans Racine qu'il faut étudier notre vers, mais souvent dans Corneille, toujours dans Molière. Racine, divin poète, est élégiaque, lyrique, épique; Molière est dramatique.[28]

[28] *Préface de Cromwell* (1827), ed. M. Souriau (Paris, 1897), p. 277.

Molière's Comic Vision

Les honnêtes gens ont leur littérature, que nous appelons la littérature classique.

(Pierre Gaxotte)[1]

(i) 'Raisonneurs' and 'honnêtes gens'

Before Molière's day, as we have seen, French comedy was lacking anything that could be called 'comic vision'. The world of the farces, and of Scarron's Jodelet plays, was a world of two-dimensional theatrical characters, a world of fantasy whose only relationship with reality was that of parody or burlesque. In Corneille's comedies, on the other hand, the characters, though more rounded and lifelike, were colourless, and the plots remained tied to the complex artificiality inherited from the pastorals; so that although his plays can be accepted as portraying reality after a fashion, we should look in vain here too (except perhaps to some extent in *Mélite* and *L'Illusion comique*) for an authentic comic vision on the playwright's part.

It must have seemed to contemporaries at the beginning of Molière's career that whatever promise this new arrival showed, there were few signs of his departing from traditional patterns of comedy established by predecessors. *L'Étourdi*, *Dépit amoureux*, *Les Fâcheux* are all recognisably in the comic idiom of 1640–58; and the comedies based on the Mascarille type of character (the same will also be true of *Les Fourberies de Scapin*) offer no more of a comic vision – that is, an identifiable philosophy of life – than *Le Menteur* or *Dom Japhet d'Arménie*. But with the creation of the Sganarelle figure; the evolution of the formula 'ridicule en de certaines choses et honnête homme en d'autres'; the transfer of the comic scene indoors; and the treating of contemporary topics such as preciosity, *honnêteté*, *dévotion* or social climbing: with such highly individual innovations, Molière fashioned a totally new type of comedy that demanded to be related to the real world outside the theatre.

[1] *La France de Louis XIV* (Paris, 1946), p. 185.

How are we to define Molière's comic vision? More than any other writer of comedies has ever done, he offers us a valid and consistent view of human nature. His major plays are of course rich enough for commentators to be able to argue about this or that detail of their interpretation; but there is general agreement about the broad lines of a coherent philosophy. This is in the first place critical, or negative, in that it holds up to ridicule certain tendencies that are unsociable, or anti-social, in character – there is a common denominator of egoism and self-interest in all the Sganarelle figures – but it is also possible to deduce from the plays a constructive social ideal: an ideal very close to that of the *honnêtes gens*. It is not put forward didactically as a programme to be followed; rather it is to be inferred as a more or less implicit social norm against which the Sganarelle figures offend.

In conveying to the spectator this positive recommendation of a social norm, one group of characters has a particular importance, namely the so-called 'raisonneurs': the Chrysaldes, Cléantes and Béraldes of Molière's theatre. From having been looked on by earlier critics as lay figures playing a role as mouthpieces of the author in an essentially didactic form of comedy, this group of characters has recently come to be seen in a more theatrical light, as taking one side in a dialectical confrontation which Molière puts before us objectively, without himself taking sides: what Moore calls 'a dialogue on humanity'.[2] Bray, who also considers these characters to be satisfactorily integrated into the dramatic scheme of the plays, goes so far as to declare: 'Il n'y a pas de raisonneurs dans le théâtre de Molière. Chaque personnage est exigé par sa fonction dramatique, non par une prétendue morale inventée par la critique.'[3]

What is the true role of the *raisonneurs*, and what do they stand for? There is a distinct family likeness between the two Aristes (in *L'École des maris* and *Les Femmes savantes*), Chrysalde (*L'École des femmes*), Cléante (*Tartuffe*) and Béralde (*Le Malade imaginaire*): all of these are mature characters 'd'un certain âge', standing somewhat to one side of the dramatic action, but showing a sympathetic interest in the fortunes of the central figure, with whom they are connected by family ties or by longstanding friendship. Philinte, the other character who is often labelled a 'raisonneur', corresponds in the main to this descrip-

---

[2] *Molière, A New Criticism*, p. 96.
[3] *Molière, homme de théâtre*, p. 32. On the function of the *raisonneur*, see also R. Fargher, 'Molière and his Reasoners' in *Studies in French Literature presented to H. W. Lawton*, ed. J. C. Ireson *et al.* (Manchester, 1968), pp. 105–20.

tion; and although he clearly belongs, like Alceste, to a younger age-group, his phlegmatic temperament seems to be that of the *raisonneur* type in general. To say that their function is merely to express the viewpoint he wants his audience to adopt, is to ascribe to Molière a very limiting and simplistic view of the comic process. On the other hand, to claim that the opening dialogue between Arnolphe and Chrysalde on cuckoldry, or that between Alceste and Philinte on sincerity, is presented in a completely neutral manner, and to maintain that the spectator is not expected to find one of the characters much more reasonable than the other, seems to fly in the face of all one's experience in the theatre; moreover, even Bray seems to concede that Cléante, at least, is an episodic character whose presence is hardly essential to the plot of *Tartuffe*. But is it not possible that there is another way to justify the existence of the *raisonneur*? If we consider Molière's comedy as having evolved as the result of a two-way process, in response to the demands of a cultivated audience who were in turn being invited to approve a new form of comic drama which went beyond these demands, then would it not be legitimate to see this group of characters, who make their appearance in the most original, and most provocative, of the plays – those that belong to the category of 'comedy of ideas' – as a sort of 'objective correlative' of the *honnêtes gens* in the audience: recognisable, sympathetic figures expressing a point of view with which they could identify? Only Philinte, it is true, is fully representative of the *honnête homme* in the exclusive, aristocratic sense of the term: he is an enlightened courtier, whereas Chrysalde, Cléante and the others are bourgeois exponents of *honnêteté*. But they all represent the virtues of moderation, tolerance, and charity; they are all good listeners, wise counsellors, not doctrinaire theorists but practical men, thoroughly integrated into the society to which they belong; and all of them are good friends who can be depended on in an emergency. It would surely not be unreasonable to see their urbane, civilised manner, and the way of life they practise, as an illustration, if not of the aristocratic social ideal formulated by the Chevalier de Méré, at any rate of the code of *honnêteté* as it was accepted by some of his less exacting contemporaries.

In one important sense, the term *raisonneur* is a misnomer; and Littré's definition: 'Personnage grave de la comédie, dont le langage est celui du raisonnement, de la morale'[4] hardly does justice to this

[4] *Dictionnaire de la langue française* (Paris, 1885–92), s.v. 'raisonneur'.

group of characters in Molière's theatre. For Molière's *raisonneurs*, though they certainly stand for *la raison* in the sense of reasonableness or common sense, should not be identified with *le raisonnement* or *la raison raisonnante*. On the contrary: it is the doctrinaire characters, the *imaginaires* who inhabit a world of their own, who constantly make dogmatic use of their reasoning faculty in an attempt to coerce others into accepting their opinions. This can be seen particularly clearly in the opening scenes of *L'École des femmes* and *Le Misanthrope*, where in each case it is Arnolphe or Alceste who takes the initiative, arguing aggressively, while the so-called 'raisonneur' adopts a defensive posture, speaking in the name of ordinary human experience in a reasonable – but by no means a rationalistic – manner:

> *Arnolphe*: Mon Dieu, notre ami, ne vous tourmentez point:
> Bien huppé qui pourra m'attraper sur ce point.
> Je sais les tours rusés et les subtiles trames
> Dont pour nous en planter savent user les femmes,
> Et comme on est dupé par leurs dextérités.
> Contre cet incident j'ai pris mes sûretés;
> Et celle que j'épouse a toute l'innocence
> Qui peut sauver mon front de maligne influence.
> *Chrysalde*: Et que prétendez-vous qu'une sotte, en un mot. . .
> *Arnolphe*: Épouser une sotte est pour n'être point sot.
>
> (*É. des f.*, lines 73–82)

> *Philinte*: Tous les pauvres mortels, sans nulle exception,
> Seront enveloppés dans cette aversion?
> Encore en est-il bien, dans le siècle où nous sommes. . .
> *Alceste*: Non: elle est générale, et je hais tous les hommes:
> Les uns, parce qu'ils sont méchants et malfaisants,
> Et les autres, pour être aux méchants complaisants,
> Et n'avoir pas pour eux ces haines vigoureuses
> Que doit donner le vice aux âmes vertueuses. . . (*Mis.*, lines 115–21)

The relationship between the *raisonneur* and the central comic character presents few problems of interpretation in most of the plays; though the reason why Chrysalde should defend, as he does, the 'douceurs' and the 'plaisirs' of cuckoldry (*É. des f.*, lines 1244ff., 1302–5) has given rise to a certain amount of theorising by the critics – as has, much more importantly, the enigmatic question of Cléante's religious standpoint. But generally speaking, there seems to be no reason why an audience of *honnêtes gens* should not have been able to identify with the point of view expressed by Cléante, Chrysalde or Béralde, since that coincided with the attitudes they acknowledged themselves, or the social ideal to which they aspired; and by the same token, they presumably found no difficulty in accepting Orgon, Arnolphe or Argan as ridiculous inasmuch as their behaviour obviously departed from these accepted norms. But the relationship between Alceste and Philinte is another matter. In Alceste, contemporary spectators found a character who seemed to be one of themselves: a courtier, a would-be *honnête homme*, and a man with a highly developed sense of honour and personal integrity; and it must be acknowledged, to judge from such comment as has been preserved, that some of them found it easier to admire Alceste than to laugh at him. That the critical debate over the interpretation of Alceste's character should still be a live issue after three centuries shows that it was not just a problem of communication between Molière and contemporary audiences; though twentieth-century spectators should be better able than their seventeenth-century counterparts to situate Alceste in the context of Molière's whole comic *oeuvre*, to perceive the filiation that links him to the early Sganarelles, and to recognise the shaky foundations of self-importance and self-interest on which his crusade for sincerity is based. But Alceste will always have his champions; and Philinte, the embodiment of moderation and common sense, the *honnête homme par excellence*, will always seem to some playgoers less attractive than his headstrong, opinionated friend. And a degree of ambiguity is inevitable: ambiguity is, indeed, inherent in the formula 'ridicule en de certaines choses et honnête homme en d'autres'; and however convinced some of us may be that Alceste remains 'ridicule', we must agree that he is by far the most rounded, the most interesting, and the most sympathetic of Molière's comic characters. As Jean Emelina puts it in a most perceptive passage:

> La simplification psychologique, dans un genre plus populaire que la tragédie, est une nécessité pour le rire et pour la satire . . . La comédie ne peut, sans risquer de se détruire, prétendre sérieusement à une authentique lucidité. Elle est l'univers rassurant et clair du manichéen. Elle est l'univers de l'invraisemblable et de l'imaginaire tant pour les êtres que pour les situations, parce que le rire se nourrit de l'irréel. L'inévitable ambiguïté des personnages d'après nature, 'ni tout à fait bons ni tout à fait mauvais', ne peut pas être son lot, car de l'ambiguïté naît le malaise. Térence, Molière ou Marivaux, par les étranges résonances que font parfois lever en nous certaines de leurs créations, montrent assez que tout réalisme psychologique, que toute finesse d'analyse au sein de la comédie risquent, fatalement, de frôler le pathétique.[5]

[5] *Les Valets et les servantes dans le théâtre comique en France de 1610 à 1700* (Grenoble, 1975), p. 219.

(ii) Towards a comic catharsis

On the one hand, we know that Molière's plays were written for a company who were the favourite entertainers of Paris and the Court in the 1660s, and were the product of an intimate relationship with the audiences of his day. On the other hand, they are more frequently, and more widely, played in the twentieth century than ever before. What problems of understanding or interpretation arise for today's spectators from the fact that these comedies were created in response to the demands of a society so different from ours?

First of all, there is a group of comedies depending on fantasy and virtuosity, whose seventeenth-century reference is almost non-existent; this group includes plays which are conspicuously successful with modern audiences, such as *Le Médecin malgré lui* or *Les Fourberies de Scapin*, and there is no reason to believe that their appeal for us today differs essentially from the appeal they had for their first audiences three hundred years ago. A second group does, it is true, present certain problems of comprehension because of the seventeenth-century setting; but all that is required of us, really, is a minimum of factual knowledge about, say, *préciosité* or the *salons*, so that *Les Précieuses ridicules* or *Les Femmes savantes* should be at least as easy of access for twentieth-century spectators as *The Recruiting Officer* or *The Rivals*. On the other hand, plays like *Dom Juan*, *Tartuffe* and *Le Misanthrope* (and one could add *L'École des femmes* and *George Dandin*) pose genuine problems of interpretation, which largely derive from changes in the intellectual and moral climate between Molière's day and our own; and in such cases a great deal must obviously depend on the way in which a director views his role in guiding the response of an audience.

There seem to be two temptations for a modern director producing Molière. One is the temptation to update, to impose on the seventeenth-century play an arbitrary link with a selected period of modern history. Veteran theatregoers will no doubt have had a chance to experience *Le Misanthrope* in Edwardian dress, *Les Femmes savantes* in the costumes of the 1920s, *Tartuffe* in the dress and decor of *la belle époque*, or other productions based on similar historical analogies. One problem with such an approach is of course the very specific nature of the contemporary references in Molière's text: to take obvious examples, what does one make of the detailed evocation of seventeenth-century fashions in Alceste's scathing portrait of

Clitandre (*Mis.*, lines 475–88) if the actors are all wearing Savile Row suits, or of the references to Descartes and other thinkers in *Les Femmes savantes* which become quite meaningless in a twentieth-century context? Perhaps the most distinguished of such productions was Jean Anouilh's *Tartuffe* at the Comédie des Champs-Élysées in 1960: set in the period around 1900, it evidently succeeded in saying something important about the continuity of certain moral and social attitudes across the centuries. But to point an analogy so clearly must result in a very limiting interpretation of Molière's play: striking as such links may be, it is surely too restricting to insist on a single modern analogue to the exclusion of others that are possibly just as valid; and this kind of updating is best left to the alert spectator's imagination as he watches the play. The second temptation, irresistible to many modern directors, is to leave the play in the seventeenth century, but to subject it to a highly subjective, often political or sociological, interpretation. This has been above all the manner of Roger Planchon's productions at the Théâtre National Populaire; and both his *George Dandin* of the late 1960s and his *Tartuffe* of the mid-seventies took the form of explicit commentaries on the class-structure of the Grand Siècle. Not only does such a tendentious approach leave far too little to the imagination of the audience, but it leads to a solemn interpretation of Molière's plays which risks turning them into humourless *drames bourgeois*. The 1979 production of *Dom Juan* at the Comédie-Française by Jean-Luc Boutté illustrated a similar approach, dictated not so much by political conviction or sociological doctrine as by a personal resolve to be different at all costs, added to a damaging lack of confidence in Molière's text.[6]

For this is the inescapable conclusion: one reason why directors find it necessary to treat Molière thus is the desire to divert the audience's attention from a text that they presumably judge to be hackneyed, out of date, or lacking in theatrical qualities. Louis Jouvet gave a clear warning to his fellow-producers in the following passage from his *Témoignages sur le théâtre*:

> Dans cet art de métamorphoses qu'est le théâtre, seules comptent les pensées du poète; elles sont la vertu du théâtre. Ce que nous appelons pensées n'est qu'un vêtement de sentiments et de sensations. Généreusement le poète nous l'offre, et chacun s'approprie ce manteau, et chacun s'en revêt à son tour, pour vouloir penser à sa manière. Ce n'est là qu'une

[6] For a vigorous critique of Planchon's *Tartuffe* allied to a common-sense interpretation of Molière's text, see R. Pommier, *Assez décodé* (Paris, 1978), pp. 99–146.

usurpation. L'usage véritable d'une pièce de théâtre est d'y réchauffer son corps et son coeur.[7]

The text is sacred: this is Jouvet's message. It must never become a *pretext* for a priori sociological doctrine, for flashy theatricality, or for gratuitous embellishments in the name of 'relevance'. There will always be difficulties, ambiguities, possibilities of various layers of meaning, in certain of Molière's plays – that is partly what gives them their special quality – but the way to arrive at a meaningful reading of the text, on stage as well as in the study, is, as Jouvet says, to 'subir l'oeuvre avant de la comprendre et de l'apprécier': patiently to elucidate and interpret the original, not to substitute for it a subjective, anachronistic version of our own invention.

It is not difficult to create a convincing decor for the indoor comedies, whose text surely demands a firm link with a certain historical reality; and that can be done without indulging in the obsessive – and obtrusive – realism of Planchon and other directors. The seventeenth-century setting, which helps to establish the social context that is so necessary to a proper understanding of *Tartuffe, Le Misanthrope, L'Avare* or *Les Femmes savantes*, is not in any way exclusive: like all comic masterpieces, Molière's great plays combine the local and the topical with the universal, the individual with the general. It is a commonplace of literary theory that tragedy deals with individuals, comedy with general types. As Diderot puts it:

> Le genre comique est des espèces, et le genre tragique est des individus . . . Le héros d'une tragédie est tel ou tel homme: c'est ou Régulus, ou Brutus, ou Caton; et ce n'est point un autre. Le principal personnage d'une comédie doit au contraire représenter un grand nombre d'hommes. Si, par hasard, on lui donnait une physionomie si particulière, qu'il n'y eût dans la société qu'un seul individu qui lui ressemblât, la comédie retournerait à son enfance, et dégénérerait en satire.[8]

Diderot is quite right in his conclusion; but perhaps the terms he uses need looking at more closely: the notions of 'type' and 'individual' tend to be accepted too uncritically. For the pure stage *types* – the braggart soldier of Renaissance comedy, the stereotyped 'characters' of the eighteenth century – remain two-dimensional, and what gives a comic character that third dimension which brings him dramatic life is the successful blend of the general type to which he belongs with the individual features that distinguish him from that type.

[7] p. 26.   [8] *Writings on the Theatre*, ed. F. C. Green (Cambridge, 1936), p. 76.

Almost without exception, the comedy of Molière's contemporaries fails to achieve such a synthesis. Orgon, Alceste or Harpagon, on the other hand, although they are rooted unmistakably in the world that Molière and his audience knew, have the same universal reference as characters like Volpone and Falstaff. As with the most memorable creations of other comic dramatists, we can put this universality to the test in the case of Molière's characters when, as sometimes happens to us all, we draw on our experience as playgoers to help us to characterise acquaintances in the real world. It is not so very unusual for us to think of people we know as 'a Falstaff' or 'a Harpagon': convincing proof that these characters possess some quality or other that transcends the boundaries of time and place.

If we recognise our neighbours, then, or at any rate traits of character that we associate with our neighbours, in figures like Harpagon or Argan, what does that tell us about the moral function of comedy? Do we recognise ourselves as well? If not, it is difficult to see how comedy could fulfil the corrective role traditionally ascribed to it, even if one were to accept the sternly moralistic approach of some nineteenth-century commentators, enshrined in Meredith's well-known description of Molière: 'Never did man wield such a shrieking scourge upon vice.'[9] But the more nearly one approaches to the notion of satire in one's definition of comedy, the more difficult it surely is to believe that the moral effect attributed to Molière's comedy works in such a way. There have been periods when dramatists have pro-claimed a fervent belief in the corrective power of the theatre, and have matched that belief in practice by writing a heavily didactic kind of play; but in Molière's case we are entitled to discount the sort of claim he puts forward in the Preface to *Tartuffe*, where he is conduct-ing a defensive campaign against those, precisely, who had accused his play of immorality. Émile Augier, for all his faith that 'de tous les engins de la pensée humaine, le théâtre est le plus puissant, voilà tout', was realist enough to concede that it is asking too much of the dramatist to demand the conversion of individuals: 'd'ailleurs le but n'est pas de corriger quelqu'un, c'est de corriger tout le monde'.[10]

In any case, even if we assume that there were real-life counterparts of Molière's characters in the society for which he wrote, are we also to assume that they went to the theatre? Can we really imagine a real-life Tartuffe (or even a real-life Orgon), a Harpagon or an Argan

---

[9] *An Essay on Comedy and the Uses of the Comic Spirit* (1877) (London, 1927), p. 33.
[10] Preface to *Les Lionnes pauvres* (1858).

among the audience for whom the plays were performed? Such moral correction was never the business of comedy; this is certainly not the way in which the moral effect of Molière's comedy operates, and Alain is surely nearer the mark when he writes:

> Ce n'est point ton semblable, cet Avare qui dit son secret, car de ton semblable tu ne connais jamais que le dehors; toutefois ce qui est mis sur cette scène, c'est ce que chaque homme connaît de lui-même. Chacun est Harpagon, chacun a pensé le 'Sans dot', mais personne ne l'a jamais dit . . .
>
> Qui n'a jamais été ridicule ne sait point rire. Au reste un tel homme n'est pas né. Si l'avarice était une sorte de maladie rare, qui donc en rirait? Et si l'on me fait un portrait d'avare, d'après l'anecdote, j'éprouverai le faible plaisir de mépriser. Mais chacun est avare, de vraie avarice, et jaloux, de ridicule jalousie; chacun est Purgon et Jourdain en importance, cent fois par jour.[11]

'We are all of us miserly, jealous, and self-important, every day of our lives. . .': this shows a similar insight to Augier's 'le but n'est pas de corriger quelqu'un, c'est de corriger tout le monde'. We are all of us implicated in the comic process: not because as individuals we are the counterparts of either the *malade imaginaire* or the pompous doctors who attend on him, but because of the common humanity we share with the rest of the theatre audience. Some of us may imagine it is easy to preserve a comfortable detachment as we watch the follies of Orgon or Monsieur Jourdain; but can we say the same thing about Alceste? Here is a very different case, for we all have moods in which we think we are better, nobler, purer than the world we live in; in which we imagine that our merits are unrecognised or unrewarded. There is something of Alceste in all of us, in our most intimate relationships with those we love as well as in the broader context of our social behaviour. How many of us have not at times thought, even if we have not given expression to the thought:

> . . . Je verrai, dans cette plaiderie,
> Si les hommes auront assez d'effronterie,
> Seront assez méchants, scélérats et pervers,
> Pour me faire injustice aux yeux de l'univers? (*Mis.*, lines 197–200)

How many of us, by the same token, have not often felt, even if we have never voiced the feeling:

> . . . C'est pour mes péchés que je vous aime ainsi . . .
> Mon amour ne se peut concevoir, et jamais
> Personne n'a, Madame, aimé comme je fais? (*ibid.*, lines 520–4)

[11] *Propos* (Paris, 1970), II, pp. 456–7.

And how many of us, if we were honest, would not have to admit to occasional fantasies such as the following:

Oui, je voudrais qu'aucun ne vous trouvât aimable,
Que vous fussiez réduite en un sort misérable,
Que le Ciel, en naissant, ne vous eût donné rien,
Que vous n'eussiez ni rang, ni naissance, ni bien,
Afin que de mon coeur l'éclatant sacrifice
Vous pût d'un pareil sort réparer l'injustice,
Et que j'eusse la joie et la gloire, en ce jour,
De vous voir tenir tout des mains de mon amour? (*ibid.*, lines 1525–32)

We can all see something of ourselves in Alceste. And we may be quite sure that in confronting us with the truth about ourselves in this way, Molière never intended either to reinforce our self-esteem or to justify our anti-social impulses. For the mirror he holds up to us is the distorting mirror of comedy, and the 'truth' is exaggerated and caricatured by the comic process; so that if we can recognise the absurdity of Alceste's behaviour, we may be led to acknowledge the absurdity of any similar tendencies in ourselves. We laugh at the critical portrait of the *honnête homme imaginaire*, and thereby express our solidarity with the civilised way of life his behaviour so constantly flouts. The confrontation with a comic exaggeration of faults latent within ourselves acts as a painless corrective: this therapeutic effect is common to all Molière's great comedies, and *Le Misanthrope* is no exception. Experience teaches us, however, that there are spectators who are resistant to this process; and Alain might have been thinking of Rousseau's reaction to *Le Misanthrope* when he wrote: 'Heureux celui qui ne sait pas être important sans être ridicule; mais ces bonnes chances ne vont pas sans un peu d'humeur. La comédie nous guérit mieux, sans la honte; car la force du spectacle fait que personne ne pense au voisin.'[12]

Are we perhaps now in a position to offer an interpretation of the comic process, to which it might not seem too inappropriate to attach the label 'a comic catharsis'? Is it possible to discern an analogue for the spectator of comedy to the purging of the passions which, from Aristotle's day onwards, has been recognised by most theorists as a valid formulation of what we experience as spectators of tragedy? The fact that Aristotle did not include his projected section on comedy in the *Poetics* has not prevented commentators from constructing the theory of comedy to which he might have given expression; and

[12] *Les Arts et les dieux* (Paris, 1968), p. 337.

W. Lane Cooper went so far as to produce a full-scale adaptation of the *Poetics*, substituting concepts appropriate to comedy for those referring to tragedy. The essence of Lane Cooper's 'Aristotelian' definition is as follows:

> A comedy is the artistic imitation of an action which is ludicrous (or mirthful), organically complete, and of a proper length . . . As for the end or function resulting from the imitation of such an object . . . it is to arouse, and by arousing to relieve, the emotions proper to comedy.[13]

And his amplification of the last phrase provides a most interesting commentary on one of the central notions of the *Lettre sur l'Imposteur*, namely 'la disconvenance':

> Here we shall assume that, as men in daily life are accustomed to suffer from a sense of disproportion, it is this that is relieved or purged away by the laughter of comedy; for comedy (witness the comic mask) distorts proportions; its essence is the imitation of things seen out of proportion. By contemplating the disproportions of comedy, we are freed from the sense of disproportion in life, and regain our perspective, settling as it were into our proper selves.[14]

As with the tragic catharsis, such a process can be interpreted in two very different ways: one, as a direct, exemplary or corrective function, and the other, as an uplifting aesthetic experience of a much less specific nature. There is a world of difference between the interpretation advanced by Corneille in his *Discours de la tragédie*:

> La pitié d'un malheur où nous voyons tomber nos semblables nous porte à la crainte d'un pareil pour nous; cette crainte, au désir de l'éviter; et ce désir, à purger, modérer, rectifier et même déraciner en nous la passion qui plonge à nos yeux dans ce malheur les personnes que nous plaignons[15]

and Racine's version of the cathartic process, surely more consistent with the mature classical spirit, according to which what is 'purged' or 'tempered' is not the specific passion portrayed on stage, but any harmful excess of the very emotions of pity and fear that have been aroused by that portrayal.[16] By the same token, what we have called the comic catharsis has been seen by many as a moralistic or didactic process, but it too can be interpreted as something much less direct and specific – and again, I have no doubt that this subtler interpre-

---

[13] *An Aristotelian Theory of Comedy, with an Adaptation of the Poetics* (New York, 1922), p. 179.   [14] *Ibid.*, p. 181.
[15] *Writings on the Theatre*, ed. H. T. Barnwell (Oxford, 1965), p. 29.
[16] Cf. *Principes de la tragédie*, ed. E. Vinaver (Manchester, 1944), p. 12.

tation is more in keeping with the fully-developed classical aesthetic. Molière's purpose in his comedies was not to 'scourge' a particular vice; it is noteworthy that when he did set out to do something like that, in *Dom Juan*, he was forced to resort to a corrective process other than that of laughter. The punishment of a *grand seigneur méchant homme* lies outside the scope of the comic catharsis, and the playwright had to use dramatic, not comic, means to achieve that end. But elsewhere, Molière's aim – to 'corriger les hommes en les divertissant' – was to amuse all his audience, and to instruct all his audience, not merely such misers, misanthropists or learned ladies as might happen to be present. The heroes of classical comedy are not annihilated, like Dom Juan, but neither are they cured. They remain the intransigent outsiders, the impenitent egoists that they have been shown to be throughout the five acts of the play. They are in a sense the imaginary scapegoats of society, and by laughing at them in the social micro-cosm of the theatre the individuals composing the audience are enabled, as Lane Cooper puts it, to regain their proper perspective: that is, to preserve a healthy view of the relationship between the individual and society. This, then, is the cathartic function of Molière's comedy: to send us all away from the play purged and regenerated, as social beings, by the restorative process of laughter.[17]

'Molière n'eût pas été classique', writes Charles Lalo, 's'il n'avait défendu la bonne société établie en son temps contre les excentriques et les snobs, comme Alceste, les femmes savantes ou les précieuses ridicules; les parasites, comme Tartuffe, Harpagon ou même Dom Juan; les usurpateurs de dignités consacrées, comme le Bourgeois gentilhomme ou George Dandin.'[18] To see Molière as exemplifying this kind of *rire conformiste* would be to take a very restrictive view both of the relationship between the individual and society in his theatre, and of the nature of classical art. As L. J. Potts has written:

> Society, in the sense in which the word defines the setting of a comedy, stands for an idea rather than for a particular set of persons. It stands for coherence; for a common body of opinions and standards and a dispo-sition to cooperate. It can be contracted to a very small class living together in a small area; it can be extended to the whole of humanity . . .[19]

---

[17] For a further development of the idea of a comic counterpart to the catharsis of tragedy, see my article 'La Notion de la catharsis dans la comédie française classi-que', *Revue des Sciences Humaines*, CLII (1973), 521–39.

[18] *Esthétique du rire* (Paris, 1949), p. 200.

[19] *Comedy* (London, 1949), p. 60.

It would no doubt have been easy for Molière, once he was firmly established in the King's favour, to write comedies appealing to a narrowly-defined, self-contained Court audience, playing on that superficial sense of the proprieties which, as Stendhal says somewhere, is always the source of the courtier's notion of the comic. If he had done no more than this, his plays would long ago have become trivial museum-pieces. Instead, his comedy reflects a larger, more generous concept of society, neither exclusively aristocratic nor exclusively bourgeois; one that owed a good deal to the civilising force of Renaissance thought that had been handed down to Frenchmen of his age by the humanist tradition of previous generations. Biographers have often sought to emphasise the significance, as a guide to Molière's fundamental philosophy of life, of his translation of Lucretius and his friendship with free-thinking disciples of Gassendi. Such factors will probably always remain speculative; but the influence of the *social* ideas of the Renaissance humanists is much more tangible, and the society reflected in his theatre has considerable affinities with the ideal envisaged by thinkers like Erasmus and Montaigne. We know that in practice the France of Louis XIV's reign had its fair share of privilege and corruption, but the selective picture given by the artists and the writers of the age was not a complete misrepresentation of reality: French classical literature emphasises the values of an ordered, civilised way of life in which men and women of culture did genuinely believe, and which many of them honestly tried to practise. This aspect of the classical ideal, as a reflection of the highest aspirations of the civilisation of an age, is one that applies as fully to comedy as to any other art form; and when we speak of 'classical comedy' in this context, we think almost exclusively of Molière.

Translation of French Passages Quoted

v 'In serious plays it is enough, if one wants to avoid censure, to say things that are sensible and well expressed; in the other kind of play, however, that is not sufficient, for people want to be amused; and it's an extraordinary undertaking to try to make the gentry laugh.'

1 Every generation, for the last three hundred years [has] transformed, or distorted, in its own way a text whose essential quality is that it is totally adaptable to each new fashion, reputable or disreputable.

2 In order to understand how *Le Misanthrope* was written, it is much less important to know whether the playwright was uncommunicative or irritable, than to establish the number of actresses in his troupe, and to assess their talents.

2 He approaches his task neither as a psychologist nor as a moralist, but as a technician.

3 Such are the flights of fancy, padded out with suggestive details, that the human imagination needs in order to make its contacts with genius stand out against the ordinariness of everyday life.

3 A comic interpretation of life implies a comic vision, which in turn implies a philosophy.

9 His acting . . . has found favour with enough spectators, to give him some pretension to be considered the best farce-player in France.

9 I have never seen her perform; but she is said to be the best actress of all. She is a member of a travelling company.

9 A young man called Molière left the lecture-rooms of the Sorbonne to follow her: he was in love with her for a long time and acted as adviser to the company, finally joining them and marrying her. He's written some plays that are not without wit. He's not a very talented actor, except in comic roles. His company is the only one that performs his plays: they are comedies.

10 Everything has to yield to our new buffoon: upon my word, his is the only theatre where the audience get a good laugh for their money. For at the Hôtel de Bourgogne, famous for its tragic acting, you only get a chance to laugh at comedy; but at the Palais-Royal, when Molière takes both comic and serious parts, you can always laugh at tragedy as well!

259

10 He was such an excellent comic actor – though but mediocre in tragedy – that those who have taken his roles since his death have been poor copies of the original.

10 It is true that Molière's talents were all for comedy. He could never achieve the truly tragic manner; and it is asserted by some that having set out to succeed as a tragic actor, he performed so poorly at the first attempt that he was not even allowed to finish. From then onwards, they say, he confined himself to comedy, in which his success was constant – though certain playgoers of refined taste accused him of being too much given to grimacing.

10 He comes on stage with his head in the air, his feet stuck out at right angles, and one shoulder thrust out ahead of him; his wig, pointing all askew in the direction he is travelling, is adorned with more laurel-leaves than a York ham. Then he stands, his hands on his hips in a most unnatural posture, and with eyes staring wildly he begins his tirade, spacing out his words with heavy breathing, for all the world as if he had the hiccups.

11 When he first went on the stage, he realised that his delivery was marked by an uncontrollable rush of words, which tended to spoil his performance. The efforts he made to check this fault produced in him a sort of heavy breathing, which was to characterise his delivery for the rest of his life. However, he compensated for this defect by a remarkable subtlety of technique; he neglected none of the accents or gestures capable of affecting his audience. He never declaimed at random, like those actors who, having no understanding of the principles of declamation, are lacking in self-control; and every detail of his performance was studied.

11 'What? D'ye call that the way to speak verse? You must be joking: what's needed is a proper emphasis. Listen to me now . . . and do you see this stance? Take good note of it. And now, let me hear you put a proper stress on the last line: there, that's the way to produce a storm of applause.'

11 'To which players will you offer it?'
'A fine question! To the Royal Players, of course! None but they are able to bring out the finer points of a text. The others are ignoramuses, who declaim just as they would converse: they are unable to make a line of verse resound, and they haven't the wit to stop in the right places. For how can one tell where the best lines are, if the player doesn't stop and signify that it's time to applaud?'

12 Their début was successful enough, the women in the company being especially applauded. But since Molière knew well enough that his troupe would never rival the Hôtel de Bourgogne in tragedy, he stepped forward at the end of the play, paying a compliment to His Majesty, and requesting that he be allowed to perform one of the trifling entertainments with which they had gained a certain renown in the provinces. He

was quite confident of success in this, for his company were trained to extemporise short comic pieces in the manner of the Italian actors.

13 The King asked [Boileau] one day who had been the outstanding writer among those who had brought distinction to France during his reign. When Boileau replied 'Molière', the King said 'I should never have guessed it; but you know more about such matters than I do.'

13 If he had not played to the gallery so much in his masterly compositions; if his portraits had not too often tended towards caricature; if he had not been so ready to forsake refined amusement for vulgar clowning, and quite shamelessly forced Terence into company with Tabarin. In the farcical sack that Scapin carries, tied round his waist, I look in vain for the author of *Le Misanthrope*.

15 His company were trained to extemporise short comic pieces in the Italian manner. There were two of these in particular that everyone in the South, not excepting persons of the gravest demeanour, never tired of watching. They were *Three Rival Doctors* and *The Schoolmaster*, both entirely in the Italian style.

16 By the sort of plagiarism of which he alone is capable, he imitated *Le Médecin volant* and other pieces of the Italian players, whom he copied not only by taking the plays that they themselves perform, but also in their manner of acting, for on his own stage he is forever aping Trivelin and Scaramouche. But what more could one expect of a man whose reputation depends on the *Memoirs* of Guillot-Gorju that he bought from the actor's widow, from which source he has taken all his own plays?

16 Molière admired Scaramouche on account of the naturalness of his acting. He often watched him play, and this enabled him to teach the best actors of his own company.

16 This actor of unique renown
By his great gifts charmed all the town.
For great Molière had him for teacher,
While he was taught by none save nature.

16 Molière, the French genius, tried never to miss a performance by Scaramouche, the Italian genius.

17 He frequents the famous Scaramouche day and night. There, a mirror in his hand, in front of the great man, the prize pupil copies every single gesture, posture or grimace of the master of comic acting, repeating these over and over again.

17 Never was comedy so well performed, nor with such consummate skill. Every actor knows how many steps he has to take, and every single glance has been reckoned up beforehand.

17 Never was anything seen so diverting as the posturings of Sganarelle behind his wife's back. His facial movements and gestures offer such a

convincing representation of jealousy that even without speaking he would be recognised as the most jealous of men.

18 We've changed our mode of operation:
Jodelet's gone out of fashion.
The one thing now we have to learn
Is truth to life at every turn.

18 Molière and his company arrived in Paris in the month of October 1658 and offered themselves to Monsieur, the King's brother, who honoured them with his protection and bestowed on them the title of his players, with 300 *livres* pension for each of them.

19 The Théâtre du Marais doesn't possess a single good actor, male or female.

19 Had not thought it necessary to take the actors' views into account in pressing on with the building plans for the Louvre.

20 But the Troupe de Monsieur remained firm to a man: all its members admired M. de Molière, their leader, in whom an outstanding professional competence was allied to personal qualities which earned their respect and affection. They all promised him that they would harness their fortunes to his own, and would never abandon him, whatever advantageous offers they might receive from another source.

20 He accuses him of marrying the daughter, and of having had the mother as his mistress. But Montfleury isn't listened to at Court.

21 My aim, Monsieur, is to mark out for you those whom I consider deserving of such favour, in keeping with your orders, so as to provide a number of writers who will proclaim the King's virtues.

21 We all fervently hope that the same royal arm that upholds the true religion will put down this impious monster and destroy for ever his insolent pretensions.

22 Once the company's reputation was established, such visits were less sought after, perhaps even avoided. Molière and his colleagues devoted themselves almost exclusively to the King and the Parisian public.

23 Those who regret that he did not write more plays like *Le Misanthrope* are making a big mistake about the nature of his comic genius.

25 It was thus Molière the playwright who provided the bread and butter for Molière the actor and his company.

25 The number of actresses Molière had at his disposal, and what they were good at.

26 To the comedy at the Palais-Royal, to see . . . Molière's *Précieuses ridicules*. Mascarille was masked, the [Vi]comte de Jodelet wore a floured face.

27 This farce is an acrobatic *tour de force*, by means of which an actor can

learn the precise measurements of a stage, the technique of rapid entrances and exits, skill at adopting multiple, and almost simultaneous, disguises, and the most outlandish theatrical tricks. The play moves on at an ever-increasing pace, leaving reality further and further behind, till we end up with a house whose windows disgorge a succession of strange figures. The stolid Gros-René is taken by surprise; as for us, we are in on the secret, we know that this is a burlesque version of the real world such as only the theatre can create.

28 'He's a blockhead who is sure to make a mess of everything but we'll have to use him since there's no-one else.'

28 Breeches, doublet and cloak, collar and slippers, all of crimson satin.

28 Breeches, doublet, cloak, collar, wallet and belt, all of musk-coloured satin.

29 'Instead of plays by Corneille, I played *L'Étourdi*, which succeeded marvellously. For no sooner had the audience seen me carrying my halberd, heard my comic way of speaking, and observed my outfit, my cap, my moustache and my ruff, than they were all delighted. At once, the boredom and displeasure that had been vexing us, disappeared; from pit to stage-seats, and stage-seats to boxes, my praises resounded without interruption, and for three whole months they went on calling for this same entertainment.'

29 The great following they had at their farce, the *Précieuses* . . . shows well enough that they are only capable of succeeding with that sort of trifle, and that a play of substance would collapse at their hands.

30 Another costume for *L'Étourdi*, consisting of doublet and breeches, with a satin cloak.

30 Picture it for yourself, Madame: his wig was so enormous that it swept the floor every time he made a bow, and his hat was so small that it was quite clear the Marquis carried it in his hand more often than on his head; his bands were sufficiently ample to make a lady's cape, and his lace canons abundant enough for children to play hide-and-seek in them. A sheaf of tassels sprouted from his pocket as from a horn of plenty, and his shoes were so covered with ribbons that I am unable to tell you whether they were of Russian leather, English calf, or morocco. All I can say is that they were six inches high, and that I was at a loss to know how such tall and slender heels could possibly carry the weight of the Marquis, his ribbons, his canons and his powder.

30 Mascarille had served his purpose: this valet to the scatter-brained hero of *L'Étourdi*, this shameless hoaxer of the Précieuses, represents Molière's youth, which was now at an end. Now he was turned thirty-eight, he needed a more mature character to play, with less of the lively practical joker about him. Sganarelle fulfils these conditions.

31 One would need the brush of Poussin, Le Brun and Mignard in order to

do justice to his admirable antics in the scene in which Sganarelle appears with his wife's relative. You never heard such a simpleton, or saw such a foolish face; and one doesn't know whether to admire the author more for the way he has written the play, or the player for the way he acts it. There was never an actor with such control over his facial expression, and in this one scene it would be true to say that he changes it a score of times . . .

33 The less a gentleman has to do with those animals called actors, the better it is for him.

35 In Tallemant's day, there were at times up to two hundred persons on stage.

36 Even though Paris seems to have been half-empty, there were nevertheless enough persons of quality to fill the boxes and the seats on stage at the Petit-Bourbon more than forty times over; and enough bourgeois to fill the pit no less often.

36 'I was seated on the stage, all set to listen to the play, which I had heard praised on all sides. The actors were just beginning, and everyone was quiet, when a man with fussy lace canons burst in noisily and in an affected manner, calling out: "Ho there! Bring me a seat at once!" The whole audience was taken aback by the noise he made, which totally ruined a particularly fine passage of the play.'

37 'The actors made to carry on with the play, but the new arrival sat down with a renewed commotion; and although he could quite well have remained at the side of the stage, he planted his chair in front, at the middle, and with his broad back showing his contempt for the other spectators, he hid the actors from three-quarters of the occupants of the pit.'

37 'And he even went so far as to recite out loud lines that he knew by heart, before the actors reached them.'

37 An intolerable abuse . . . it spoils everything, and you need only one insolent spectator to put the whole place in an uproar.

37 How often, when the actor reaches a phrase such as 'Here he comes', 'I see him coming', have we not seen arriving, instead of the character so announced, well-appointed, fashionably-dressed men, seeking their seats on the stage even after several scenes have been played?

37 The people's friend . . . [charms] the rabble with coarse, vulgar expressions.

38 The seats on stage [were] so completely filled, that persons of the highest quality had to resort to the pit.

39 'What, Marquis, are you one of those gentlemen of fashion, then, who will not admit that the pit can have any judgement, and would be vexed at laughing together with them, even at the best joke in the world? I saw

one of our friends on stage the other day, who was making himself look ridiculous in just that way. He listened to the whole play with the most sombre expression, and whenever the others laughed, this merely made him frown the more. At each burst of laughter he would shrug his shoulders and look at the pit with a scornful expression; and sometimes, when his anger got the better of him, he would shout down to them: "Laugh then, laugh, damn you!" It was a second comedy, to see our friend's bad temper.'

39 'I beg you to realise, Monsieur Lysidas, that courtiers have just as much discernment as other men; that one can show sound judgement when dressed in Venetian lace and plumes, as well as if one wears a short wig and plain bands. Know, too, that the real test of all your plays is the judgement of the Court; it is the taste of the Court that you must study if you want to succeed. Nowhere else are sounder decisions made; and without counting the store of learning that is to be found there, the simplest common sense, aided by the frequenting of so many people of breeding, produces a kind of intelligence which beyond any doubt is more reliable in matters of judgement than all the rusty pedantry of your professional scholars.'

39 'You must learn, Marquis . . . that sound judgement is not the prerogative of a particular section of the audience, and that to have paid half a sovereign instead of fifteen pence is no guarantee of good taste. Standing or seated, one may form a wrong opinion; and in general terms I should be inclined to trust the judgement of the pit, since of those who compose that part of the audience not a few are knowledgeable enough to judge a play by the rules, while the rest judge in the best way of all, which is to let the play speak for itself, and not be swayed by blind prejudice, partisan indulgence, or ridiculous scruples.'

40 The conversational style of the best elements at Court, matching the written style of the best contemporary authors . . . When I say the Court, I mean men and women, and many persons of the city where the monarch resides, whose manners, by their intercourse with the Court, come to share a similar polish.

40 'Outside Paris, there is no salvation for a gentleman' . . . Outside Paris, there is no salvation for the fair sex, or for the gentry.

40 However refined the Court of Lorraine may be, . . . I can recall having seen better company in the gutters of Paris than I have yet met in the Duchess's *salon*.

42 At the fourth performance of *Le Misanthrope,* Molière gave his *Woodcutter* with it, and this provided the bourgeois of the rue Saint-Denis with a good laugh. That made them like *Le Misanthrope* better, and gradually it came to be regarded as one of the best plays ever written.

43 The finance minister offered this imposing company . . . the most magnificent hospitality, the good food being accompanied by entertain-

ment consisting of an agreeable ballet, a play, and a profusion of fireworks . . . In a word, this fête was embellished with every conceivable delight, and Their Majesties . . . expressed their perfect contentment.

44 The intention was to give a ballet as well; however, since there was only a small number of good dancers, it was necessary to space out the scenes of dance, and it was decided to make these scenes the interludes of the play, to give time for the same dancers to reappear in different costumes. And so that these interludes should not break the continuity of the play, they were incorporated as fully as possible into the subject, so as to make ballet and play into a single entertainment.

45 The Duc de la Feuillade . . . devised a form of vengeance as unworthy of a man of his condition as it was unwise. Seeing Molière pass by one day, he greeted him effusively, as if wanting to embrace him; and when Molière bent his head, he took hold of it, crying 'Cream tarts, Molière, cream tarts!' and rubbed his face against his buttons – which, as these were hard and sharp, left his face scratched and bleeding. The King, seeing Molière the same day, was very indignant, and showed his displeasure towards the Duke, who learned at first hand how high Molière stood in the King's favour.

45 This play was very popular, and very successful in Paris before being played at Court. Everyone recognised M. de Montausier, and claimed it was he whom Molière had portrayed in Alceste. Montausier, learning this, was so angry that he threatened to have Molière given a good thrashing.

45 [He] withdrew abruptly, saying he would not perform this office with a mere actor.

45 It's true, we appear to be favoured by the nobility, but they merely want to use us for their pleasure. It's a miserable condition, to be at the mercy of their slightest whim.

46 He began by saying 'a man of my sort', and passed from that to saying 'a man of my condition'. He wants to be taken for such; and none of those to whom he lends money, or who are guests at his table (which is excellent) is prepared to dispute it.

46 There is a region where joy is visible, but affected, and unhappiness hidden, but real. Who would believe that the vogue for entertainment, the enthusiastic reception of the plays of Molière and Arlequin, the banquets, the hunting, the dancing, the military tattoos – that all these delights masked so many anxieties, worries and intrigues, so many hopes and fears, so many burning passions and affairs of the utmost seriousness?

46 In one sense, the most honourable reproach one can bring against someone, is to say that he is ignorant of the life of the Court. To say this, is to heap all sorts of virtues on his head.

46 Paris fills one with distaste for the provinces; the Court disillusions one with Paris, and cures one of a taste for the Court. A healthy mind acquires at Court a taste for solitude and the quiet life.

46 When a poet came to the Prince de Condé, offering him an epitaph he had written on Molière, the Prince replied: 'I would very much rather it had been Molière bringing me one he had written on you.'

48 In the Jesuit colleges, the basic exercise was that of *praelectio*. The master reads a passage, elucidates it, comments on it, paraphrases it; the pupil copies it out, learns it by heart, and adopts it as a subject for imitation and rewriting, and as a topic for Latin prose composition.

49 Whereas the boys shut their books on leaving college, many girls opened theirs when they left the convent.

49 This glorious office that has freed me from the demeaning activity of writing poetry.

49 Noting in Molière the responsiveness and insight necessary to study philosophy, was pleased to teach him.

50 And whatever you do, be careful not to lose the reputation of gentleman that you have at Court, merely in order to receive from a mercenary publisher the name of foolish and wretched author.

50 How can it be that a man . . . who is not positively obliged to become an author by the King's command, or on pain of death, should wish to forsake the condition of gentleman in order to assume the title of impertinent and foolish scribbler among the doctors and the scholars?

50 It is enough to be a merchant in order to be regarded with contempt. Thus, the merchant forsakes commerce to retire to the country, or else buys an office in order to escape from his servitude.

50 In France, the only titles that are respected are military ones: those conferred by letters and other liberal professions are despised, and a man of quality who is a skilled author is regarded as having forfeited his nobility. I know for a fact that the d'Urfé family are ashamed of their ancestor Honoré d'Urfé because he was the author of *L'Astrée*.

51 Chapelain, Conrart and Balzac, with the whole Academy behind them, could not have had such a powerful influence on taste had it not been for the Hôtel de Rambouillet, which afforded them access to the ear of polite society.

53 I am only too aware of the relationship that exists between the true and the false *précieuses*, between the perfection of the original and the shortcomings of the imitation.

53 The company of *précieuses* is nothing more than a small gathering of persons, of whom some, possessing true delicacy, have produced in the rest an affectation of delicacy that is quite ridiculous.

53 Let us consider various other kinds of bore, among whom I would place the *précieuses*: the false ones, of course, whose only virtue is to be found in their language, or jargon, and their affected manners of speech and behaviour. These are not the *précieuses* of true quality, of whom there are two or three in Paris, and who are respected as much as any princess.

53 The *précieux* phenomenon, if one thinks about it, carries within it its own corruption and produces quite spontaneously its own caricature. Not only is the sublime closely allied to the ridiculous, but it must remain rarefied: once it becomes the object of a fashionable cult, it is soon absorbed by that which it aimed to avoid. Moreover, the subtle art of lending enchantment to everyday life depends not only on good intentions: it also needs tact, good taste, delicate imagination, a true nobility of intellect and behaviour.

55 Though I would certainly want women to know more than they commonly do, I do not by any means want them to act or speak as ladies of learning. I should like it to be said of a person of my sex that she knows a hundred things she does not boast of, that she has a well-developed mind, is familiar with the best works of art, speaks and writes well, and has some experience of society; but I do not want it to be possible to say of her that she is a learned lady. Not that she who is not called learned may not know as much as, and more than, those on whom that dread title is bestowed; the difference is that she makes better use of her intelligence, and is skilled in hiding that which the others are forever displaying.

55 What discipline could be introduced to the disorder of marriage, in order to soften the rigour of its slavery, the harshness of its fetters – and what is perhaps worse than both together: the length of time that both can last? . . . Ought one to say: to contract marriage with, or against, a husband?

56 An early feminine intelligentsia, which was to stake the first claims on behalf of women: the right to divorce, to sexual fulfilment, to education and training, to employment, and to political activity.

56 The epithet 'ridiculous' is the product of anti-feminist bias.

56 A *précieuse*, a survivor of the once-famous company whom Molière discredited at a stroke of his satirical pen.

57 The true gentleman is he who never boasts about anything.

57 When I think of the profound reflection mathematics requires, how one is forced to withdraw from a life of action and pleasure to devote oneself entirely to this pursuit, what it has to offer seems dearly bought, and one must feel an excessive love of truth to seek it at such a price . . . Let me confess: there is no tribute I would not pay to the great mathematicians, provided I do not have to be one myself. I marvel at their discoveries, and at their learned works; but I am sure that it is enough for persons of sense to be able to employ them judiciously; for to speak truly, we should

be more concerned with enjoying the world about us than with its understanding.

57 It is a misfortune for a gentleman to have the appearance of a professional; and when one suffers this handicap, one must endeavour to get rid of it at once.

57 Who, confined within the limits of his art . . . , shows apart from this neither judgement, nor memory, nor spirit, nor character, nor personality . . . a musician, for instance, who when he has charmed me with his playing, appears to pack himself away in the same case as his lute.

57 You know that . . . I sometimes wield a painter's brush, against the custom in France, which is that a gentleman should be ignorant of everything.

58 The military profession is the finest in the world, one must agree; but in fact, a gentleman has no profession. Although he may have a perfect understanding of a certain subject, and even be obliged to devote his life to it, this should not be apparent from his appearance or from his conversation.

58 It is the quintessence of all virtues; and those who do not possess this quality are poorly received by persons of good taste. Even when they speak of matters of general interest, they commonly do it so ungraciously that they are quite insufferable. The calling of gentleman is really that of man in general, since it consists of living and conversing in the most reasonable human way with one's fellows.

58 An *honnête homme* is also a man who displays the most agreeable qualities of the man of the world. In this sense, an *honnête homme* is the same thing as a man whose galant, refined conversation fits him for polite society.

58 'You are a rogue.'
'Excuse me, sir, I am an honest man.'

'Virtue without wealth is a useless commodity: money suffices to turn a villain into an honest man.'

'Nothing is easier, when one is rich, than to be an honest man; it's when one is poor that it becomes difficult.'

59 'Someone has stolen money from you?'
'Yes, you rogue; and I'll have you hanged, if you don't give it back.'
'Heavens! don't handle him so roughly: I can tell by his bearing that he's an honest man.'

'I should have more regard for a labourer's son who was an honest man, than for a king's son who led the kind of life you lead.'

59 'And whatever you do, be careful not to lose the reputation of gentleman that you have at Court.'

59 One is not accepted in society as being knowledgeable about poetry, unless one displays the label of poet, mathematician or whatever it may be. But the true all-rounder does not need a label, and hardly differentiates between the occupation of poet and that of embroiderer. All-rounders are not known as poets, geometricians, etc., but they are all these things, and are capable judges of all such activities . . . So it is false praise when a man is greeted on arrival as someone who is particularly proficient with regard to poetry; but it is a bad sign if he is not appealed to for his views, when the conversation turns to the discussion of a poem.

60 'How now, Monsieur Gorgibus, does your daughter piss no more than these few drops? She's a pretty poor pisser, your daughter is: I can see I shall have to prescribe a piss-making potion.'

60 'Nurse, sweet nurse, my medicine is the humble slave of your wet-nursery, and I should adore to be the infant fortunate enough to suck the milk of your charming favours.'

60 Even in comedy, crudity must be veiled; and Molière, even Molière himself, learned this lesson in *Le Malade imaginaire* . . . In this play, there is an apothecary, M. Fleurant, with an off-hand, insolent manner, who comes along, syringe in hand, to give the imaginary invalid an enema. A man of good sense, brother to this would-be invalid . . . , persuades him not to take it, at which the apothecary flies into a rage, and utters all the impertinences such people are capable of. At the first performance, the sensible brother replied to the apothecary: 'Go to, sir, it's easy to see your ordinary converse is with men's backsides.' (I hope your Lordship will pardon such a coarse word: I quote it merely to condemn it.) All the spectators on this first occasion were indignant, whereas they were delighted at the second performance to hear the reply: 'Go to, sir, it's easy to see your ordinary converse is not with men's faces.' It is the same thing, said with refinement.

61 'I see him reproving everything, and he even takes a considerable interest in my wife, for the sake of my honour. He tells me of all those who make sheep's eyes at her, and proves himself six times more jealous than myself.'

62 'Sire, my father is dead; these eyes have seen his blood flowing in copious streams from his generous side: his blood which has so often defended your walls; his blood which has so often won battles for you; his blood which even now that it has been spilled, fumes with anger at having been spilled in a cause other than your own . . .'

62 Any laughter too pronounced, the sort produced by low comedy, is unsuitable for men of intellectual distinction; on the other hand, the sublime . . . bores them. It is precisely the exclusion of these two extremes that defines Molière's comedy: neither Turlupin nor Lysidas.

63 The famous Molière died last Friday . . . apart from his profession, he was very much a gentleman.

63 Molière declaimed on stage as a player; but in real life he spoke as a gentleman, and had all the feelings of a gentleman. In short, he had nothing against him but his profession.

64 This great actor, and incomparably greater playwright, lived in close communion with the Italians, for they were excellent actors and lived a thoroughly decent life.

64 In addition to the qualities needed by the poet and the actor, he had those that go to make the gentleman. He was generous, a good friend, decent and honourable in all he did, modest in the way he received praise, learned without showing it, and so easy and agreeable in conversation that his company was sought by the leading personalities of Court and Town.

64 He was noticed at Court as a decent and gentlemanly person, never presuming either on his talent or on his popularity, adapting well to the temperament of those among whom he was forced to live, and having an admirable, generous disposition: in short, he possessed all the attributes of a thorough gentleman.

64 It is as well to remember that the Court on which we model ourselves is an assembly of all sorts of persons; that some are merely passing through, others have but recently arrived, and the most part, even if born at Court, are not to be imitated.

65 Molière, born with an upright character, and whose own behaviour was simple and natural, had little patience with the zealous, flattering, slandering, restless, importunate, treacherous manners of the Court.

65 He was a man of probity, with feelings one rarely meets among persons of his birth.

65 He was an actor, that is to say a member of an ignoble profession, to whom the style and title of 'Monsieur' is quite inappropriate . . . Truth to tell, it is intolerable to read, on opening this book, 'The Life of Monsieur de Molière'.

65 Molière had been nominated to fill the next vacancy in the Académie Française, and this body had agreed to a compromise with regard to his profession: Molière would henceforth have acted only in roles of high comedy. But his sudden death deprived him of a well-deserved honour, and the Academy of one well qualified to join its number.

68 'It's not at all incongruous that a person should be ridiculous in certain matters and a respectable man of honour in others.'

68 'It's an extraordinary undertaking to make the gentry laugh.'

69 'Do you think it's a trifling matter to offer something of a comic nature to a gathering like this; to try to make people laugh who fill us with respect and laugh only when they want to?'

69 The continual bursts of laughter coming from the pit.'

69 Isn't it better to be bored like a gentleman, than to be amused like a fool?

69 A laboured, or a misplaced, joke has its just deserts when it is ignored or scorned. A joke must be natural, and in keeping with the subject: let it only be noble, decent and gentlemanly, and I consider there is nothing more agreeable than such jesting.

70 Jesting is fashionable, indeed, but laughter, like joking, soon tires; and though amusement is almost the only consideration at Court, those bent on pleasure are sometimes not loth to listen to someone who talks in a serious, measured way, so as to satisfy his hearers and not bore them.

70 So I advise gentlemen, and particularly ladies, of breeding, to aim to please rather than to amuse; for many things amuse, which we do not approve of, whereas we do approve of everything that pleases us.

70 One of the authors Boileau liked best was Terence. He said he was an author whose expressions are all directed at the reader's heart; he does not try to make us laugh, like so many other comic writers: his only aim is to say things that are reasonable, and whatever he says is in keeping with nature, which he always portrays in an admirable manner . . . In a word, said he, it is remarkable that this poet, writing after Plautus, who was so dear to the popular audiences, should have effaced his rival by choosing the least certain road to success. For the Roman people . . . wished to laugh at all costs; and Terence was admirable in that he accommodated the people to his taste instead of accommodating his own taste to that of the people; and thereby, said Boileau, Terence has the advantage over Molière; the latter certainly paints portraits from life, but less so than Terence, since he often compromised with his noble genius to produce coarse jokes for the people, instead of the people of taste for whom one should write.

71 The gentry will find as much to divert them here, as those who want to laugh without hindrance; and who often, when they have laughed, find no sense in the economy of a play, for they are loth to listen to anything serious.

71 [Molière,] in order to improve his case, wants to make us believe that the French wish only to laugh; but this shows he holds them in poor esteem, since he does not hold them capable of appreciating fine things.

71 He who makes others laugh rarely earns their esteem.

71 I doubt . . . whether excessive laughter is suitable for men.

71 [Plays] like this seem more diverting to me, even though one laughs less openly. I find that they are more diverting, that they are more agreeable, and that one constantly laughs with the laughter of the mind.

72 A kind of comedy which does not seek to arouse excessive laughter in a

vulgar crowd, but which persuades that crowd, in spite of itself, to laugh with elegance and wit.

72 The gentleman smiles with an inward smile, so much to be preferred to open laughter.

72 M. Boileau . . . told me there were two kinds of laughter, one the product of surprise, and the other causing an inward satisfaction, and making us laugh the more effectively in that it is based on reason. For, he said, the natural effect of reason is to please us, and when you see on stage a coherent action, with characters well portrayed, you cannot but applaud, if not with violent bursts of laughter, at any rate with a feeling of inner satisfaction. The sort of buffoonery that arouses laughter has some merit, it is true; but compared with the pleasure produced by a natural character, well portrayed, it is a bastard beside a legitimate child.

73 That, sir, is my opinion of *The Misanthrope in Love*, which I find all the more admirable in that the hero amuses without being ridiculous, and makes the gentry laugh without producing the sort of cold, vulgar jokes that we commonly see in comedies.

73 'Let me tell you at once that this malady of yours provides amusement wherever you go, and that this great invective against the manners of our day makes you appear ridiculous in many people's eyes.'

74 'In my view it is easier to express fine sentiments in stilted phrases, to challenge Fortune in well-turned verses, to rail at one's fate and to accuse the gods, than to penetrate human folly in agreeable terms, and to reproduce on stage the faults of men around you.'

75 In a few masterpieces, he succeeded in investing the most commonplace things with a remarkable authority. He set those who laugh – that is the common run of men – against the isolated exceptions; or rather, he set himself against them, with the common herd.

75 Laughter is a reflex action, related to vomiting and a fit of the shivers.

75 This judgement by means of our laughter expresses the highest function of our intelligence.

76 The peasant or the drunkard may provide a few scenes for the writer of farce, but they hardly enter into true comedy.

76 They are excellent players, who possess very mediocre plays.

77 The novelty of this kind of comedy, unprecedented in any language, and the natural style which produced a portrait of the manners and speech of gentlefolk, were no doubt the reason for the success and reputation of the play. It was unknown for a comedy to provoke laughter without ridiculous characters such as clownish servants, parasites, braggart captains, pedant doctors and so forth. This one achieved its effect by the vivacious mood of characters of a higher social rank than those one sees in Plautus and Terence, who are merely shopkeepers.

77 An imitation of life, a mirror of custom, and the image of truth . . . a picture of life that shows the fortunes of private persons, without any danger . . . a dramatic poem, eventful, in a popular style, and with a happy ending.

78 Is it impossible to amuse oneself in good French and in a reasonable manner . . . ? To say nothing worse about this kind of amusement, it smacks of comedy rather than of civil intercourse, and of farce rather than of comedy. This is not amusement fit for a gentleman.

78 By the best comedies, I mean plays which portray the passions in a galant manner, plays in which one finds fine sentiments, judicious moral truths, witty sallies: in short something to instruct as well as entertain us. I number among them the masterpieces of the great Ariste [Corneille], whose *Menteur* will suffice to contrast with all the wretched comedy Zoïle [Molière] gives us.

78 'And this Monsieur de la Souche, then, who is so intelligent, and who seems so serious at times: does he not descend to something too extravagantly comic in Act V, when he declares his love to Agnès with such violence, rolling his eyes to such excess, uttering those ridiculous sighs and shedding those silly tears that make all the audience laugh?'

79 Who had replaced clowns with gentlefolk.

80 Comedy of the period 1640–60 seems to have been essentially one of fantasy and play. Fantasy in the invention of interesting, or romantic, situations: Spanish authors provided numerous models, but our own authors went much further in their ingenuity . . . Fantasy, too, in the creation of grotesque or bewildering characters: the Italian-type puppets are taken and given epic proportions . . . Fantasy, again, in the verbal play . . . : there is no kind of juggling with words that isn't to be found in the plays of this period.

81 He owes as much to French farce as to the Spanish *comedia*.

81 'Ho, there, Foucaral! Dom Roc Zurducaci! Dom Zapata Pascal! Or Pascal Zapata, for it's immaterial whether Pascal goes in front or behind. Ho! my retainers! my suite! Oh, the wretches, the scoundrels, the traitors, the imbeciles! Let all my servants take note that my patience is wearing thin: the wretches will learn that as from today I dismiss them all.'

81 In short, Scarron does not manage to resolve the duality that is typical of the comedy of his times: plot and comic content are juxtaposed, but are not integrated into a homogeneous whole. Even controlled and orchestrated by Jodelet, the comic effects remain so to speak a superficial veneer.

82 'This lover swooned away as soon as he saw me: what features, O my beauty, has Heaven endowed you with? I cannot set foot outside my door without my beauty being responsible for someone's death. And I am at a

loss to know what path to follow: the world will come to an end, if I stay alive . . . '

83 All those who are offended by his success take a malicious pleasure in bringing him down to the level of a comic actor specialising in farce, and unable to do justice to works of real merit, like tragedies. It is an excellent way of getting rid of this unwelcome intruder, to relegate him to a small corner of what we should nowadays call 'sub-literary' comedy.

87 To avoid starving, he ended up writing comic parts for himself: Molière in spite of himself.

89 'I have a certain valet called Mascarille, who passes in some folk's eyes as a kind of wit: for there is no more common coinage than wit nowadays. He's a fanciful character, who has conceived the idea of trying to be accepted as a man of breeding. He goes in for galant behaviour and for writing verse, and he scorns other valets, going so far as to call them coarse fellows.'

89 'No: my honour is at stake. No-one shall say that he gets the better of me in matters of skill: in my profession of arch-intriguer, such obstacles merely irritate me, and make me the more determined to display the talents with which Heaven has endowed me.'

91 Molière himself played Scapin: did he possess the physical strength for this role? . . . The character of Scapin requires not only the mobility of a virtuoso actor, but a dancer's agility as well . . . We may wonder whether in acting this part, Molière was not over-taxing his strength. This would explain why he never tried, during the remaining twenty months of his life, to appeal against the first verdict of the public: the role was too demanding for him.

92 Everyone is talking of Scapin, who surpasses even Till Eulenspiegel, that model for all joyous pranksters, by the extraordinary range of his tricks and stratagems.

92 Everyone knows how these two plays were condemned by persons of taste and judgement. But the general public, for whom Molière had written them, flocked to see the plays, and saw them with considerable pleasure.

92 A corruptor of youth, who has fallen foul of the law.

92 His face is hardened by a certain deceitful violence. He combines traits of the real scoundrel, the demagogue and the potential rioter. Harlequin's slapstick in his hands could well take the form of a cudgel. The sound of his name is more ominous than that of Mascarille.

93 'You have just learned down at the harbour that my father is back?'
'Yes.'
'That he is coming home this very morning?'
'This very morning.'

'And that he is coming home in order to marry me off?'
'Yes.'
'To the daughter of Seigneur Géronte?'
'Of Seigneur Géronte.'
'And that this girl has been sent for from Tarento for this purpose?'
'Yes.'
'And the news comes from my uncle?'
'From your uncle.'
'To whom my father told it by letter?'
'By letter.'
'And my uncle, you say, knows everything there is to know about us?'
'Everything there is to know.'

93 'To tell the truth, few things are impossible to me, when I exert myself. Heaven has endowed me with a fair talent for all the witty inventions, the ingenious gallantries to which the common folk in their ignorance give the name of cheats; and I can say without boasting that there has seldom been a man who was more skilled than myself at tricks and intrigues, and who has gained more glory at this noble profession.'

94 'What on earth was he doing in that galley?'

94 'Chance has produced the very result that parental wisdom planned to bring about.'

94 Mascarille was only a stage valet. Scapin is much more than that: at certain moments we suspect him of being his creator's mouthpiece; and that is no doubt the key to the secret, but clear, affinity that links him with Beaumarchais's Figaro.

94 The final triumph of the proletariat.

95 'I know that your mind, fertile in tricks, has never found any difficulty in anything, that you can well be called the king of servants, and that all over the world . . . '

95 'After this rare exploit, I want to be painted as a hero, crowned with laurel, and with letters of gold beneath my portrait: "Long live Mascarille, the prince of tricksters!"'

95 'To tell you the truth, there are few things that are beyond me . . . '

96 'Wait. Hold yourself upright. Tilt your cap at a provocative angle. Thrust one foot forward, with hand on hip. Let your eyes flash fiercely. Take a few steps like a player king. That's good. Follow me. I have certain secrets for disguising your face and your voice.'

96 'Let me show my valiance in avenging my disgrace.'

96 'As for men of choleric temperament, I detest them with all my heart, and it is peaceful men that I love. I don't go around giving blows, for fear of receiving them; and my principal virtue is my easygoing disposition.'

96 'For my part I believe, on mature reflection, that it is better to be a cuckold than to be a dead man.'

96 'Nevertheless, I can feel my gall rising, and prompting me to some manly act. Yes, my anger consumes me; I have been a coward too long: I am determined to avenge myself on the thief. And to begin with, in the full flush of my ardour, I will affirm on all sides that he has been sleeping with my wife!'

97 Never was there a finer spectacle, never was a play better acted, and never were verses more universally esteemed. Sganarelle plays this scene on his own, rehearsing in his mind all that is generally said about a cuckold, together with his own reasons for not being too concerned about it; [and] he manages so well, that his arguments might well be of some consolation to those that are of the fraternity.

99 'Was anyone ever more certain than I was of being a cuckold? You see that in such cases appearances can mislead. Remember my example; and even if you see everything, don't believe a thing!'

99 And even if you know everything, don't say a word!

99 Lack of moderation, of which he is unlikely to cure himself.

100 'Ha, my lovely, we can now begin to be happy together. You will no longer have the right to refuse me anything, and I shall be able to do whatever I like with you, without anyone objecting. You will be all mine from head to foot, and I shall be master of everything: of your lively little eyes, your saucy little nose, your appetising lips, your lovable ears, your pretty little chin, your little round breasts, your . . . In a word, your whole person will be at my disposal, and I shall have the right to caress you in any way I please.'

100 'What pretty package have we here? Nurse, sweet nurse, my medicine is the humble slave of your wet-nursery, and I should adore to be the infant fortunate enough to suck the milk of your charming favours.'

101 'Power in all things is on the side of the husband.'

102 'Among her possessions, even should she want them, she must not have writing-desk, paper, ink or pen: in well-regulated households it is the husband who writes what needs to be written.'

102 'She whom the bond of marriage has placed in a husband's bed must realise that in spite of today's fashions, that husband has taken her for himself alone.'

102 'When, like me, anyone has married a faithless wife, the best thing he can do is to throw himself into the river head first.'

102 'This marriage will fulfil all your desires, and bring you every sort of pleasure and satisfaction. In your mutual ardour you will live together like two children, like two turtle-doves.'

103 'Ah! you are a devout man, and you lose your temper!'

103 'Let me tell you at once that this malady of yours provides amusement wherever you go, and that this great invective against the manners of our day makes you appear ridiculous in many people's eyes.'

104 'So much the better, by God! that's just what I want. It's an excellent sign, and I'm delighted. And men as a whole are so odious to me that I should be sorry to be wise in their eyes.'

104 'Betrayed on all sides, overwhelmed with injustices, I shall turn my back on this horrible, vice-ridden place, and seek out somewhere on earth a solitary place where it is possible to be a man of honour.'

104 A long tradition, not only scholarly but scholastic, insists that Molière's theatre be studied as a series of plays, each of which has its own meaning and value; accordingly, the single play tends to become the ideal unit of analysis.

105 'Now, my heart, be firm: no human weakness!'

105 'I am not kind; I can be cruel when I want to be.'

106 You must surely admit that Molière learned the finer secrets of his art in Plautus and Terence.

106 Aristophanes had no influence on living literature.

109 The beginnings of a character comedy and the sketch of a portrait of avarice.

109 The household god tells us: Euclio has inherited his miserliness, and succumbs to a family failing . . . However, in the rest of the play, this trait is not given enough emphasis . . . The whole action of the Latin play, instead of depending on character, springs from the pot of gold: watched, hidden, coveted, stolen and finally returned. It is a situation, not a vice, that is portrayed.

110 The *Aulularia* has only the outward appearance of a character comedy. And the proof that Plautus was not aiming so high is that this is the only one of its kind among his plays. No others have this appearance of high comedy; in no others do we wonder whether he was out to personify a human failing, a dominant passion, in his central character. His most important plays do not rise above comedy of manners.

113 His fondness for poetry made him keen to read the classical poets with great care. He knew them well, especially Terence: he chose him as the best model he could find, and never did anyone imitate him so well.

115 The principle established above enables us to say that woman is cold and moist, for the purpose for which nature has created her; and since she is cold she must be weak, and hence timid, fearful, suspicious, distrustful, cunning, deceitful, flattering, mendacious, quick to take offence, vindictive, cruel, unjust, avaricious, ungrateful and superstitious. And her

moist nature makes her inconstant, unreliable, faithless, impatient, easily influenced, compassionate and talkative.

115 Teach self-knowledge, which is the height of all wisdom, and knowledge of others, which is the mark of true understanding.

116 The most important of the hybrid passions are shame, impudence, pity, indignation, envy, rivalry, jealousy, repentance and surprise. For shame is a mixture of sorrow and of the fear that is produced by infamy. Impudence is composed of pleasure and of the boldness that is needed to do dishonourable things.

116 It is a fact, then, that the body undergoes a change when the mind is stirred by emotion; and that there are hardly any actions of the mind that do not produce physical impressions. These may well be called characters, since they show the effects of such actions, and display their image.

116 There is no passion without its distinctive character.

117 Theophrastus treated things in a more philosophical manner: he merely considered the universal, whereas you have descended into the particular. You have drawn your portraits from nature: Theophrastus' are drawn from general ideas. Yours resemble certain individuals, and one can often identify them. Those of Theophrastus resemble only man in general. For that reason they will always be lifelike; but it is to be feared that yours will lose some of their brilliant life, when they can no longer be compared with their originals.

118 'Yes, that great physician, in his chapter on the nature of animals, says . . . a score of good things. And since the humours that possess a certain affinity have a lot in common – as for instance, melancholy is the opposite of joy; or bile, spreading through the body, makes us turn yellow; or again, there is nothing more opposed to health than sickness – therefore, we can say, following this great man, that your daughter is very ill.'

118 'I call it a hypochondriacal melancholy, to distinguish it from the two other kinds; for the renowned Galen established in his learned manner three forms of the illness we call melancholy – so called not only by the Romans but also by the Greeks, which is very relevant to our concerns: the first, deriving from the distemper of the brain itself; the second, produced by the blood, which has been rendered atrabilious; the third, called hypochondriacal – and this is ours – which proceeds from the disorder of the belly and the lower regions, especially the spleen, whose excessive heat and inflammation conveys to our patient's brain an excess of thick, fuliginous vapours, whose dark, malign properties produce a malfunctioning of the sovereign faculty, causing the malady of which, by our reasoning, we have shown him to be possessed and stricken.'

119 '. . . Court and Town offer me on all sides objects capable of stirring my bile. I am possessed by a black humour, by a profound chagrin . . .'

119 'My phlegmatic temperament is just as capable of philosophy as is your bilious nature.'

120 A dissertation I have written in dialogue form . . . I shall not repeat in this Preface what can be read in the *Critique*.

120 Designed to reply to my censors and justify my play.

120 'Ridiculous in certain matters and a respectable man of honour in others.'

120 'Doesn't Arnolphe offer his money to Horace too readily? And since his is the ridiculous character of the play, was it necessary to make him behave like a man of honour?'

121 'And this Monsieur de la Souche, then, who is so intelligent and who seems so serious at times: does he not descend to something too extravagantly comic in Act V, when he declares his love to Agnès with such violence, rolling his eyes to such excess, uttering those ridiculous sighs · and shedding those silly tears that make all the audience laugh?'

121 A portrait of the manners and speech of gentlefolk.

123 'And the sincerity of which he is so proud contains something noble and heroic. It's a rare enough virtue nowadays, and I should like to see it in everyone as it is in Alceste.'

123 'Ridiculous in certain matters and a respectable man of honour in others.'

124 'It's an extraordinary undertaking to try to make the gentry laugh.'

124 'Rolling his eyes to such excess, uttering those ridiculous sighs and shedding those silly tears that make all the audience laugh.'

125 I think too highly of you to believe that you did not laugh, at least in your mind.

125 It's remarkable that this period – almost the whole – of Molière's career should start with *Le Cocu imaginaire* and should finish with *Le Malade imaginaire*. The epithet could be applied to all the versions of Sganarelle: the 'imaginary', whereas Mascarille was the imaginative one.

125 'Arnolphe, or the imaginary husband'; 'Jourdain, or the imaginary man of quality'; 'Orgon, or the imaginary man of religion'; 'Chrysale, or the imaginary man of courage'; 'Alceste, or the imaginary *honnête homme*'.

125 *Imaginary*: existing only in the imagination, having no existence in nature . . . Existing only in the imagination; not real.

126 Look . . . how he wilts beneath the weight of his happiness; see the cold, aloof manner he adopts with those who are no longer his equals; he does not reply to their greeting, he does not see them; the salutations and caresses of the great, who are no longer so far removed from him, complete his downfall; he becomes confused and disoriented; it is a temporary derangement.

280

126 'What good does it do you if a man caresses you, swears friendship and faith, professes a zealous and tender regard for you, and praises you to the skies, if he goes off and behaves in the same way to every worthless fellow? No: nobody who values himself could possibly desire a friendship prostituted in this way; and even the most vain among us would find flattery pretty unpalatable if it had to be shared with all and sundry. Personal esteem must be discriminating, and to profess esteem for everyone is to esteem nobody at all. Since you yourself are inclined to affect these vices of our age, by God! you will have to part company with me. I reject the sort of easy affability that makes no distinction of persons. I wish to be distinguished; and let there be no doubt about it: the friend of everyone is no friend of mine!'

126 'There's nothing more to be said: my daughter will be a marchioness in spite of everyone; and if you make me angry, I'll see she becomes a duchess!'

127 'Power in all things is on the side of the husband.'

127 'The obedience that the soldier, trained in his duty, shows towards his leader, that the servant shows towards his master, a child towards his father, or the humblest monk towards his father superior, falls a long way short of the docility, the obedience, the humility and the deep respect that a wife should show towards her husband, her leader, and her lord and master.'

127 'The greater our love, the less we must flatter the person we love. The truest love is the one that pardons no faults; and if I were you, I should dismiss all those spineless lovers who followed all my fancies, and whose servile flattery merely played up to every extravagant whim I might have.'

127 '. . . On condition that you loyally abide by my plan to renounce human society, and that you agree to follow me at once to the country retreat where I have sworn henceforth to live.'

128 'Finally, Heaven inspired me to have him to live with me, and since then everything seems to prosper here. I see him reproving everything, and he even takes a considerable interest in my wife, for the sake of my honour. He tells me of all those who make sheep's eyes at her, and proves himself six times more jealous than myself.'

128 '. . . Seeing myself in a state of weakness and ill-health, I want to surround myself with a son-in-law and his family connections who are doctors, so that they can provide me with resources against my illness, and so that I can have to hand in my own family the consultations, the prescriptions and the cures that I need.'

128 'This Monsieur Trissotin who is the subject of such complaint against us, and who has the misfortune not to be in your good graces, is the man I have chosen as a husband for her, and I am a better judge than you of his worth. Argument is useless, and I have made up my mind.'

128 'The beauty of my cashbox!'

129 'And what about Tartuffe? . . . Poor fellow!'

129 'Stand a little further back, Madam.'
'I beg your pardon?'
'One step further back, please.'
'But why?'
'Go back a bit, so that I can get the third one in.'

129 'It's all up with me: I can feel the Faculty of Medicine taking its revenge
. . . You heard, brother, the extraordinary illnesses he threatened me
with . . . He said I would be beyond all hope within four days.'

129 The main theme of Molière's comedy is the interplay between folly and
cunning.

132 The attitudes, movements and gestures of the human body are laughable
in proportion as the body concerned makes us think of a machine.

132 The mechanical encrusted on the living.

132 'What on earth was he doing in that galley?'

133 'What you say is too utterly bourgeois . . .'
'Such behaviour is too shopkeeperly for words . . .'
'People who are quite lacking in the rudiments of polite behaviour'
'What frugality of dress, and what a famine of conversation!'
'A delicate ear suffers furiously at the pronouncing of such words.'

133 'I am dressed today like the gentry . . .'
'Do the gentry also learn music?'
'Do the gentry have [concerts]?'
'Do the gentry really wear the flowers upside-down?'

134 The actor was still aspiring to success in tragedy.

135 In *Dom Garcie*, the determining causes of the hero's jealousy are always
external; the jealous outbursts are produced, like Lélie's blunders, by
extraordinary coincidences, such as would make even the most trusting
lover jealous.

135 'I can already see by the way he is looking at me, that the letter has upset
him. What an extraordinary temperament is his! . . . You seem to reply
in a very different tone, and your expression is suddenly changed. I find
this transformation very surprising: what can have caused it? Pray tell
me.'
'It is caused by a disease that has suddenly attacked my heart.'

'Ah, foolish Prince: let this letter cure your disease, for it existed only in
your mind.'

136 Arnolphe and Alceste are Dom Garcie all over again, devoured by the
same jealousy.

137 'Marrying a stupid girl is a way of avoiding being a stupid husband.'

137 Well worth our esteem, and deserving our affection.

137 A clever creature, well versed in the art of duping her jealous guardian without seeming to, and who already practises to perfection the charming tricks that lovers get up to.

138 To complete their image of the playwright, the Romantics in a sense needed a Molière who was a cuckold, or at least tormented by jealousy. This unhappy condition was essential to his genius.

138 The tortures of jealousy may have caused Othello and Alceste to spring, fully armed with sword and dagger, from the godlike brains of their creators.

139 'For the ungovernable turmoil of my heart could not have been hidden from her eyes; it would have revealed the anguish from which I am suffering . . . O fateful absence! Ill-omened journey!'

139 'Heavens, how my heart suffers!'
'What! does the star which constantly persecutes me give me no time to recover?'
'Day and night, without ceasing, I will fondle you, caress you, kiss you, devour you.'

140 'Oh! I am speechless; I'm suffocating, so provoked am I, and I'd like to tear all my clothes off!'

140 Arnolphe's sufferings, expressed as they usually are in the vocabulary of tragedy, strike us by their arbitrariness and disconnectedness. Even though they may be genuine, and justified by circumstances, they always seem to us to be incongruous and absurd.

140 'That's enough: I'm the master, I speak. Go along now: I will be obeyed.'

141 'You can behave just as you like. I shall raise no objection, and that's plain enough.'

141 The tone of comedy is left far behind . . . The comic effect is secondary here. What matters is the anguish of this human being, tormented, shattered, flayed alive as it were.

142 'I declare he seems to me to have quite lost his reason.'
'He is a little unbalanced on certain matters.'

143 'By God! it's a scandal, an outrage, to stoop to insincerity of this sort; and if I had had the misfortune to behave in such a way, I should go off and hang myself in shame.'

143 'For my part, I don't see that it's a hanging matter; and I beg you to allow me a stay of execution, so that I need not go off and hang myself just yet.'

143 'Let me tell you at once that this malady of yours provides amusement

wherever you go, and that this great invective against the manners of our day makes you appear ridiculous in many people's eyes.'

144 'So much the better, by God! that's just what I want. It's an excellent sign, and I'm delighted. And men as a whole are so odious to me that I should be sorry to be wise in their eyes.'

144 This Philinte is the wise man of the play: one of those 'gentlemen' of high society, whose maxims are remarkably like those of a scoundrel; one of those meek and mild persons who always judge that everything around them is well, because it is in their interest that nothing should be better; who are always content with other people in general, because they take no interest in other people in particular; who, seated at a well laden table, declare that it is quite false that the common people go hungry; who, their own pockets well filled, think it in poor taste to argue in favour of the poor; who, from the security of their own house, would see the rest of humanity robbed, pillaged, massacred, without a protest; for the Lord has endowed them with an admirable capacity for bearing the ills of others with patience.

144 'I wish to be distinguished; and let there be no doubt about it: the friend of everyone is no friend of mine!'

144 Alceste is an *honnête homme*. He does not want either to do without men or to eliminate them. He wants to live with them in good faith, sincerity, decency. He wants to be able to esteem them . . .

145 'That unbending virtue of our forefathers.'

145 'The man dressed in green ribbons.'

146 The *honnête homme* . . . was a man of the world who was also a man of honour.

146 'You are an *honnête homme*, and you lose your temper!'

146 '. . . A solitary place where it is possible to be a man of honour.'

147 It is a false kind of praise when it is said of a man, as he enters a room, that he is skilled in poetry; but it is a bad sign when it is a question of judging the merit of certain verses, and he is not appealed to for his opinion.

147 'In a word, I am yours to dispose of as you will; and since you are renowned for your judgement, in order to cement this new bond of friendship between us I wish to show you a sonnet I have recently written, and to ask you if it is fitting that I expose it to public view.'

147 Poetry requires a particular talent, which does not always go hand in hand with common sense. Now it is the language of the gods, now the language of fools; seldom is it the language of an *honnête homme*. Not that there isn't something genteel about the ability to compose agreeable verses; but we must remain masters of our talents, otherwise our mind is

usurped by an alien presence that does not allow us a proper degree of freedom.

147 'A gentleman should always keep a tight rein on any impulses he may feel to become an author.'

147 'Has spoiled many a gentleman.'

148 'Believe me, you must resist these temptations, and keep such occupations hidden from the public gaze. Do not sacrifice, I urge you, the good name you possess at Court, in order to exchange it, at the hand of a greedy publisher, for that of wretched and ridiculous author.'

148 '. . . I remarked one day, to someone whose name I will not disclose . . .'

148 'I did not say that.'

148 'This figurative style of which authors are so proud, departs completely from truth and common sense; it's just playing with words in a most affected way, and nature never expressed itself so. The execrable taste of our day makes me apprehensive . . .'

149 'But who is going to plead your case for you?'

149 'Who? Why, reason; justice; equity!'

149 'In my quiet way, I take men as I find them.'

149 'What! shall I see myself betrayed, ambushed, robbed, without . . . By God! I'll be quiet, I'm so put out by such an impertinent argument!'

150 'I do not possess sufficient control of my tongue. I should not be responsible for what I might say, and I should bring all sorts of trouble down on my head.'

150 'Sir, you do me too much honour.'

150 'I, Madam! And why should I pretend to such favours? What service have I ever rendered the state? What have I done, I ask you, so note-worthy that I can complain at Court that nothing is done for me?'

150 'My fault, I confess, is to be rather more sincere than I should.'

150 'Heaven did not bestow on me a temperament compatible with the atmosphere of Courts. I do not possess the virtues that would enable me to succeed there. My chief talent is to be sincere and outspoken; the ability to make dupes of others is a skill I lack; and anyone who is unable to hide his true thoughts ought not to stay long at Court.'

151 'But, Madam, in saying that, do you reflect that this lady is your friend?'

151 'In matters such as you are hinting at, doubt is much more disturbing than anything else; and for my part I should like only to be told that which can be made clear to me without ambiguity.'

151 Let me repeat: to make of Célimène a systematic liar and cheat is to bring the play down to the level of an elegant drawing-room comedy on

'pre-cuckolding'. To accept Célimène at her word, as it seems only fair to do, is to emphasise the richness of the play in terms of Molière's psychological intuition as well as of the comic impasse to which this gives rise.

152 'The sincere vows, . . . the profound love, the respectful homage, the dutiful and assiduous service, that my heart will offer up to you as sacrifice.'

153 'Ye heavens! how can I control my anger?'
'How now! what is this disorder in which I see you? What is the meaning of these sighs, and the sombre looks you keep giving me?'
'That all the horrors the human mind is capable of are as nothing compared with your infidelity; and that fate, all the demons of Hell, and a hostile Providence have never created anything so wicked as you.'
'Well, I must say that is a charming way to pay court to me.'
'It's not a time for joking, and this is no laughing matter. Rather you should be blushing: you have every reason to, for I have reliable witnesses of your treachery . . .'

153 'My star warned me of what I had to fear . . .' This word 'star', spoken by a romanesque prince, sounds more natural than it does when repeated by Alceste.

154 'Betrayed on all sides, overwhelmed by injustice, I shall turn my back on this horrible, vice-ridden place.'

154 'No, I beg you, make this letter innocent if you can: my love is ready to back you up. If you can only manage to appear faithful, I will make every effort to believe you so.'

154 'Really, you are quite unbalanced in these outbursts of yours, and you don't deserve the love I bear you. Tell me, I pray you, why I should be obliged, for your sake, to stoop to the ignominy of pretence; and why on earth, if my affections were engaged elsewhere, I should not say so with complete frankness.'

155 'Ah! there is nothing like the extremity of the love I bear you: so eager is it to prove itself, that it even indulges in hostile fancies about you. I wish nobody else found you attractive; I wish you were reduced to a state of wretched poverty, and that Heaven had given you no advantages either of birth or of fortune, so that you could be rescued from such a deplorable fate by the great sacrifice of my love, and so that I should have the glory and the satisfaction of seeing you owe everything to my devotion.'

155 'What an extraordinary way of wishing me well!'

156 When Molière has punished the flirt – or worse – of his *Misanthrope* by having her letters to all her lovers read out in public, he leaves her humiliated by the treatment he has meted out to her; and he is absolutely right to do so. He abandons this cruel widow of vicious habits, a true woman of the Court, for whom there is no excuse, the tormentor of a man of honour – he abandons her to our contempt, and this is a mark of his stern morality.

156 The marvel of your art was to have created the Misanthropist in such a way that there is nobody, apart from the wicked, who would not like to be Alceste with all his foibles.

156 'It's also partly because of your censorious nature that I loved you, as a reaction. At the age of twelve I was in love with Alceste in our French literature class!'

156 Alceste cannot possibly be to us what he was to the seventeenth century.

157 That, Sir, is my view of *Le Misanthrope*, which I find the more admirable, in that the hero amuses us without being too ridiculous, and that he makes the gentry laugh without uttering low jokes, which is the fashion in most comedies. Plays like this seem more diverting to me, even though one laughs less openly. I find that they are more diverting, that they are more agreeable, and that one constantly laughs with the laughter of the mind. In spite of his folly, if that is the right name for his temperament, the Misanthropist has the character of an *honnête homme*.

158 The celebrated Molière hasn't disappointed us in the promise he made some four years ago to put on a comedy at the Palais-Royal that should be formally quite perfect.

158 Those which are judged the best of his plays, like *Le Misanthrope*, *Tartuffe* and *Les Femmes savantes*, are masterpieces which can never be sufficiently admired.

159 'Those disgusting syllables, which shock us even in the most elegant words.'

159 'I like his vortices.'
'I prefer his shooting stars.'

159 'Our forefathers were men of common sense in this, when they said that all a woman needed to know was how to distinguish a doublet from a pair of breeches.'

159 'In my view, a woman should have a general education; but I do not want to see in her the detestable mania of learning for learning's sake; and I would far rather that when she is in company, she should disclaim knowledge of the things she does know.'

159 Even though I wish women were generally more knowledgeable, I do not want them to act or speak like learned ladies.

160 'I am the favourite of Heaven, and the dread of all the earth; the enemy of peace, and the thunderbolt of war; the object of desire to women and of terror to men, and I bring in my wake bloodshed and horror. Mars begot me on a proud Amazon, and I was suckled on lion's milk. Men talk of the miracles performed by the infant Hercules, when he killed two serpents in his cradle. But he was inferior to me, for when I was tired of being suckled one day, I strangled my nurse.'

160 'Ye gods! how I am to be feared! Surely there is nothing more deadly to

mankind than my beauty! When I was born, nature prided itself on creating a masterpiece; but this merely hastened its ruin. It would be easier to number the leaves of the forest, the grains of sand on the shore, the ears of wheat at harvest-time, the flowers covering the earth in spring, the icicles in winter, the grapes in the autumn or the very stars in the sky, than to count the lovers whose death I have caused.'

161 'One is so formed, I hope, that one can say there is no shortage of admirers in one's train; and Dorante, Damis, Cléonte and Lysidas can all bear witness to one's charms.'
'These persons all love you?'
'With all their heart.'
'They have told you so?'
'None has had the temerity to do so. They have all respected me so much, that they have never breathed a word of their love. But their mute interpreters have all been busy, offering me the homage of their hearts.'

161 'The animal part, whose gross appetites bring us down to the level of the beasts.'

161 There is no doubt that of the three learned ladies [Armande] was the most odious to Molière in her claim to spurn the laws of nature. Bélise is merely grotesque; Philaminte is difficult to put up with, but Armande, with her patronising aloofness, represents the denial of all that is feminine.

162 These two greying lovers are touching, not laughable.

162 It is not necessary to conclude that Molière wanted Philaminte played as a caricature. All that was necessary was for the character to be somewhat masculine. It is likely that Hubert was well able to avoid extremes in a kind of impersonation that he could no doubt make convincing enough.

163 'It's you I'm addressing, sister.'

163 His view of comedy changed markedly after *L'Avare*, and especially in the last years of his life . . . the poet seems to have rejected, by 1672–3, the rule of the segregation of genres.

163 A structure which has some affinity with that of the *comédie-ballet*.

163 Ballet-sequences, in the dialogue as well as in the visual spectacle, follow almost continuously one after the other throughout these four hundred lines.

164 Jerkin and breeches of black velvet with a pale blue floral design; short jacket of gold and purple muslin, with ornamental buttons, a gilded silk cord, garters, aiguillettes and gloves.

165 One of the most sublime elements of true morality.

165 Ridicule is therefore the outward form attached by Providence to everything that is unreasonable, to bring it to our notice and oblige us to shun it. In order to recognise this ridicule, we must recognise the reasonable,

of which it is the opposite, and understand what it consists in. Its essence
is nothing other than congruity, and its external manifestation is propriety, the famous 'what is fitting' of the ancient world; so that propriety, in
relation to congruity, is what Platonists say that beauty is in relation to
goodness: that is to say, the flower, the tangible physical exterior.
Propriety is the apparent reason, congruity the essential reason. Hence
what is fitting always depends on some reason of congruity, just as that
which shocks denotes a certain incongruity, or in other words in the same
way that the ridiculous denotes a certain lack of reason.

166 When one hears this sort of decision, our surprise forces us to laugh,
because there is nothing that leads more readily to laughter than a
surprising disproportion between what we hear and what we see.

166 Just as reason produces in our mind a blend of joy and esteem, so the
ridiculous produces a blend of joy and scorn.

166 In the same way that Christian truths command our love and respect,
the errors which are their opposite deserve our scorn and displeasure, for
there are two things in the truths of our religion: divine beauty, which
makes us love these truths, and a holy majesty, which makes us respect
them. Similarly, there are two things in error: impiety, which makes us
hate it, and incongruity, which renders it ridiculous.

168 The next day there was a new comedy, written by an actor called
Molière. He's a fellow with a prodigious wit; and like the ancient
authors, he ridicules the vices of his age in all his plays.

168 Anyone who is born a Christian and a Frenchman is subject to considerable constraints as a satirist. All the important subjects are forbidden; he may tackle them occasionally, but he will soon turn to insignificant matters, and try to enhance them by his literary talent and his
style.

169 This play does not exceed the limits of decent, acceptable satire.

169 Not true *précieuses*, but their crude imitators, who deserve to be ridiculed.

170 'Good Heavens! if everyone was like you, we should soon reach the end of
a novel! It would be a fine thing if Cyrus were to marry Mandane
straightaway, and if Aronce and Clélie were to marry without any
preliminaries!'

170 'Indeed, Uncle, my cousin is perfectly right. How on earth can one
receive the addresses of suitors who have no idea of galant behaviour? I
dare wager that they have never seen the map of Tender-love, and that
the topography of that country is quite unknown to them.'

172 And you will be better able to pay your court, if you adopt the disguise of
a marquis. You know, of course, what is necessary for that, and you
won't overlook any details of dress or manners. Your hat must be
embellished with feathers by the score; your wig must be of superb

quality; your bands must impress by their volume, and your doublet by its smallness . . .

172 To arouse laughter by trivial jokes and word-play.

172 'He makes them laugh at one another and call each other Turlupins, as they have done at Court since Élomire performed his *Critique*.'

173 "Sdeath! when I take a critical look at myself, I cannot see anything to disturb my composure. I am not without money, I am young, and my family has some pretensions to blue blood; so that there are few offices to which my rank does not entitle me to aspire. As for courage, which is rightly esteemed above all else, it is well known (I say this in all modesty) that I do not lack it; and I have defended my honour with vigour and panache. I am equally well known for my wit; for my taste; and for my ability to pass instant judgement on anything under the sun. At all the new plays, where I am to be seen seated on stage among the spectators of fashion and taste, I give the lead in saluting all the best passages with approving comments and loud applause.'

173 'But at least tell me, Madam, by what magic spell your Clitandre has gained your favours? What merit, what sublime virtue, entitles him to the honour of your esteem? Did the long nail he wears on his little finger earn him the high place he enjoys in your regard? Did you surrender, like the rest of the fashionable world, to the outstanding merit of his blond wig? Was it perhaps his ample bands that earned your love? Was it his mass of ribbons that charmed you? When he became your slave, was it the quality of his large petticoat-breeches that evoked a response? Or did perhaps the way he laughs, and his falsetto voice, find the secret way to please you?'

174 'This kind of satire has the manners of the day as its target, and only hits individuals indirectly. We should not be too ready to apply to ourselves what is intended as censure of a general nature; and let us profit from the moral teaching, if we can, without assuming that it is addressed to us. The ridiculous portraits we see on stage should be viewed with equanimity by everyone. They are public mirrors, in which it is unnecessary to show that we recognise ourselves; and we acknowledge faults as our own, when we protest at their correction.'

174 Of marrying the daughter, and having had the mother as his mistress.

175 That a man who frequents the highest circles at Court, and whom Mademoiselle honours with the name of friend, could possibly be the object of such a savage satire.

175 'Very well, let me refer you to the author of the *Satires*.'
'I'll refer you to him as well.'

176 'Learn, I pray you, that it is not your place to use such a word with a person of my quality; that although you may be our son-in-law, there is a great distance between us, and it is for you to know your place.'

177 "Swounds! I should strangle her with my own hands, if she were to forfeit her mother's honour.'
     "Sdeath! I should run them both through with my sword, my daughter and her lover, if she had besmirched her honour.'

178 'My vows? I never pronounced them freely, and they were obtained from me by force. Did you ever stop to ask my consent before our marriage; did you consider whether I wanted to marry you? You consulted only my parents: it is they whom you really married, and so it is to them you should complain if you have any grievances. As for myself, who never asked you to marry me, and whom you took without regard for my feelings, I maintain that I am not obliged to submit to your wishes like a slave; and I intend, so please you, to enjoy what is left of my youth, to take advantage of such freedom as my age and condition allow me, to see something of the world of fashion, and to experience the pleasure of being courted. Make up your mind to this; it serves you right, and you should thank Heaven I am not capable of anything worse.'

178 'I declare that I have no intention of renouncing the world, and of burying myself alive in a husband.'

178 They took advantage of my youth and my submissiveness, and I was buried alive in the marriage-bed of Évandre's son.

179 'When, like me, anyone has married a faithless wife, the best thing he can do is to throw himself into the river head first.'

179 A play with a subject so diverting
     Will even amuse the Stoics, that's certain;
     Is it so funny, then? Not half!
     The veriest sobersides would laugh.

180 This adventure, no less disconcerting for ordinary human values than the predictions of today's science fiction.

182 'In most love-affairs, such a disguise would not be very successful; and the person of a husband is not universally the most favoured.'

182 'Truly, Amphitryon, you must be jesting to talk like that; and if anyone were to hear you, I should be afraid they might think you had taken leave of your senses.'

182 'All these subtleties are merely frivolous excuses; and when one is already angry, such talk only makes matters worse.'

183 'I come down towards the beloved object who alone has power to charm me; not without feeling a certain surprise that I need to disguise myself in order to be loved. But in my true guise, mortal men could not suffer for long the full blaze of my splendour, which would blind them. So when I have dealings with the fair sex, I veil the divine majesty that is mine; and as a result I can pass for a human being, albeit a nonpareil.'

183 'When one has the good fortune to grace an elevated rank, all one's

actions are fine and admirable; and depending on one's position in the world, what one does may well be called by a different name.'

184 'There is nothing dishonourable about sharing with Jupiter; and it can only be a source of pride to find oneself the rival of the king of the gods.'

184 'Lord Jupiter knows how to sugar the pill.'

184 'My lords, do you want my advice? Do not waste time on such congratulation: this would not be wise, for compliments in these circumstances are likely to be embarrassing.'

184 It was a savage business, which seriously offended the Queen, Mlle de la Vallière, Mme de Montausier, M. de Montespan and many others. Molière would not have undertaken this cruel assassination without prompting. One can see him deploring his servile position. But what could Molière-Sosie do? He was a servant, and must continue to serve. For he had only his master to support him, and the rest of the Court against him.

185 'She must not take the liberty of dying without the doctor's permission.'

186 'He was dressed like a doctor, so I thought I had to mention money to him.'

186 'But you can see that emetic wine is making a big noise nowadays. Its miracle cures have converted even the most sceptical; and only three weeks ago I myself witnessed a most remarkable case.'
'What was that?'
'A man had been at death's door for a week. They didn't know what to prescribe, for none of the medicines had any effect; and at last they decided to prescribe emetic wine.'
'And he was cured?'
'No, he died.'
'Truly a remarkable result.'
'Why! he had been unable to die for a whole week, and this enabled him to die straightaway! Can you imagine anything more effective?'

187 'They come to seek me out from all quarters; and if things continue like this, I propose to stick to medicine all my life. It seems to me the best of all professions; for, whether you perform well or badly, you receive the same pay; poor workmanship never has harmful consequences for a doctor, who is free to treat his patients as he pleases. A shoemaker can't spoil a piece of leather, when he's making a pair of shoes, without having to pay for it himself; but a doctor can spoil a human being with impunity. The mistakes are never ours: it's always the fault of the man who dies. In a word, what I like about this profession is that dead men observe the greatest possible discretion: you never hear them complaining of the doctor who killed them.'

187 'But, Sir, this is a practice I don't understand. Why bleed someone who is not ill?'

'That is of no consequence: it's a beneficial practice. And just as we drink to prevent future thirst, so we need to be bled to prevent future illness.'

187 'I tell you your daughter is dumb.'
'Yes, but pray tell me the cause of this.'
'Nothing easier: she is dumb because she has lost the faculty of speech.'
'Very well; but why has she lost the faculty of speech?'
'All the best authorities will tell you that it's because the tongue has been prevented from functioning.'

188 What was even more laughable was that these masks bore such a likeness to M. Guénaut, M. Esprit and M. des Fougerais, that everyone took them to be the models. M. Guénaut took this as a joke, but it was no laughing matter for M. Esprit.

189 Whatever salutary improvement is produced in us by chance, by nature, or by some other unknown cause (whose number is infinite) is unfailingly attributed by doctors to their art. All the fortunate things that happen to a patient under their treatment, are ascribed to their own success.

189 'The great weakness of men is their strong attachment to life; and we doctors exploit this with our pompous jargon, and take advantage of the veneration of our profession that is produced by this general fear of death. Let us retain the high esteem that human weakness accords us, and present a united front to our patients, so as to claim for ourselves the favourable outcome of the illness, while imputing to nature all the failures of our art. Let us not, I say, be so foolish as to destroy the fortunate prejudice which, however ill-founded, provides a living for so many people.'

189 'You should never say "So-and-so died of a fever, followed by pneumonia", but "He died of four doctors, followed by two apothecaries."'

189 'Don't forget the man whose death you caused last week.'
'Remember the lady you despatched to the other world a few days ago.'

190 'God forbid, Sir, that I should presume to add anything to what you have said! You have discoursed so well on the signs, the symptoms and the causes of Monsieur's illness; your reasoning is so admirably learned that it is quite impossible that he should not be deranged, as a result of melancholic hypochondria; and even if he were not, he would have to become deranged, because of the excellent things you have said, and the admirable quality of your argument. Yes, Sir, you have portrayed most graphically all the properties of this illness: there could be no wiser or more learned reasoning than your exposition of the diagnosis, the prognosis and the therapy; and all that is left for me to do is to congratulate Monsieur on his good luck in falling into your hands, and to tell him how fortunate he is to be mad, so as to experience the pleasantness and the effectiveness of the remedies you have so judiciously proposed.'

191 'What I understand, brother, is that I have never seen anyone less ill than you, and I should be delighted to have a constitution like yours.'

191 In one sense Argan's illness is very real: it is not an imaginary illness, but an illness of the imagination, whose most important and most serious symptom is that anyone suffering from it is convinced he is ill.

191 It would be wrong to consider these doctors as ignoramuses; their consultations on Argan's case are coherent, and entirely consistent with current medical practice . . . There is no doubt that the case corresponds to a known condition, accepted by seventeenth-century medical science.

192 'It's not doctors he's ridiculing, but the absurdity of medical science.'

192 'Their whole art is nothing but play-acting.'

192 'But let's talk about it, brother. You don't believe in medicine?'
'No, brother, and I don't see that such a belief is essential for one's salvation.'
'What! you refuse to believe in something everyone has believed in, throughout the ages?'
'Far from believing in it, I find it one of the biggest of human absurdities; and if one looks at it philosophically, there is no more far-fetched mummery. I can't think of anything more absurd than one man setting out to cure another.'
'And why shouldn't one man be able to cure another?'
'Because, brother, the workings of the human machine have so far remained mysteries to which men do not possess the key; and nature has veiled our sight so that we are unable to discern anything.'
'Doctors are ignoramuses, then, in your view?'
'That's right. Most of them know the ancient tongues; they can speak fine Latin, and name the illnesses in Greek, define and categorise them. But as for curing them, they haven't the slightest idea!'

193 I leave nature alone, supposing that it is provided with claws and teeth to defend itself against attack, and to preserve that structure whose dissolution it seeks to avoid. I am afraid that instead of coming to its aid when it is at grips with a serious illness, we merely assist its enemy, and increase the forces against which it must strive.

193 'But what, finally, is to be done when one is ill?'
'Nothing, brother.'
'Nothing?'
'Nothing. Simply keep calm. Nature itself, if it is left alone, will be able to correct any disorder. It's our anxiety, our impatience, that spoil everything; and nearly everyone dies of the cure rather than of the illness itself.'
'But you must agree, brother, that nature can be helped by certain things.'
'These are pure fancies, brother, that we love to cherish; and men have always imagined things that they end up by believing because they

console us, and we should like them to be true. When a doctor speaks of helping and reinforcing nature . . . , he is indulging in the fantasies of medical science. But when you come to facts and experience, things are very different: it's like waking up from a beautiful dream with the disappointment of having believed in it.'

194 I have been told that Molière kept an eye on the doings of these gentry, and that he planned to unmask their plots in a comedy he proposed to write to entertain the Court.

195 'What I like about him – and in this he follows my example – is that he follows unquestioningly the opinions of the ancients, and that he has always refused to understand, or to listen to, the reasoning or the experiments in favour of the so-called discoveries of our day concerning the circulation of the blood, and other opinions of the same kind.'

196 'No, in spite of everyone you shall seek her company.'

196 'Poor fellow! Let's draw up a document at once, however mortified envy may be!'

198 'According to different needs, a technique exists to enable us to relax the constraints of conscience, and to adjust the evil consequences of an action with the purity of our intention.'

199 The Tartuffes were able, in secret, to obtain Your Majesty's favour; and the originals succeeded in having the copy suppressed.

199 [The] famous originals of the portrait I wanted to paint.

200 'Ah! if only you had seen how I made his acquaintance!'

200 'I see him reproving everything, and he even takes a considerable interest in my wife, for the sake of my honour. He tells me of all those who make sheep's eyes at her, and proves himself six times more jealous than myself.'

201 'I've seen it, I tell you; seen it with my own eyes; seen it, do you hear? Must I tell you fifty times, and shout until I'm hoarse?'

201 'Good Lord, appearances are often misleading; and one shouldn't always judge by what one sees.'

201 'Laurent, put my hair-shirt and my scourge away, and pray for the guidance of Heaven in everything you do.'

201 'These words are spoken by a villain.'

201 It's true that M. Purgon is sincere, whereas Tartuffe is a hypocrite. But would a comedy that had presented a M. Purgon in religious matters have differed significantly, as far as the comic meaning is concerned, from the *Tartuffe* we possess?

202 Christian isolation becomes the model for comic isolation.

202 'Whoever follows his teaching enjoys perfect peace, and looks on the rest of the world as dung. Yes, I am becoming a different man under his guidance: he teaches me to have affection for nobody, and releases me from all friendships. I could see brother, children, mother and wife die in front of my eyes without caring a scrap.'

202 'What human feelings those are, brother!'

203 It is not for the theatre to discuss such matters.

203 Without changing the intellectual world-order.

203 If Molière had dared to make his Tartuffe a priest who . . . seduces a woman under the cover of the language of devotion . . . and succeeds in ruining a whole family; if, far from being punished at the end against all probability in order to conform to our pitiful dramatic conventions, this fraudulent priest had triumphed . . ., then *Tartuffe* would have become a work of great public importance, worthy of conveying moral instruction to an enlightened nation.

206 'You see in my master, Dom Juan, the greatest scoundrel the world has ever known, a mad dog, a devil, a Turk, a heretic, who believes neither in Heaven nor in the Saints, nor in God nor in werewolves; who truly lives the life of a mindless animal, one of Epicurus's pigs, a veritable Sardanapalus; whose ears are closed to all the Christian remonstrances one may make, and who treats all our cherished beliefs as nonsense.'

206 'There's nothing so pleasant as to triumph over the resistance of a fair person, and on this subject my ambition is that of conquerors who fly from one victory to another, and whose ambition knows no bounds. Nothing can check the impetuous ardour of my desires: I feel driven to possess the whole earth; and like Alexander, I wish there were other worlds elsewhere, so that I could extend my amorous conquests.'

206 '. . . It's as if you had learned all that by heart: you speak just like a book.'

207 'I could not bear to see in them such a good understanding: my desires were aroused by resentment, and I took great pleasure in the idea of disrupting this harmony, and breaking off their relationship, which offended the delicacy of my feelings.'

207 'Do you know, I still experienced a certain feeling for her: the novelty of our situation gave me a bizarre pleasure, and her casual dress, her languid air and her tears revived some part of my extinct passion.'

207 'That is merely a sketch of the character; and to produce a finished portrait, many other brush-strokes would be necessary.'

207 'One of the greatest errors to be found among men.'

207 'Two and two make four, and four and four make eight.'

208 'It's a trifle; we may have been deceived by the light, or led astray by some mist which clouded our sight.'

208 'The profession of hypocrite offers marvellous advantages today. It's an art whose imposture always meets with respect; and even when it is found out, nobody dares speak out against it. All other vices are subject to censure, and anyone may attack them openly; but hypocrisy is a privileged vice, which is able to silence its critics, and to enjoy a sovereign impunity.'

209 'It shall not be said of me, whatever happens, that I am capable of repenting.'

210 A badly constructed play; an unactable part.

213 Ballet is to comedy what death is to tragedy: the leap into the beyond, the completing of a trajectory from which there is no return, no possible readjustment to the everyday world.

213 To reconcile in a single entertainment the most farcical sort of comedy, an element strongly suggestive of dance, and a convincing portrayal of human nature.

215 As for *Psyché*, it is opera before its time, and this work contains in advance all the features one looks for in the operatic genre.

218 A curious combination, in which the King was both a spectator at the play, and a performer in the ballet.

219 'Let us crown this marvellous day by a spectacular pageant.'

221 Each scene of the *Bourgeois* demonstrates, with remarkable verve and precision, a trait of character or feeling reduced to its simplest essence. And this essence is expressed by means of a dramatic action which prefigures the ballet sequence.

221 The four apprentice tailors take part in a joyful dance.

221 Into which something of the dress and manners of the Turks might be introduced.

222 'Ah! everyone is sensible now.'

222 'Isn't it dangerous to pretend to be dead?'

223 'Long live, long live, long live a hundred times, our new doctor, who speaks so eloquently! May he continue for a thousand years to eat, and drink, and bleed his patients, and kill them!'

228 'Indeed, I speak without affectation.'
'It is obvious that that is the case, Madam, and that everything in you is natural. Your speech, the tone of your voice, your expression, your walk, and your behaviour and your dress: everything has an air of good breeding about it, by which everyone is charmed. I am all eyes and ears to study you; and I am so full of you, that my aim is to imitate you as closely as I can.'
'You are mocking me, Madam.'

'Far from it, Madam. Who would want to mock you?'
'I am not a good model, Madam.'
'Indeed you are, Madam.'
'You flatter me, Madam.'
'Not at all, Madam.'
'Spare me, I pray you, Madam.'
'But I am sparing you, Madam, and I do not say half of what I really think.'

229 'Heavens! what do I hear! All that was needed to complete the picture was for you to turn hypocrite, and this is the crowning abomination. This is too much for me, Sir, and I can't refrain from speaking my mind. Do what you like: beat me, thrash me, kill me if you want: I have to speak out, and do my duty as a faithful servant. Know then, Sir, that the pitcher goes so often to the well that at last it is broken; and as that writer says whose name I don't know, man is in this world like a bird on the branch; the branch is attached to the tree; whoever holds on to the tree is guided by good principles; good principles are better than fine words; fine words are spoken at Court; at Court one finds courtiers; courtiers follow the fashion; fashion is produced by fantasy; fantasy is a faculty of the spirit; the spirit is the source of life; life ends in death; death puts us in mind of Heaven; Heaven is above the earth; the earth is not the sea; the sea is subject to storms; storms bring destruction to ships; ships need a good pilot; a good pilot needs wisdom; wisdom is not found in the young; the young owe obedience to the old; the old love wealth; wealth makes wealthy men; wealthy men are not poor; the poor know necessity; necessity knows no law; he who knows no law lives like a brute beast; and as a result, you will be damned to hell-fire.'

229 'Do you take me for a man entirely governed by money, a man swayed by self-interest, a man with a mercenary soul? Let me tell you, my friend, that if you were to offer me a purse full of *pistoles*, and if that purse was in a rich box, that box in a precious casket, that casket in an admirable chest, that chest in a curious cabinet, that cabinet in a magnificent room, that room in a pleasing apartment, that apartment in a splendid castle, that castle in a peerless citadel, that citadel in a famous city, that city in a fertile island, that island in an opulent province, that province in a prosperous kingdom, and that kingdom in the whole world; and if you were to give me the world in which was that prosperous kingdom, in which was that opulent province, in which was that fertile island, in which was that famous city, in which was that peerless citadel, in which was that splendid castle, in which was that pleasing apartment, in which was that magnificent room, in which was that curious cabinet, in which was that admirable chest, in which was that precious casket, in which was that rich box containing the purse full of *pistoles*, I should not care a fig for your money or yourself!'

230 'It is not just that I am his father, Sir, but I can say that I am pleased with him, and all who know him speak of him as a lad quite without malice.

He's never had a very lively imagination, or the quick wit displayed by some; but that is what has always led me to augur well of his judgement, a quality necessary to the practice of our art. When he was small, he was never quick and alert; he was always docile, quiet and taciturn, never opening his mouth and never playing at childish games. We had the utmost difficulty in teaching him to read, and even when he was nine, he didn't know his alphabet. "Good", I said to myself, "the late-flowering trees bear the best fruit; it's much harder to write on marble than on sand, but what you write endures much longer; and his slow understanding, his laboured imagination, are the sign of a sound judgement in the future."'

230 'Rhythmical prose, a kind of free verse, such as pleasure and necessity might suggest to two people who are speaking spontaneously.'

231 'I display for a certain person all the tender ardour that can be imagined; I love nothing but her in the world; I have nothing but her in my mind; she is the object of all my devotion, my desires, my joy; I talk, think and dream of her alone, I live for her, my heart beats for her – and this is how I am rewarded for so much affection!'

231 'Is there anything, Covielle, like the treachery of my faithless Lucile?'
'Or like that of my scamp of a Nicole, Sir?'
'After all the ardent sacrifices, the sighs and the vows I have devoted to her charms!'
'After all the devoted care, and the services I have rendered her in the kitchen!'
'All the tears I have shed at her feet!'
'All the buckets of water I have fetched her from the well!'
'All the ardour I have displayed, in loving her more than myself!'
'All the heat I have endured, in turning her spit for her!'

232 'I loved you with an extreme tenderness; nothing in the world was as dear to me as you; I neglected my duty for you, everything I did was for you; and all the reward I ask is that you should amend your ways, and forestall your damnation.'

232 'Ah! how little we know what we are about when we choose not to leave Heaven to decide what favours we receive, when we insist on knowing better, and on importuning Heaven with our blind desires and our thoughtless demands! I yearned for a son with unbelievable ardour; I constantly prayed for a son with the most extreme devotions; and this son, whom I obtained by importuning Heaven, is the chagrin and the torment of my life, of which I thought he would be the joy and consolation.'

233 Molière had written *L'Avare* in prose, intending to put it into verse later; but it seemed so good that the actors wanted to play it as it was, and nobody ever dared touch it afterwards.

233 'I am tired of your dissolute behaviour . . . Birth counts for nothing

without virtue . . . On the contrary, the resulting scandal is very much to your discredit.'

233 Generally speaking, Molière's prose is pretentiously poetic, full of *précieux* expressions and of ready-made lines of verse. *Le Sicilien*, for instance, is a little play absolutely full of blank verse.

233 *L'Avare*, like several of Molière's other prose plays, is almost entirely in blank verse. The rhythm and measure of verse are there: all that is missing is rhyme.

234 The style of *Le Sicilien* is remarkable . . . together with its comic appeal, it possesses a sort of poetic manner that seems to express romance in a kind of song.

234 'The night is as black as an oven. The heavens are dressed like Scaramouche tonight, and I don't think there's a single star showing the tip of its nose.'

234 'Whatever isn't prose, is verse; and whatever isn't verse, is prose.'

234 Free verse is more flexible than the alexandrine, especially Molière's alexandrine; it lends itself to delicate nuances, and breaks the action down into minute details. The text closely follows the movements of mind and body.

235 In a handful of words, and with simple elegance, Terence says what Molière says with a wealth of metaphors which border on the meaningless. I like his prose much better than his verse. For instance, *L'Avare* is better written than his plays in verse. True, French versification hampered him; indeed, he was more successful in *Amphitryon*, where he chose to write in irregular verse.

235 'And when I myself wanted to oblige you to refuse the marriage you had been offered, what did my insistence convey to you, if not the interest I chose to show in you, and the displeasure I should feel if the union that had been decided on should share the possession of a heart I desired for myself alone?'

236 'The few years one may have to one's name more than yourself are hardly enough to take such pride in.'

236 Célimène's language is perfectly clear, and shows a basic honesty in spite of her coquetry . . . Arsinoé's replies, on the other hand, flounder in syntactical complexities of which one soon loses the thread.

236 'Yes, I should deceive you if I spoke otherwise: sooner or later, we shall certainly part company.'

236 'No: without getting angry, pray justify to me the terms of this letter.'

236 'Provided your heart lends its support to my plan to flee the whole human race.'

237 'But I did not lend my ear to these spiteful tongues.'

237 Although [it] is by Molière, it is absolute nonsense.

237 He speaks the language of his day, that is all.

237 'At meal-times, he insists on placing him at the head of his table, and happily watches him eat as much as six men. He has him served with the best morsels of every dish; and if he happens to belch, he says "God bless you!"'

237 'It's not for the wife to lay down the law; and I'm all for letting the husband be top dog.'

237 'Ah, Myrtil, take care of what you are doing. Do not offer hope to my heart, for it might receive it too gratefully; and if it were to vanish afterwards like a flash of lightning, this would make my disappointment most bitter.'

237 'Léon calls me, and the throne awaits me, in vain. The crown offers little to satisfy me, and its splendour appeals to me only if it gives me the joy of crowning the object of my love, and of making amends by this just tribute for my offence against her rare merits.'

238 'What! does the star which constantly persecutes me give me no time to recover?'

238 'Ye heavens! how can I control my anger?'

239 'It is enough to see that others esteem it.'
'They must have the knack of pretending: I haven't.'
'Do you think you're favoured with so much wit?'
'I'd have a great deal more, if I praised your verse!'

'The ballad, however, is found charming by many.'
'That doesn't prevent me finding it unattractive.'
'It's no worse at all for that little misfortune.'
'It has a remarkable appeal for pedants.'
'And yet it appears that it's not to your liking.'

239 'If she has a pale complexion, she is compared to the whiteness of jasmine; if she's hideously dark, she's an adorable brunette; if she's skinny, she has a slender grace; if fat, she is credited with a majestic bearing; if she lacks grace, and is careless of her person, she is called a casual beauty. The giantess is praised as a goddess; the dwarf, as an epitome of all heavenly charms. The proud woman has a heart fit for a queen; the cunning woman is celebrated for her wit, and the fool for her kind nature. One who talks too much has a lively temperament; one who never talks at all is of a modest disposition. Thus does a lover, carried away by his passion, love even the very faults of his mistress.'

240 'Tell me, Agnès, did he not take something else of yours? Eh?'
'Well, he . . .'
'What?'
'Took . . .'

'Well?'

'The . . .'

'Come now!'

'I do not dare, and you will be angry with me . . .'

240 'You know that I have always confided in you. Do please . . .'

'No, for all I care you shall be tartufficated!'

241 'I can relieve you of these absurd fears, Madam, and I am skilled in the art of overcoming scruples. Heaven forbids certain satisfactions, it is true; but it is possible to reach a compromise. According to different needs, a technique exists to enable us to relax the constraints of conscience, and to adjust the evil consequences of an action with the purity of our intention. You shall be instructed in these secrets, Madam; all you need do is to let yourself be guided. Satisfy my desire, and have no fear: I will be responsible for everything, and will take everything on myself.'

241 'And what do you claim that a fool will be able to do . . . ?'

'Marrying a stupid girl is a way of avoiding being a stupid husband.'

'What? Can you not bring yourself, once and for all, to act like a man?'

242 'This is a delicate matter, Sir; and we always want to be flattered about our talent. But one day I happened to say to someone, whose name I will not reveal, who had shown me some verses he had written, that a man of taste should always keep a strict control on the temptation we may feel to become writers; that one should always keep in check one's zeal for the display of such amusements; and that such a great readiness to show one's work can be a source of considerable embarrassment.'

242 'He himself gave me an account of the affair.'

'My affection is ready to lend you my support.'

'He releases me from all friendships.'

'Do you think his passion for you is so strong, and that his affection for me is quite extinguished?'

242 Never did any writer's language, whether in verse or in prose, adhere so closely to the rhythms of thoughts and feelings.

243 For proof that the genius of our poetry presents few obstacles to the free expression of all that is true, it is perhaps not in Racine that French verse should be studied, but sometimes in Corneille, and always in Molière. Racine, that divine poet, is elegiac, lyrical, epic; Molière is dramatic.

244 The *honnêtes gens* possess their own literature, which we call classical literature.

245 There are no 'philosophers' in Molière's theatre. Each character fulfils an essential dramatic function, not a so-called moral function invented by the critics.

246 A serious character who appears in comedy, and whose language is that of reason and morality.

247 'Good Lord, my friend, do not worry about me: he will be a clever man who can catch me out! I know the subtle wiles of women, and the ruses they adopt in order to fool us; and how easily we are taken in by their tricks. I have taken my precautions against such accidents, and the girl I am going to marry has all the innocence that is needed in order to protect my forehead against the workings of a malign fate.'
'And what do you claim that a fool will be able to do . . . ?'
'Marrying a stupid girl is a way of avoiding being a stupid husband.'

'And are all poor mortals, without exception, included in your dislike? Surely there must be, in this day and age . . . '
'No, my dislike is general, and I hate all humanity: some because they are malevolent and wicked, and the others because they are friendly towards the wicked, and do not feel for them the vigorous hatred that vice should produce in the minds of the virtuous.'

248 Psychological simplification, in a genre more popular than tragedy, is necessary to produce either laughter or satire . . . Without running the risk of destroying itself, comedy cannot aspire to a genuine lucidity. It is the reassuring world of the Manichaean. It is the world of the improbable and the imaginary, as regards both characters and situations, because laughter feeds on the unreal. The inevitable ambiguity of lifelike characters, neither wholly good nor wholly bad, cannot be a feature of comedy, for ambiguity gives rise to uneasiness. Terence, Molière or Marivaux, by the curious resonances that certain of their characters sometimes produce in us, prove that all psychological realism, all subtle analysis in comedy inevitably runs the risk of bordering on the pathetic.

250 In that art of metamorphosis, the theatre, only the thoughts of the poet count: they are the virtue of the theatre. What we call thoughts is only a cloak of feelings and sensations. The poet generously offers this cloak to us, and everyone borrows it, each one in turn putting it on, so as to be able to think in his own way. That is a mere usurpation. The true use of a play is to warm one's body and one's heart.

251 To experience the work before understanding and appreciating it.

251 The comic genre is concerned with man in general, tragedy with individuals . . . The hero of a tragedy is a certain man: he is either Regulus, or Brutus, or Cato, and nobody else. The chief character of a comedy, on the contrary, must represent a large number of people. If by mischance he was given such a specific personality that there was only one individual in society who resembled him, then comedy would be returning to its infancy, and degenerating into satire.

252 Of all the instruments of human thought, the theatre is definitely the most powerful . . . besides, the object is not to correct someone, it is to correct everyone.

253 This Miser who takes us into his confidence cannot be your fellow-being, for we only ever know the exterior of our fellow-beings. No: what is shown on stage is what every man knows of himself. Everyone is Harpagon; everyone has thought 'Without a dowry!', but no-one ever said it . . . He who has never been ridiculous, is unable to laugh. Besides, no such man has ever existed. If miserliness was a sort of rare illness, who would laugh at it? And if I am shown a portrait of a miser, according to the classical anecdotes, I shall have the feeble pleasure of despising him. But each of us is a miser, with real miserliness, and jealous, with ridiculous jealousy; each of us is Purgon and Jourdain in self-importance, a hundred times a day.

253 'I shall see, in this affair, whether men have such effrontery, whether they can be so wicked, perverse and criminal, as to treat me with injustice in the eyes of the whole world.'

253 'It's for my sins that I love you so much . . . My love is quite inconceivable, and no-one has ever loved as I do, Madam.'

254 'I wish nobody else found you attractive; I wish you were reduced to a state of wretched poverty, and that Heaven had given you no advantages either of birth or of fortune, so that you could be rescued from such a deplorable fate by the great sacrifice of my love, and so that I should have the glory and the satisfaction of seeing you owe everything to my devotion.'

254 Happy is he who is unable to be self-important without being ridiculous; but such good fortune is not always free from chagrin. The theatre is a better cure, for it brings no shame: the power of the spectacle means that nobody thinks of his neighbour.

255 The pity we feel at a misfortune into which we see our fellow-men fall, makes us fear a similar fate for ourselves; this fear leads to the wish to avoid it; and this wish enables us to purge, modify, and even eradicate in ourselves the passion which we have seen to be the cause of the misfortune of those we pity.

256 Molière would not have been a classical writer, if he had not defended the established society of his day against the eccentrics and the snobs, like Alceste, the learned women or the *précieuses*; the parasites like Tartuffe, Harpagon or even Dom Juan; those who usurp dignities and status, like the bourgeois nobleman or George Dandin.

Appendix I Chronological list of Molière's plays, with the parts played by Molière

	Date of first performance	Title	Acts	Verse or prose	Place	Part played
1	?	La Jalousie du Barbouillé	1	prose	(provinces)	Le Docteur (?)
2	?	Le Médecin volant	1	prose	(provinces)	Sganarelle
3	(Nov 1658)[1]	L'Étourdi	5	verse	Petit-Bourbon	Mascarille
4	(Dec 1658)[1]	Dépit amoureux	5	verse	Petit-Bourbon	Albert
5	Nov 1659	Les Précieuses ridicules	1	prose	Petit-Bourbon	Mascarille
6	May 1660	Sganarelle, ou le Cocu imaginaire	1	verse	Petit-Bourbon	Sganarelle
7	Feb 1661	Dom Garcie de Navarre	5	verse	Palais-Royal	D. Garcie
8	June 1661	L'École des maris	3	verse	Palais-Royal	Sganarelle
9	Aug 1661	Les Fâcheux	3	verse	Vaux-le-Vicomte	various
10	Dec 1662	L'École des femmes	5	verse	Palais-Royal	Arnolphe
11	June 1663	La Critique de l'École des femmes	1	prose	Palais-Royal	Le Marquis (?)
12	Oct 1663	L'Impromptu de Versailles	1	prose	Versailles	Molière
13	Jan 1664	Le Mariage forcé	1	prose	Louvre	Sganarelle
14	May 1664	La Princesse d'Élide	5	2-v, 3-p	Versailles	Moron
—	May 1664	(Tartuffe)[2]	3	verse	Versailles	Orgon
15	Feb 1665	Dom Juan	5	prose	Palais-Royal	Sganarelle
16	Sept 1665	L'Amour médecin	3	prose	Versailles	Sganarelle
17	June 1666	Le Misanthrope	5	verse	Palais-Royal	Alceste
18	Aug 1666	Le Médecin malgré lui	3	prose	Palais-Royal	Sganarelle
19	Dec 1666	(Mélicerte)[2]	2	verse	Saint-Germain	Lycarsis
20	Dec 1666	La Pastorale comique	1	verse	Saint-Germain	Lycas
21	Jan 1667	Le Sicilien, ou l'Amour peintre	1	prose	Saint-Germain	Dom Pèdre
22	Jan 1668	Amphitryon	3	verse	Palais-Royal	Sosie
23	July 1668	George Dandin	3	prose	Versailles	G. Dandin

24	Sept 1668	L'Avare	5	prose	Palais-Royal	Harpagon
25	Feb 1669	Tartuffe	5	verse	Palais-Royal	Orgon
26	Sept 1669	Monsieur de Pourceaugnac	3	prose	Chambord	Pourceaugnac
27	Feb 1670	Les Amants magnifiques	5	prose	Saint-Germain	Clitidas
28	Oct 1670	Le Bourgeois gentilhomme	5	prose	Chambord	Jourdain
29	Jan 1671	(Psyché)[3]	5	verse	Tuileries	Zéphire
30	May 1671	Les Fourberies de Scapin	3	prose	Palais-Royal	Scapin
31	Dec 1671	La Comtesse d'Escarbagnas	1	prose	Saint-Germain	(no part)
32	March 1672	Les Femmes savantes	5	verse	Palais-Royal	Chrysale
33	Feb 1673	Le Malade imaginaire	3	prose	Palais-Royal	Argan

[1] Already performed in the provinces before this date.
[2] Incomplete.
[3] Written in collaboration with Corneille and Quinault.

Appendix II **List of members of Molière's company, with summary biographical information.**

This list gives the names of all those who were associate members of the company at any time between 1658 (date of the return to Paris) and Molière's death in 1673. Associate members each received a share (in certain cases a half-share; Molière himself was granted a double share from 1661 onwards) of the company's profits. The list also indicates the roles each is known to have created: roles given in italics can be assigned only with varying degrees of probability. Numbers refer to the titles of Molière's plays as listed in Appendix I.

Béjart, Joseph (b. 1606(?); d. 1659). Eldest member of the family who, with Molière, formed nucleus of L'Illustre Théâtre. Had an impediment of speech. With Molière in provinces, but died soon after return to Paris. Roles of *Pandolfe* (3), Éraste (4).

Béjart, Madeleine (b. 1618; d. 1672). Associated with Molière professionally throughout his career with Illustre Théâtre, in provinces, and in Paris from 1658 to her death, exactly a year before his own. His mistress for many years, and alleged by pamphleteers to be the mother, not the elder sister, of his wife Armande. A dependable business woman, and mainstay of the company. Had some literary ability (her adaptation of Guérin de Bouscal's *Dom Quichot* was played by the company). Roles predominantly, but not exclusively, those of *suivantes*: Marinette (4), Madelon (5), Elvire (7), Lisette (8), *Une Bohémienne* (13), Philis (14), Lisette (16), *Jacqueline* (18), *La Nuit* and *Cléanthis* (22), Frosine (24), Dorine (25), Nérine (26), *Aristione* (27).

Hervé, Mlle (Geneviève Béjart, known as) (b. 1624; d. 1675). Associated with Molière throughout his career, though she had only a half-share in the Paris company. Minor roles, with possible exception of *Bélise* (32).

Béjart, Louis (b. 1630; d. 1678). Retired from Molière's company 1670. Limped as result of an accident (hence premature retirement with pension: first member of Troupe du Roi to be treated thus). Molière exploited his limp for dramatic purposes in e.g. *Des Fonandrès* (16), La Flèche (24). Other roles: *Anselme* (4), Porteur de chaise (5), Alcantor (13), Théocle (14), *Dom Louis* (15), Dubois (17), *Oronte* (26). Also roles of elderly women: Mme Pernelle (25).

Dufresne, Charles (b. 1611(?); d. 1684(?)). Leader of Duc d'Épernon's company, which amalgamated with survivors of Illustre Théâtre at Nantes in 1646. Molière gradually assumed responsibility for company, but Dufresne stayed with him until shortly after return to Paris in 1658.

de Brie (Edme Villequin, known as) (b. 1607; d. 1676). With his wife, was a member of Molière's company from 1650. Specialised in valets and similar roles: Villebrequin (1), La Rapière (4), Almanzor (5), Villebrequin (6), Notaire (10), *Alcidas* (13), La Ramée (15), *Anselme* (24), M. Loyal (25), Maître D'Armes (28), Le Fleuve (29), *Purgon* (33).

de Brie (Catherine Leclerc, known as) (b. 1630(?); d. 1706). Joined Molière with her husband in 1650. Mainly a *jeune première*: *Lucile* (2), Célie (3), *Lucile* (4), Cathos (5), Isabelle (8), *Orante* (9), Agnès (10), Cinthie (14), Mathurine (15), *Éliante* (17), Martine (18), Isidore (21), Claudine (23), *Élise* or *Mariane* (24), Mariane (25), Julie (26), Dorimène (28), Vénus (29), Armande (32), *Béline* (33).

Du Parc (René Berthelot, known as) (d. 1664). Was in Duc d'Épernon's company with Molière from 1647. Left Molière at Easter 1659 to follow his wife to Marais theatre; returned Easter 1660, and remained in company until his death. Played Gros-René parts (2,4,6), and also Le Barbouillé (1), Ergaste (8).

Du Parc (Marquise-Thérèse de Gorla, known as) (d. 1668). Joined Molière's company when she married Du Parc in 1653. Left the company in 1659, returning in 1660. A good dancer, and a gifted tragic actress. Was Racine's mistress, and left Molière for the Hôtel de Bourgogne in 1667 after breach between Molière and Racine at time of *Andromaque*. Died in childbirth (Racine was accused of poisoning her). Roles of Célie (6), Climène (9), Climène (11), Dorimène (13), Aglante (14), *Elvire* (15), *Arsinoé* (17), Mélicerte (19).

La Grange (Charles Varlet, known as) (b. 1635; d. 1692). Joined company Easter 1659, becoming secretary and business manager. Succeeded Molière as *orateur* 1664. Sent on mission to King at Lille during ban on *Tartuffe*. Author of *Registre* of company; co-editor of *Oeuvres* of Molière 1682. Largely responsible for preservation of company after Molière's death. Mainly *jeune premier* roles (until arrival of Baron): *Valère* (1), La Grange (5), Lélie (6), Valère (8), Éraste (9), Horace (10), *Marquis* (11), Lycaste (13), Prince d'Ithaque (14), • Dom Juan (15), *Clitandre* (16), *Acaste* (17), Léandre (18), Myrtil (19), Corydon (20), Adraste (21), *Mercure* (22), *Clitandre* (23), *Cléante* or *Valère* (24), Valère (25), Éraste (26), Sostrate (27), Cléonte (28), Prince (29), Léandre (30), *Clitandre* (32), Cléante (33).

Du Croisy (Philibert Gassot, known as) (b. 1626(?); d. 1695). Joined Molière Easter 1659. Wide range of roles: Du Croisy (5), Lysidas (11), Marphurius (13), *M. Dimanche* (15), *Oronte* (17), Géronte (18), Second Berger (19), M. de

Sotenville (23), *Maître Jacques* or *Valère* (24), Tartuffe (25), Sbrigani (26), Maître de Philosophie and Covielle (28), Jupiter (29), *Géronte* (30), Harpin (31), Vadius (32), *Béralde* or *Notaire* (33).

Du Croisy (Marie Claveau, known as) (d. 1703). Joined Molière with her husband Easter 1659, but never made much of a mark. Was reduced to a half-share in 1662, and her contract was not renewed in 1665.

Jodelet (Julien Bedeau, known as) (d. 1660). Achieved a considerable reputation as a comic actor (with floured face) at Hôtel de Bourgogne and Marais theatres in middle decades of century. Joined Molière at Easter 1659: played Vicomte de Jodelet (5), and died shortly after.

L'Espy (François Bedeau, known as) (d. 1663). Brother of Jodelet, was with him at Hôtel de Bourgogne and Marais, and joined Molière at same time in 1659. Roles: *Gorgibus* (5), *Gorgibus* (6), *Ariste* (8).

Molière, Mlle (Armande Béjart, known as) (b. 1642/3; d. 1700). Joined the company on her marriage to Molière, February 1662. Sang and danced gracefully, and was soon given *premiers rôles* in comedy: *Léonor* (8), Élise (11), Princesse d'Élide (14), *Charlotte* (15), Célimène (17), Lucinde (18), Climène (21), Angélique (23), *Élise* or *Mariane* (24), *Lucette* (26), Lucile (28), Henriette (32), Angélique (33).

La Thorillière (François Le Noir, known as) (b. 1626(?); d. 1680). Joined Molière's company from Marais theatre 1662; soon after Molière's death, left to join Hôtel de Bourgogne. Played kings in tragedy, *raisonneurs*, and some comic roles: Géronimo (13), *Philinte* (17), Hali (21), *Jupiter* or *Amphitryon* (22), Lubin (23), Cléante (25), *Dorante* (28), Silvestre (30), *Trissotin* (32). Took over Argan (33) after Molière's death.

Brécourt (Guillaume Marcoureau, known as) (b. 1638; d. 1685). Joined Molière from Marais theatre 1662, but left 1664 for the Hôtel de Bourgogne. Author of comedies. Roles: *Alain* (10), Dorante (11), Pancrace (13).

Hubert, André (d. 1700). After several years at Marais theatre, joined Molière in 1664. A varied range of roles: Iphitas (14), *Pierrot* (15), *Clitandre* (17), *Maître de Musique* (28), Tibaudier (31), Diafoirus (33). Succeeded Louis Béjart as Mme Pernelle (25), and created other roles of elderly women: *Mme de Sotenville* (23), *Lucette* (26), Mme Jourdain (28), Philaminte (32).

Baron (Michel Boiron, known as) (b. 1653; d. 1729). According to Grimarest, joined Molière in 1666, playing *Myrtil* (19), but left the company after a quarrel with Molière's wife. What is certain is that he was recruited from the provinces in 1670, and played Cupidon (29) and *jeune premier* roles such as *Cléonte* (28), *Octave* (30). However, he was also Ariste (32) and possibly *Fleurant* (33). Replaced Molière as Alceste (17) in 1672, and took this and other roles of Molière's from 1680 onwards. He was to write successful comedies, and was the outstanding actor in the early decades of the Comédie-Française (founded 1680).

Beauval (Jean Pitel, known as) (b. 1635(?); d. 1709). Joined Molière's company 1670; left after Molière's death for Hôtel de Bourgogne. Minor roles, especially the *niais*: Bobinet (31), *Garçon Tailleur* (28), *Notaire* (32), Thomas Diafoirus (33).

Beauval, Mlle (Jeanne-Olivier Bourguignon, known as) (b. 1655; d. 1720). Joined Molière with her husband (they were granted one-and-a-half shares between them) in 1670, and left the company when he did, in 1673. Said to have had an idiosyncratic laugh, which is featured in Nicole (28) and Zerbinette (30). Other roles: Julie (31), *Martine* (32), Toinette (33).

La Grange (Marie Ragueneau, known as) (b. 1639; d. 1727). The daughter of Ragueneau, the stage-struck pastrycook who may have been a member of Molière's company in the provinces. Employed as *receveuse* and *vendeuse* (and possibly as Mlle de Brie's maid), she may also have played *Marotte* (5) and *Georgette* (10). Joined the company with a half-share on marrying La Grange in 1672; played Comtesse d'Escarbagnas (31).

In addition to the associate members, there were the following 'gagistes' (who were paid a fixed sum each time they performed):

Croisac (Nicolas Bonenfant, known as). Had been a member of Illustre Théâtre in 1643, and director of his own company in 1657. Was with Molière 1658–9.

Prévost, Marin. Occasional roles with Molière's company up to 1666.

Crosnier, Jean (b. 1643(?); d. 1709). Was 'garçon de théâtre' at the Palais-Royal 1662–7, employed as *décorateur*.

Du Perche (Jacques Crosnier, known as). Like his brother, was 'gagiste' with Molière 1662–7.

Châteauneuf, Charles (?) or Henri (?). Probably employed as 'gagiste' from 1670; played Lycas (29). From 1670 to 1672, his wage was paid out of the one-and-a-half shares of Beauval and his wife; in 1672, when Mlle La Grange joined the company on her marriage, it was decided that Châteauneuf's wage should be deducted from the one-and-a-half shares of La Grange and his wife.

Villiers (Jean Deschamps, known as) (b. 1648(?); d. 1701). Acted with provincial companies throughout his career; was brought from the provinces by royal edict in 1672 to serve as 'gagiste' with Molière's company. Remained at the Palais-Royal for a few months only.

A tradition that Molière's servant La Fôret played *Martine* (32) does not appear to be well founded.

Appendix III **Analysis of performances by Molière's company**

From the *Registre* kept by La Grange from Easter 1659 onwards, supplemented where necessary from other sources, we obtain a record of 1624 performances of Molière's own plays, and 779 performances of works by other authors, in the period of almost fourteen years up to Molière's death. These totals include both performances at Molière's Paris theatres (the Petit-Bourbon and the Palais-Royal) and private performances at Court or at various princely houses; though it should be noted that in the case of *visites*, the *Registre* sometimes fails to record the name of the play or plays performed.

		Performances	
(a) Plays by Molière	in Paris	at Court etc.	Total
La Jalousie du Barbouillé[1]	6	2	8
Le Médecin volant	14	2	16
L'Étourdi	64	13	77
Dépit amoureux	67	10	77
Les Précieuses ridicules	56	15	71
Sganarelle ou le Cocu imaginaire	123	20	143
Dom Garcie de Navarre	9	4	13
L'École des maris	108	18	126
Les Fâcheux	105	16	121
L'École des femmes	88	14	102
La Critique de l'École des femmes	37	6	43
L'Impromptu de Versailles	20	9	29
Le Mariage forcé	36	6	42
La Princesse d'Élide	25	9	34
Dom Juan	15	—	15
L'Amour médecin	63	4	67
Le Misanthrope	62	—	62
Le Médecin malgré lui	61	1	62
Mélicerte	—	1	1

311

La Pastorale comique	–	1	1
Le Sicilien	20	1	21
Amphitryon	53	2	55
George Dandin	39	4	43
L'Avare	47	2	49
Tartuffe[2]	82	12	94
Monsieur de Pourceaugnac	49	1	50
Les Amants magnifiques	–	5	5
Le Bourgeois gentilhomme	48	1	49
Psyché	82	–	82
Les Fourberies de Scapin	18	–	18
La Comtesse d'Escarbagnas	18	1	19
Les Femmes savantes	24	1	25
Le Malade imaginaire	4	–	4
	1443	181	1624

[1] Appears in *Registre* as *La Jalousie de Gros-René*.
[2] Known performances of the three-act version of 1664 are included in the total.

(b) Plays by other authors[1]	Date of first (Paris) performance by company	Performances in Paris	Performances at Court	Total
Le Docteur amoureux (f., anon.)	Oct 1658	1	—	1
Nicomède (t., P. Corneille)	Oct 1658	6	—	6
Héraclius (t., P. Corneille)	Apr 1659	14	—	14
Les Visionnaires (c., Desmarets de Saint-Sorlin)	Apr 1659	20	1	21
Jodelet ou le Maître valet (c., Scarron)	Apr 1659	15	—	15
Rodogune (t., P. Corneille)	May 1659	20	—	20
Cinna (t., P. Corneille)	May 1659	7	—	7
Dom Japhet d'Arménie (c., Scarron)	May 1659	31	4	35
Mariane (t., Tristan l'Hermite)	May 1659	23	—	23
Le Menteur (c., P. Corneille)	May 1659	22	—	22
Pompée (t., P. Corneille)	May 1659	3	—	3
Gros-René écolier (f., anon.)	May 1659	2	1	3
La Mort de Chrispe (t., Tristan l'Hermite)	June 1659	5	—	5
Scévole (t., Du Ryer)	June 1659	3	—	3
Dom Bertrand de Cigarral (c., T. Corneille)	June 1659	11	2	13
Venceslas (t., Rotrou)	June 1659	13	—	13
Le Gouvernement de Sancho Pansa (c., Guérin de Bouscal)	June 1659	30	1	31
Le Cid (t., P. Corneille)	July 1659	4	—	4
Jodelet prince (c., T. Corneille)	July 1659	15	2	17
Horace (t., P. Corneille)	July 1659	2	—	2
L'Héritier ridicule (c., Scarron)	Aug 1659	28	1	29
Le Campagnard (c., Gillet de la Tessonnerie)	Sept 1659	3	—	3
La Folle Gageure (c., Boisrobert)	Sept 1659	13	1	14
Pylade et Oreste (t., Coqueteau de la Clairière)	Nov 1659	3	—	3
Alcionée (t., Du Ryer)	Dec 1659	1	—	1
Zénobie (t., Magnon)	Dec 1659	7	—	7

Don Quichotte, ou les Enchantements de Merlin (c., Guérin de Bouscal²)	Jan 1660	3	—	3
La Vraie et la fausse Précieuse (c., Gilbert)	May 1660	9	—	9
Le Docteur pédant (f., anon.)	June 1660	3	—	3
Les Amours de Diane et d'Endymion (t., Gilbert)	June 1660	11	—	11
Huon de Bordeaux (t.c., Gilbert)	Aug 1660	19	1	20
La Pallas (f., anon.)	Aug 1660	1	1	2
Les Charmes de Félicie (p., Montaubon)	Sept 1660	6	—	6
Gorgibus dans le sac (f., anon.)	Jan 1661	5	1	6
Plan-plan (f., anon.)	Feb 1661	3	—	3
Le Tyran d'Égypte (t.c., Gilbert)	Feb 1661	11	—	11
Les Trois Docteurs (f., anon.)	March 1661	1	—	1
Le Riche impertinent (c., Chappuzeau)	May 1661	8	—	8
Le Fagotier (f., anon.)	Sept 1661	1	—	1
Les Indes (f., anon.)	Sept 1661	1	—	1
Sertorius (t., P. Corneille)	June 1662	38	4	42
La Soeur (c., Rotrou)	Oct 1662	4	1	5
Arsace (t., de Prade)	Nov 1662	6	—	6
Tomaxare (t., de Boyer)	Nov 1662	15	—	15
Bradamante ridicule (c., anon.)	Jan 1664	8	1	9
Le Grand Benêt de fils aussi fort que son père (c., Brécourt)	Jan 1664	9	2	11
La Farce de la casaque (f., anon.)	May 1664	1	—	1
La Thébaïde (t., Racine)	June 1664	20	4	24
La Coquette ou le Favori (t.c., Mlle Desjardins)	Apr 1665	26	1	27
La Mère coquette (c., Donneau de Visé)	Oct 1665	28	—	28
Alexandre (t., Racine)	Dec 1665	9	—	9
Attila (t., P. Corneille)	Mar 1667	23	3	26

La Veuve à la mode (c., Donneau de Visé)	Apr 1667	25	1	26
Délie (p., Donneau de Visé)	Oct 1667	17	1	18
L'Accouchée ou les Embarras de Godard (c., Donneau de Visé)	Nov 1667	18	1	19
Cléopâtre (t.c., La Thorillière)	Dec 1667	12	1	13
La Folle Querelle ou la Critique d'Andromaque (c., Subligny)	May 1668	27	–	27
Le Fin Lourdaud (f., anon.)	Nov 1668	30	–	30
Les Maux sans remèdes (c., Donneau de Visé)	Jan 1669	2	–	2
Le Désespoir extravagant (c., Subligny)	Aug 1670	16	–	16
Tite et Bérénice (c.h., P. Corneille)	Nov 1670	21	–	21
Les Maris infidèles (c., Donneau de Visé)	Jan 1673	4	–	4
		743	36	779

1 f. = farce; t. = tragedy; c. = comedy; p. = pastoral; t.c. = tragicomedy; c.h. = 'comédie héroïque'. Some of the anonymous farces are likely to have been early works of Molière's.
2 Adapted by Madeleine Béjart.

Bibliography

I: Modern editions of seventeenth-century texts

(a) Molière
Oeuvres, ed. E. Despois and P. Mesnard, 10 vols., Paris, 1873–1900.
Oeuvres complètes, ed. R. Jouanny, 2 vols., Paris, 1962.
Oeuvres complètes, ed. G. Couton, 2 vols., Paris, 1971.

Amphitryon, ed. P. Mélèse, Geneva, 1946.
L'Avare, ed. C. Dullin, Paris, 1946.
   ed. P. J. Yarrow, London, 1959.
Le Bourgeois gentilhomme, ed. H. G. Hall, London, 1966.
Dom Juan, ed. W. D. Howarth, Oxford, 1958.
   ed. G. Sandier, Paris, 1976.
L'École des femmes and *La Critique de l'École des femmes*, ed. W. D. Howarth, Oxford, 1963.
L'École des maris, ed. P. H. Nurse, London, 1959.
Les Femmes savantes, ed. H. G. Hall, London, 1974.
Les Fourberies de Scapin, ed. J. T. Stoker, London, 1971.
Le Malade imaginaire, ed. P. H. Nurse, London, 1965.
Le Misanthrope, ed. G. Rudler, Oxford, 1947.
Les Précieuses ridicules, ed. M. Cuénin, Geneva, 1973.
Tartuffe, ed. H. Ashton, Oxford, 1946.
   (mise en scène de R. Planchon), ed. A. Simon, Paris, *c.* 1976.

(b) Molière in English translation
The Misanthrope and Other Plays (*The Sicilian, Tartuffe, A Doctor in Spite of Himself, The Imaginary Invalid*), trans. J. Wood, Harmondsworth, 1959.
The Miser, The Would-be Gentleman, That Scoundrel Scapin, Love's the Best Doctor, Don Juan, trans J. Wood, Harmondsworth, 1968.

The Misanthrope, trans. R. Wilbur, New York, 1954.
The Misanthrope, English version by T. Harrison, London, 1973.
Tartuffe, trans. R. Wilbur, London, 1964.

(c) Other authors
Corneille, *L'Illusion comique*, ed. R. Garapon, Paris, 1957.
Desmarets de Saint-Sorlin, *Les Visionnaires*, ed. H. G. Hall, Paris, 1963.
Le Boulanger de Chalussay, *Élomire hypocondre* in *Molière Mocked: Three Contemporary Hostile Comedies*, ed. F. W. Vogler, Chapel Hill, N.C., 1973.

Bibliography

La Querelle de l'École des femmes, ed. G. Mongrédien, 2 vols., Paris, 1971.

Scarron, *Dom Japhet d'Arménie*, ed. R. Garapon, Paris, 1967.

Tallemant des Réaux, *Historiettes*, ed. A. Adam, 2 vols., Paris, 1960–1. \

II: Bibliographical and documentary aids

Jurgens, M. and Maxfield-Miller, E., *Cent ans de recherches sur Molière, sur sa famille et sur les comédiens de sa troupe*, Paris, 1963.

Lacroix, P., *Bibliographie moliéresque* (2nd edn), Paris, 1875.

La Grange, *Le Registre de La Grange, 1659–1685*, ed. B. E. and G. P. Young, 2 vols., Paris, 1947.

Mélèse, P., *Le Théâtre et le public à Paris sous Louis XIV, 1659–1715*, Paris, 1934.

Répertoire analytique des documents contemporains d'information et de critique concernant le théâtre à Paris sous Louis XIV, Paris, 1934.

Mongrédien, G. (ed.), *Recueil des textes et des documents du xviie siècle relatifs à Molière*, 2 vols., Paris, 1966.

Saintonge, P., 'Molière', *A Critical Bibliography of French Literature*, ed. D. C. Cabeen and J. Brody, III, *The Seventeenth Century*, Syracuse, N.Y., 1961, pp. 226–43.

Thirty Years of Molière Studies: A Bibliography, 1942–71 in R. Johnson *et al.* (eds.), *Molière and the Commonwealth of Letters*, Hattiesburg, Miss., 1975, pp. 747–826.

Saintonge, P. and Christ, R. W., *Fifty Years of Molière Studies: A Bibliography, 1892–1941*, Baltimore, 1942.

III: Critical and historical works

Actes des journées internationales Molière (1973), (*Revue de l'Histoire du Théâtre*), Paris, 1974.

Adam, A., *Histoire de la littérature française au xviie siècle*, 5 vols., Paris, 1948–56.

Arnavon, J., *La Morale de Molière*, Paris, 1945.

Auerbach, E., 'La Cour et la ville' in *Vier Untersuchungen zur Geschichte der französischen Bildung*, Berne, 1951, pp. 12–50.

Baumal, F., *Molière auteur précieux*, Paris, 1923.

Bergson, H., *Le Rire* (1899), Paris, 1949.

Bray, R., *Molière, homme de théâtre*, Paris, 1954.

Brereton, G., *French Comic Drama from the Sixteenth to the Eighteenth Century*, London, 1977.

Brisson, P., *Molière: sa vie dans ses oeuvres*, Paris, 1942.

Chapman, P. A., *The Spirit of Molière: An Interpretation*, Princeton, 1940.

Chappuzeau, S., *Le Théâtre français* (1674), ed. G. Monval, Paris, 1875.

Cooper, Lane, *An Aristotelian Theory of Comedy, with an Adaptation of the Poetics*, New York, 1922.

Cosnier, C., 'Jodelet: un acteur du xviie siècle devenu un type', *Revue d'Histoire Littéraire de la France*, LXII (1962), 329–52.

Deierkauf-Holsboer, S. W., *L'Histoire de la mise en scène dans le théâtre français à Paris de 1600 à 1673*, Paris, 1960.

Descotes, M., *Les Grands Rôles du théâtre de Molière*, Paris, 1960.

Molière et sa fortune littéraire, Bordeaux, 1970.

Emelina, J., *Les Valets et les servantes dans le théâtre comique en France de 1610 à 1700*, Grenoble, 1975.

Eustis, A., *Molière as Ironic Contemplator*, The Hague, 1973.

Fernandez, R., *La Vie de Molière*, Paris, 1929.

Garapon, R., *La Fantaisie verbale et le comique dans le théâtre français*, Paris, 1957.

Le Dernier Molière, des 'Fourberies de Scapin' au 'Malade imaginaire', Paris, 1977.

Gill, A., 'The "Doctor in the farce" and Molière', *French Studies*, II (1948), 101–28.

Gossman, L., *Men and Masks: A Study of Molière*, Baltimore, 1963.

Greene, E. J. H., *Menander to Marivaux: The History of a Comic Structure*, Edmonton, Alberta, 1977.

Grimarest, *La Vie de M. de Molière* (1705), ed. G. Mongrédien, Paris, 1955.

Guicharnaud, J., *Molière: une aventure théâtrale*, Paris, 1963.

(ed.), *Molière: A Collection of Critical Essays*, Twentieth-Century Views, Englewood Cliffs, N.J., 1964.

Guichemerre, R., *La Comédie avant Molière, 1640–1660*, Paris, 1972.

Gutwirth, M., *Molière ou l'invention comique*, Paris, 1966.

'*Tartuffe* and the Mysteries', *PMLA*, XCII (1977), 33–40.

Hall, H. G., 'The Literary Context of Molière's *Le Misanthrope*', *Studi Francesi*, XIV (1970), 20–38.

'Molière Satirist of Seventeenth-Century French Medicine: Fact and Fantasy', *Proceedings of the Royal Society of Medicine*, LXX (1977), 425–31.

Herzel, R. W., 'The Décor of Molière's Stage: The Testimony of Brissart and Chauveau', *PMLA*, XCIII (1978), 925–53.

Hodgart, M., *Satire*, London, 1969.

Howarth, W. D., *Life and Letters in France: The Seventeenth Century*, London, 1965.

'La Notion de la catharsis dans la comédie française classique', *Revue des Sciences Humaines*, CLII (1973), 521–39.

'Alceste, ou l'honnête homme imaginaire', *Actes des journées internationales Molière* (1973) (*Revue de l'Histoire du Théâtre*), Paris, 1974, 93–102.

(ed.), *Comic Drama: The European Heritage*, London, 1978.

and Thomas, M. (eds.), *Molière: Stage and Study: Essays in honour of W. G. Moore*, Oxford, 1973.

Hubert, J. D., '*L'École des femmes*, tragédie burlesque?', *Revue des Sciences Humaines*, XCVII (1960), 41–52.

Molière and the Comedy of Intellect, Berkeley, Cal., 1962.

Jasinski, R., *Molière et le Misanthrope*, Paris, 1951.

Jouvet, L., *Témoignages sur le théâtre*, Paris, 1952.

Kern, E., '*L'École des femmes* and the Spirit of Farce', *Esprit Créateur*, XIII (Fall 1973), 220–8.

Kohler, P., *L'Esprit classique et la comédie*, Paris, 1925.

Lancaster, H. C., *A History of French Dramatic Literature in the Seventeenth Century*, 9 vols., Baltimore, 1929–42.

Lanson, G., 'Molière et la farce', *Revue de Paris* (May 1901), 129–53.

Bibliography

Larthomas, P., *Le Langage dramatique*, Paris, 1972.
Lough, J., *Paris Theatre Audiences in the Seventeenth and Eighteenth Centuries*, London, 1957.
'Molière's Audience', *Durham University Journal* (1974), 257–65.
Seventeenth-Century French Drama: The Background, Oxford, 1979.
McBride, R., *The Sceptical Vision of Molière*, London, 1977.
Meredith, G., *An Essay on Laughter and the Uses of the Comic Spirit* (1877), London, 1927.
Michaut, G., *La Jeunesse de Molière*, Paris, 1923.
Les Débuts de Molière à Paris, Paris, 1923.
Les Luttes de Molière, Paris, 1925.
Mongrédien, G., *Les Grands Comédiens du xviie siècle*, Paris, 1927.
La Vie littéraire au xviie siècle, Paris, 1947.
La Vie quotidienne des comédiens au temps de Molière, Paris, 1966.
Moore, W. G., *Molière: A New Criticism*, Oxford, 1949.
'Dom Juan Reconsidered', *Modern Language Review*, LII (1957), 510–17.
'Molière's Theory of Comedy', *Esprit Créateur* (Fall 1966), 137–44.
'Comedy, Cruelty and Molière', *London Magazine* (June–July 1975), 77–83.
Morel, J., 'Molière ou la dramaturgie de l'honnêteté', *Information Littéraire*, XV (1963), 185–91.
'Médiocrité et perfection dans la France du xviie siècle', *Revue d'Histoire Littéraire de la France*, LXIX (1969), 441–50.
Nurse, P. H., 'Essai de définition du comique moliéresque', *Revue des Sciences Humaines*, CXIII (1964), 9–24.
Pelous, J.-M., 'Les Métamorphoses de Sganarelle: la permanence d'un type comique', *Revue d'Histoire Littéraire de la France*, LXXII (1972), 821–49.
Römer, P., *Molières 'Amphitryon' und sein gesellschaftlicher Hintergrund*, Bonn, 1967.
Rojtman, B., 'Alceste dans le théâtre de Molière', *Revue d'Histoire Littéraire de la France*, LXXIII (1973), 963–81.
Scherer, J., *La Dramaturgie classique en France*, Paris [1950].
Structures de Tartuffe, Paris, 1966.
Thibaudet, A., 'Le Rire de Molière', *Revue de Paris*, XXIX (1922), 99–125.
'Molière et la critique', *Revue de Paris*, XXXVII (1930), 365–94.
Thomas, M., 'Philinte and Éliante', *Molière: Stage and Study*, ed. W. D. Howarth and M. Thomas, Oxford, 1973, pp. 73–92.
Vedel, V., *Deux Classiques français vus par un critique étranger: Corneille et son temps; Molière*, Paris, 1935.
Wadsworth, P. A., *Molière and the Italian Theatrical Tradition*, n.p., 1977.
Waterson, K., *Molière et l'autorité: structures sociales, structures comiques*, Lexington, Ky, 1976.
Wheatley, K., *Molière and Terence*, Austin, Texas, 1931.
Wiley, W. L., *The Early Public Theatre in France*, Harvard, 1959.

Index